Biker Gangs and Transnational Organized Crime

Second Edition

Thomas Barker
Professor Emeritus, School of Justice Studies, Eastern Kentucky University

ELSEVIER

AMSTERDAM • BOSTON • HEIDELBERG • LONDON
NEW YORK • OXFORD • PARIS • SAN DIEGO
SAN FRANCISCO • SINGAPORE • SYDNEY • TOKYO

Anderson Publishing is an imprint of Elsevier

Acquiring Editor: Pamela Chester
Development Editor: Ellen S. Boyne
Project Manager: Punithavathy Govindaradjane
Designer: Russell Purdy

Anderson Publishing is an imprint of Elsevier
225 Wyman Street, Waltham, MA 02451, USA

Library of Congress Cataloging-in-Publication Data
Barker, Thomas.
  [Biker gangs and organized crime]
  Biker gangs and transnational organized crime / Thomas Barker. – Second edition.
    pages cm
  Revised edition of the author's Biker gangs and organized crime, published in 2007.
  ISBN 978-0-323-29870-4
  1. Motorcycle gangs–United States. 2. Motorcycle gangs. 3. Organized crime–United States. 4. Organized crime. 5. Transnational crime. I. Title.
  HV6439.U5B38 2015
  364.106'6–dc23

                                                                              2014014131

British Library Cataloguing in Publication Data
A catalogue record for this book is available from the British Library

ISBN: 978-0-323-29870-4

For information on all Anderson publications
visit our website at http://store.elsevier.com

Biker Gangs and Transnational Organized Crime

Contents

Acknowledgments ix

Online Resources xi

CHAPTER 1 **Introduction** 1

Overview 1

Guiding Principles for the Second Edition 2

    Criminal Organization Continuum of Outlaw Motorcycle
Clubs 2

    Network Approach to Organized Crime 2

    Structural Complexity of Biker Gangs 6

    A Note on Methodology 7

CHAPTER 2 **Enter the One-Percenters** 9

Introduction: Clubs or Gangs 9

Motorcycle Clubs 11

    Conventional Motorcycle Clubs 13

    Outlaw Motorcycle Clubs 13

Hollister Motorcycle Incident/Riot 1947: Birthplace of the
American Biker 17

Moral Panics and Folk Devils 19

    Bikers as Folk Devils 21

Riverside Motorcycle Riot (1948) 22

Cyclists Raid 23

The Wild One: First of the Biker Movies 24

Hells Angels Motorcycle Club and the One-Percenters 25

    Ralph "Sonny" Barger 26

    Oakland HAMC Chapter: The Early Years 27

    One-Percent Bikers 28

    HAMC in the Mid-1960s 29

Altamont Speedway—One-Percent (1%) Bikers on Display 30

CHAPTER 3 **Evolution from Clubs to Gangs** 35

One-Percenters' Creed 35

Introduction 35

Outlaw Motorcycle Gangs 36

    U.S. Criminal Justice View 36

Club Reaction to Gang Label 44

    Recognition That Some Are Criminals 44

Gang Label Has Real Consequences for Members 47

Club/Gang Interactions with Other Motorcyclists and
Citizens 49
    Tread Softly in the Presence of a One-Percenter Outlaw
    Biker 49
Are All Outlaw Motorcycle Clubs (1% Clubs) Criminal
Gangs? 52

CHAPTER 4   **Outlaw Motorcycle Club: Criminal Organization**
       Continuum **73**
       Criminal Organization Continuum 73
       Dimension: Extent of Members' Involvement in Organized
       Crime 76
          Becoming a Member of an Outlaw Motorcycle Club-Four
          Stages 76
          Leaving a One-Percent Club 85
          Members' Criminal Behavior 86
          Focus: Club/Gang Criminal Activity 96
       Dimension: Leaders' Involvement in the Planning and
       Execution of Criminal Activities 98
       Criminal Organization Continuum of Outlaw Motorcycle
       Clubs 100

CHAPTER 5   **United States Outlaw Motorcycle Gangs: Big Five,**
       Major Independents, and Others **103**
       Introduction 103
       The Big Five One-Percent Biker Gangs 104
          Hells Angels Motorcycle Club/Gang (HAMC) 104
          Bandidos Motorcycle Club/Gang 107
          Outlaws Motorcycle Club/Gang 110
          Pagans Motorcycle Club/Gang 111
          Sons of Silence Motorcycle Club/Gang 113
       Puppet/Support Gangs 114
       Major Independents 117
          The Mongols MC 118
          Warlocks MC 120
          Vagos Motorcycle Club 122
          Wheels of Soul 124
       Black or Interracial One-Percent Outlaw Motorcycle Clubs 125
          Blacks in the One-Percent Biker Subculture 125
          Black Outlaw Motorcycle Gangs 127
       Basic Organizational Structure of Outlaw Motorcycle Gangs 131

CHAPTER 6   **U.S.-Based OMGs: Criminals Without Borders** **133**
International Expansion 133
International Organizations: Interpol and Europol...............134
    Interpol 135
    Europol 135
U.S.-Based Biker Gangs with Chapters Outside the
Continental United States 140

CHAPTER 7   **The Hells Are No Angels: Organized Crime, Death,
and Mayhem in Canada** **145**
Introduction 145
Criminal Intelligence Service Canada 146
    CISC Annual Report—1997 147
    CISC Annual Report—1998 147
    CISC Annual Report—1999 148
    CISC Annual Report—2000 150
    CISC Annual Report—2001 151
    CISC Annual Report—2002 152
    CISC Annual Report—2003 154
    CISC Annual Report—2004 154
    CISC Annual Report—2005 and Beyond..................155
The End of the Canadian Biker War..............................155
Continued Efforts Against Canadian OMGs 156
Drug Smuggling into the United States from Canada 159
Canadian OMG Violence..160
    Canadian Bandidos Massacre..................................160
More Recent Actions Against Biker Gangs 166

CHAPTER 8   **Bikies Down Under—OMGs in Australia
and New Zealand** **169**
Australia...169
    Australian Outlaw Motorcycle Gangs.......................169
    Australian Bikies: 1% Bikers and 100% Violent Criminals ...175
    Australian Bikies by State 177
    Official Response to Australian Bikie Gangs...............180
    Recent Developments Down Under.............................183
New Zealand 185
    The Rise of the Outlaw Clubs 1960-1980 187
    New Zealand's Actions Against Patched Gangs, Including
    OMGs...189

The Organized and Financial Crime Agency of New Zealand
(OFCANZ)..190
New Zealand District Councils...191

CHAPTER 9   **Back Patch Clubs in the United Kingdom**.................**193**
United Kingdom 193
Hells Angels Expansion into the U.K 196
Biker Alliance Against HAMC...198
Outlaws Expansion 200

CHAPTER 10 **Outlaw Motorcycle Gangs in Europe** **203**
Introduction...203
Germany 205
Nordic Countries: The Great Nordic Biker War 207
    Denmark...208
    Norway...210
    Sweden...212
    Finland...213
The Netherlands...213
Other European Countries 215
    France...215
    Spain...215
    Southeast Europe 216
The Rest of the World 216

CHAPTER 11 **Conclusions**..**219**
Responding to OMG Expansion 227

Appendix A   **By-Laws—Bandidos Motorcycle Club, 1999**..........**229**

References **233**

Index **249**

Acknowledgments

The author would like to thank all the unnamed persons who helped me in my research into the world of outlaw bikers. That list includes students, colleagues, undercover officers, and bikers. I would also like to thank the staff at Elsevier, especially Pam Chester and Ellen Boyne. Ellen, your friendship, guidance, and help have always made the publishing process easier to navigate. My wife and best friend, Betsy, has provided her usual support and encouragement. I express my gratitude to BSJ, who made it all possible.

Online Resources

Thank you for selecting Anderson Publishing's *Biker Gangs and Transnational Organized Crime*, 2nd edition. To complement the learning experience, we have provided online tools to accompany this edition.

Please consult your local sales representative with any additional questions. You may also e-mail the Academic Sales Team at textbook@elsevier.com.

Qualified adopters and instructors can access valuable material for free by registering at: http://textbooks.elsevier.com/web/manuals.aspx?isbn=9780323298704

Introduction

KEY TERMS

criminal exploitable ties

Criminal Organization Continuum

economic criminal organizations

horizontal differentiation

network approach to organized crime

organized criminal gang

single-purpose gangs

social criminal organizations

spatial differentiation

vertical differentiation

OVERVIEW

One-percent bikers and outlaw motorcycle gangs (OMGs) began in the United States and at one time were solely considered an American phenomenon and problem (Barker, 2007). This limited view changed markedly in the last 30-plus years as U.S.-based motorcycle gangs spread their criminal tendrils throughout the world to the extent that some U.S.-based clubs—Hells Angels MC, Outlaws MC, Bandidos MC—now have more chapters outside the United States than within U.S. boundaries. With this expansion, U.S.-based motorcycle gangs evolved from local to regional, then national, and now international/transnational criminal gangs. For example, the president of the Nicaragua chapter of the U.S.-based Vagos MC was convicted of murdering the "Godfather" of the San Diego Hells Angels in a shootout at a Nevada casino and sentenced to life imprisonment (Sonner, 2013, August 7). The slain Hells Angels chapter president was the fifth-ranking Hells Angels leader. The international Vagos leaders approved his murder during the Vagos national meeting at the casino. Complicating the transnational crime problem posed by U.S.-based biker gangs, indigenous OMGs from outside the United States are spreading beyond their borders and in several cases setting up chapters in the United States. They are following the lead of the

U.S.-based biker gangs and becoming transnational. In the twenty-first century, one-percent biker gangs are a transnational organized crime reality.

The extension of the one-percent lifestyle, culture, and criminal behavior has not been without violence and death as the U.S. clubs have met resistance from indigenous one-percent clubs not in awe of their foreign interlopers. The wars and violence between competing U.S. and indigenous biker gangs in Canada, Australia, England, and the Scandinavian countries have exceeded those of prior organized crime groups in terms of the dead and injured, the weapons used, and the public settings in which they take place. Adding fuel to the fire of increased violence, the U.S. biker gangs have carried their "at home" enmities for other U.S. biker gangs with them and fought with each other over territory, crime markets, drug routes, and perceived real or imagined incidents of disrespect.

The end result of this transnational expansion of biker gangs has been an exponential increase in international OMG organized crime and a level of violence that has called for extraordinary measures by national and international law enforcement authorities and other government agencies, causing many to pass bans on membership or wearing colors.

The second edition of this book, recognizing the movement to transnational organized crime by U.S.-based OMGs, reexamines the "roots" of the one-percent lifestyle in the United States and the distinction between motorcycle clubs and motorcycle gangs, including a discussion of the Big Five biker gangs, their puppet and support clubs, and the major independent biker gangs. The expansion of U.S.-based biker gangs throughout the world is examined with special attention to selected countries where OMGs have become major organized crime problems.

GUIDING PRINCIPLES FOR THE SECOND EDITION

Criminal Organization Continuum of Outlaw Motorcycle Clubs

The discussion that follows will expand the **Criminal Organization Continuum** of outlaw motorcycle groups, ranging from clubs at one end to gangs on the other end, developed in the first edition. Basic to this continuum is the distinction between conventional and deviant motorcycle clubs and the evolution of a select group of bikers who are labeled *one-percenters*. Closely examined are one-percent clubs known as OMGs organized and devoted to crime for profit. We will identify the dimensions along which we classify OMGs and identify the major OMGs and their puppet/support gangs whenever possible. As the discussion crosses "the pond," we identify the major biker gangs in Canada, Australia, the United Kingdom, Europe, and the rest of the world.

Network Approach to Organized Crime

As in the first edition, guiding the inquiry is the network approach to organized crime proposed by Klaus von Lampe. A noted German organized crime researcher, von Lampe says that there are two areas of consensus in the study of organized crime: (1) no one doubts that organized crime exists; however, and (2) there is no generally accepted definition of organized crime (von Lampe, 2003). Von Lampe opines that many researchers use the concept of "illegal enterprise," examining the activities and not the structure as a starting point. Using this approach, criminal enterprises (organized crime) exist when groups of criminals provide an illegal good or service on an ongoing basis, best exemplified by groups such as drug trafficking organizations (DTOs). Von Lampe says that classifying organized criminal behavior by enterprise/activity avoids the conspiracy theory involved in ethnically defined criminal organizations and the use of fuzzy and hard-to-define terms of the enumeration method of mandatory and optional criteria possessed by organized crime groups. However, there are problems with this approach.

The enterprise theory, with its emphasis on market, fails to address predatory and fraudulent crimes with no primary market orientation (such as investment fraud—Ponzi schemes, mortgage fraud, etc.), and quasi-government or parasitic power syndicates that occupy strata above criminal groups (e.g., political machines) engaged in illegal business transactions, such as those addressed by Block (1983) in his seminal study of organized crime in New York from 1930 to 1950. Von Lampe proposes a new concept— "criminally exploitable ties"—in describing a network approach that provides for a better understanding of organized crime (von Lampe, 2003:10). His analysis assumes that crimes such as drug trafficking or investment fraud; criminal collectives such as "mafia syndicates"; and criminogenic milieus or systematic conditions, such as corrupt alliances of businessmen, politicians, and public officials, all begin with participants connected through criminally exploitable ties that combine into criminal networks. These criminal networks are sets of actors connected by ties that in some way support the commission of illegal acts. Criminal networks constitute "the least common denominator of organized crime" (von Lampe & Johansen, 2004:167). This leads to the four principles in the network approach of organized crime.

First Principle

All group crime begins with a dyadic network between individuals with criminally exploitable ties.

According to the **network approach to organized crime**, the basic unit in any form of criminal cooperation is a criminally exploitive tie linking two actors. Each actor in the basic network has latent or manifest criminal dispositions that come together when the opportunities arise, and there is a common basis of trust. Each actor could already be an individual criminal; however, a network between them will not be formed without common trust. Trust is necessary for two actors to engage in criminal behavior in order to minimize the risks involved in illegal transactions. Those risks include the increased risk of detection and prosecution that comes with "partnering up." After all, one has to be sure that the partner is not an undercover officer or an informant, loose-lipped, or in any way unreliable, because agreements between criminal partners cannot be enforced in a court of law. Of course, this trust can be misplaced or break down under the pressure imposed by law enforcement authorities, but it will have to be perceived to be there by both parties when the network begins. This leads to the second principle.

Second Principle

Networks between criminal actors will depend on a common basis of trust.

Trust is formed in a number of ways. Trust in the criminal milieu can be based on one's reputation among criminal actors, especially in OMGs. Prospective members in biker clubs/gangs are chosen from that group of bikers known to have the reputation as "righteous bikers." This common basis of trust can also be found in some sort of bonding relationship, such as ethnicity, kinship, childhood friendship, and prison acquaintanceship. Furthermore, this bonding relationship can be formed by affiliation or membership in secret societies such as the Sicilian Mafia, Chinese Triads, or Japanese Yakuza, or in subcultures that share a specific set of values and code of conduct much like street gangs and one-percent motorcycle clubs. Groups such as street gangs and one-percent biker clubs are recognizable to each other by reputation, distinctive clothing, behavior patterns, argot, or tattoos. As social groups, they adhere to mutual support and noncooperation with law enforcement and other formal social control agents.

The common basis of trust can also develop over time as actors come together in legal and or illegal business relationships. These ties will not be as strong and intense as those of ethnicity, kinship, affiliation, and membership, and they will often be ephemeral. They may also be more common in certain organized criminal activities such as drug trafficking (see Desroches, 2005; Box 1.1).

Single-purpose gangs have limited supporting networks and organization, and the criminal activity they engage in is only constrained by opportunity and inclination. Typically, single-purpose gangs have little or no continuity—arrested members are not replaced (Barker, 2012). Aggressive law enforcement action against single-purpose gangs usually eliminates them. The single purpose does not endure with the turnover of members into an organized criminal gang—that is, unless the single-purpose gang morphs into an **organized criminal gang**. Organized criminal gangs have extensive supporting networks and long histories of criminal activity, a defined membership, and use violence in the furtherance of their criminal behavior and quest for power. Examples of these organized criminal gangs include adult street gangs, prison gangs, OMGs, and DTOs (Barker, 2012).

BOX 1.1 ORGANIZED CRIME IN THE UNITED STATES—NETWORKS

Organized crime in the United States today is a multiethnic enterprise, comprised of many different groups, most of them quite small, which emerge to exploit criminal activities (e.g., fraud, smuggling, stolen property distribution, and so on). Many of these groups are short-lived, comprised of career criminals who form temporary networks with desired skills (e.g., forgery, smuggling connections, border and bribery connections, etc.) to exploit a criminal opportunity (the Single Purpose Criminal Gangs identified by Barker, 2012). These *networks* often dissolve after the opportunity has been exploited as the criminals seek new opportunities that may employ different combinations of criminals.

Source: Albanese, 2004:13. (Italics added).

Adult street gangs such as the "super gangs" of Los Angeles and Chicago and the transnational street gangs like 18th Street and Mara Salvatrucha (MS 13); prison gangs such as the Mexican Mafia, Aryan Brotherhood, the Black Guerilla Family, and the transnational Barrio Azteca and Hermanos de Pistoleros Latinos; and OMGs are unique within the category of organized criminal gangs because they share common characteristics (Barker, 2012). These criminal gangs make a clear distinction between themselves and others—they are truly "outsiders" in society. They express this distinction between themselves and others with symbols, colors, tattoos, argot, and dress. They also share the distinctive characteristics of all criminal gangs. The members of these groups are involved in various types of crimes for profit, and engage in violence.

Criminal organizations such as organized criminal gangs evolve out of dyadic criminal networks and are defined as a set of three or more people linked by **criminal exploitable ties**. They have to evolve out of the dyadic setting due to the size and complexity of networks necessary for some crimes. When the dyadic relationship requires a third person, the nucleus for organized crime and organized criminal gangs appears. In addition, in order to be an organized crime gang, these social networks must engage in ongoing or recurring illegal acts. Obviously, two criminals would not be enough to engage in all the activities necessary in organized crime, such as drug trafficking. Organized crime requires conspiracies between criminal actors. Illicit goods must be found, grown, or otherwise produced, and transported; customers must be found, identified, or cultivated; law enforcement must be avoided or neutralized; and profits must be laundered, shared, and divided. Furthermore, many criminal activities are spatially separate—regional, national, and transnational. All these tasks require combinations of individuals linked together by criminally exploitive ties—criminal organizations.

Third Principle

A criminal organization consists of a combination of individuals linked through criminally exploitable ties.

Many crimes require organization and structure: drug and weapons trafficking, protection/extortion rackets, organized retail theft (ORT), human trafficking, disposal of stolen goods, gambling, prostitution, money laundering, and the production and distribution of pornography. Von Lampe provides a typology of criminal organizations according to the functions they serve and their degree of structural complexity (von Lampe, 2003). He goes on to say that criminal organizations serve one of three functions: economic, social, and quasi-governmental. We will discuss the economic and social functions because they have the most direct bearing on OMGs. **Economic criminal organizations** are those set up for the sole purpose of achieving material gain through crime, such as gangs of burglars, robbers, DTOs, or an illegal casino. As we shall see, some motorcycle "clubs," such as the Pennsylvania Warlocks MC, the Canadian Rock Machine MC, the Mongols MC, and the Bandidos MC, came into being for the sole purpose of making money through criminal behavior. At times, chapters of many OMGs act or have acted as economic criminal organizations. For example, according to Canadian law enforcement officials, the Quebec Nomads Hells Angels as an economic criminal organization had $18 million in drug sales from November 10 to December 19, 2000 (Cherry, 2005:168). They sold 1916 kg of cocaine in addition to other drugs.

On the other hand, **social criminal organizations** support the economic criminal activities of their members only indirectly. Membership creates and promotes a sense of solidarity and belonging—trust establishes contacts, gives status within a criminal milieu, and provides a forum for sharing information, both criminal and noncriminal—and promotes a deviant ideology. In other words, membership establishes and intensifies criminally exploitable ties and makes possible criminal networks that can extend regionally, nationally, and internationally for some clubs. There is little doubt that many biker clubs started out as special interest clubs devoted to partying and riding; their criminal activities were not structured or organized, rather they were confined to individuals or small groups of members. That has changed for many clubs or chapters of clubs, such as the "Big Five" motorcycle gangs (Hells Angels, Outlaws, Bandidos, Pagans, and the Sons of Silence) and their puppet/support clubs. The criminal members took, and take, advantage of the structure and social nature of the clubs to further their criminal interests.

Fourth Principle

Social criminal organizations, such as one-percent biker clubs, indirectly support the criminal activities of their members.

Following the logic of von Lampe's argument that a social criminal organization supports the criminal activities of its members when groups of individuals with criminally exploitive ties come together within a common basis of trust, the manner in which one-percent club members are selected, including their criminal backgrounds, the socialization process for new members, and the peer group and leader support that arises for certain criminal behavior, is important to understanding OMGs.

We argue that one-percent biker groups can be placed on a continuum from gangs on one end to clubs on the other, with social criminal organizations in the middle. Those clubs that evolve into social criminal organizations that support the criminal activities of individuals or groups set the stage for the development of OMGs. This evolution led to a number of these OMGs becoming involved in organized criminal activities on a national and international/transnational scale.

Structural Complexity of Biker Gangs

Biker criminal organizations vary by structural complexity: horizontal differentiation, vertical differentiation, and spatial differentiation. **Horizontal differentiation** refers to the extent that the biker criminal organization has subdivided tasks among its members; that is, its division of labor. Crimes are committed by OMG members and also "farmed" out to puppet/support clubs or gang associates, depending on the skills necessary. **Vertical differentiation** is evidenced when a president leads a typical chapter; beneath him are a vice-president, a treasurer. and a sergeant at arms. The support and facilitation of the "club's" criminal activities by these leaders is an important dimension in determining where the "club" is placed on the Criminal Organization Continuum. **Spatial differentiation** depends on the number of locations in which the organization operates. Motorcycle gangs are spatially located throughout the United States and the rest of the world. In addition, related to their structural complexity, motorcycle clubs have written constitutions and by-laws in order to appear outwardly legal even though their members engage in a variety of criminal activities. Club spokesmen (there are no spokeswomen in these misogynistic groups) point to these constitutions and by-laws as proof that they are merely motorcycle clubs who happen to have a few members who commit crime. This argument does not sway law enforcement authorities and others who know that other notorious criminal gangs such as the Mexican Mafia and Aryan Brotherhood also have constitutions and by-laws, along with a number of adult criminal gangs.

A Note on Methodology

Research on subjects who belong to deviant groups is difficult under any circumstances but research on outlaw motorcycle group members is even more difficult and potentially dangerous for the researcher and the subjects. The usual data collection methods—survey instruments, interviews, observations—are often not feasible. Studies of deviant activities that also involve biker groups often exclude them from the study because of the difficulties involved in studying them. In Desroches' study of drug trafficking, biker gang members refused to be interviewed (Desroches, 2005). A Canadian study of HIV-related risk factors among erotic/exotic dancers excluded "women who dance in bars controlled by motorcycle gangs, commonly referred to as biker bars" (Lewis & Maticka-Tyndale, 1998:2). The clubs do not want to be studied and, because of their criminal activities, maintaining strict access to club business is an attempt to frustrate the information-gathering efforts of law enforcement agencies. Through the years I have been told on numerous occasions "Tom, that is club business and not yours." Quinn (1983), in his seminal study on "one-percenters," found that "[a]s secret societies there are rules, inhibitions, and severe sanctions (i.e., expulsions and death) prohibiting discussions of any and all club affairs with non-members." Another researcher found that "[b]iker gangs are tight-knit, regimented organizations that demand a high degree of conformity to norms [their deviant norms] and exert strong control over individual members" (Desroches, 2005:7). Furthermore, much of the official information on OMGs produced by government agencies is considered to be law enforcement–sensitive and not for public dissemination.

For the reasons outlined above, this book is based on a combination of quantitative and qualitative research methods such as the journalistic accounts and autobiographies of former and present biker gangs. In the last ten years, there has been an avalanche of these "crooks books," spurred on by the best-selling success of Ralph

"Sonny" Barger's (the Hells Angels icon) autobiography in 2002. These "crooks books" all discount the criminal activities of motorcycle clubs and claim that they are not gangs but brotherhoods of motorcycle riders. Nevertheless, they are a good data source on the secret lifestyle, criminal behavior, and rationalizations common among the one-percenters once the careful reader wades through the "BS." The author also has carefully examined the limited academic/scholarly works, including dissertations and theses, available law enforcement/government reports, and articles from newspapers gathered during an examination of ten-plus years of Google alerts. Data was also gathered from biker websites, including numerous Internet motorcycle club websites. The author and several of his graduate students performed a ten-year content analysis of biker court cases—federal and state—from a LexisNexis search. The work is also based on "interviews/conversations" with current and past biker club members and law enforcement officers and almost 40 years of studying crime, criminals, and organized crime.

Enter the One-Percenters

KEY TERMS

biker movies

Boozefighters Motorcycle Club

conventional motorcycle clubs

folk devils

Hells Angels Motorcycle Club (HAMC)

Hollister Motorcycle Incident/Riot

moral panics

one-percent bikers

outlaw motorcycle clubs (OMCs)

outlaw motorcycle gangs (OMGs)

Riverside Motorcycle Riot

> The club [Hells Angels] in and of itself is not a criminal organization. It's never been proven to be a criminal organization.
>
> George Christie Jr.—2006 (Heinz, 2006)

INTRODUCTION: CLUBS OR GANGS

The number one question in any discussion of one-percent clubs, also known as **outlaw motorcycle clubs** (OMCs), is are they motorcycle clubs, i.e., voluntary social organizations built around the love of motorcycles that happen to contain "some" criminal members, or are they criminal gangs, aka **outlaw motorcycle gangs** (OMGs), whose members just happen to ride motorcycles and are organized and devoted to crime for profit? If they are criminal gangs, they are certainly unique, but not the only ones among criminal groups that call attention to themselves with websites, patches and tattoos, written constitutions and by-laws, trademarked names and logos, and publicity campaigns. The most important symbol for OMC members is the "patch," which consists of three pieces, a top rocker identifying the gang by name, a gang logo, and a bottom rocker identifying the gang or chapter location. This "patch" is sewn onto a sleeveless leather or denim vest, often referred to as a "cut." The "cut" is worn at all gang meetings and functions. Most OMCs have rules dictating that the "cut" must always be worn when riding their motorcycle but never when in a "cage" (car). In addition, OMC members, especially those known as one-percenters, will have the MC (motorcycle club) badge and a 1% or 1%er badge symbolizing that the wearer is an outlaw or one-percenter.

Our purpose will be to provide a plausible answer to the question: are the OMCs clubs or gangs? That is, if an answer is possible. There is no argument that at some time every member of an OMC will engage in, or has engaged in, criminal activity common among their deviant lifestyle (disorderly conduct, intoxication, drug taking, assaults, etc.). However, more salient to our inquiry is: how many members of these supposed clubs have engaged in crimes common to criminal organizations, such as trafficking in drugs, weapons, humans, and other contraband; money laundering; aggravated assaults; and murder. Are the outlaw one-percent clubs composed of autonomous individuals engaging in occasional crimes, some serious and some not, or a criminal association pursuing crime for profit in an organized fashion?

Today, in the age of the transnational biker criminal, one-time president of the Ventura, CA, Hells Angels and national and international Hells Angels president George Christie's self-serving statement cited at the beginning of the chapter does not stand up under the bright light of inquiry. Christie was referring to the Hells Angels, the largest and most well-known OMG. As one Canadian judge stated:

> I am certain that the jury would have no difficulty in concluding that the Manitoba Chapter of the Hells Angels Motorcycle Club was a criminal organization.
>
> (Caine, 2012:185)

Other one-percent club spokesmen make the same self-serving utterances. Nevertheless, the facts stand in contradiction to the egocentric proclamations of many one-percent club spokesmen. It is true that no one court has the power to declare the Hells Angels or any other OMC to be a criminal organization in every city, state, region, or country in which the club has a chapter or chapters. However, numerous chapters of the Hells Angels Motorcycle Club (HAMC), the largest of the OMGs in the world, along with chapters of other OMCs have been declared to be criminal organizations in U.S. courts and courts in other countries throughout the world. In the largest outlaw biker trial to ever take place, following the completion of Operation Springtime in Quebec, Canada, the prosecutor made the following statement to the jury in closing:

> I will repeat again that being part of the Hells Angels is not a crime in itself. But we have surely proven to you that the organization is a gang in the sense of the Criminal Code, and that it is a criminal organization. A criminal organization does not exist on its own. It is the members who compose it that commit the crimes.
>
> (Cherry, 2005:372)

The trial that followed the Montreal Biker War, which left 160 dead, resulted in the conviction of eight defendants, Hells Angels and members of their puppet/support club the Rockers MC, for being members of a criminal organization and committing crimes in furtherance of this criminal organization. It was well known, even before the trial, that the vicious and racist Maurice "Mon" Boucher, the Montreal Hells Angels leader, had created the Rockers to expand the drug-trafficking activities of the Hells Angels and act as a "farm team" for murderers and assassins in the Biker War. Furthermore, OMC members of some clubs, including HAMC members in the United States and other countries, have publicly stated in court that they belong to a criminal organization and had committed crimes in furtherance of that club/criminal organization.

The club/gang controversy is not the only contradiction that belies the motorcycle club nature of one-percent biker gangs. The popular adage among **one-percent bikers**—All bikers are not club members; but all club members are bikers—is no longer accurate for the chapters of some clubs whose members do not even own or ride bikes. In these instances the "bikers without bikes" are criminals using the "power of the patch" attached to being a member of a one-percent motorcycle gang to further their criminal pursuits. The patch is an important part of the bikers' philosophy of intimidation by reputation. Australian biker expert, Arthur Veno describes the new bikies [Australian term for bikers] as "Nike Bikies" because they wear Nike tennis shoes instead of riding boots (Kleinig, 2009, November 28). As we will see, this is not confined to Australia. He reports that the new clubs have dropped the riding rules and made the ownership of motorcycles optional. Furthermore, in those rare outlaw clubs where all the members are not engaged in serious criminal activity, the "non-criminal" members are accessories and fellow conspirators to the criminal behavior of their "brothers" for concealing and not reporting the crimes committed.

To fully grasp the difference between motorcycle clubs and motorcycle gangs, we must examine the differences between conventional motorcycle clubs and deviant motorcycle clubs and where the one-percent OMCs fit in the deviant (not according to the norm) motorcycle club grouping.

MOTORCYCLE CLUBS

Millions of Americans ride motorcycles, and those riders are a diverse group; however, since the first American "motor-driven cycle," the Indian, was built in 1901 by bicycle manufacturer George Hendree and his engineer Oscar Hedstrom in Springfield, Massachusetts, motorcycle riders have tended to form clubs, or voluntary social organizations based on their common interest in riding the iron machines (Hayes, 2011). At first the clubs were composed of foolhardy men racing these dangerous and unwieldy machines; then, in 1903, the fledgling American motorcycle scene changed dramatically. In 1903, William Harley and his friends Arthur and Walter Davidson launched the Harley-Davidson Company in Milwaukee,

Wisconsin, building a motorized bicycle that soon changed the machines and the way the machines were used, and this brought about a change in the riders and how they grouped together. William Harley and the Davidson brothers had no way of knowing at the time that "Harley" would come to describe a way of life and create a loyalty where men and women of all ages and races would tattoo the Harley-Davidson bar and shield on their bodies and Harley shops all over the world would sell Harley-Davidson bandanas, jackets, shirts, and even underwear emblazoned with the H-D logo. That was in the future, but first the motorized bicycle in the hands of the skilled Harley-Davidson workers morphed into a motorcycle with a powertrain consisting of a single-cylinder gasoline engine displacing 26.24 in.[3] with a direct drive transmission, leather belt primary drive, back brakes, and three dry cell batteries for ignition (Davidson, 2002). The chassis that this powertrain rested on resembled a bicycle, but it was certainly different. The chassis had a single loop frame, no suspension, a 51-in. wheelbase, a one-gallon gas tank, and 28-in. front and rear tires. The new motorcycle chassis and powertrain changed the manner in which the machines were used.

The new Harleys soon began to dominate the sport of motorcycle racing, and in the 1920s Harleys were used more and more as a means of transportation and for pleasure rather than racing (Davidson, 2002). Horse-drawn carriages and the latest invention, electric-powered trolleys, dominated transportation in the City of Milwaukee while the Harley-Davidson Company was manufacturing the iron machines. Individual travelers had a limited range of options—ride a horse, ride a bicycle, or walk. The adventurous of that day who desired to travel between cities or farther had to take the train. There were few highways, and coast-to-coast travel was a challenge. Motorcycles soon made it possible to ride within cities, between cities, and across the country for transportation or pleasure. In 1915, Della Crewe and her dog "Trouble" rode a 1914, side-car equipped, two-speed Harley-Davidson twin 5,378 miles from Waco, Texas, to Milwaukee to New York City (Hayes, 2010). The same year, Effie Hotchkiss and her mother, sitting in a sidecar, became the first women to ride across the United States. The sidecar also allowed for the entire family to share the motorcycle experience.

The motorcycle riders changed as women and other family members began riding motorcycles. The clubs they formed also changed. In 1924, the American Motorcycle Association (AMA) was formed, providing the main motorcycle racing sanctioning body, and soon began promoting what was known as "gypsy tours" that were, according to Hayes (2010), "statewide, good-clean-fun, jamboree-picnic soirees, which proved to be the ground-seed for events like the Sturgis Rally" (p. 43). Unbeknownst to anyone at the time, the AMA would soon play a huge role in the definition of what became known as OMCs. Following the formation of the AMA, groups of motorcycle riders organized clubs that are broadly classified as either conventional or OMCs (Barker, 2007). By the 1930s, the AMA had chartered 300 motorcycle clubs (Fuglsang, 1997). These AMA clubs represented the "responsible" motorcycle riders and had strict dress codes. Clubs that obtained a charter from the AMA were considered legal clubs; the others were classified as "outlaws" (Wolf, 1999). The "outlaw" label in this case meant non-AMA, not criminal. However, what was in effect a deviant label had consequences: outlaw clubs were not allowed to participate in AMA-sanctioned events such as mixers, charity events, races, and hill-climbing contests.

Conventional Motorcycle Clubs

Members of **conventional motorcycle clubs**, representing all races and sexes and riding all makes of motorcycles foreign and domestic, behave according to the norms of society and join together based on their common interest in motorcycles, riding together for pleasure and companionship. The early organized conventional clubs began a tradition of sponsoring mixers, charity events, and hill-climbing contests. They promoted responsible motorcycling as a family activity. The family-oriented ethic exists today in conventional motorcycle clubs. Today's conventional clubs, as did the early clubs, join traditional motorcycle associations such as the AMA and the Canadian Motorcycle Association (CMA). Historically, the members of conventional clubs come from different social strata and dress differently and act differently from outlaw club members.

The 13 Rebels Motorcycle Club, a conventional club established in 1937, touts itself as a family-oriented motorcycle club adhering to the conventional principles of: No Drugs, No Crimes, No Intimidation, Support Our Military, Support of Community, Support Our Brotherhood, and Have a Good Time. Their motto according to their website is "Not to bully the weak. Not to fear the powerful" (www.13rebelsmc.org). In a glaring departure from the OMGs to be discussed later, the 13 Rebels MC publicly state in their Code of Conduct that members will not sell drugs or commit crimes and that any member convicted of these offenses will be expelled from the club. This conventional club does not claim any territory. On the other hand, territorial/turf disputes lead to violence between and among OMCs. The American Cruisers Motorcycle Club, another conventional club, states that they are "a non-territorial, family oriented organization that supports our family, communities, military, and our country" (www.americancruisars.us). This motorcycle club also removes any member involved in illegal activities.

Outlaw Motorcycle Clubs

At about the same time as the appearance of the "outlaw" label, groups of motorcyclists began to appear in the motorcycle-friendly weather of Southern California in the early 1930s (Barker, 2007). Depression-stricken "Okies," looking for work and riding motorcycles because they were cheap transportation, appeared on the scene. Although most were loners who rarely stayed in one town for long, some banded together in the squalid Southern California industrial districts and formed loose-knit motorcycle clubs. Riding together in groups, these outsiders worked menial jobs and lived a deviant lifestyle of drinking and rowdy behavior, with some dealing in stolen motorcycle parts and other criminal pursuits (Yates, 1999). Harley-Davidson motorcycles were the most popular and abundant bikes at that time, so Harleys became the motorcycles of choice for these groups—for both possession and theft. Yates (1999) claims that this solidified the Harley-Davidson's identification as an outlaw machine. These outlaw clubs—non-AMA sanctioned or chartered—were often more like gangs than clubs and were also different in dress and behavior from the AMA conventional clubs. Their appearance foreshadowed the development of OMGs and the one-percent biker.

The steady growth of AMA-chartered conventional clubs and outlaw clubs continued into the early 1940s. At first, outlaw clubs, still in the minority, were not much of a threat to conventional motorcycle clubs or the image of motorcycle riders in general, but this changed in the late 1940s. Following World War II, outlaw clubs began disrupting AMA-sanctioned events and the label "outlaw" motorcycle clubs took on a new meaning and changed the public image of motorcycle riders. Although no one person was responsible for the change, "Wino Willie" Forkner has come to represent the change and the men who brought it about.

The Original Wild One: "Wino Willie" Forkner

In the early 1940s, conventional motorcycle clubs like the 13 Rebels and the Three Points existed in the Los Angeles area (Reynolds, 2000). Club members were riders with wives and kids who wore flashy sweaters and ties and had their bikes tuned for competition racing. A hard-drinking young motorcyclist named "Wino Willie" Forkner joined the 13 Rebels Motorcycle Club and rode with them for two years before the attack on Pearl Harbor. The young Forkner, who was to become a legend in outlaw motorcycle history, acquired his nickname at the age of 12 because of his affinity for red wine. After Pearl Harbor, the dipsomaniac Forkner joined the Army Air Corps and was manning a 0.50 caliber machine gun on a B-24 Liberator for the next 30 months (Reynolds, 2000). During that period, Wino Willie flew numerous missions in the South Pacific, made corporal, and lost his stripes because of a drunken episode in which he trashed a bar and got thrown in jail. In the summer of 1945, the hell-raising Wino Willie returned to California and rejoined the 13 Rebels, most of whom had spent the war years working in the area's aircraft manufacturing plants. It was not long before Wino Willie felt the loss of his bonds with the military and began having difficulty settling into the routine of a nine-to-five job, a mortgage, and the stresses of family life, and this led to a search for new adventures.

Forkner, according to his widow, Teri, was like many of the returning veterans "back from the war and letting off steam" (Bill Hayes Video Interview: The Original Wild Ones, 2003). "Letting off steam" for these veterans supposedly meant riding their bikes and drinking together in an attempt to recreate the camaraderie and excitement they had experienced in battle. Previous military service, especially combat experience, and the resulting postwar dissatisfaction, according to popular wisdom, plays a huge part in the creation of one-percent bikers and OMCs, with some writers considering it the defining factor. However, only a minute number of these returning veterans formed or joined OMCs. Military service may indeed be a factor, but how much of a factor is an empirical question. The relationship between military service and OMC membership may be spurious. There may be factors more important, or in addition to military or combat experience, that explain the early development of OMGs. Further confusing this facile explanation is that OMCs are found all over the world and their development does not appear to be related to military service. Alain (1995) says that there have been organized biker gangs in Canada since the 1930s. I am not aware of any studies of the military experiences of one-percent bikers in or outside the United States. Many of the members found in OMCs, past and present, were never in the military and could not join the military if they wanted to because of their criminal and psychological backgrounds. Furthermore, as discussed later, some of those who were instrumental in the early growth and establishment of OMCs were "veterans" in name only, such as Sonny Barger, the most celebrated Hells Angels leader, or were "kicked" out of the military because of their aberrant behavior. It appears that the veteran composition of most U.S.-spawned OMCs has drastically changed from the period right after World War II. That should not come as a surprise to anyone because practically all U.S. men who were in the age group 18-40 during that period and who were physically fit were under arms. Now, back to Wino Willie Forkner.

In the summer of 1946, Forkner and his drinking buddy and fellow 13 Rebels member Blackie were "letting off steam" in their favorite watering hole, the All-American Bar, when they decided to show up at a 13 Rebels–sponsored quarter-mile race in San Diego after an all-night drinking session (Reynolds, 2000:34-36). Forkner and Blackie sat in the stands and watched what they thought was a boring race. Thoroughly plastered and frustrated, Wino Willie decided to liven things up. Forkner drove his bike through the wooden gate leading from the parking lot onto the track. The drunken Forkner burst onto the track in a shower of shattered wood and loud applause from the audience who shared his view of the race. Forkner roared down the straightaway and made four laps around the track before losing control and turning his bike over. The subdued whirling dervish was promptly arrested and hauled off to jail. After a weekend in jail, Forkner pleaded guilty to trespassing and being drunk and disorderly. He hitchhiked back to Los Angeles and faced an enraged group of 13 Rebels members. The club members demanded his 13 Rebels sweater and threw him out of the club. The unrepentant Forkner reportedly returned the sweater after defecating on it (Reynolds, 2000:36). Wino Willie's legend was born and the evolution to one-percent biker clubs had begun.

The Boozefighters Motorcycle Club (1946)

The angry Wino Willie decided to put the 13 Rebels and the raceway fiasco behind him by drinking and sulking at the All-American Bar (Barker, 2007; Reynolds, 2000:36-38). Forkner began drinking with three former servicemen, including one who had lost both legs during the war. As the alcohol flowed and the night went on, the four inebriated bikers decided to form a new motorcycle club, but they could not come up with a name. Overhearing the animated discussion, an All-American regular named Walt Porter lifted his head off the bar and called out, "Call it the Boozefighters." At the time, the four bikers thought that was a perfect name for some reason. Happenstance ruled over reason. During the following weeks, Wino Willie and his fellow Boozefighters recruited 16 other members. All the new members of the **Boozefighters Motorcycle Club** were World War II veterans except a teenager named Jim Morrison (not, of course, the Morrison of The Doors fame). When it came time to choose officers, Forkner declined to be president, and C.B. Clauson, a former paratrooper, was elected president. The Boozefighters even applied for AMA membership, but were turned down by the AMA president, who allegedly said: "No goddamn way I am giving a name like that a charter" (Forkner, 1987). By 1947, three charters of the Boozefighters MC had formed in Los Angeles, San Pedro, and San Francisco (see Figure 2.1).

The Boozefighters MC was one of the first, but not the only, outlaw (non-AMA sanctioned–club formed by ex-servicemen "letting off steam"). Numerous World War II veterans joined outlaw clubs and called themselves the Galloping Goose (see Box 2.1), the Pissed Off Bastards of Bloomington (POBOB) (name later changed to Pissed Off Bastards of Berdoo), Satan's Sinners, and the Market Street Commandoes. Conventional clubs used simple and innocent-sounding names like the Road Runners, the Glendale Stokers, and the Side Winders. On occasion, these

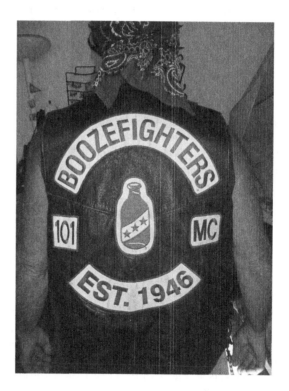

FIGURE 2.1

A Boozefighters back patch. The Boozefighters MC was one of the first outlaw clubs formed by ex-servicemen.

Photo courtesy of the Boozefighters Motorcycle Club and Bill Hayes.

conventional clubs engaged in reckless street races, but their behavior was harmless compared to the sometimes violence-prone behavior of the new outlaw clubs (Yates, 1999). To further distinguish themselves from AMA-club members who wore ties and racing caps, the outlaw veterans were unkempt in appearance and rowdy in behavior. With these groups, the stage was set for the creation of a new label—OMCs.

BOX 2.1 GALLOPING GOOSE MC AS A CRIMINAL ORGANIZATION

The Galloping Goose, formed by World War II veterans, has evolved into a criminal organization/criminal gang. The Galloping Goose MC and its affiliate El Forastero MC are involved in organized crime activities in the Midwest. In 2009 members of both motorcycle gangs pleaded guilty to conspiracy to distribute methamphetamine in the Kansas City, Kansas, area. Testimony at trial revealed that members of both gangs were required to pay annual dues and attend a certain number of runs (motorcycle trips) each year. On each run, the members were required to pay money that was pooled, or collected by each club chapter, then forwarded to the specific Galloping Goose or El Forastero charter (chapter) that hosted the particular motorcycle run to purchase methamphetamine, cocaine, and marijuana. Those drugs were maintained in run bags, which were distributed to all club members that attended the run.

Source: DOJ 12 (2009, June 3) and DOJ 13 (2009, November 25).

One event is considered to be the incident that changed the social definition of outlaw clubs: the **Hollister Motorcycle Incident/Riot** in 1947. Yates (1999) opines that it was at Hollister that OMCs made their national debut.

HOLLISTER MOTORCYCLE INCIDENT/RIOT 1947: BIRTHPLACE OF THE AMERICAN BIKER

The events, real, imagined, and contrived, that took place in the small California town of Hollister, the garlic-growing capital of the United States, during the 1947 July 4th weekend would lead to a staged photograph, which inspired a short story that led to a movie. The movie influenced a genre of biker movies and media publicity that ultimately constructed a new social definition of outlaw bikers. Fuglsang (1997:5) opines: "the events [with liberal media help] of Hollister began a long process that transformed a small group of Southern California bikers and free spirits into a national scourge." Although there are numerous versions of what took place during that weekend, Reynolds's account, relying on the observations of those present (including Wino Willie), appears to be accurate (Reynolds, 2000:45-58). The AMA had been conducting "gypsy tours" since their inception. These events were long-range rides to motorcycle rallies across the United States. In 1947, the West Coast town of Hollister, California, was chosen as the site for the gypsy tour and would draw in bikers from across the country. Hollister was (and still is) a big motorcycle town in the 1940s, with 27 bars and 21 gas stations. However, the town had only had six police officers. Hollister held its first gypsy tour in 1936 and held regular motorcycle races and hill climbs. The events scheduled for this gypsy tour included hill climbs, a slow race, dig-out race, and a flat-track race with a winning $1,200 purse. The residents were not expecting any trouble at the 1947 rally.

Members of all three Boozefighters MC chapters made plans to attend the motorcycle rally. The Los Angeles members, including Wino Willie, met on Thursday evening at the All-American to prepare for the ride to Hollister. Preparation included drinking at the All-American, riding to Santa Barbara for more drinks, and then riding to San Luis Obispo, where they became too drunk to continue. The Los Angeles Boozefighters "slept it off" in a bus terminal for three hours and roared off to King City, where they stopped at a liquor store to finish "preparing" for the ride into Hollister. By the time they arrived in Hollister, several thousand (actual number unknown) motorcyclists were already there and thoroughly "prepared." It was not long before intoxicated bikers turned the blocked-off main thoroughfares into drag-racing strips and stunt-riding exhibitions. Many of the local residents joined in the drag racing and merrymaking. The local bars were making a killing and were not complaining.

Members of conventional clubs were at the nearby Bolado Racetrack, which was filled to capacity for the scheduled races. Wino Willie's former club members from the 13 Rebels were competing in the races, and at least one member went home with a trophy (see Figure 2.2).

The hard-core bikers of Wino Willie's new club, the Boozefighters, and the other hell-raising outlaw clubs such as the POBOB were driving the town's six police officer's crazy. Soon the jail was filled to capacity with drunken motorcyclists, including

FIGURE 2.2

The Hollister trophy.

Photo courtesy of the 13 Rebels MC and National President Michael Mirando.

Wino Willie. Wino Willie was arrested for inciting a riot when the police mistakenly thought he was trying to incite the crowd into breaking the arrested bikers out of jail (Bill Hayes Video Interview: *The Original Wild Ones*, 2003). He was actually talking the mob out of the jailbreak.

While the commotion was going on, a photographer for the *San Francisco Chronicle*, who was there to cover the gypsy tour, decided to take a picture of a drunken motorcyclist. For some unknown reason, he staged a photograph, even though there were plenty of drunken motorcyclists available. The photographer, Barney Peterson, and a colleague sat a Harley-Davidson motorcycle on top of a pile of beer bottles and persuaded an intoxicated biker in a leather jacket coming out of a bar to sit astride the bike (see Box 2.2 and Figure 2.3). The picture never appeared in the *San Francisco Chronicle*, but it later became one of the most famous pictures in motorcycle history after the Associated Press picked it up and printed it in *Life* magazine.

BOX 2.2 EYEWITNESS ACCOUNT

The day after everyone had left, near my store there were two guys taking a photograph. They brought a bunch of empty beer bottles out of an alley and put them all around a motorcycle and put a guy on it. I'm sure that's how it was taken because they wanted to get up high to take the shot and they borrowed a ladder from me. (The photo appeared on the cover of *Life* magazine. Photo actually appeared on page 31 of *Life's* July 21, 1947, issue.)

Source: *Hayes (2005:181) (Ron Yant, Hollister appliance store owner)*.

On Sunday night, the thoroughly exhausted and disgusted Hollister police officers called for help from the California Highway Patrol (CHP). Forty CHP officers arrived at dusk and were met by hundreds of drunken motorcyclists. The majority of the motorcyclists were combat veterans like the Boozefighters and POBOBs and were used to following orders. The CHP lieutenant in charge ordered his men to break out the tear gas guns, and they began moving the compliant bikers toward the end of town. The lieutenant spotted a group of musicians unloading their instruments for a dance at the American Legion Hall and ordered them to set up in the street on a flatbed truck and play for the crowd. The crowd started dancing and continued dancing into the night under the watchful eyes of the CHP. While the drunken bikers danced, the local Chief of Police went to all the bars and closed them at midnight, two hours early. The "riot" was over, but the exaggerated and distorted publicity of the incident was just beginning. The media blitz that followed the alleged Hollister "riot" would create a new moral panic and "folk devil"—the biker.

MORAL PANICS AND FOLK DEVILS

"Moral panic" and "folk devil" are terms first defined by Stanley Cohen (1972) in his seminal work *Folk Devils and Moral Panics: The Creation of the Mods and Rockers*. Cohen described the media's exaggerated and sensationalized coverage of the Mods and Rockers (British rowdy juveniles identified by their dress). According to Cohen, a **moral panic** is created when false or exaggerated perceptions of some behavior or groups of persons, particularly minority groups or subcultures, lead to the conclusion that the behavior of the group is particularly deviant and poses a threat to society. This is not to say that the behavior of the group or members of the group is not deviant or does not pose a threat, but only that this threat is over-sensationalized, often leading to changes in the law and dealing with the group too harshly.

Historically, egregious examples of moral panics leading to harsh and despicable treatment of so-called **folk devils** have occurred in the United States, none more shocking than the racial cleansing of African-Americans from communities in Indiana (Washington County, 1864; Vermillion County, 1923), Texas (Comanche County, 1886), Tennessee (Polk County, 1894; Unicoi County, 1918), Missouri (Lawrence County, 1901), Kentucky (Marshall County, 1908; Laurel and Whitley Counties, 1919), Arkansas (Boone County, 1905 and 1909; Sharp County, 1906), Georgia (Forsyth County, 1912), and North Carolina (Mitchell County, 1923). In each of these racial cleansing incidents, a member of the black community (folk devils) committed a real or imagined crime against a member of the white community, usually the rape or attempted rape of a white woman, creating a moral panic (Jaspan, 2007). As a result of the moral panic, the folk devils—the black community—were violently "run" out of town. The violent event occurred, and the blacks were given a choice: Leave or die. Due to the times and the limited media sources, the moral panic in each of these racial cleansing episodes was primarily influenced by word of mouth with limited newspaper coverage, or the newspaper coverage was scarce or no longer extant. Obviously, today's mass media can create moral panics and folk devils that have a more far-flung impact than the small communities mentioned above. One can argue that the media's response to the tragic attacks on September 11, 2001 (9/11) and the so-called "War on Terror" have created new folk devils—terrorists—and a new moral panic that has led to new laws such as the USA PATRIOT Act, which some believe goes too far and is being used against individuals with no ties to terrorism.

There have been numerous examples of folk devils and moral panics created by sensationalized media coverage in recent years, including school shootings, such as the Columbine High School massacre that led to "zero tolerance" against imagined deviance by some students; daycare sexual abuse in the 1980s leading to the conviction of several innocent child care providers; child pornography on the Internet leading to several state laws declared unconstitutional by the U.S. Supreme Court; and sexting by school kids leading to a proliferation of laws and in-school restrictions, many of dubious utility and legality. There has been an explosion of sexual pedophile laws that, in an attempt to protect innocent children, have led to several named laws that put restrictions on all types of sexual offenders, even those convicted of statutory rape or urinating in public. We should also mention the recent moral panics created by the latest folk devils—illegal immigrants—resulting in several states passing their own immigration laws. The National Rifle Association (NRA) and other anti-gun control advocates argue that the shootings at Sandy Hook Elementary School in 2012 and other recent events have created a moral panic calling for restrictions of U.S. Second Amendment rights. Moral panics have also been created over violent video games and other role-playing games. The list of real or potential modern moral panics could go on ad infinitum, including the same-sex marriage controversy.

Cohen (1972:9) opined that certain youth cultures, such as the Teddy Boys (UK), the Mods and Rockers (UK), the Hells Angels, the Skinheads, and the Hippies, created moral panics with their deviant and delinquent behavior, and groups of people, such as communists, blacks, foreigners, immigrants, satanic worshippers, homosexuals, and bikers after the "Hollister Riot," have been socially constructed into folk devils.

Bikers as Folk Devils

Reynolds (2000) says that the Hollister incident would have been forgotten except for the picture and caption that appeared in the July 21, 1947, edition of *Life* magazine (see Figure 2.3).

FIGURE 2.3

The staged photograph at the Hollister Motorcycle Incident that set the tone for viewing bikers as folk devils.

The picture appeared in the July 21, 1947, edition of *Life* magazine.

On the Fourth of July weekend, 4,000 members of a motorcycle club roared into Hollister, California, for a three-day convention. They quickly tired of ordinary motorcycle thrills and turned to more exciting stunts. Racing their vehicles down the main street and through traffic lights, they rammed into restaurants and bars, breaking furniture and mirrors. Some rested a while by the curb. Others hardly paused. Police arrested many for drunkenness and indecent exposure but could not restore order. Finally, after two days, the cyclists left with a brazen explanation. "We like to show off. It's just a lot of fun." But Hollister's police chief took a different view, "It's just one hell of a mess."

Parts of the short article that accompanied the picture were true: bikers did race up and down Main Street, fights broke out, at least one biker did ride into a bar, some furniture was broken, 49 did get arrested, and 19-year-old Jim Morrison, the only nonveteran Boozefighter, was arrested for indecent exposure as he urinated in a truck's radiator in a drunken attempt to cool it down. However, there was no riot, and there were not 4,000 members of a motorcycle club. In fact, no motorcycle club of the time had 4,000 members. Even the write-up itself, an extreme exaggeration, could not raise to the level of riot. The "so-called Battle of Hollister was at best a skirmish and at the least a glorified drunken binge" (Yates, 1999:17). What may be the ultimate irony of this staged picture is that it is so famous and received so much publicity, but it is only one of the three pictures that appeared in the "Picture of the Week" section of that *Life* magazine. The first picture in the series of pictures shows four dead black prisoners lying on the ground of a Georgia prison camp. According to the accompanying article, on July 11, 1947, 27 black prisoners in the Thalman, Georgia, camp refused to work until they could air their grievances to a visiting prison inspector. The warden ordered that they be fired on, resulting in seven dead and eight injured. This picture of the prison massacre and the Georgia prison incident received no more publicity, but the Hollister "riot" and the staged picture would become part of outlaw motorcycle history and the bedrock for media attention. Did a new folk devil—the bikers—push the old folk devils out of the media's spotlight? Not yet entirely, but the stage had been set for the next motorcycle riot and the cheap media exploitation and sensationalism that followed.

RIVERSIDE MOTORCYCLE RIOT (1948)

Drunken motorcyclists, whether outlaw club members or not, were not through disrupting AMA-sponsored events. According to Reynolds, during a Labor Day [sic, it was actually July 4th] gypsy tour rally in Riverside, California, in 1948 more than 1,000 drunken motorcyclists recreated the scene that had occurred at Hollister one year earlier—this time with violent consequences. At the **Riverside Motorcycle Riot**, where there was plenty of drag racing and partying, an Air Force officer and his wife, trying to get through, honked at the pack of drunks blocking the street. The mob smashed the car windows, punched the driver, and manhandled his frightened wife (Reynolds, 2000:60). While this was occurring, one of the drunken riders wiped out on his bike, killing his girlfriend, who was riding with him. Boozefighters were in the area but not involved in the incident. However, local newspapers reporting the incident carried pictures of two Boozefighter members drinking beer and sitting on their bikes. The caption under the picture read that they were members of the same group who "started the Hollister Riot the previous year" (Reynolds, 2000:60).

Bill Hayes, a Boozefighter member called by some "The world's most literate biker," gives an entirely different account (Hayes, 2005). Quoting the undersheriff at the time, Hayes says that there were no traffic accidents in the city of Riverside that July 4th weekend and that most of the arrests that occurred were downtown when the motorcyclists were out of town participating in AMA events. The undersheriff goes on to say "that the nation-wide sensational publicity given the 4th of July weekend in Riverside, California, was neither honest nor factual" (Abbott, 1948, in Hayes, 2005:44-45). The only death, according to the undersheriff, that occurred in the county that weekend occurred when a motorcyclist ran into a bridge abutment "nearly a hundred miles from Riverside." The only injury occurred when a city park worker awoke a sleeping motorcyclist and got punched in the nose. Furthermore, the picture of the Boozefighters appearing in the newspapers had actually been taken a year earlier at Hollister. Undersheriff Abbott in his notarized report made a statement important to the one-percent label that would be applied to OMGs later on (see Box 2.3). Nevertheless, the national story coming on the heels of the Hollister "riot," whether it was true or false, led to a motorcycle short story that would create a genre of low-budget exploitation biker films that would cement bikers as folk devils and a part of modern pop culture.

BOX 2.3 STATEMENT OF UNDERSHERIFF ROGER L. ABBOTT

Definitely, a change in attitude and acts of the **one-percent** of irresponsible, intemperate and sometimes vulgar motorcyclists hiding behind the cloak of the ninety-nine percent of motorcyclists must be accomplished (emphasis added) (see Hayes, 2007 in Veno, 2007, for the entire notarized statement of Undersheriff Roger L. Abbott).

CYCLISTS RAID

In 1951, *Harper's Magazine* published a short story by Frank Rooney entitled "Cyclists Raid." The story was an exaggerated account of the Hollister incident and would have been forgotten except for the movie it inspired—*The Wild One*. The short story's plot is about an unnamed motorcycle gang taking over and terrorizing a small town somewhere on the West Coast. The assault by the leather-jacketed motorcyclists leads to the accidental death of the daughter of a hotel owner. Filmmaker Stanley Kramer read "Cyclists Raid" and decided to make a movie based on the story. He, writer Ben Maddow, and film star Marlon Brando spent three weeks interviewing ex-Boozefighters before filming started (Stidworthy, 2003). The resulting screen adaptation ushered in a new genre of biker movies.

THE WILD ONE: FIRST OF THE BIKER MOVIES

The 1954 movie, *The Wild One*, starring Marlon Brando, became a cult movie and solidified the image of bikers as folk devils and spread their cultural life style and dress throughout the world. In the movie, Brando as Johnny, the leader of the Black Rebels Motorcycle Club, leads a group of nomadic bikers into a conservative rural town. To set the stage for the shocking events that were to explode on the screen, the movie opened with: "This is a shocking story. It could never take place in American towns—but it did in this one. It is a public challenge not to let it happen again." Following the theme of postwar dissatisfaction and a spirit of rebellion against conventional mores having a part in the formation of OMCs, Johnny uttered the most famous line in the movie. When asked by an excited town's girl reading the back of his leather jacket, "Black Rebels Motorcycle Club, that's cute! Hey Johnny, what are you rebelling against?," Johnny laconically replies, "Whaddya got?" The mood now fixed, the macho, leather-clad bikers terrorize the local "squares" with their outrageous behavior (Osgerby, 2003). Lee Marvin, playing a decorated World War II Marine, leather-jacketed and riding a chopped Harley (Johnny rode a Triumph), is Johnny's arch-rival and leader of the biker club, the Beetles. After the film's release, hundreds of American bikers would emulate Brando and Marvin in dress and behavior. The Australian biker expert Arthur Veno asserts that motorcyclists across the Western world "saw the Hollywood version of an outlaw motorcycle rebel" and copied their attitudes, clothes, disrespect for society, and the way they treated women (Veno, 2003:30). According to Veno, motorcycle clubs in England, Australia, Canada, South Africa, New Zealand, Germany, Denmark, and Italy mimicked the screen outlaw bikers.

The Wild One was the first of a wave of exploitive movies that portrayed bikers as the new American outlaws. All these low-budget "drive-in" **biker movies** had the same basic plot: individualistic bikers—new outlaws—battling a corrupt, unfeeling, and conformist society (Wood, 2003). The movies were exploitation films based on sensational print media stories, and they were successful because "outlaw motorcycle gangs were a hot topic with many titillating and exploitable elements" (Synder, 2002:12). The most commercially successful biker movie was the cult classic *Easy Rider* (1969), starring veteran biker actors Peter Fonda and Dennis Hopper. The characters played by Fonda and Hopper traveled the country as hippies on bikes, visiting communes, smoking marijuana, taking LSD, and eventually being murdered by hippie-hating southern rednecks. The one-percent biker clubs were evolving at the same time as the biker movies.

HELLS ANGELS MOTORCYCLE CLUB AND THE ONE-PERCENTERS

The history of one-percent motorcycle clubs is ultimately a narrative of the HAMC. The name "Hell's Angels," although now copyrighted (without the apostrophe) by the HAMC, dates back at least to World War I. There was reportedly even an AMA-sanctioned Hell's Angels riding club in Detroit in the 1920s. The name was first used in movies in a 1930s Howard Hughes film, starring an 18-year-old Jean Harlow. The film was about two brothers who left their studies at Oxford to join the Royal Air Force and fight the Germans in World War I. A squadron of General Clair Chenault's famous "Flying Tigers" in China used the name, as did 12 different bomber squadrons in World War II (Reynolds, 2000). Its use as the name of a motorcycle club appears to be a matter of happenstance as was the naming of the Boozefighters MC.

One year after the Hollister incident, the World War II veterans OMC, the POBOB (there is now a chapter in California), had disbanded, partly because of the bad publicity from the sensationalized Hollister "riot." Reynolds (2000) contends that Arvid Olsen, a former squadron leader with the "Flying Tigers," suggested the name "Hell's Angels" for a new motorcycle club that he and several other former POBOB members decided to form in 1948 in San Bernardino, California. The official history of the HAMC appearing on the Hells Angels website says that Olsen gave the name but did not join the new club. The new members chose as a logo a grinning skull wearing a pilot's helmet with attached wings. A decade later the name and logo would be adopted by a group of motorcycle-riding young toughs and thugs in Oakland, completing the one-percent bikers progression.

During the next decade, HAMC charters (the use of charters follows the AMA tradition, other clubs use chapters) formed throughout California as nomadic members moved from one city to the next: in 1954, a charter/chapter was formed in San Francisco (former members of the Market Street Commandoes—World War II veterans) and Sacramento and North Sacramento charter/chapters were formed in 1957 (Reynolds, 2000:107-108). The 1957 Sacramento Hells Angels charter/chapter was formed out of the Hell Bent for Glory OMC started by two teenage toughs, James "Mother" Miles and his younger brother Pat. It was common then, and now, for groups of young toughs, responding to the media and pop culture to form clubs and, in the case of motorcycle riders, to declare themselves OMCs with bizarre and threatening names. As exemplified by the Hell Bent for Glory motorcycle clubs, some clubs, then and now, are assimilated or "patched over" by larger and more organized OMGs. The publicity surrounding the 1966 funeral of "Mother" Miles, the largest funeral in Sacramento up to the time, included a picture in *Life* magazine. These Hells Angels charters/chapters were more like separate clubs operating autonomously and independent of each other, often not knowing of the others. One man, Ralph "Sonny" Barger, is credited with bringing the chapters (chapters will be used from this time on, following the common designation) together creating the largest motorcycle club in the world.

Ralph "Sonny" Barger

Ralph "Sonny" Barger, the son of an alcoholic father and a negligent mother, is often referred to as the founder of the HAMC. As we have seen, this is not accurate. The charismatic Sonny Barger, although the most well-known Hells Angel with his own website, was only ten years old when the first HAMC chapter was formed in 1948. According to his best-selling autobiography, he grew up in the blue-collar jungle of Oakland, California, and joined the Army in 1955 with an altered birth certificate (Barger, Zimmerman, & Zimmerman, 2000). Less than a year later, the Army discovered his actual age and discharged him, making Barger technically a veteran. When he returned to Oakland, there were conventional and deviant motorcycle clubs in the city. According to Barger, there were numerous motorcycle clubs, like the Oakland Motorcycle Club, that were family clubs, and there were also "freewheeling clubs" like the Oakland Panthers. Barger joined the Panthers but soon left because they did not provide enough action. He looked for a more action-oriented club to join.

Once more, serendipity charted the course for the evolution of one-percent motorcycle clubs. Barger found a new wild bunch of motorcyclists with whom to ride. This group of young toughs, responding to the media portrayal of motorcycle gangs, declared themselves to be a motorcycle gang and looked for a name to use as a common identifier. One of Barger's riding buddies "wore a modified Air Force–like patch he found in Sacramento, a small skull wearing an aviator cap inside a set of wings" (Barger et al., 2000:30). The young "outlaws" thought the patch was cool and decided to name their club Nomad Hells Angels after the patch. In April 1957, the club had patches made based on the design (which later became the easily recognizable copyrighted HAMC death's head). Sometime later Barger met another biker wearing the very same Hells Angels patch. This Angel filled Barger in on the history of the club formed in San Bernardino in 1948, including the other chapters and the rules, regulations, and procedures for becoming a Hells Angels chapter. Angels from the SoCal (Southern California) chapter visited the quasi–Hells Angels in Oakland. A series of meetings later and the Oakland Chapter of the HAMC came into being. In 1958, Sonny Barger became president of the Oakland Chapter; he then became President of the National Hells Angels Motorcycle Club and changed the HAMC forever. Although the Hells Angels' basic organization was in place when Barger took over as Oakland president, under his leadership and guidance new rules were added pertaining to new members, club officials, and induction of new charters/chapters. With Barger at the helm, the HAMC would expand into the largest and the most well-known motorcycle club in history. They would also become more like a criminal gang than a motorcycle club. However, along the way there were bumps, including movement into drug dealing, adoption of the one-percent label, adverse publicity, and the Altamont Speedway homicide.

Oakland HAMC Chapter: The Early Years

Early outlaw clubs like the Boozefighters were formed by veterans; later, outlaw clubs, particularly the one-percent clubs, would not be veteran-centered and would be in the tradition of the Sacramento Hells Angels chapter, formed by young toughs and criminals or those with criminal tendencies. Even motorcycle clubs formed by veterans such as the Bandidos (Marine veteran), Sons of Silence (Navy veteran), and the Florida Warlocks (Navy veteran) would soon evolve into gangs and criminal organizations. Some point to the veteran status of the founders of the Bandidos, Warlocks, and Sons of Silence as an indicator that these clubs were founded and soon "overflowed with highly disciplined, profoundly alienated, Vietnam Veterans who had been inoculated with violence, calloused against mere materialism, and greeted upon their return with contempt and scorn" (Davis, 2011). The founders of the Bandidos, Warlocks, and Sons of Silence were Vietnam-era veterans, as were most of the young men of their social class at that time. However, these founders did not experience the horror of combat, and there is no evidence that they were in any way alienated by their service experiences or the horror of combat. Donald Eugene Chambers, the former Marine founder of the Bandidos, according to one former Bandidos member, only saw Vietnam combat on TV (Winterhalder, 2005). The other founders were Navy veterans during the Vietnam War and it is extremely unlikely that they came close to the horror of combat. These "facts" once again cast doubt on the relationship between veteran status and membership in OMGs and call for an empirical examination of the issue. I would suspect that the rolls of law enforcement agencies at that time (post–World War II and post-Vietnam) were also filled with veterans. Furthermore, the young toughs who formed the Oakland Hells Angels in no way resembled the supposedly disaffected World War II veterans who were the core of the early outlaw clubs.

The Oakland Angels were "outlaws" regardless of whether they belonged to the AMA. For example, George "Baby Huey" Wethern, a high school dropout who received an undesirable discharge from the U.S. Air Force, became the vice president of the Oakland Hells Angels in 1960 (Wethern & Colnett, 1978). Wethern, like Barger and many of the other Oakland Angels, was not comparable in military service to those who formed the first HAMC in 1948. Veteran status does not appear to be a necessary condition for joining or being predisposed to join an OMC, but being a criminal or having criminal or violent tendencies does.

Wethern describes the early Angels as "basically honest blue-collar or unskilled workers looking for excitement" (Wethern & Colnett, 1978:50). The Oakland

Hells Angels at that time were a nascent version of what criminologist Klaus von Lampe refers to as a social criminal organization (von Lampe, 2003). A social criminal organization is one that indirectly supports the criminal behavior of its members. The bond of trust between members in a social criminal organization reduces the likelihood of any one member; even a fellow member that does not approve of certain criminal acts, "ratting out" or disapproving of a fellow member's criminal activities. In other words, they look the other way in silence (more on this later when we discuss the criminal activities of OMGs). In von Lampe's network approach to organized crime, the basic unit in any form of criminal cooperation occurs when two actors are linked together by criminally exploitable ties (latent or manifest criminal dispositions that come together when the opportunities arise and there is a common basis of trust) (von Lampe, 2003; von Lampe & Johansen, 2004). His network approach assumes that crimes such as drug trafficking or investment fraud; criminal collectives such as mafia syndicates syndicate, street gangs, OMGs, and prison gangs (see Barker, 2007, 2012); and criminal collectives such as corrupt alliances of businessmen, politicians, and public officials, all begin with participants connected through criminally exploitable ties that combine to form criminal social networks. Furthermore, the networks established as the OMGs expanded statewide, regionally, nationally, and internationally allowed for the criminal tendrils of U.S.-based OMGs to blanket the world.

Many of the early members of the Oakland Hells Angels chapter, although they may have been "basically honest blue-collar or unskilled workers looking for excitement," as Wethern alleges, also shared criminally exploitable ties. This was to become clear as the Hells Angels moved into drug dealing and the vice-president, Wethern, and the president, Sonny Barger, became major drug dealers. At this point, the Oakland Hells Angels were a criminal gang, not a motorcycle club. Wethern also describes an ominous event—the first club-sanctioned execution of a member in 1968 (the first of many brother-on-brother murders). Paul A. "German" Ingalls, a 21-year-old transfer from the Omaha Hells Angels chapter, was force-fed "reds" (barbiturates) until he went into a coma and died. Ingalls was tried, convicted, and executed by his "brothers" for committing a capital offense— stealing the president's, Sonny Barger's, coin collection (Wethern & Colnett, 1978:154-155).

One-Percent Bikers

"We're the one-percenters, man—the one-percent that don't fit and don't care… we're royalty among motorcycle outlaws," claimed a Hell's Angel.

(quoted in Thompson, 1966)

Wethern describes a historic meeting that was "sort of like the Yalta conference" in 1960, held at the home of Frank Sadilek, the president of the San Francisco Hells Angels chapter. At the meeting were Hells Angels leaders from across the state and former warring California biker club leaders—of the Gypsy Jokers, Road

Rats, Galloping Goose, Satan's Slaves, the Presidents, and the Mofos. The purpose of the meeting was to discuss police harassment, but discussion soon turned to recent hostile comments by the AMA.

FIGURE 2.4

The 1% patch has been accepted by the one-percenters as a badge of honor, and is often represented in tattoos sported by biker club members.

Photos courtesy of the U.S. Department of Justice.

"To draw a distinction between its members and us renegades, the AMA had characterized ninety-nine percent of the country's motorcyclists as clean-living folks enjoying pure sport. But it condemned the other one-percent as antisocial barbarians who'd be scum riding barbarians riding horses or surfboards too" (Wethern & Colnett, 1978:54). The clubs decided to accept the one-percent label (1%) as a tribute and not as an insult and adopt the "1%" patch to identify themselves as righteous outlaws. Wethern and Sonny Barger were the first to get the "1%" tattoos (see Figure 2.4).

HAMC in the Mid-1960s

The HAMC began to receive a lot of adverse publicity during the mid-1960s, culminating in the famous Altamont homicide (discussed later). The long-haired, leather-jacketed, Nazi symbol–wearing outcasts on two-wheels lived up to their folk devil label as they were thrust into the national limelight by the alleged rape of two Monterey, California, teenagers in 1964 (Reynolds, 2000; Thompson, 1966; Veno, 2002). On Labor Day (September 19, 1964), an estimated 300 Hells Angels from throughout California went on their annual run to Monterey. While in a local bar, two girls and five teenage boys started hanging around with them. Later that night, sheriff's deputies responded to a call to some sand dunes where the Angels were camping. When the deputies arrived, they found the young girls hysterical, one naked and the other wearing a ripped sweater. The 14- and 15-year-old girls claimed they had been assaulted by up to 20 Hells Angels. Four Angels were arrested. The event exploded onto the national headlines. Hunter S. Thompson, the gonzo journalist and author of the classic and seminal work on the Oakland Hells Angels and the first to use the term outlaw motorcycle gangs in print, says that the event made the Hells Angels national celebrities (folk devils). Later, the girls stated that they and their teenage friends had willingly followed the Angels from the bar to their camp to drink wine and get high. Three weeks later the case was dismissed for lack of evidence, but the dismissal did not receive national publicity. Legend has it that the Angels first moved into drug dealing to pay legal fees associated with the defense of the four arrested Angels.

The California Attorney General, Thomas Lynch, responding to pressure from the alleged Monterey "rape," contacted state law enforcement agencies and asked for data on the Hells Angels. In 1965, the "famous" Lynch report was released. Although the report was largely fiction compiled from questionable police files, it again thrust the Hells Angels into the national limelight as stories of their alleged debauchery appeared in *Time, Life,* and *Esquire.* Movie director Roger Corman, sensing opportunity, quickly put together (in 15 days at a budget of $360,000) another biker film, *The Wild Angels,* starring Peter Fonda and Nancy Sinatra, in 1966 (Osgerby, 2003). Corman even hired a group of Ventura, California, Hells Angels as extras. The film was as "shocking" as it was awful in its violation of social taboos, including men kissing each other, wild partying—drinking and taking drugs—in a church, scenes of sexual violence, a swastika draped over a coffin under a crucifix, and roughing up a priest, all to the sound of wild bongos. The film was widely panned by the movie industry but became a huge commercial success, setting the stage for even more successful biker movies such as *Easy Rider,* mentioned earlier.

ALTAMONT SPEEDWAY—ONE-PERCENT (1%) BIKERS ON DISPLAY

The popularity of the biker movies declined at the same time that the image of the Hells Angels and one-percent bikers (1%) became clear—at the Altamont Speedway on December 6, 1969. The Rolling Stones, described at that time as the greatest rock-and-roll band in the world, were finishing a tour of the United States. The band, criticized for the high prices charged for their performances during the tour, decided to thank the public and assuage their guilt by giving a free concert in San Francisco at its conclusion (Baers, 2002). The event was plagued with problems from the outset. It was first scheduled to be held in Golden Gate Park, but the large number of people expected led the San Francisco City Council to turn down the permit four days before the concert. Sears Point Speedway, outside San Francisco, was then chosen. While the scaffolding, generators, and sound equipment were being assembled at Sears Point, the owners demanded an exorbitant bond to protect them from liability, so the deal fell through. Less than 48 hours remained before the announced concert date when the Altamont Speedway owner, Dick Carter, volunteered his property for free, thinking that he would receive a vast amount of publicity for his benevolence. Carter was right, but it was not the publicity he expected. December 6, 1969, was to become the most violent day in rock history and was later hailed as the real and metaphysical end to the 1960s counterculture (Baers, 2002). The true viciousness of the Hells Angels was also exposed that day at Altamont, revealing them to be "really as dangerous as everyone said they were" (Morton, 1999).

The Rolling Stones hired the Hells Angels for $500 worth of beer to act as security for the event. All that beer was probably not the deciding factor for the Hells

Angels, who were anticipating all the money they could score for drug sales during the concert. The naïve British rock group had previously used the London, England, Hells Angels chapter for a concert without any problems. The relatively harmless London Angels shared only the club name with their alcohol-drinking, marijuana-smoking, and acid-dropping "brothers" in California. The California Angels believed that the way to handle security was to beat the crowd with lead-filled pool cues, throw full cans of beer at them, or drive motorcycles into the crowd. Violence began almost immediately. During the first set by Santana, inebriated and whacked-out Angels began provoking fights with the enthusiastic and also inebriated and equally whacked-out audience. Whenever anyone ventured too close to the stage, they were intercepted by pool cue–waving Hells Angels. Jefferson Airplane began their set as the Angels arranged themselves on stage. Several Angels jumped off the stage into the crowd and began beating and stomping real and perceived troublemakers. Singer Marty Balin, personally knowing several of the Angels, jumped off the stage to stop the violence. His futile effort was akin to jumping into a shark-feeding frenzy. Balin was knocked unconscious and stomped repeatedly. The Angels calmed down under the mellow country rock of the Flying Burrito Brothers, but they continued drinking, smoking marijuana, and dropping acid, setting the stage for the final act.

The Rolling Stones made a serious miscalculation by waiting for an hour and a half before taking the stage. They wanted to make their entrance as dramatic as possible for maximum effect, a rather dumb move given what had already taken place. The crowd grew restless and the Angels continued to get stoned. When the band took the stage, small fights began to break out in front of the stage. Although what happened next is a matter of controversy, it was recorded on film for the documentary *Gimme Shelter*. The Rolling Stones had contracted with the filmmaking crew of David Maysles, Albert Maysles, and Charlotte Zwerin to document the last weeks of the Stones concert in America. According to one version of what happened, the racist Angels spotted a young black man, 18-year-old Meredith Hunter, with a young white girl. According to Michael J. Baers, the Angels, after spotting Hunter, jumped off the stage and began savagely beating, stomping, and stabbing him (Baers, 2002). Allegedly Hunter drew a gun in self-defense. The gun was taken away from him, and the crazed Angels continued their assault and would let no one come to Hunter's aid until he bled to death. The Rolling Stones carried on with the song they were singing, and when they finished they fled to a waiting helicopter.

Hells Angels' icon Sonny Barger provides a different, but no less violent, account of the events at Altamont Speedway that fateful night. He says that he and the other Oakland Hells Angels arrived late in the afternoon, some three hours after the concert started (Barger et al., 2000). The crowd parted and let them ride to within four feet of the front of the stage. So far, his account squares with the film footage. Barger says that there had been several fights before they arrived—one being the incident where singer Marty Balin had been knocked unconscious, which was also on the film footage. Barger explains this incident as being the result of Balin disrespecting an Angel. According to Barger, while the rest of the Angels sat on the stage drinking beer waiting for the Rolling Stones to come on, "some of the people who had been pushed around got mad and started throwing bottles at us and messing with our bikes" (Barger et al., 2000:164). The film does show the crowd very close to the bikes in front of the stage, but there is nothing showing any bottles being thrown at the Angels on the stage. Admittedly, the final documentary was edited, but it never shows the crowd assaulting the Angels with bottles or anything else. Barger and the Hells Angels jumped into the crowd, "grabbing some of the assholes vandalizing our bikes and beat the fuck out of them" (Barger et al., 2000:164). This assault on the crowd does appear. Barger says that shortly after the incident "a topless fat girl" tried to get on the stage, and he walked over and kicked her in the head. In the documentary, a totally nude girl is shown attempting to climb on the stage, but the crowd pulled her back. Barger then says that Keith Richards announced to the crowd that the band was going to stop playing if the violence did not stop—verified by the film. Barger says that "…I stood next to him and stuck my pistol into his side and told him to start playing his guitar or he was dead." On the film, a Hells Angels is seen talking to Keith Richards, but there is no indication of a pistol.

Barger offers little sympathy for Meredith Hunter, whom he says rushed the stage with a gun in his hand. It is at this point that Barger's description of what happened that night varies from what is in the film footage. There is no evidence that the homicide victim, Meredith Hunter, ever approached the stage with a gun in his hand. From here on, Barger's description of the events lacks credibility. Barger says that Hunter got up on the stage, was knocked off, and the gun fired, hitting an Angel. Because the Angel was a fugitive and only received a flesh wound, according to Barger he was not taken to a doctor or emergency ward. Barger says he didn't see the stabbing; Hunter was already stabbed when Barger got to him, so the Angels picked him up and turned him over to the medics. Whether or not one accepts Barger's account of the stabbing (as stated, viewing the *Gimme Shelter* documentary does not support much of his account), his version of the actions of the Hells Angels on that fateful day reveals them to be very violent individuals ill-suited to provide security at any public event.

The gun disappeared after the stabbing and was recovered several days later by Barger and sent to attorney Melvin Belli with the fingerprints wiped off (Reynolds, 2000). San Francisco Hells Angel Allen Passaro, age 22, was charged with stabbing Hunter five times and brought to trial. The film clip from the documentary was played for the jury several times. The documentary does show Hunter with a gun in his hand, but it does not show him on the stage or firing the gun. In any event, the jury found Passaro not guilty, leading the Hells Angels to boast that they were bigger than the law. Passaro was found dead years later floating in a ravine, but not before being charged with participating in a criminal enterprise (HAMC) through a pattern of racketeering activity.

Just how ill-suited these violent Hells Angels were for security duties is revealed in a speech given by a psychoanalyst who had worked with Allen Passaro (the psychoanalyst does not give Passaro's name, but it is clear it is him) in the early 1960s at Hope Place, a community mental health center in New York's East Village

(Lasky, 2002). Among those treated at Hope House were a group of really "bad boys" who were members of the New York chapter of the Born Killers Motorcycle Gang (believed to be a pseudonym for the Aliens MC) who had their clubhouse nearby. These gang members, according to Lasky, were notorious for their criminal behavior and acts of sadism and violence, including one of them tearing the throat out of the Hope House pet kitten, with his teeth. Lasky says that the members of the Born Killers glorified in "terrorizing anyone who was not a Born Killers member; that included both the street kids and the staff of Hope House" (Lasky, 2002:4). One particular member of the Born Killers (presumably Passaro), although exceptionally violent and sadistic, entered into a six-week period of "twice weekly supportive psychotherapy" on the condition that it be kept from his buddies. Lasky admits that his patient scared him and was made to lock up his "gun, knife, chains, razor-sharp belt buckle, brass knuckles, and any other weapon" before their sessions. Lasky says that the patient mysteriously disappeared after the six-week period, and Lasky forgot about him until seeing the movie that had been made at the Rolling Stones' Altamont concert. Lasky stated in his speech: While watching the stabbing of Meredith Hunter "…who do you think I saw doing the stabbing? Right. My former patient" (Lasky, 2002:6).

Passaro's violent tendencies are confirmed by another account. According to Reynolds (2000), Passaro did not even own a motorcycle when he was voted in as a member of the San Francisco Hells Angels. He was told to get one before he became an official member. Passaro called a man who had a Harley advertised in the paper, went to see him, beat the man unconscious, and stole the bike. Barger also makes it clear that he was aware of the violent nature of the Angels when he comments on their selection as security: "Soon enough, the Stones would find out that California Hells Angels were a little bit different from their English counterparts of the day." As Rolling Stones guitarist Mick Taylor said, "These guys in California are the real thing. They're very violent" (Barger et al., 2000:160). The intervening years have not changed that much. The Hells Angels and other one-percent biker clubs that came after them are still very violent and criminal.

Evolution from Clubs to Gangs

KEY TERMS

American Motorcycle Association (AMA)

Double-O-Alliance

gang colors

International Outlaw Motorcycle Gang Investigators Association (IOMGIA)

one-percenters (1%ers)

National Gang Intelligence Center (NGIC)

Vietnam Vets MC

ONE-PERCENTERS' CREED

One-percenters are the one percent of us who have given up on society and the politician's one-way law. We're saying we don't want to be like you. So stay out of our face. It's one for all and all for one. If you don't think this way, then walk away, because you are a citizen and don't belong with us.

Statement attributed to Bandido Motorcycle Gang founder Donald Eugene Chambers (Winterhalder & De Clerco, 2008:xv).

INTRODUCTION

It has been more than 50 years since the first outlaw motorcycle clubs roared onto the American motorcycle scene. These motorcyclists sought their identity in the outlaw label, which at that time meant not being associated with, or sanctioned by, the **American Motorcycle Association (AMA)**. The outlaw bike riders wanted to be seen as different from conventional riders who sought AMA approval and were bound to traditional society and its rules and laws. Members of outlaw motorcycle clubs were proud of their outcast sameness. These outlaw motorcycle clubs morphed into the infamous **one-percenters (1%ers)** after the incidents of Hollister and Riverside and once again reveled in their sameness and exclusion from society and its mores and laws. Then, they, the outlaw clubs, in a sense, finally "got what they asked for"—exclusion from society—when

35

U.S. law enforcement labeled them "criminal organizations whose members use their motorcycle clubs as conduits for criminal enterprises" and designated outlaw motorcycle clubs as outlaw motorcycle gangs (OMGs), who used the club label as a screen for criminal behavior and the organizational structure of the clubs to facilitate their criminal enterprises. In effect, U.S. law enforcement said that the outlaw motorcycle clubs and their members were more like criminals than motorcyclists. As these OMGs expanded outside the Continental United States (CONUS), the criminal label followed in the wake of their criminal activities. The U.S.-based outlaw motorcycle clubs, now criminal gangs, became universally recognized as international crime threats. Nevertheless, as the OMG tag expanded nationally and internationally, outlaw motorcycle "club" spokespersons vociferously argued that they were not criminal organizations or gangs and resisted the new gang label as passionately as they had embraced the outlaw label. The claims of being clubs, not gangs, fell largely on deaf ears outside the outlaw motorcycle community. The credibility of their self-serving statements was undermined by the observation that many of those offering up these egocentric statements were, like Hells Angels leaders George Christie and Sonny Barger, convicted felons with long criminal histories who often regaled others with their criminal pasts. For example, a Texas cop once asked Sonny Barger, a self-proclaimed American legend, why he and his fellow bikers were carrying big knives. Barger replied: "Because we are all felons and we can't carry a big gun like you" (Barger et al., 2000:3).

The debate between outlaw motorcycle club members and the law enforcement community over the gang label continues unabated today. Members claim that outsiders, particularly law enforcement, fail to see the true picture. "It's a motorcycle club [Hells Angels] with criminals in it, not a criminal organization. That's an important distinction" (Edwards, 2013:273). This quote is from Lorne Campbell, a 46-year one-percent Canadian biker—30 years with Satan's Choice as an officer and enforcer before becoming a member of the Hells Angels. Campbell is an admitted murderer, and the book portrays him as an extremely violent man with a quick temper, a drug dealer, a weapons trafficker, and an ex-con. Is there a distinction between a motorcycle club with criminals in it and a criminal organization, or is the supposed distinction a matter of semantics? Some outlaw motorcycle clubs have members committing crimes on an individual or small group basis supposedly without the knowledge or overt support of the entire membership, and some outlaw motorcycle clubs are criminal gangs organized for crime for profit using the club marker as a screen and conduit for criminal behavior. Are both examples to be considered criminal gangs?

OUTLAW MOTORCYCLE GANGS

U.S. Criminal Justice View

Law Enforcement (Local and National)

LOCAL

The term outlaw motorcycle gangs (OMGs) was first used by Kentucky native and gonzo journalist Hunter S. Thompson in his 1966 seminal work on the Hells Angels

Motorcycle Club—*Hell's Angels: The Strange and Terrible Saga of the Outlaw Motorcycle Gangs*. Law enforcement began to use this pejorative label as the former hell-raising and nonconforming motorcycle clubs, particularly the notorious media sensation the Hells Angels Motorcycle Club, moved into criminal activity, particularly drug dealing, and became more like gangs (organized for crime as profit) than clubs of motorcycle enthusiasts (Barker, 2007). Local law enforcement agencies, not federal authorities, were the first to treat the outlaw (one-percent, not AMA-sanctioned) motorcycle clubs as organized crime groups. In 1976 and 1977, the Orange County, California, Sheriff's Department had an undercover female deputy riding with a Hells Angels member (Detroit, 1994). The undercover operation led to the indictment of 77 bikers, 19 of them Hells Angels members, for charges ranging from drug trafficking to murder. The Hells Angels posted a $25,000 reward for the deaths of the deputy and the Hells Angels member she rode with. The California Hells Angels imported a New York Hells Angels contract killer to kill both of them. The deputy left California and located in another state under an assumed name, and the club informer later died in a motorcycle accident under suspicious circumstances. Several of the Angels brothers who caused the penetration were murdered. In 1981, on the other side of the country, an investigation by the Fayetteville, North Carolina, Police Department into thefts of Harley-Davidson motorcycles and insurance fraud led to a local Hells Angels chapter (Johnson, 1981). The investigation resulted in arrests in 20 states.

It was not long before outlaw motorcycle clubs other than the Hells Angels were soon classified as OMGs. The Ohio Attorney General listed 29 OMGs, including the Hells Angels, Outlaws, Pagans, Avengers, and Iron Horsemen, operating in Ohio (Organized Crime Consulting Committee, 1986). The report described a 1982 raid of a drug factory run by the Avengers MC where 50 pounds of methaqualone powder were found. The same report stated that 12 homicides in northern Ohio had been linked to the Hells Angels and the Outlaws Motorcycle Club. Another 1982 law enforcement report listed the criminal activities of major OMGs as manufacturing and distribution of narcotics, prostitution, weapons-related violations, extortion, murder, arson-for-hire, pornography, protection rackets, loan sharking, interstate transportation of stolen property and stolen vehicles, and insurance fraud (Davis, 1982). The profits from these illegal activities were being invested in legitimate businesses, a characteristic of other organized crime entities, such as the Mafia. Federal law enforcement agencies, recognizing the national threat as these organized crime activities crossed state boundaries, moved against the OMGs.

NATIONAL

The FBI began targeting the outlaw motorcycle clubs now officially known by law enforcement agencies as OMGs (see Box 3.1) in 1981 under the Organized Crime Program and RICO (Racketeer Influenced Criminal Organization) statute. The FBI defines a criminal organization as a group of individuals with an identified hierarchy engaged in significant criminal activity (McFeeley, 2001). The RICO statute allowed for the prosecution of OMGs following the enterprise theory of investigations, which called for identifying the hierarchy and network between members. Common to such investigations are the use of cooperating witnesses, informants, undercover agents, and—most importantly—court-approved electronic surveillance. To prosecute a gang under RICO requires showing that: (1) an enterprise exists (gangs, by definition, qualify as enterprises), (2) that the enterprise affects interstate commerce (obviously all drug and weapons trafficking crosses state lines), (3) that the defendant was associated with the enterprise (colors, tattoos, and avowed membership prove association), (4) that the defendant engaged in a pattern of racketeering activity (wiretaps and undercover operations are used here), (5) that the defendant conducted the racketeering activity of the enterprise by committing at least two racketeering activities (examples include: any act or threat involving murder, kidnapping, gambling, arson, robbery, bribery, extortion, dealing in obscene matter, or dealing in narcotics or other dangerous drugs) within two years of each other (Barker, 2012:272). In 1979, federal authorities decided to take action against the Hells Angels as a criminal organization, not as individual criminals. However, they underestimated the Hells Angels and the complexity of making a plausible RICO case that a jury would believe. This first federal action under the RICO statute against the Hells Angels and Sonny Barger resulted in a nine-month trial and a mistrial. The government tried again, and a second mistrial was declared (Barger et al., 2000). The HAMC is still celebrating this as a victory over the federal government. However, later prosecutions under RICO have been more successful against the HAMC and other OMGs, as well as other adult criminal gangs such as street gangs and prison gangs (Barker, 2012). In 1981, the FBI raided a Hells Angels arsenal in Cleveland, Ohio, and found a large quantity of explosives and automatic weapons, including hand grenades and antitank rockets (Organized Crime Consulting Committee, 1986). The explosives and weapons were reportedly to be used in their war with the Outlaws MC. A two-year undercover investigation by an FBI agent begun in 1982, known as "Operation Roughrider," involved 11 HAMC chapters in seven states and led to the arrests of 125 members and associates (Operation Roughrider, 1985). Starting a trend that continues to this day, several of the Hells Angels informed on their "brothers" for lighter sentences (Reynolds, 2000). The longer sentences allowed under RICO prosecutions encourage "ratting" out accomplices, and the first "rat" gets the best deal. Drugs confiscated during this operation included: methamphetamine, cocaine, marijuana, hashish, PCP, and LSD. Also, beginning in 1982, a member of the HAMC Alaska chapter, Anthony Tate, became an FBI informant and remained one for three years. The resulting arrests of 35 Hells Angels included the National President, Sonny Barger (Reynolds, 2000). Tate was paid $250,000 and now reportedly lives in Europe under an assumed name.

BOX 3.1 OUTLAW MOTORCYCLE GANGS

Outlaw motorcycle gangs (OMGs) are organizations whose members use their motorcycle clubs as conduits for criminal enterprises. OMGs are highly structured criminal organizations whose members engage in criminal activities such as violent crime, weapons trafficking, and drug trafficking.

Source: U.S. Department of Justice.

The FBI also moved against other Outlaw Motorcycle Gangs. A 1982 RICO prosecution against Outlaws MC members from Florida, Georgia, North Carolina, and Tennessee involved white slavery and transporting women across states lines for immoral purposes (Smith, 2002). The National President of the Pagans Motorcycle Club, Anthony "Tiny" Martinez, was killed in a shootout with the FBI on Interstate 80 near Hubbard, Ohio, in 1984 (Organized Crime Consulting Committee, 1986). He had $69,820, a 9-mm pistol, and a machine gun in his possession when stopped. The Pagans leader was "on the run" for failure to appear in a federal court in Delaware on the RICO charges of drug trafficking and operating a continuing criminal enterprise. The 1986 President's Commission on Organized Crime listed OMGs as being active in the United States during the 1980s. By the beginning of the 1990s, OMGs were recognized as an emerging new type of organized crime by law enforcement officials and others. They appeared in the Congressional Record as such in 1991, and the RICO prosecutions picked up speed (Brenner, 2002:4).

Today, in the United States, RICO prosecutions are law enforcement's best weapons against all adult criminal gangs, including OMGs. In order to begin a RICO prosecution, the indictment must specifically allege that there is a criminal enterprise, that that enterprise is engaged in specific criminal acts involving interstate commerce, and the part each criminal actor plays in the furtherance of the criminal acts. For example, Box 3.2 on Double-O-Alliance presents portions of the RICO indictment of what is known as the **Double-O-Alliance**, a 2009 criminal enterprise between the Chicago Outlaws Motorcycle club and the traditional Chicago organized Mafia crime group known as the Outfit or the mob.

BOX 3.2 DOUBLE-O-ALLIANCE—COOPERATION BETWEEN CRIMINAL ORGANIZATIONS

I The Enterprise

1. There existed a criminal organization, that is, a group of individuals consisting of defendants (The leader of the enterprise was also the leader of the Chicago Outlaws MC. His name and the names of the other 6 defendants are removed), and others known and unknown.

2. This criminal organization, including its leadership, membership, and associates, constituted an "enterprise" as that term is used in Title 18, United States Code, Section 1961 (4) (hereinafter, the "enterprise"), that is, a group of individuals associated in fact, which enterprise was engaged in, and the activities of which affected, interstate commerce.

3. The members of the enterprise constituted an ongoing organization whose members functioned as a continuing unit for the common purpose of achieving the objectives of the enterprise. The purposes and goals of the enterprise included but were not limited to the generation of income for its members through various illegal activities.

4. The illegal activities of the enterprise included, but were not limited to (a) committing armed robberies and thefts from jewelry stores, businesses, and private residences; (b) transporting stolen goods across state lines; (c) committing thefts, and obtaining stolen items, from interstate shipments of goods; (d) purchasing, possessing, and selling stolen goods; (e) using threats, violence, and intimidation to advance the interests of the enterprise's illegal activities;

Continued

BOX 3.2 DOUBLE-O-ALLIANCE—COOPERATION BETWEEN CRIMINAL ORGANIZATIONS—Cont'd

(f) committing arson; (g) operating and facilitating illegal gambling businesses, which included the use of video gambling machines; (h) obstructing justice and criminal investigations by tampering with and intimidating witnesses; (i) obstructing justice and criminal investigations by gathering information concerning the fact of, and extent of, ongoing federal criminal investigations from, among other sources, corrupt local law enforcement officers and law enforcement databases; and (j) traveling in interstate commerce to further the goals of the gambling enterprise.

5. In order to carry out its activities, the enterprise utilized individuals employed by, and associated with it, who had varying roles and responsibilities.
6. Defendant [ranking member of the Chicago Outfit], directed and guided certain of the enterprise's illegal activities.
7. Defendant [leader of the Chicago Outlaws MC] also occupied a leadership role in the enterprise. He supervised the activities of the enterprise, identified targets for robbery and other illegal enterprise activity, and directed the activities of others employed by, and associated with, the enterprise.
8. Defendant [Chicago Outfit] served the enterprise by, among other things, participating in robberies, by assembling explosive materials into a bomb, and participating in the bombing of C&S Coin Operated Amusements.
9. Defendant [police officer] was a Berwyn police officer who served the enterprise by, among other things, acting as a courier for stolen money; conducting physical surveillance of potential targets of illegal enterprise activity under the guise of carrying out his duties as a police officer; participating in an attempted armed robbery; and providing information concerning ongoing law enforcement investigation into illegal enterprise activity, including the bombing of C&S Coin Operated Amusement.

Source: *Adapted from United States of America v. Mark Polchan et al. No. 08 CR 115.*

The Outlaw MC leader was sentenced to 60 years in prison upon conviction. The Chicago Outfit "boss" received a 25-year sentence and the corrupt police officer, after pleading guilty, was sentenced to four years in prison.

International recognition (to be discussed later) of the OMG criminal threat proceeded along with RICO prosecutions and the expansion of U.S.-based OMGs outside the United States.

Court's View (National and International)

Christie's 2006 statement, quoted earlier, that the club (Hells Angels) had never been proven to be a criminal organization was no longer accurate two years after he made it. In 2008, a California jury found that his Ventura, California, Hells Angels chapter was a criminal organization according to California criminal statutes (Hernandez, 2008, December 17). The same jury found that a Ventura Hells Angels member had committed a bar assault for the benefit of, in association with, and at the direction of the Hells Angels. The same month, three California members of the

Mongols MC admitted to participating in a criminal street gang in the shooting of a Hells Angel member (Garmine, 2008, December 18). The verdicts in California were not aberrations confined to that state. In 2009, an Arizona jury declared the Hells Angels a criminal street gang when a member was convicted of aggravated assault and acting for the benefit of a criminal street gang (Anon. 12, 1999, October 6). This particular verdict demonstrates the violent nature of OMG members. The Arizona Hells Angels members attacked and severely beat a man who accidently bumped into them in a bar. They kicked and punched a man on the floor and struck him with beer bottles until a woman threw herself on the victim and screamed for them to stop.

International courts have also ruled on outlaw motorcycle clubs, particularly the Hells Angels, as criminal organizations. In 2011, after a marathon court trial, members of a Toronto, Canada, Hells Angels chapter were found not guilty of being members of a criminal organization; however, they were found guilty of conspiracy to traffic the date rape drug GHB (gamma hydroxybutyrate) (Edwards, 2012a, June 7). The same Canadian court ordered that the fortified clubhouse of the gang be forfeited to the Crown, demonstrating that the court did not think the "club" fit the narrow legal definition of a criminal organization under Canadian law but the defendants and their fellow bikers were considered criminals and dangerous. In January 2013, eight Hell Angels members went on trial in Tromos, Norway, for their involvement in organized narcotics trafficking from Oslo to northern Norway. They were charged under Norway's so-called "mafia paragraph" dealing with organized crime and criminal organizations. After a six-week trial, all eight were found guilty. According to newspaper accounts, the court found that there was "no doubt" that the eight defendants' membership in, or relationship to, the Hells Angels club had considerable impact on how their criminal acts were planned and organized (www.newsinenglish.no). The court found that the Hells Angels club had a structure and hierarchy (president, enlisted members, prospects, and "hangerarounds") that determined specific tasks and made decisions within the club. The court also found that the Hells Angels clubhouse in Oslo was where the eight defendants planned their criminal activities with the president always present. The prosecutions' criminal organization network allegation was based on a two-year telephone surveillance resulting in 24,000 text messages and 35,000 phone conversations.

Other Government Agencies' Views
INTERNATIONAL
Other government entities, particularly licensure and regulatory agencies, have declared the Hells Angels Motorcycle Club a criminal organization. The Canadian Immigration and Refugee Board (IRB) declared that being a member of the Hells Angels Motorcycle Club is reason to deport noncitizens (Humphries, 2012). The IRB ruled: "The business of the Hells Angels is crime." In support of the finding, the IRB cites police statistics showing that in Ontario, Canada, 67.2% of the Hells

Angels members had criminal convictions, 43% drug-related. Thus far, four Hells Angels members have been deported. One who was deported in 2010 had come to Canada from Scotland in 1969 when he was seven years old but had never become a Canadian citizen.

Political entities such as cities, states, and countries have passed bans on the wearing of club identifiers in public and some have gone so far as to place restrictions on membership in outlaw motorcycle clubs/gangs. For example, Queensland, Australia, has proposed legislation that would prohibit anyone in a criminal organization—in other words a bikie (Australian term for bikers) gang—from owning a firearm, or working in security or as a nightclub bouncer, or holding a liquor license. Queensland has recently enacted a law making it an offense for three or more members of a criminal bikie gang to be together in one place (Prain, 2013, November 14). The Finks MC of Queensland recently "patched over" to the U.S.-based Mongols MC, and three members of the new Mongols gang were the first outlaw bikies to be charged under the new law (Stolz & Pierce, 2013, November 14). It does not matter where they are found associating together; these three bikies were spotted together at the Gold Coast's luxurious Palazzo Versace Hotel. This new legislation has implications for all motorcycle riders. Recently, the Bundaberg, Australia, police showed up at a cancer fundraiser sponsored by a conventional motorcycle club and confiscated all the entry forms and took them to police headquarters. The police wanted to check to see if three or more bikie gang members were in attendance (Prain, 2013, November 14). They are awaiting trial. South Australian Police are in the process of having the Finks MC declared a criminal organization and then following up with applications against the Hells Angels and the Rebels MC (Hunt, 2013). The Supreme Court and the High Court had declared previous anti-bikie legislation invalid, but after amendments to the legislation the police are going to try again.

In the United Kingdom, the Warwickshire Police are continuing their efforts to ban the annual Hells Angels Bulldog Bash even though there was little trouble at the latest festival. British police have designated 1% outlaw motorcycle clubs as organized crime groups. The police allege that the Bulldog Bash, a motorcycle rally that has been run for 20 years, is a fundraiser for an organized crime group, the Hells Angels, and point to the murder of an Angel returning home from the festival by seven rival members of the Outlaws MC in 2007. Other countries have designated 1% outlaw motorcycle clubs as criminal groups and banned them from entry into the country. The Scandinavian Hells Angels were coming to Iceland to celebrate New Year's Eve with their prospect chapter (first step in club status) but were turned back at the Keflavik International Airport. Iceland will not allow known 1% OMG members into the country at any time. In 2007, police at the Keflavik airport detained eight visiting Hells Angels and deported them the next day. Iceland considers Hells Angels members to be a threat to national security because of the club's history of crime and violence, whether or not the individual member has a criminal record.

The wearing of **gang colors**, in addition to causing conflict between rival clubs/gangs, has an intimidating effect on nonmembers, leading to bans in public places, such as bars and restaurants. The Canadian Province of Saskatchewan has a law against wearing gang "colours" in bars. The Crown argues that gang "colours" have an intimidating effect on people who see them and the government has the objective of limiting intimidation (Adam, 2009). Members of the Saskatoon Hells Angels are currently challenging the law. A Canadian judge recognized that gang symbols are used to intimidate nonmembers and as a means to extort money from others (Humphreys, 2009). Two Hells Angels went to a man's house to shake him down for selling black-market satellite TV equipment—they were wearing their colors, a belt buckle with the death's head on it, a T-shirt with the death's head logo, and a necklace with the same logo. The judge in his ruling said:

> They deliberately invoked their membership in the HAMC with the intent to inspire fear in their victim. They committed extortion with the intent to do so in association with a criminal organization, the HAMC to which they belonged.

In Sydney, Australia, bikies are banned from wearing their colors in The Star Casino, and hundreds of known bikies are specifically banned from entering the casino (Anon 24, 2013, November 16). The bikies were using the casino as a de facto meeting place and money-laundering facility. It was also alleged that they were robbing patrons that won large sums of money.

United States

The Hells Angels are banned from wearing their colors to the Ventura, California, County Fair. They have gone to court to have this ban lifted. A Hells Angels member is suing the city of San Francisco because he was ejected from Candlestick Park for violating the "code of conduct" against wearing "offensive clothing" (Rosenberg & Melvin 2013, November 8,). The "offensive clothing" in question was his denim jacket with Hells Angels colors on the back. He took the denim jacket off and attempted to reenter with a T-shirt with the Hells Angels logo on the back, and once again was rejected. Following the 2011 fatal shooting of the San Jose, California, Hells Angels chapter president by the president of the Vagos, Nicaragua, chapter in the Nugget Casino in Reno, Nevada, during the annual Street Vibrations festival, festival organizers have banned the wearing of "colors" by the Hells Angels, Vagos, Mongols, Bandidos, Las Vegas Gents, and Green Machine Nation motorcycle clubs (AP 1, 2013, September 26).

Color bans of this nature will likely expand in the future here and abroad as more jurisdictions define the clubs as gangs or criminal organizations. Furthermore, the community of motorcycle riders recognizes the known violent nature of OMGs. As we shall see, motorcycle gang members, conventional club riders, and non–bike riders are forewarned by motorcycle spokespersons. Figure 3.1 shows a typical "no colors" sign at a bar frequented by bikers.

FIGURE 3.1

Establishments that are often frequented by bikers often post "no colors" signs to forewarn bikers not to sport gang colors.

Photo courtesy of Jill Kiley.

CLUB REACTION TO GANG LABEL

Recognition That Some Are Criminals

Most 1% club spokesmen admit that some members of their "supposed" clubs commit or have committed criminal acts; however, they insist that there are a few bad apples in every organization and the organization is not responsible or to be blamed for their behavior. The standard answer is that crime is not "club business" but the "personal business" of the "bad apple" minority in some chapters. The best answer that can be gotten from members or former members of 1% outlaw clubs is to deflect the gang label to other clubs: "other clubs do [commit crimes], but not us." A former Outlaw MC "boss" (chapter and regional president) when writing about the "needle law" (members could not engage in intravenous drug use) wrote:

> "It didn't mean a brother couldn't sell needle drugs. What a man did on his own time was his own business. The club [Outlaws MC] never demanded anyone, at least while I ran with them, to sell dope or to be involved in any criminal activity for that matter. Don't get me wrong, we were often involved in a variety of illegal pursuits, which was the nature of the life outside the law and ethics of normal society. It's important to restate that the club does not require its members to sling dope and give percentages to the treasury, as I've heard said. Many folks, including a large number in the law enforcement community seem to have that impression. *Perhaps that's because it is true of some motorcycle clubs. It wasn't true of either of the two of which I was a member*"
>
> (emphasis added, Spurgeon, 2011:247-248)

The same Outlaw MC boss said later "Because of the drug trade, many members of the club were learning to become businessmen rather than bike riders" (Spurgeon, 2011:253).

These statements are best understood as impression management techniques attempting to divert attention away from the members' and leaders' involvement in serious crimes in addition to those crimes normally associated with the biker lifestyle. The one-percent clubs proudly proclaim their outlaw status and exclusiveness while eschewing the gang label. One-percent bikers wear the 1% patch on their clothing and bodies and proudly declare that they live outside society's norms, laws, and values. Biker expert Yves Lavigne opines that one-percent bikers "are dedicated to a criminal lifestyle" and the "1% patch…is a declaration that dishonesty is a way of life."

Every member of a one-percent motorcycle club, even those most often labeled outlaw motorcycle gangs, such as the Hells Angels, Outlaws, Bandidos, Pagans, and Sons of Silence, is not a "convicted" criminal. Some club/gang members are actually in occupations that do not allow for criminal convictions. For example, the FBI reports that Hells Angels members, including an Army lieutenant colonel, have served in Iraq (Marin, 2007). Canadian and Dutch military servicemen are reported to be HAMC members. One of the Hells Angels killed in the 2002 Laughlin shootout at Harrah's Casino between the Hells Angels and the Mongols was a member of the U.S. Coast Guard. In 2002, the president of the Hells Angels London, England, chapter led a phalanx of motorcycles during Queen Elizabeth's Golden Jubilee parade. The former president of the Guildford, Australia, Hells Angels chapter was employed as a technical expert on vehicle and industrial safety equipment at the New South Wales Roads and Traffic Authority (Maxton, 2009). He was also involved in a Sydney Airport brawl between the Hells Angels and the Commancheros MC. Following the bloody brawl, he was suspended from his employment for three months with pay as New South Wales (NSW) authorities investigated his actions. He has since been fired and is planning an appeal. There are other examples of one-percenter club members who have not been convicted of any crime. There is always the possibility that a member of an OMG who has not been arrested, tried, and convicted of a criminal offense is a criminal actor who has just not yet been caught. There are numerous examples of 1% OMG members who are, in outward appearances, law-abiding citizens, except for being a member of a motorcycle club with a notorious reputation, until the "hammer falls." For example, a well-known Gary, Indiana, criminal defense attorney and member of the Wheels of Soul MC, who claim to be the largest mixed-race 1% outlaw club in the United States, was recently convicted of racketeering conspiracy charges and sentenced to 23 years for his part in a multistate racketeering conspiracy by the gang (DOJ 7, 2013, April 23).

If the outlaw "clubs" are not criminal organizations or supportive of members' criminal activities, one would expect club discipline following criminal convictions, especially organized criminal behavior by the "clubs" leaders as is common in conventional motorcycle clubs. A senior Vancouver, Canada, Hells Angels member testified that the club did not condone lawbreaking (Edwards, 2009a, 2009b). The judge was not swayed by this testimony and replied that three-quarters of the alleged "club" members have criminal records and that the Hells Angel member could not cite one instance in which a club member had been expelled for committing a crime. The judge pointed out that current or former police officers are not allowed to be members, supporting the perceived danger that police officers allowed to be members would arrest or report the criminal activities of other club members. On rare occasions OMGs will expel a member when the notoriety of the criminal act exceeds even the bounds of their violent world. This occurred in 2004, when a full-patched Bandido Motorcycle Club member, Richard Merla, a chapter's sergeant at arms, well known for his bad temper and violence, brutally stabbed to death a former International Boxing Federation Super Flyweight champion, Robert Quiroga, in San Antonio, Texas. Quiroga was a hometown hero and a celebrated icon in the Hispanic community. Merla killed Quiroga after an all-night drinking session, in which Merla says the former boxer disrespected him and "nobody disrespects a Bandido" (see History Channel, 2008). Merla was expelled from the Bandidos, and the Bandidos National president publicly stated that Merla acted on his own without the knowledge or consent of the "club."

"Club" members of commonly designated OMGs on occasion recognize and acknowledge that they are criminal gang members, and that gang membership has real consequences:

> This ain't no club, Rocky [patched member of the Mongols Motorcycle Club] continued. We're outlaws. I've had to do things that would send me to prison for years if I got caught. You ready for that? Would you kill for the Mongols? Because that's what you might have to do. We're outlaws, Billy [ATF agent who infiltrated the Mongols and became a patched member]. You need to know that. You need to be sure. You need to understand what you're getting into.
>
> (Queen, 2005:51)

Ralph "Sonny" Barger, the iconic Hells Angels leader who led the HAMC in its expansion outside of California and nationwide and then outside the United States and is still referred to as "Chief" by members, admits that the supposed club at one time was a criminal organization, but he claims that the gang has since changed its ways: "The seventies were a gangster era for us [Hells Angels Motorcycle Club]. I sold drugs and got into a lot of shit" (Barger et al., 2000:252). Barger says that he "sold heroin from the late sixties into the early seventies directly to junkies. Sometimes I had other junkies selling it too" (Barger et al., 2000:81). Barger divides the evolution of the HAMC into four eras: First Era—1950s-1960s, freewheeling and partying; Second Era—1970s, gangster era; Third Era—1980s, pay-back era, we "were paying for every motherfuckin' crime we committed and some we didn't;" Fourth Era—Twenty-first century, the club has come full circle and returned to its freewheeling and partying ways. The facts certainly support that the HAMC has been a criminal organization since Barger and his fellow HAMC members sold drugs in the late 1960s and continued their criminal activities in the 1970s, 1980s, and 1990s; however, there is no evidence that the "club" has renounced its gangster ways in the twenty-first century. There is a plethora of supporting evidence that the Hells Angels as a criminal gang is a transnational crime threat today and has been one for decades.

GANG LABEL HAS REAL CONSEQUENCES FOR MEMBERS

The gang label is resisted because outlaw motorcycle club members know it has real consequences in how they are treated by law enforcement and society in general. The "club" members want the power and notoriety that come with wearing the patch but not the adverse consequences. The notorious reputation of many one-percent clubs and their known criminal and violent behavior labels members as criminals and gang members even if they are not directly implicated in criminal activity. For example, the State of Washington is moving to revoke the state gambling license of a Hells Angels member who was the security supervisor of a state-licensed casino (Anon. c. 2007). Videotapes show the security supervisor wearing his colors (vest containing club's three-piece patch; see Figure 3.2) while working. Washington considers the Hells Angels Motorcycle Club to be a "criminal offender cartel"; therefore, members are not eligible for licensure in the tightly regulated gambling industry. The security supervisor was, at the time, vice-president and acting president of the Washington Nomads Hells Angels Chapter based in Spokane. Members of the Nomads chapter, including the president—and former West Coast Hells Angels President—and four members, are on trial for trafficking in stolen motorcycle parts, robbery, racketeering, and murder. The security supervisor is not charged in this particular case, but he is suffering the consequences of belonging to a designated criminal gang. The Ontario, Canada, Court of Appeals has ruled that a bar owner can be denied a liquor license simply because he is a member of the Hells Angels (Small, 2013, March 19). In Britain, a Hells Angel press officer was revealed to be a BBC reporter and was promptly fired from BBC Wales TV and Radio Wales (Salkeld, 2010, January 13). According to the BBC, he had breached their code of conduct that requires that journalists must disclose their interests and get permission before representing outside organizations. Even associating with or being in their presence can taint the way nonmembers are viewed by the media or the public. Hells Angels members attended the funeral of a murdered Vancouver, Canada, teen-ager leading to speculation that the father of the teen was a member of the gang or her death was somehow related to the Hells Angels (Olivier, 2010, October 3). According to the Angels, they were there in sympathy for the father who had grown up with several members.

The social stigma that attends the club's (gang's) criminal reputation affects non-club members who associate with club/gang members, as well. The U.S. correspondent for the Swedish newspaper *Expression* was fired for his close associations with the former leader and founder of the Swedish Hells Angels (Reporter fired over Hells Angels contacts, 2009, June 4). A California diesel mechanic is complaining that he has become a police target, including having a hole put in the side of his trailer as the police executed a search warrant because he worked on the diesel truck of the president of the Santa Barbara Hells Angels and gave him a ride home (Hernandez, 2009). There appears to be evidence that supports his claim. International tennis player Australian Bernard Tomic, ranked number 46 in the world in 2013, has received media attention because of his links to the Gold Coast Bandidos chapter.

FIGURE 3.2

Selected one-percent club colors.

Photos courtesy of the U.S. Department of Justice.

It was reported that his Facebook profile picture showed him standing beside the national Bandidos sergeant at arms. He was shown partying with Bandidos in their clubhouse.

The social stigma attached to outlaw clubs extends to all one-percent clubs that are linked in any way to OMGs. A former Capitol Police Department lieutenant has sued the Capitol Police Department for discrimination, alleging that he was suspended and later dismissed because he was a member of the one-percent Southern Maryland Tribes Motorcycle Club (TMC). The Capitol Police Department, according to the suit, alleged that the TMC is a racially charged motorcycle gang with ties to the Hells Angels (Siegelbaum, 2012, May 15).

One-percent outlaw club membership can and does taint "good deeds." The outlaw clubs routinely participate in charitable events such as Christmas toy events. Law enforcement groups say they do this to mask their true nature or rehabilitate their criminal reputation. Jay Dobyns, an undercover ATF agent who infiltrated the Arizona Hells Angels, recently stated: "The public doesn't see Cynthia Garcia [mother of two stomped and stabbed by Angels for disrespecting them in their clubhouse] being stomped to death, they just see Hells Angels delivering gifts to sick kids at Christmas. They are very good at propaganda" (Scotland on Sunday, 2009). The Queensland, Australia, Police Minister says that because some members of the Australian bikie gangs—Rebels, Bandidos, Finks, Outlaws, and Hells Angels—are murderers, rapists, robbers, and drug traffickers—charities should stop accepting their donations (Viellaris, 2007, April 1). The police minister says that the donations give the gangs an undeserved "veneer of respectability."

Even when local authorities have had no trouble with a one-percent outlaw club, they prepare for trouble at charitable events because of the reputation of the clubs/ gangs. The New Jersey Hells Angels held their 2009 annual Hells Angels Summer Bash at the Eagles Lodge in Bridgewater, New Jersey. The annual bash raises money for the club and its charitable causes, including raising money for a girl suffering from a rare form of cancer. The Bridgewater chief of police had 15-20 officers stationed nearby and uniformed personnel (some in camouflage), SWAT vehicles, and a mo- bile command post stationed three blocks away. The chief readily admitted that the New Jersey Hells Angels had committed no acts of violence that he knew of, but he had heard stories of past violent acts and he had to be prepared (Grant, 2009). The same precautions are taken by law enforcement agencies at almost all runs and events by one-percent clubs, and there are enough violent acts by and between the clubs/gangs to justify such vigilance.

CLUB/GANG INTERACTIONS WITH OTHER MOTORCYCLISTS AND CITIZENS

Tread Softly in the Presence of a One-Percenter Outlaw Biker

Outlaw motorcycle club/gang members ride among, but not with other motorcyclists, and these bike riders must be constantly wary in their presence. The supposed "bad apples" alluded to by "club" spokesmen are often career criminals and/or violent men selected and recruited because of their known reputations for violence and/or criminal behavior. As Australian biker expert Arthur Veno says: "Violence is central to club life. It's implicit in the rules, the way members live, and their interactions with other clubs" (Veno & Gannon, 2009:139). One-percenter outlaw clubs and members have been fighting with one another since their formation. These altercations have ranged from bare-knuckle combat between individuals, to street rumbles between groups of com- peting gangs, to shoot-outs and bombings in public places. Unfortunately, violence, or the potential for violence, extends to all those who innocently or unintentionally en- counter them. Those who travel and visit the "bar-room" milieu of the one-percenter outlaw clubs must be continually on guard for potential violence. A certain number of the 1% club members are, and always have been, bullies who join the club to have their brothers finish the fights their mouths or attitudes get them into. Courage for them comes in the beer they drink and the presence of like-minded intimidators. Dave Nichols is a noted motorcycle expert, author of several biker books, and editor-in-chief of *Easyriders*, a premier motorcycle magazine. In his discussion of the "one-percenter code," he provides examples of the potential violence that can be encountered by coming in contact with a one-percenter, however innocently (see Box 3.3).

Nichols also goes on to caution how to look at a one-percenter: "Never 'eye fuck' a one percenter. (Act respectful and sincere around bikers. Don't challenge them with your eyes … or anything else for that matter. It will just end up getting you thumped.") (Nichols 2012:67).

BOX 3.3 RULES TO BE FOLLOWED WHEN IN THE PRESENCE OF A ONE-PERCENTER

... Never touch a one percenter. Never touch a one percenter's cut or patch. Even brushing by in a crowded room could get you beat up.

Never touch a one percenter's motorcycle unless you enjoy getting yourself a proper beating. Make sure your girlfriend never touches or sits on anyone's bike but your own.

Don't think that wearing a support shirt buys you anything. You are not a member, you are a civilian. Never wear a support shirt anywhere that a warring club can see, or you're dead meat.

Keep your thoughts to yourself. Until you show yourself as being about something and not one of the walking dead [citizens], one-percenters don't give a shit what you think.

Never disrespect a one percenter's ol' lady (girlfriend or wife). Period.

Never interrupt two or more patch holders when they are having a conversation. This is disrespectful.

Source: Modified from Nichols, 2012:111.

These rules are not without merit, especially considering that when one outlaw biker begins "thumping" a real or imagined rules transgressor, all his "brothers" present are expected to jump in, no questions asked. Outlaw bikers are notorious for ganging up and "putting the boots" to others for any perceived act of disrespect. A real problem exists when the uninitiated are purposely or accidently in the presence of an outlaw biker and do not know the rules or even know there are rules. They, 1% outlaw bikers, decide when and if there is a problem. A motorist in Cardiff Bay, South Wales, in the United Kingdom was stopped and filling up his vehicle at a petrol station when a group of Hells Angels pulled up (Anon. 11, 2012, August 1). One of the Angels approached and asked, "Have you got a problem?" [If a man approaches wearing outlaw biker colors and asks if you have a problem, you have a problem.] The Angel punched him with a gloved hand [probably loaded with metal], causing severe facial fractures that resulted in three metal plates in his face. The Hells Angel member arrested for the assault claims that he is not the one that struck the blow, but he knows who did. The Hells Angels member said if he revealed the identity of the assailant, who is also a Hells Angel, he would be kicked out of the club.

A California motorcyclist was riding down Interstate 580 when he was surrounded by a group of Sonoma County Hells Angels (Rossmann, 2008, September 8). One of the Angels came up to him as he was exiting the highway and told him to let the Hells Angels get off first. The luckless motorcyclist was then bumped and wrecked. A San Jose, California, man observed a line of 20 motorcycles riding two abreast in the fast lane of Highway 101. When he observed that the motorcycle riders were flying the colors of the Hells Angels and a support 1% club, the Original Kings, he decided to use his cell phone to make a video of the caravan. The 19-year-old man was so intent on videotaping the riders that he failed to see the traffic in front of him slow down. When he did realize that he was going to rear end the cars in front of him, he quickly swerved to the left, hitting and wrecking into several of the gang members. The uninjured outlaw bikers beat and stomped him in retaliation. By the time the police and EMS workers arrived, most of the uninjured bikers had left.

The motorist, whose name was not released because of *concerns* for his safety, could not identify any of his assailants [a smart move on his part].

In June 2006, a New Hampshire man, a self-employed contractor and father of two, wore a Hells Angels T-shirt that he had recently purchased [such items are readily available on the Internet and at motorcycle rallies] into Three Cousins Pizza and Lounge, which was well known as an Outlaws MC hangout, even though his friends had tried to talk him out of it because of the danger involved. Inside the bar was the sergeant at arms for the New Hampshire Outlaws chapter, a violent man with five previous felony convictions. The man's friends again tried to get him to take the shirt off or turn it inside out as they saw the Outlaw becoming agitated. The man refused and said he didn't care. The Outlaw left the bar and came back with a semiautomatic pistol and fired three shots, one striking the man as he tried to run away. The bar was full when the shooting took place, but the majority of the customers belonged to a tribe well known to the police, the Know Nothing Tribe (I didn't see nothing, I didn't hear nothing, I don't know nothing). One of those who did see something was murdered shortly after. In spite of this, the Outlaw was convicted and sentenced to 45-90 years for the cold-blooded murder. The Outlaw enforcer showed no emotion at his sentencing and raised his hands in a thumbs-up signal and said to his supporters [at least six New Hampshire Outlaws in full colors] present "I love you" and "Call me later" (Marchocki, 2007, May 11).

There are some outlaw club members who are so dangerous and violent that any contact with them is problematic. An enforcer for the Victoria, Australia, Hells Angels with the nickname of "Skitzo" was arrested for punching a 62-year-old woman in the face over an argument over his lost dog (Oakes, 2013, June 5). Skitzo's dog ran away during a storm and was found by the woman who put up posters of the dog in the neighborhood trying to find the owner. Skitzo saw the posters, went to the woman's house, took umbrage when she asked for proof of ownership, and punched her. Two armed men later showed up at the woman's house and told her not to report the assault to the police. A disturbing case of biker violence occurred in Apopka, Florida, in 2009. A man got into an argument in a bar and was asked to leave. On his way out of the parking lot, he hit a parked motorcycle belonging to a member of the Warlocks MC. The gang member jumped into the bed of a friend's pickup truck and chased the ejected bar patron. When the gang member and his friend got close, the biker jumped out of the bed and shot the ejected bar patron in the head, killing him (Jacobson, 2009, September 15). A recent example of random one-percent biker violence occurred in what is considered to be a safe area for bikers. Two Hells Angels members (they were wearing their colors) severely beat a 22-year-old man sitting at the bar in Johnny's Bar—a historic biker bar considered to be the birthplace of the American biker in Hollister, California—during the Hollister Motorcycle Rally (Beardsley, 2013, July 10). The young man, talking to his friends, was sucker punched by one Angel and then kicked by both while he was on the floor. Witnesses and the victim had no explanation for the attack.

Club members are known to intimidate proprietors and workers in business establishments when they are in a pack. A long-time member and "boss" of the Outlaws MC describes a stop at a small convenience store in North Florida by a pack of Outlaws returning from a member's funeral. He describes how the cashier was so overwhelmed by the "starting and stopping of the pumps, then pulling away, making room for the next guy" that there was no way for him to keep track of the sales. The Outlaws walked through the store openly shoplifting, drinking beer, eating potato chips, and whatever they wanted. They dared the cashier to call the cops. The Outlaw leader says that this "was the most hilarious gas stop I have ever witnessed" (Spurgeon, 2011:90). He goes on to say that they laughed about it the rest of the day.

ARE ALL OUTLAW MOTORCYCLE CLUBS (1% CLUBS) CRIMINAL GANGS?

There is no scientifically accurate accounting of the number of one-percent outlaw motorcycle clubs nationally or internationally, and how many of them fall into the category of OMGs is equally difficult to determine. The definition of what is and what is not an OMG is complicated by the lack of a common definition, and there is no one recognized source for information on one-percent clubs. Further complicating data collection is the ephemeral nature of motorcycle clubs, including one-percent clubs. Outlaw motorcycle clubs spring up and fade away for a variety of reasons—waning interest, petty jealousies among members, law enforcement pressure, disbanded forcefully or by persuasion by other more established one-percent clubs. Often, outlaw clubs last only as long as the founding members or leaders remain in the club. At times, groups have declared themselves to be motorcycle gangs, even though no members have motorcycles. The Epitaph Riders of New Zealand did this in 1969 (Gilbert, 2013:72). The Notorious MC of Sydney, Australia, is a more recent example of a motorcycle club without motorcycles. The Mongols are also allowing members without bikes in Australia. Very few of these chimerical biker clubs stay around long enough to become organized criminal gangs or recognized by the motorcycle community as bona fide "righteous" outlaw motorcycle clubs. This constantly changing phenomenon is repeated as motorcycle clubs/gangs are created, disbanded, or assimilated into other clubs. On the other hand, some establish formal rules, membership criteria and fees, and an organizational hierarchy that allows for leadership succession. Once established, these righteous clubs jealously guard their identity, symbols, and territory, eventually becoming organized OMGs in their own right, or assimilate into other more dominant OMGs. They follow what has become known as the Hells Angels Model since the mid-1950s. As we have seen, the 1957 Hell Bent for Glory Motorcycle Club evolved into the Sacramento Hells Angels. The 1958 Hells Angels Motorcycle Club formed by Sonny Barger and his group of friends originally came into being from a cabal of young motorcycle-riding "hell raisers" and toughs deciding to come together and form a motorcycle club with a common identity and symbol—Nomad Hells Angels. Once Barger and his fellow desperadoes learned of the original Hells Angels formed in 1948, they became a charter/chapter of the initial Hells Angels. This put into motion the organization and expansion of the Hells Angels Model and its imitation by other outlaw clubs.

In spite of the difficulties of accurately portraying the secret and deviant outlaw motorcycle club/gang world, there are several sources that attempt to compile lists of one-percent clubs or OMGs, although for different reasons, and they often contradict one another. A recently published book, *The One Percenter Encyclopedia: The World of Outlaw Motorcycle Clubs from Abyss Ghosts to Zombies Elite* (Hayes, 2011), is the first attempt to list the one-percent clubs by a well-known one-percent biker, but even this groundbreaking effort does not include all the one-percent clubs and includes clubs that are not one-percent or outlaw clubs. Hayes's encyclopedia, written for the general motorcycling audience, purportedly examines the "worldwide" population of one-percenter clubs and examines "the origins, histories, legends, and current keepers of the 'one-percenter' lineage; the powerful brotherhoods that are the outlaw motorcycle clubs" (Hayes, 2011:6). There are a total of 395 motorcycle clubs listed in this work, including several so-called pioneer clubs, such as 13 Rebels MC, which is neither a one-percent nor an outlaw club. *The One Percenter Encyclopedia* also includes several that are, according to the encyclopedia, AMA-sanctioned clubs (Baltimore Ramblers—Charter Member of the AMA; Custom Riders MC—AMA charter; Free Spirits MC—AMA-chartered and "all ties to the 1% world ended totally and completely" in the 1960s (p. 79). Historically, as stated earlier, the designation of outlaw clubs has been non-AMA chartered. In addition to the Free Spirits MC, the *Encyclopedia* lists motorcycle clubs that the author admits are not 1% clubs; for example, the Buffalo Soldiers MC, EYE of RA ("While certainly not an outlaw club, this organization has 'connections' to the one percent world," p. 73); Flying Wheels MC ("A three piece patch, but they don't consider themselves one percenters," p. 76); Fly-in Wheels MC ("not a one percent club," p. 76); Hell Razors MC—two clubs—South Africa and United Arab Emirates ("While neither may actually be a one percent club in the strictest sense, the name alone is worth a mention," p. 103); and the most obvious non–one-percent club listed in the encyclopedia, the Devil Dolls MC—an all-female club. Females are not allowed to be members of outlaw motorcycle clubs since the mid-1960s when Sonny Barger purged the female Hells Angels and banned women from membership. From information supplied, or not supplied, in the *Encyclopedia*, it is difficult to determine the actual number of clubs listed that are not one-percenters or outlaws.

Hayes is a one-percent biker, an author of several books on the one-percenter lifestyle, is considered an authority on outlaw bikers, and his encyclopedia and his other works are significant contributions to the literature on biker clubs. However, his writings, including the *Encyclopedia*, are biased toward the outlaw motorcycle "club" definition and eschews the use of the gang label in any shape or form when discussing one-percenters. Hayes's dismissal of the gang label is typical of the groupthink present in the "one-percent world" to deal with the cognitive dissonance of obvious "club" criminality, including organized crime. Those of this ilk accept only information that supports their preconceived notion of outlaw motorcycle clubs and dismiss counterevidence. For example, Dr. Stephen "Skinz" Kinzey, Associate Professor of Kinesiology at California State University, San Bernardino, and president of the local chapter of the Devils Deciples Motorcycle Club, wrote the Foreword for *The One Percenter Encyclopedia*. The International Outlaw Motorcycle Gang Investigators Association (IOMGA) lists the Devils Diciples Motorcycle Club as an OMG, and Kinzey is currently charged with leading a motorcycle gang and a methamphetamine sales ring. He is charged with street terrorism, conspiracy, and possession of a controlled substance for sale. A raid of his home yielded a pound of methamphetamine, rifles, handguns, and body armor. A tap on Kinzey's cell phone captured text messages between him and dealers and suppliers (Willon, 2011, November 6). Before joining the Devils Diciples, Kinzey joined the Boozefighters Motorcycle Club, another OMG listed by the IOMGA, when he was teaching at the University of Mississippi in 1997 (see Box 3.4).

BOX 3.4 DEVIL'S DICIPLES AS A CRIMINAL ORGANIZATION

The national president of the Devil's Diciples MC of Mt. Clements, Michigan, was indicted for being a violent felon in possession of body armor. The national president had been previously convicted of a violent felony crime, making it illegal for him to possess body armor. Seventeen other Devil's Diciples members were also indicted for using a communication facility in furtherance of drug trafficking. During the course of the investigation, the following were seized from the Devil's Diciples MC: 42 firearms, 3000 rounds of ammunition, 3 bulletproof vests, $12,000 in U.S. currency, 1.5 pounds of meth, 55 pounds of marijuana, 1000 Vicodin/OxyContin pills, and 15 casino-style slot machines.

Source: U.S. DOJ 11, 2009, April 4.

Hayes's book spends a good deal of its content criticizing the second list: the *2010 Edition U.S. Outlaw Motorcycle Gangs*, produced by and for the International Outlaw Motorcycle Gang Investigators Association (IOMGIA), a professional law enforcement organization. The IOMGIA's website states: "The International Outlaw Motorcycle Gang Investigator's Association is a professional organization made up of federal, state and local law enforcement and prosecution personnel." Its purpose is to "provide a conduit for information exchange, updated training, and international network building among its estimated 600 members." It has been in existence since 1974. The IOMGIA publication is produced for the law enforcement community and does not explain the process for selecting OMGs to be listed. Table 3.1 presents the U.S. outlaw motorcycle gangs arranged by the number of individual gangs or gangs with chapters in the 50 states; in descending order the top 10 OMGs present in the 50 states are: the **Vietnam Vets MC**—37 states; the Hells Angels MC—22 states; Outlaws MC—19 states; Bandidos MC—16 states; Black Pistons—15 states; Boozefighters—14 states; Sons of Silence—11 states; Pagans MC—11 states; High Plains Drifters MC—11 states; and Wheels of Soul—11 states.

The listing of the Vietnam Vets MC as the sixth largest OMG in the United States is an enigma and could be an indication of "group think" by the IOMGIA and other law enforcement agencies—all outlaw motorcycle clubs are criminal organizations/gangs involved in organized crime. They are not found in a search of the Department of Justice, Federal Bureau of Investigation (FBI), or Bureau of Alcohol, Tobacco, Firearms, and Explosives (BATF) websites, nor does a Google search for Vietnam Vets MC criminal activities bring up any criminal activities. The Vietnam Veterans MC appears only once in Massachusetts in the National Gang Intelligence Center's listing of OMGs by state and will be examined later. They are a three-piece patch club but claim not to be a 1% club; nevertheless, the IOMGIA classifies them as a criminal organization (see Box 3.5 and Figure 3.3).

Table 3.1   U.S. Outlaw Motorcycle Gangs. IOMGIA—2010

OMG	Present in States
Vietnam Vets MC	37
Hells Angels MC	22
Outlaws MC	19
Bandidos MC	16
Black Pistons MC	15
Boozefighters MC	14
Sons of Silence MC	11
Pagans MC	11
High Plains Drifters MC	11
Wheels of Soul MC (Black)	11
Iron Horsemen MC	9
Mongols MC	8
Warlocks MC	8
Set Free Soldiers MC	8
Brotherhood	8
Vagos MC	7
Devils Diciples MC	7
Grim Reapers MC	6
Galloping Goose MC	6
Diablos MC	6
Renegades MC	5
Sundowners MC	5
Tribe MC	5
Brothers Speed MC	4
Hells Lovers MC (multi-ethnic)	4
Red Devils MC	4
Invaders MC	4
Kingsmen MC	4
Avengers MC	4
Legacy Vets MC	4
Amigos MC	4
El Foresteros MC	4
Tribesmen MC	3
Iron Coffins MC	3
Bandeloros MC	3
Cross Roads MC	3
Breed MC	3
Mountain Men MC	3
Loners MC	3
Chosen Few MC (Black)	3

Continued

Table 3.1 U.S. Outlaw Motorcycle Gangs. IOMGIA—2010—cont'd	
OMG	**Present in States**
Highwaymen MC	3
Outcasts MC	3
Hermanos MC	3
Hombres MC	3
40 Clubs in 2 states	(40)
157 Clubs in 1 state	(157)
241 Different OMGs	494 Chapters in 50 states

BOX 3.5 MISSION OF VIETNAM VETS MC

Our Mission

The Viet Nam Vets Motorcycle Club (VNVMC) is an international organization with members in Europe, Canada and the United States.

The VNVMC is made of both in-country and Vietnam-Era Vets. We are bonded by history and united by principles to from a proud and unique Biker Brotherhood: "The Viet Nam Vets Motorcycle Club."

We have pledged to contribute our energy, time, and resources to build a better future for all veterans and their families.

Our prime objective is to do everything within our power to bring our POW/MIA Brothers home and to insist that our government provide accountability for each of these patriots.

Members of the Viet Nam Vets Motorcycle Club continue to honor our solemn oath to defend and protect the Constitution of the United States against all enemies, both foreign and domestic.

We also make every effort to reach out to other Viet Nam Veterans with whatever assistance we can provide. Whether it be helping them understand their rights and benefits, or helping them wrestle with the bureaucratic system.

We often sponsor awareness events within our communities to help bring to light the plight of often forgotten Veterans.

Our Brothers share a strict set of codes, ethics, and values.

We do not get involved with the private business of other motorcycle clubs or their problems.

We strive to respect the freedom of the wind and the road.

"We are the Brotherhood of the Wind."

Source: VNMC/illinois.com/our_mission.html/.

Box 3.6 shows the individual states with their OMGs according to the IOMGIA.

According to the IOMGIA, California leads the nation with 58 different OMGs, followed by Florida with 27 different gangs. Massachusetts and New York each have 22 OMGs, followed by Connecticut, Minnesota, and Wisconsin with 20 different OMGs. Texas and New Mexico each have 19 different OMGs. Vermont, according to the IOMGIA, has the least number of OMGs in the United States: 2.

There are two official government listings of OMGs—**National Gang Intelligence Center (NGIC)** and the U.S. Department of Justice. Congress established the NGIC in 2005 to assist U.S. law enforcement agencies in dealing with street, prison, and OMGs by acting as a "repository and dissemination hub for gang intelligence" (National Gang Intelligence Center, 2011:3). According to the NGIC report, there are approximately 1,140,344 members of street, prison, and OMG gangs in 33,000 gangs in the United States. This includes an estimate of 44,108 members in 2,965 OMGs (National Gang Intelligence Center, 2011:10). This is the largest estimate of U.S. Outlaw Motorcycle Gangs that I am aware of and, unfortunately, the NGIC does not list the gangs. However they do say that "OMGs include One Percenter gangs as well as support and puppet gangs." The data on the number of OMGs and gang members for the NGIC Report, *2011 National Gang Threat Assessment: Emerging Trends*, comes primarily from the National Drug Intelligence Center (NDIC) and its National Drug Threat Survey (NDTS). This survey is a stratified random sample of nearly 3,500 state and local law enforcement agencies. The data provides estimates of the threat posed by various drugs, the availability and production of illicit drugs, as well as the role of street gangs and OMGs in drug trafficking. The data reported on in the 2011 report came from weighted national, regional, and state-level statistical estimates of the 2010 responses from 2,963 law enforcement agencies out of a sample of 3,465 agencies. Boxes 3.7 and 3.8 show that respondents report that there are 230 OMG chapters from 63 different OMGs reported to be involved in drug trafficking in 49 states (no reporting from Vermont).

FIGURE 3.3

Vietnam Vets and "Property of Vietnam Vets" insignias at the Arizona Military Hero's Poker Run.

Photo courtesy of Phoenician Patriot, en.wikipedia.org.

BOX 3.6 OMGs BY STATE—IOMGIA

OMGs by State

2010 Edition: U.S. Outlaw Motorcycle Gangs—IOMGIA

ALABAMA (7)
  Bandidos
  Outlaws
  Vietnam Vets
  Pistoleros
  Alabama Riders
  Devils Diciples
  Black Pistons

ALASKA (5)
  Devils Horsemen
  Hells Angels
  Vietnam Vets
  Pan Handlers
  Sentinels
  Scooter Tramps

ARIZONA (16)
  Hells Angels
  Mongols
  Vagos
  Huns
  Set Free Soldiers
  Lucifers Crew
  Cochise Riders
  Soul Brothers
  Nomads
  Devils Diciples
  Loners
  Chosen Few
  Vietnam Vets
  Legacy Vets
  Hawg Ridin Fools
  Spartan Riders

ARKANSAS (11)
  Banchees
  Diablos Lobos
  Boozefighters
  Road Barons
  Vietnam Vets
  Outlaw
  Bandidos
  Sons of Silence

CALIFORNIA (58)
  Grand Fathers
  Jus Brothers
  Unknown Locos
  Bravados
  Devils Diciples
  Border Bandits
  Diablos
  Sons of Hawaii
  Crucifiers Riderz
  Maldidos
  Mescaleros
  Ramblers
  Humpers
  Lost Souls
  Hell Bent
  Nuggets
  Righteous Ones
  Ghost Mountain Riders
  Top Hatters
  Amigos
  Heathens
  Hessians
  Amons
  Saints S/S Sinners
  Ressurection
  Red Nation
  Against the Wall
  Sundowners
  Misfits
  Iron Horsemen
  Saints
  Galloping Goose
  Boozefighters
  Peckerwoods
  Sadistics
  Military Misfits
  Loners
  Solo Angels
  Ozark Riders
  Mongols

BOX 3.6 OMGs BY STATE—IOMGIA—cont'd

Southside Crew
Hells Angels
Black Pistons
COLORADO (18)
American Iron
Flying Wheels
Free Tomorrow
Valiants
Iron Horsemen
High Plains Drifters
Diablos Lobos
Outlaws
Hells Lovers
Mongols
Invaders
Bandidos
Sundowners
Boozefighters
Vietnam Vets
Set Free Soldiers
Sons of Silence
Destroyers
CONNECTICUT (20)
Hells Angels
Vietnam Vets
Boozefighters
Charter Oaks
Chosen
Combat Vets
Compadres
Cross Roads
Diablos
Dismantlers
Forbidden
Helter Skelter
Hole in the Wall
James Gang
Lost Tribe
Phantom Lords
Reservoir Dogs
Righteous and Unruly
Red Devils
Outlaws

P.O.B.O.B.
Vagos
Soul Brothers
Green Machine
Vietnam Vets
Set Free
Soldiers
Bay Riders
Heavy Hitters
Hell Bound
Most Envied
West Coast O.G.
Violators
Skeleton Crew
Henchmen
Vituscans
Molochs
Wanted
FLORIDA (27)
Breed
CC Riders
Rock Machine
Brotherhood
Cobras
Cruisers
Black Pistons
Mongols
Phantoms
Fly In Wheels
Highwaymen
Rough Riders
Iron Coffins
Outcasts
Sundowners
Boozefighters
Renegades
Kingsmen
Semanon
Mystic Seven
Tribesmen
Nam Knights
Warlocks
Sons of Silence

Continued

BOX 3.6 OMGs BY STATE—IOMGIA—cont'd

DELAWARE (6)
- Wheels of Soul
- Tribe
- Thunderguards
- Warlocks
- Vietnam Vets
- Pagans

IDAHO (10)
- The Others
- Brotherspeed
- I-84 Roadbrothers
- Vagos
- Empties
- Highwaymen
- Vietnam Vets
- The Selects
- Bandidos
- Phuk

ILLINOIS (19)
- Brotherhood
- Cross Roads
- Death Marauders
- D.C. Eagles
- Hombres
- Dirty Dozen
- Wheels of Soul
- Furgawe Tribe
- Invaders
- Devils Diciples
- Outcasts
- Scorpions
- Grim Reapers
- Black Pistons
- Hells Lovers
- Sons of Silence
- Hells Angels
- Vietnam Vets
- Outlaws

INDIANA (14)
- Mongols
- Brotherhood
- Black Pistons
- Wheels of Soul
- Grim Reapers
- Vietnam Vets
- Outlaws
- Pagans

GEORGIA (8)
- Iron Cross
- Outcasts
- Black Pistons
- Rappers
- Saints
- Set Free Soldiers
- Outlaws
- Vietnam Vets

HAWAII (10)
- Na Kulana
- Alii
- Koa Puna
- Devils Breed
- Jesters
- Vagos
- Bandidos
- Legacy Vets
- Vietnam Vets
- Set Free Soldiers

IOWA (8)
- El Foresteros
- Believers
- Handlebar Jockeys
- Circle of Pride
- Bond Slaves
- Sons of Silence
- Vietnam Vets
- Raptorz

KANSAS (7)
- Rouges
- Boozefighters
- Galloping Goose
- El Foresteros
- Diablo Locos
- Mextecas
- Vietnam Vets

KENTUCKY (10)
- Black Pistons
- Custom Riders
- Iron Horsemen

BOX 3.6 OMGs BY STATE—IOMGIA—cont'd

Iron Horsemen
Invaders
Diablos
Sin City Deciples
Hells Angels
Outlaws
Boozefighters
Sons of Silence
Vietnam Vets

MAINE (7)

Exiles
Saracens
Mountain Men
Iron Horsemen
Diablos
Hells Angels
Outlaws

MARYLAND (11)

Vietnam Vets
Pagans
Blitzgrieg
Derelicts
Iron Horsemen
Kingsmen
Phantoms
Tribe
Thunderguards
Wheels of Soul
Hells Angels

MASSACHUSETTS (22)

Hells Angels
Vietnam Vets
Outlaws
Black Pistons
Chieftons
Diablos
Domners
Freewheelers
Headsmen
Phantom
Lords
Pale Riders
Red Emeralds
Red Devils

Grim Reapers
Outlaws
Pagans
Hells Angels
Wheels of Soul
Vietnam Vets
Sons of Silence

LOUISIANA (11)

Grey Ghost
Banshees
Galloping Goose
LA Riders
Bandidos
Vietnam Vets
Satans Tramps
View Deux Tramps
Hole-Da-Wall
Sons of Silence
Hells Angels (pending confirmation)

MINNESOTA (20)

Thunderbirds
Warlords
Brotherhood
Peacemakers
Hells Outcasts
Fossils
Midnight Riders
EL Forersteros
Galloping Goose
Ice Cold Riders
BPMs
Street Soldiers
TRU Breed
Themadones
Los Valentes
Wheels of Soul
Sons of Silence
OL Timers
Boozefighters
Bond Slaves

MISSISSIPPI (7)

Sons of Silence
Asgards
Boozefighters

Continued

BOX 3.6 OMGs BY STATE—IOMGIA—cont'd

Rum Pot Rustlers
Sidewinders
South Shore Hawgs
Tribesmen
Victors
Violators
Long Riders
Devils Diciples

MICHIGAN (11)
Avengers
Brotherhood
Black Pistons Scorpions
Devils Diciples
Iron Coffins
Sin City Deciples
New Attitude
Wild Bunch
Highwaymen
Warlocks
Zulus

MONTANA (12)
Boozefighters
Amigos
Cossacks
Bad Company
Hermanos
Galloping Goose
Brotherspeed
Mongols
Set Free Soldiers
Bandidos
Vietnam Vets
Barons

NEBRASKA (9)
Brudenschaft
Defiant Few
Tribesmen
Valhallas
Iron Rage
Bandidos
Flat Landers
Vietnam Vets
Hells Angels

Pistoleros
The Family
Bandidos
Vietnam Vets

MISSOURI (16)
Midwest Drifters
Boozefighters
Vietnam Vets
EL Forseteros
Galloping Goose
New Breed
Hells Lovers
Road Saints
Rock Machine
Sin City Deciples
Invaders
Saddle Tramps
Brothers Word
Statesmen
Wheels of Soul
Set Free Soldiers

NEW YORK (22)
Kingsmen
Demon Knights
Chosen Few
Highwaymen
Bridge Runners
Rare Breed
Iron Horsemen
Set Free Soldiers
69 ers
Mortal Skulls
Road Vultures
Brotherhood
Satans Soldiers
Black Pistons
Vietnam Vets
Unforgiven
Condemned Few
Warlocks
Vicious Circle
Hells Angels
Outlaws

BOX 3.6 OMGs BY STATE—IOMGIA—cont'd

NEW HAMPSHIRE (12)
  Diablos
  Outlaws
  Hells Angels
  Chieftans
  Combatants
  Unruly
  Cross Roads
  Flying Iron
  Iron Eagles
  Milford & Co
  Mountain Men
  Road Kings
NEW JERSEY (6)
  Breed
  Warlocks
  Wheels of Soul
  Hells Angels
  Iron Demons
  Satans Soldiers
NEW MEXICO (19)
  Maldidos
  Huns
  Regulators
  Paisanos
  Los Traviesos
  High Plains Drifters
  Black Berets
  Los Carnales
  Narbonas
  Los Hermanos
  German M/C
  Pacoteros
  Los Compadres
  German Army Vets
  Solados
  Bandeloros
  Native Thunder
  Vietnam Vets
  Bandidos
OHIO (18)
  Journeymen
  Pagans
  Iron Horsemen

Pagans
NORTH CAROLINA (11)
  Desperados
  Renegades
  Veterans Nomads
  Red Devils
  Steel Rebels
  Boanerges
  Iron Tribe
  Black Pistons
  Hells Angels
  Outlaws
  Pagans
NORTH DAKOTA (7)
  Norsemen
  Spartans
  Silent Thunder
  Dakota Riders
  Sons of Silence
  Vietnam Vets
  Pagans
SOUTH CAROLINA (12)
  Warlocks
  Trinity
  Hammerheadz
  Steele Stallions
  Wild Bunch
  Southern Vikings
  Spartans
  Man O War
  Odds Few
  Rolling Rebels
  Hells Angels
  Dire Wolfz
SOUTH DAKOTA (6)
  Deadmen
  EL Foresteros
  Hermanos
  Ghost Dance
  Vietnam Vets
  Bandidos
TENNESSEE (10)
  Grim Reapers
  Limited Few

Continued

BOX 3.6 OMGs BY STATE—IOMGIA—cont'd

Swordsmen
Avengers
Devils Diciples
Renegades
Sin City Deciples
Avengers
Renegades
Brotherhood
Black Pistons
Wheels of Soul
Iron Coffins
Vietnam Vets
Hells Angels
Outlaws
Boozefighters

OKLAHOMA (10)
Set Free Soldiers
Mongols
Loners
Rogues
Forsaken Few
Hessians
Grim Reapers
Bandidos
Outlaws
Vietnam Vets

OREGON (5)
Gypsy Jokers
Free Souls
Brother Speed
Outsiders
Vagos

PENNSYLVANIA (11)
Hells Angels (frozen)
Iron Horsemen
Breed
Kingsmen
Tribe
Black Pistons
Warlocks
Wheels of Soul
Vietnam Vets
Outlaws
Pagans

Henchmen
Iron Cross
Ghost Riders
The Family
Iron Horsmen
Outlaws
Black Pistons
Vagos

TEXAS (19)
Dorsai
Cossacks
Rightous Ones
Banshees
Reapers
Companaros
Freewheelers
Amigos
Tiberones
German Army Vets
Mexhetexos
German M/C
Hombres
Scorpions
Boozefighters
Bandeloros
Los Carnales
Vietnam Vets
Bandidos

WEST VIRGINIA (10)
Apache
Avengers
Tribe
Brothers of the Wheel
Last Rebels
Titans
Barbarians
Ghost Riders
Hells Angels
Pagans

WISCONSIN (20)
Chosen Few
Brotherhood
Black Pistons
Diablo Locos

BOX 3.6 OMGs BY STATE—IOMGIA—cont'd

RHODE ISLAND (5)
  Boozefighters
  Highway Drifters
  Red Devils
  Hells Angels
  Vietnam Vets
UTAH (11)
  Brotherspeed
  Vagos
  Bandeloros
  Hermanos
  Barons
  Kerberos
  Sundowners
  Bandidos
  Destralos
  Vietnam Vets
  Legacy Vets
VERMONT (2)
  Mountain Men
  Vietnam Vets
VIRGINIA (17)
  Illusions
  Renegades
  Warlocks
  Tribe
  Ching-A-Lings
  Vietnam Vets
  Mongols
  Outlaws
  Deranged Few
  Scorpions
  Merciless Souls
  Pagans
  Devils Grip
  Untamed
  Desperados
  Wheels of Soul
  Messengers
WASHINGTON (15)
  Free Souls
  Resurrection
  Dirt and Grime
  Gypsy Jokers

  Outcast
  D.C. Eagles
  SFB
  EL Foresteros
  Dorsai
  Heathens
  Road Dogs
  Hells Lovers
  Sin City Diciples
  Immortals
  Sundowners
  BPM
  Zodiacs
  Mextecas
  Outlaws
  Vietnam Vets
WYOMING (10)
  Grim Reapers
  Ching-A-Lings
  Vietnam Vets
  Bandidos
  Knights
  Destroyers
  UMF
  Los Lobos
  Legacy Vets
  Wehrmacht

Continued

BOX 3.6 OMGs BY STATE—IOMGIA—cont'd

Amigos
Hombres
Canyon Riders
Gurio
Questerlos
Unforgiven
Brotherspeed
Outsiders
Bandidos
Vietnam Vets
Hells Angels

BOX 3.7 OMGs BY STATE—NGIC

OMGs by State
2011 National Gang Threat Assessment: Emerging Trends, NGIC

ALABAMA (10)
  Black Pistons
  Devils Disciples (sic)
  Hells Lovers
  Outcasts
  Pistoleros
  Outlaws
  Sin City Disciples
  Tribe
  Wheels of Soul
ALASKA (1)
  Hells Angels
ARIZONA (3)
  Hells Angels
  Mongols
  Vagos
ARKANSAS (4)
  Bandidos
  Outlaws
  Sons of Silence
  Wheels of Soul
CALIFORNIA (6)
  Desperados
  Hells Angels
  Kings of Call
  Mongols

  Vagos
  Wheels of Soul
COLORADO (5)
  Bandidos
  Hells Angels
  Mongols
  Outlaws
  Sons of Silence
DELAWARE (1)
  Pagans
FLORIDA (8)
  Bruise Brothers
  Outlaws
  Pagans
  Phantom
  Renegades
  Sons of Silence
  Vagos
  Warlocks
  Zulus
GEORGIA (5)
  Black Pistons
  James Gang
  Outcasts
  Outlaws
  Vagos

BOX 3.7 OMGs BY STATE—NGIC—cont'd

HAWAII (1)
  Vagos
IDAHO (3)
  Bandidos
  Brothers Speed
  Vagos
ILLINOIS (5)
  Black Pistons
  Hells Angels
  Outlaws
  Sons of Silence
  Wheels of Soul
INDIANA (7)
  Black Pistons
  Devils Disciples (sic)
  Hells Angels
  Mongols
  Outlaws
  Sons of Silence
  Wheels of Soul
IOWA (14)
  Branded Breed
  Chosen Few
  Custom Riders
  El Foresteros
  Grim Reapers
  Hells Angels
  Iron Horse
  Matadors
  Midnight Riders
  Outlaws
  Rebel Knights
  Sons of Freedom
  Sons of Silence
  Vagos
KANSAS (3)
  Bandidos
  El Foresteros
  Sons of Silence
KENTUCKY (6)
  Hells Angels
  Iron Horsemen
  Outlaws
  Pagans

  Sons of Silence
  Wheels of Soul
LOUISIANA (3)
  Bandidos
  Pack of Bastards
  Sons of Silence
MAINE (4)
  Hells Angels
  Iron Horsemen
  Outlaws
  Saracens
MARYLAND (10)
  Blitzkreg
  Hells Angels
  Iron Horsemen
  New Blood
  Outlaws
  Pagans
  Phantoms
  Thunderguards
  Warlocks
  Wheels of Soul
MASSACHUSETTS (9)
  Hells Angels
  James Gang
  Long Riders
  Mongols
  Outlaws
  Phantom Lords
  Road Demons
  Ruthless for Life
  Vietnam Vets
MICHIGAN (7)
  Avengers
  Devils Disciples
  (sic)
  Forbidden Wheels
  Highwaymen
  Jokers
  Outlaws
  Rebels
MINNESOTA (2)
  Hells Angels
  Sons of Silence

Continued

BOX 3.7 OMGs BY STATE—NGIC—cont'd

MISSISSIPPI (3)
  Bandidos
  Sons of Silence
  Vagos
MISSOURI (3)
  El Forresteros
  Mongols
  Outlaws
NEBRASKA (5)
  Bandidos
  Hells Angels
  Iron Eagles
  Outlaws
  Pagans
NEVADA (3)
  Bandidos
  Mongols
  Vagos
NEW HAMPSHIRE (4)
  Hells Angels
  Iron Eagles
  Outlaws
  Pagans
NEW JERSEY (2)
  Hells Angels
  Pagans
NEW MEXICO (2)
  Bandidos
  Vagos
NEW YORK (6)
  Hells Angels
  Outlaws
  Pagans
  Vagos
  Warlocks
  Wheels of Soul
NORTH CAROLINA (4)
  Hells Angels
  Misplaced Souls
  Outlaws
  Red Devils
NORTH DAKOTA (1)
  Sons of Silence
OHIO (19)
  Avengers

Black Pistons
Brothers
Brothers of the Hammer
Derelects
Diamond Dogs
Dirt and Grime
Hells Angels
North Coast
North Coast XII
Outlaws
Pagans
Satans
Sin City Disciples
Strays
The Breed
The Brothers
Wheels of Soul
Zulus
OKLAHOMA (3)
  Bandidos
  Mongols
  Outlaws
OREGON (2)
  Mongols
  Vagos
PENNSYLVANIA (10)
  Barbarians
  Hells Angels
  Outlaws
  Pagans
  Sin City Disciples
  Tribe
  Vagos
  Wardogs
  Warlocks
  Wheels of Soul
RHODE ISLAND (2)
  Hells Angels
  Vagos
SOUTH CAROLINA (5)
  Band of Brothers
  Hells Angels
  Outlaws
  Red Devils
  Warlocks

BOX 3.7 OMGS BY STATE—NGIC—cont'd

SOUTH DAKOTA (2)
  Bandidos
  Vagos
TENNESSEE (3)
  Confederate Sons
  Outlaws
  Renegades
TEXAS (4)
  Bandidos
  Ironriders
  Los Compadres
  Vagos
UTAH (4)
  Bandidos
  Mongols
  Sons of Silence
  Vagos
VERMONT
  No Reporting
VIRGINIA (17)
  Black Pistons
  Ching-A-Lings
  Ghost Riders
  Hells Angels
  Illusions

  Iron Coffins
  Marauders
  Mongols
  Nomads
  Outlaws
  Pagans
  Renegades
  Scorpions
  Titans
  Tradesmen
  Tribe
  Warlocks
WASHINGTON (4)
  Bandidos
  Hells Angels
  Mongols
  Outlaws
WEST VIRGINIA (2)
  Pagans
  Warlocks
WISCONSIN (2)
  Black Pistons
  Outlaws
WYOMING (1)
  Bandidos

BOX 3.8 OMGs IN 49 STATES INVOLVED IN DRUG TRAFFICKING—NGIC

OMGs Identified by NGIC—2011

Avengers
Bandidos
Band of Brothers
Barbarians
Black Pistons
Brothers
Brothers of the Hammer
Bruise Brothers
Ching-A-Lings
Confederate Sons
Derelicts
Devils Disciples

Diamond Dogs
Dirt and Grime
El Foresteros
Forbidden Wheels
Ghost Riders
Hells Angels
Hells Lovers
Highwaymen
Illusions
Iron Coffins
Iron Eagles
Iron Riders

Continued

BOX 3.8 OMGs IN 49 STATES INVOLVED IN DRUG TRAFFICKING—NGIC—cont'd

James Gang	Road Demons
Jokers	Ruthless for Life
Long Riders	Saracens
Los Compadres	Scorpions
Marauders	Sin City Disciples
Mongols	Sons of Silence
Misplaced Souls	Strays
Nomads	The Breed
North Coast	The Brothers
North Coast XII	Thunderguards
New Blood	Titans
Outcasts	Tradesmen
Outlaws	Tribe
Pagans	Vagos
Phantoms	Vietnam Vets
Phantom Lords	Wardogs
Pistoleros	Warlocks
Rebels	Wheels of Soul
Red Devils	Zulus
Renegades	Total—63

As can be seen in Table 3.2, the rank order of states with chapters of different OMGs is quite different from the list presented by the IOMGIA. An explanation of these differences is not readily available, other than to say that the figures reported by the IOMGIA are based on 241 OMGs with 494 chapters, and those of the NGIC are based on respondents' reports of 230 chapters from 63 different OMGs. Further complicating the competing results is a methodological issue. The NDTS data for the NGIC results comes from a stratified random sample of 3,465 law enforcement agencies, and we have no information of how the IOMGIA data were generated.

Table 3.2 Rank Order of States with Different OMGs	
IOMGIA Listing	**NGIC Listing**
CALIFORNIA—58	OHIO—19
FLORIDA—27	VIRGINIA—17
MASSACHUSETTS and NEW YORK—22	IOWA—14
CONNECTICUT, MINNESOTA, WISCONSIN—20	PENNSYLVANIA—10
TEXAS and NEW MEXICO—19	MICHIGAN—7

The listing of OMGs appears on the website of the U.S. Department of Justice (DOJ) (see www.justice.gov/criminal/ocgs/gangs/motorcycle.html). The website begins with a definition: "Outlaw Motorcycle Gangs (OMGs) are organizations whose members use their *motorcycle clubs as conduits for criminal enterprises*" (emphasis added). The DOJ then discusses the number of clubs: "There are more than 300 active OMGs within the United States, ranging in size from single chapters with five or six members to hundreds of chapters with thousands of members." Then, the DOJ reports that certain OMGs—the Hells Angels, Mongols, Bandidos, Outlaws, and Sons of Silence—"pose a serious national domestic threat and conduct the majority of criminal activity linked to OMGs, especially activity relating to drug-trafficking and, more specifically, to cross border drug smuggling. Because of their transnational scope, these OMGs are able to coordinate drug smuggling operations in partnership with major international drug-trafficking organizations" (DTOs). Obviously, the DOJ considers OMGs to be criminal organizations using their "clubs" or club designation as a conduit or mask for criminal activities. Furthermore, the DOJ considers the five OMGs named above—Hells Angels, Mongols, Bandidos, Outlaws, and Sons of Silence—to be international crime threats acting in consort with major DTOs. In addition to the five OMGs listed above, the DOJ lists the Pagans MC as a domestic OMG with criminal ties to traditional organized crime groups in Philadelphia, Pittsburgh, and New York; the Vagos MC as a domestic and international crime threat; and the Black Pistons MC, an official Outlaws MC support club, with chapters in the United States, Canada, and Europe.

Thus far, the available literature on OMGs does not provide for a clear answer to the question: Are all outlaw motorcycle clubs (1% clubs) criminal gangs? The answers vary from none are criminal gangs (Hayes) to all are criminal gangs (IOMGIA, NGIC, and DOJ). Realistically, the first answer—none—is too restrictive and flies in the face of available evidence of organized criminal activities by well-known 1% clubs. The answer that all outlaw motorcycle clubs are criminal gangs is faulty as well because it is too broad. There are OMGs or chapters of these OMGs that identify themselves as one-percenters that are not involved in organized criminal activity. The question—Are all OMGs (1%) criminal gangs?—is an empirical question depending on the clubs' or chapter of a clubs' placement on a Criminal Organization Continuum.

Outlaw Motorcycle Club: Criminal Organization Continuum

KEY TERMS

core values of outlaw bikers

crooks' books

hangarounds

National Alliance of Gang Investigators Association

ongoing instrumental enterprises

out in bad standing

out in good standing

patchholders

righteous bikers

spontaneous expressive acts

CRIMINAL ORGANIZATION CONTINUUM

Whether any particular outlaw motorcycle club or a chapter of a motorcycle club is an outlaw motorcycle gang lies along a Criminal Organization Continuum depending on two dimensions: the extent of the members' involvement in organized crime and whether the club's officers and leaders are involved in the planning and execution of these criminal activities. These two dimensions will separate clubs with criminals in it from criminal gangs whose members are working as a collective to seek profit from crime. Because of these social dynamics and their effect on how we classify motorcycle clubs along the continuum, the selection and socialization process common to outlaw motorcycle clubs and the resulting formal and informal group networks of criminal actors are paramount to an understanding of biker organized crime and outlaw motorcycle clubs as gangs—criminal organizations.

Cooperation among criminal actors and networks of criminal actors is important to an understanding of organized crime entities, especially those that cross spatial boundaries, because crimes, such as drug, weapon, and human trafficking; protection rackets; organized retail theft; extortion rackets; disposal of stolen goods; gambling; prostitution; and the production and distribution of pornography, require social networks, structure, and organization to be successful.

For example, to engage in drug trafficking on a consistent basis there has to be a social network of criminal actors to produce, import, and distribute the drugs. Once produced and distributed to markets, the drugs must be sold and proceeds collected; someone has to protect the criminal organization and keep out competitors; the money must be laundered; and members must be paid. To facilitate this social network, there must be some hierarchy of actors with identifiable duties, a criminal structure, and organization. Box 4.1 provides an example of the social networks involved in an outlaw motorcycle gang—Outlaws MC.

BOX 4.1 OUTLAWS MC AS A CRIMINAL ORGANIZATION

The national president of the American Outlaw Association (Outlaws Motorcycle Club) was sentenced to 20 years in prison for leading a violent criminal organization. According to court testimony, the Outlaw's national president oversees a highly organized criminal enterprise with a well-defined, multilevel chain of command. As national president, the defendant declared war on the Hells Angels Motorcycle Club and ordered violent acts on rival gang members. At trial, he was convicted of conspiracy to commit racketeering and violent acts. There were 24 Outlaw MC members and three Pagan MC members charged in the original indictment; thus far, 20 have pled guilty or were convicted at trial. The 24 Outlaw MC members, including numerous leaders, came from multiple states—Wisconsin, Maine, Montana, North Carolina, Tennessee, South Carolina, and Virginia. The three Pagan MC members came from Virginia. Court records revealed that the Outlaws planned and executed violence against several rival motorcycle clubs. In one incident, the Pagans MC members joined the Outlaw MC members in an assault against rival members. During a charitable event known as the Flood Run, Outlaw MC members brutally beat Hells Angels MC members and stole their patches or colors. Court testimony also revealed that the Outlaws MC regularly distributed narcotics and used firearms or other dangerous weapons.

Source: *Department of Justice. Press Release.* April 8, 2011 and *FBI-Washington Field Office. Press Release.* June 15, 2010.

On the other hand, group members, or the "club" as a collective, do not commit all crimes that occur within an outlaw motorcycle club. Individual club members can and do commit crimes such as robberies, thefts, and other unsophisticated crimes, sometimes without the knowledge and help of other members or the club as a collective. The club apologists and club spokesmen would have us believe that this is the case whenever criminal activity occurs within an outlaw motorcycle club— clubs with criminals in it. It is possible that outlaw motorcycle clubs exist where individual or spontaneous criminal behavior is the norm, that is, bad apples in the club. However, individual criminal actors, the so-called bad apples of the club, cannot engage in organized crime without help, a detail often overlooked or ignored. Therefore, we must examine group behavior.

Quinn and Koch (2003) point out that the informal groupings within clubs are a topic often neglected in the discussion of biker clubs. These informal groupings encourage or discourage certain forms of criminality and facilitate the growth/evolution of criminal networks necessary for organized crime. At the group level in biker clubs/gangs, where members are selected from a deviant population and socialized by a deviant group once selected, it is common for cliques of like-minded members, sharing latent or manifest criminally exploitable ties—defined as latent or manifest criminal dispositions—to come together and commit crimes when the opportunities arise and there is a common basis of trust. The criminal conspiracies formed by these groups within outlaw motorcycle clubs are examples of what von Lampe refers to as social criminal organizations, that is, ones that indirectly support the criminal behavior of the members. The bond of trust between members in a social criminal organization reduces the likelihood of any one member, even a fellow member that does not approve of certain criminal acts, "ratting out" or openly disapproving of a fellow member's criminal activity—they look the other way in silence in order to remain a member of the club. Therefore, some outlaw motorcycle clubs have chapters that are social criminal organizations—motorcycle clubs with criminal members that receive tacit support from their "brothers" not, or not yet, involved in serious criminal activity.

Quinn and Koch (2003) and Barker (2007) also recognize that some motorcycle clubs are economic criminal organizations—criminal gangs—at inception or over time. For example, World War II veterans, seeking a renewed sense of the camaraderie experienced during the war, formed the original Hells Angels Motorcycle Club in 1948; however, the modern Hells Angels Motorcycle Club (HAMC) turned to organized criminal activity as an economic criminal association/gang under the leadership of Ralph "Sonny" Barger in the mid- to late 1960s. On the other hand, some outlaw 1% clubs or chapters of clubs began as and still remain criminal organizations/gangs. There is evidence to support the law enforcement community's allegation that the Bandidos MC (originally formed to control drug trafficking in the Southwest), the Order of the Blood MC (formed by an Aryan Brotherhood member after his release from prison), the Mongols MC (formed by Hispanic gangbangers from Los Angeles), and the Pennsylvania-based Warlocks MC (formed by young gangsters required to perform crimes as initiation) came into being for the purpose of committing organized crime activities. They were criminal organizations/gangs at formation—gangsters on wheels. If a club began as a criminal organization or evolved into a criminal organization, it is highly likely that it will remain so because of the process through which individual bikers become members (see Box 4.2).

BOX 4.2 BANDIDOS MC AS A CRIMINAL ORGANIZATION

DENVER September 27, 2011—Members of the Bandidos motorcycle gang, and their associates, all of whom were charged with trafficking in methamphetamine and cocaine, were arrested early this morning without incident by approximately 50 agents and officers affiliated with or supporting the Metro Gang Task Force. The arrests follow a grand jury indictment obtained on September 13, 2011, which was sealed until the defendant's arrest. Similar enforcement actions took place this morning in Dallas, San Antonio, and Austin, Texas. Defendants were allegedly members or associates of the Bandidos Motorcycle Club.

According to court documents recently filed in U.S. District Court in Denver, the Bandidos motorcycle organization is a self-styled "1%" "outlaw" motorcycle organization. The Bandidos are known as a criminal organization comprised of more than two thousand members and associates with more than 90 chapters in the United States, Canada, Europe, and elsewhere.

Source: *The United States Attorney's Office—District of Colorado. Press Release.* September 27, 2011.

DIMENSION: EXTENT OF MEMBERS' INVOLVEMENT IN ORGANIZED CRIME

Becoming a Member of an Outlaw Motorcycle Club—Four Stages

The selection and socialization process common to becoming a member of an outlaw motorcycle club sets in motion the formation of the formal and informal group networks that create, facilitate, and perpetuate the criminal behavior of outlaw motorcycle club members (see Table 4.1). This selection and socialization process has resulted in some outlaw motorcycle clubs and their chapters becoming criminal gangs that will remain such until they are disbanded voluntarily or by force of law.

Table 4.1 Four Stages in Becoming a Patchholder	
Stage	**Purpose**
Righteous Biker	Committed to the biker lifestyle—necessary but not sufficient criteria
Friend of Club/Hangaround	Form affective bonds with members
Striker/Prospect/Probate	Probationary period. Socializing, learning, and testing stage
Initiation/Patchholder	Membership
Source: Adapted from Wolf, 1991:34.	

First Stage—Righteous Biker

A biker is more than a male who rides a motorcycle. He is a deviant minority within the four million American motorcycle riders. At national motorcycle rallies (Hollister, Daytona, Laconia, Sturgis), he rides among, but not with, the other motorcyclists. All the other motorcyclists know who the bikers are by their bikes, attire, and attitude and leave them alone. Joans, noted author and biker expert, says that he, the biker, is "tough, paid his dues, ready to fight, hard drinker, doper and shitkicker" (Joans, 2001:65). His main interest in life is motorcycles and motorcycling, with his bike the defining component of his life. Bikers read biker magazines, attend rallies, ride on runs, and attend meetings on biker issues such as helmet reform laws. They wear the clothes of the bike world and sport the tattoos. They know bikes and work on bikes. Their looks, demeanor, and attitude set them apart from mainstream society. Bikers have chosen a life/world that revolves around riding a motorcycle, but all of that does not assure them entry into a one-percent biker club if that is what they want. Being a biker is a necessary, but not sufficient, status to be invited to begin the process or "hangaround" with outlaw club members.

Bikers are deviant motorcyclists within the larger community of motorcycle riders and outlaw motorcycle club members; one-percenters are an even smaller minority of deviant bikers, known loosely as "**righteous bikers**." In order to become an outlaw club member, the biker must be recognized as a "righteous biker" or demonstrate that he can become a righteous biker—committed to the biker lifestyle and the mutual support ethic—to even be considered for club membership (Veno, 2003). In the words of Hells Angels icon Sonny Barger:

> We don't recruit, we recognize—that's the best way to describe the growth of our club. What we look for in prospective members is that they are not only proficient bike riders, but also strong, self-reliant, loyal, confident and trustworthy....
>
> (Shaylor, 2004:10-11)

First, a righteous biker is riding a Harley-Davidson motorcycle or other brand of American iron. It is their most prized—and maybe their only significant—possession. Biking for them is a lifestyle that includes values, norms, and a specialized argot. The righteous biker must ride the right machine and love biking, but to be considered for a club he must be willing and able to enter into what is known as the brotherhood of one-percent bikers. According to club members, the overriding value of one-percent bikers is brotherhood—the mutual support ethic. It is the cement that holds the club together. The principles upon which this supposed brotherhood is based are loyalty, masculinity, discipline, independence, and courage (Veno, 2003). The righteous biker must exhibit evidence of these values to be considered for membership. Brotherhood is a social network, shared to some extent with and among all righteous bikers, but that sense of brotherhood is, according to club members, strongest among outlaw club members. Ultimately, it is this spirit of trust, qua brotherhood, among real or perceived "brothers" in a secret and deviant subculture that makes the formation of criminal networks within one-percent clubs possible (see Box 4.3). It is a sociological fact that peer group support can create, encourage, facilitate, sustain, and perpetuate deviant behavior between and among members of a group, especially a closed and secret group. In the case of outlaw motorcycle clubs, we not only have closed and secret groups but groups that are well known for their deviant and/or criminal behavior and one with a highly selective selection and socializing process.

BOX 4.3 CODE OF BROTHERHOOD

Brotherhood is love for members of the club.... You know there's going to be a brother there to give you a hand when you need it. There's going to be a brother there to lend you five bucks for gas when you want to go for a ride. There's going to be a brother to talk to when you need someone to talk to ... You never have to worry because there's always going to be someone there to back you, and you know it.

Source: Adapted from Wolf, 1991:96—Onions, Rebels MC.

Hells Angels celebrity and former chapter president Chuck Zito says that one-percent bikers have their own brotherhood that includes a passion for riding motorcycles and an outlook on life that is hard to explain (Zito & Layden, 2002). That sense of brotherhood, he says, includes their own rules, their own code of ethics, and their own definition of right and wrong. Their subcultural code does not allow redress of wrongs through the criminal justice system. Zito goes on to say that the Hells Angels are "an international brotherhood ... the world's largest extended family (Zito & Layden, 2002:117). However, there is often trouble in the family and the Hells Angels are considered to be the largest outlaw motorcycle gang, not club, in the world (see Box 4.4). As an example, in the Netherlands, 15 Hells Angels members were tried for killing three other chapter/charter members, including the chapter's president (Anon. 14, 2005, January 21). The killings allegedly took place in the clubhouse and were in retaliation for a 300-kilogram theft from a Colombian drug gang.

BOX 4.4 HELLS ANGELS MC AS A CRIMINAL ORGANIZATION

COLUMBIA, SC—As a result of a cooperative federal, state, and local investigation, 16 members and associates of the Hells Angels were convicted in federal court of crimes related to a racketeering conspiracy (Racketeer Influenced and Corrupt Organization Act, also known as RICO....). Previously, 12 other members and associates pleaded guilty and were sentenced.

Members and associates of the Hells Angels South Carolina Charter operated from Lexington to Rock Hill, South Carolina. As part of the coordinated criminal activity, the group engaged in drug dealing, money laundering, firearms trafficking, use of firearms in relation to crimes of violence and drug dealing, attempted armed robbery, arson, and other offenses. The Hells Angels' leadership coordinated the criminal activity and received kickbacks or cuts of the proceeds generated by members and associates of the Hells Angels.... Throughout, as [two leaders] explained in recorded conversations, members of the Hells Angels were to pay a cut of their profits from illegal activity to the Hells Angels and its leadership.

Source: *FBI Columbia Division—District of Columbia.* June 19, 2013.

Whether the idealized expression of brotherhood is more rhetoric than reality is an empirical question that will be examined later, but there is little doubt that it is portrayed to be an important value for one-percent bikers and a recurring theme in their culture. In any event, if the righteous biker has impressed club members, he may be given the opportunity to proceed to the next stage, at which he is said to begin to form the bonds of brotherhood with club members (Wolf, 1991:60-87).

Second Stage: Friend of the Club/Hangaround

"Friends of the club" fall into two categories: those who have no intention of becoming members, and those who have expressed an interest in joining the club. The first category includes people who have no intention of becoming members but want to establish friendship ties to the club or its members (Wolf, 1991). These friends of the club may later become known as associates of the club and even participate in the illegal activities of the club or individual members (after they develop trust relationships with individuals or groups of members). The second category includes those who have expressed an interest in joining and have been told to hang around until "we get to know you." In any event, the process to become a friend of the club is the same for both categories.

To enter the world of one-percent bikers, a righteous biker must establish a friendship bond with a member and have that member sponsor him. Members also approach righteous bikers with a good "rep" in the biker community and offer to sponsor them for membership. This is the initial screening process and can have bad or good consequences for the sponsor. If the sponsor finds and puts forward righteous bikers who are good friends and later become "class" members or worthy associates, his reputation is enhanced among his brothers. However, if the sponsored friend turns out to be without "class," a less-than-righteous biker, a doper, an informant, or an undercover cop, the sponsor's reputation will suffer, and he may lose his patch, get stomped, or be killed, depending on the circumstances.

The sponsor brings the name of the potential friend up in a regular "church" meeting and makes his case for the guest. Following approval of the members, the guest is extended an invitation to become a friend of the club. Depending on the club, the by-laws prescribe the vote required for an invitation all the way from no negative votes to no more than two negative votes. Friends of the club will be invited to attend club parties, runs, and other club activities, but because the friend of the club is not a member, he cannot vote, attend meetings, or be involved in club business. For many friends of the club, the relationship stays at this level. However, people in the second category of friends of the club—those wanting to join—may be invited to begin the slow assimilation process of becoming a striker/prospect/probate.

Many clubs require a striker/prospect/probate to fill out an application form so they can perform background checks (Veno, 2003:55). William "Billy" Queen, an undercover ATF agent who joined the Mongols Motorcycle Club reports that the three-page form he was required to fill out was as extensive as any he filled out in law enforcement (Queen, 2000). Queen had to supply social security number, driver's license, veterans administration records, telephone numbers and addresses for relatives, high school records, and W-2s for five years (2005). The Mongols gave the application to a private investigator to check him out. In spite of all this, the ATF agent became a patched member, secretary-treasurer, and vice president of his Mongol chapter (see Boxes 4.5 and 4.6). Veno (2003:55) cites the case of an Australian club that uses voice-stress analysis testers when interviewing nominees. If everything checks out, the nominee's sponsor must again bring up the prospective member at a meeting for approval by the membership. If approved, the new striker will be given the club's bottom rocker, which he sews on his leather or denim vest and begins the prospect/striker stage.

BOX 4.5 MONGOLS MC AS A CRIMINAL ORGANIZATION

DENVER—A three-year investigation resulted in this morning's takedown of a biker gang in Denver [October 21, 2008]. Mass arrests related to the Mongols outlaw motorcycle gang were also made in Los Angeles, where 79 defendants are being prosecuted, 73 of whom face Racketeering Charges (RICO). Federal search and arrests were executed in seven states: Colorado, California, Nevada, Oregon, Washington, Florida, and Ohio. In addition to the arrests, agents and officers executed six federal warrants throughout the Denver area....

The Mongols are an outlaw motorcycle gang that was formed in Montebello, California in the 1970s. There are as many as 600 members nationwide. Many of the Mongols were allegedly recruited from some of the most violent street gangs....

Source: *Adapted from The United States Attorney's Office—District of Colorado. Press Release. October 21, 2008.*

BOX 4.6 MONGOLS MOTORCYCLE GANG MEMBER SENTENCED TO LIFE IN PRISON FOR MURDERING PRESIDENT OF SAN FRANCISCO HELLS ANGELS

SAN FRANCISCO—Christopher Bryan Ablett, a/k/a "Stoney," a member of the Modesto Chapter of the Mongols outlaw motorcycle gang was sentenced today to serve two concurrent life sentences, and one life sentence to run consecutively.... The sentence was imposed for the defendant's gang-related murder of Mark "Papa" Guardado, the president of the San Francisco Chapter of the Hells Angels....

"The defendant killed a complete stranger for no other reason than his membership in a rival motorcycle gang," U.S. Attorney Haag said....

Evidence at Ablett's trial showed that during a trip to San Francisco to visit a friend, Ablett was armed with a foot-long military knife and a 0.357 Magnum revolver, and brought along a Mongols full-patch vest and a T-shirt that only a full member of the Mongols is allowed to wear. According to testimony from Bureau of Alcohol, Tobacco, Firearms and Explosives (ATF) gang expert, Special Agent John Ciccone, and former Mongols undercover ATF Special Agent Darrin Kozlowski, the Mongols are an organized criminal motorcycle gang whose primary rival is the Hells Angels motorcycle gang.

When Guardado learned that Ablett was wearing a Mongols patch shirt in a bar in the Mission, Guardado went to the street outside the bar and approached Ablett. A fight broke out, and Ablett stabbed Guardado four times and shot him twice, killing him. According to the testimony of FBI Special Agent Jacob Millspaugh, the case agent, Ablett's phone records showed that he spent the next several hours calling people who were identified as members of the Mongols.

Following the trial, on February 22, 2012, the jury rejected Ablett's claims that he acted in self-defense, in defense of his friends, and in the heat of passion. The jury also found that the defendant murdered Guardado to maintain or increase his position in the Mongols, and the Mongols engaged in racketeering activities.

Source: *U.S. Department of Justice. United States Attorney. Northern District of California. Press Release.* May 15, 2012.

Third Stage—Striker/Prospect/Probate

The striker period is a socializing process (see Box 4.7). One-percent club bikers use it as a learning and testing period to ensure that the prospect adheres to the **three core values of outlaw bikers:** (1) love of biking, (2) love of brothers, and (3) love of club (Wolf, 1991). For those clubs that are becoming or have become criminal organizations, this process is used to identify possible informants or undercover officers and to insure that the prospect has a needed criminal skill (e.g., dope dealer, meth cooker, marijuana grower, or an accomplished thief). The gangs are also looking for possible members who have contacts in places that aid criminal acts e.g., law enforcement or regulatory organizations, licensing agencies, contacts with other criminal organizations, etc.), or will cooperate in criminal activities or at least do nothing deemed to be rash when they occur. Through the years, there have been allegations that clubs/gangs have required prospective murderers to commit murders in order to be considered. Sandy Alexander, the tyrannical president of the Manhattan chapter, demanded absolute loyalty from all his subordinates and allegedly required all prospects to pick a target for murder from a list maintained by the club. The murder had to be witnessed by another member or the prospect had to supply flawless documentary evidence. Only those who accept the club's attitudes and values, including criminal tendencies in gangs, are selected as strikers and now the group as a collective can test and observe for evidence that supports the decision for or against membership.

BOX 4.7 PURPOSE OF PROSPECTING

Prospecting is not an initiation as you would find in a fraternity. It is instead a period of training that is sustained until the prospect, in every sense, conducts himself as a patchholder. It's a time in which:

The man's attitude is conditioned so that he displays a sense of responsibility and respect toward the patchholders of the club, without which he will not develop a sense of brotherhood.

He is educated in the basic MC (motorcycle club) protocol and etiquette.

He is given time to develop the habits that are basic to good security and good communication.

To get the man into the habits of participating.

To give his family time to adjust to the demands of the club.

To experience and learn an essential degree of humility.

To become accustomed to trusting the judgment, at times blindly, of those patchholders who will someday be his brothers.

Source: *Adapted from Hangaround/Prospect information document of a Big Five Motorcycle Club. Must remain anonymous.*

Prospecting is an intense process requiring close personal interaction between the striker and other club members; therefore, unless the club is in a war with rivals requiring the immediate infusion of immediate fighters, clubs will only have one or two prospects at any given time (Wolf, 1991). At times, some clubs have moved beyond the goal of socializing prospective members and moved into the realm of bizarre and brutal treatment. During the 1970s, an English 1% motorcycle club's (Sons of Hell MC) prospecting process was described as a "nothing short of a series of near-death experiences" (www.sonsofhellhistory.co.uk/701.html). Prospects were beaten, stabbed, hung from trees, routinely humiliated, and mentally abused. The brutal and vicious patchholders would routinely set prospects on fire and have them put out the flames without help. On the club's official website, there are two pictures of a prospect being set on fire and running to find something wet to jump in. One can imagine the effect such abuse had on righteous bikers who were asked to join the club. The brutal treatment of prospects by the California Mongols in the 1980s affected recruitment to such an extent that the outlaw club instituted a national policy of not assaulting prospects. Few righteous bikers wanted to endure a nightly beating to become a Mongols member. Depending on the club, the striking phase will last from three months to two years and will always include the summer riding season. A series of testing situations, including helping in or observing criminal activities in some clubs, determines how well the prospect lives up to the core values of the outlaw biker's world.

CORE VALUE—LOVE OF BIKING

The striker has already demonstrated that he is, on the surface, a righteous biker. He had to be to be invited to be a friend of the club. Now, he is going to be evaluated on his commitment to biking. Strikers are required to have their bikes up and running during the entire prospect period, and they have to attend every meeting, party, bike event, or gathering of any kind where club patchholders are present (see Bandidos By-laws in Appendix A). The prospect will make every national and regional club run and attend every funeral. During these situations, his potential brothers are evaluating his riding behavior, the number of miles he puts on his speedometer, the weather conditions under which he will ride, and his overall mechanical skills. The striker must be capable of taking care of his bike. One-percent bikers do not call AAA for a tow or to change a tire. They do not put their bikes in the local garage for maintenance. Patchholders will help the striker or teach him to make major repairs or modifications. That is part of the brotherhood, but the striker must show his commitment to biking by knowing the basic aspects of motorcycle maintenance.

CORE VALUES—LOVE OF BROTHERS AND LOVE OF CLUB

The learning and testing for the core values of love of brothers and love of club are intertwined. The first act of love of club the striker must demonstrate is the pledging of his bike and title during the striking period (see Bandidos By-laws in Appendix A). It shows that he loves the club more than his identity by offering his most prized possession as proof of his commitment to becoming a member. Should he fail to complete the striking period, his chances of losing his bike are real and virtually certain.

The size of individual chapters, usually from six to 25 members, allows for face-to-face personal relationships among members. Therefore, the learning and testing process for a striker is the responsibility of all club members as well as the sponsor. In addition, because each member is going to vote on the prospect, the striker is expected to get to know and interact with each member on a personal basis (Wolf, 1991:101).

The club tests the striker's willingness to follow orders from his brothers through a series of duties he must perform. The striker is responsible for cleaning the clubhouse and making sure that the refrigerator is fully stocked with beer, even if he has to buy it himself. In addition, he stands guard at the clubhouse and makes periodic security checks during meetings. During club runs, he sets up tents, gathers firewood, and keeps the fire going. He may even drive the "crash truck," which carries the beer, spare motorcycle parts, weapons, and dope on runs. Strikers are designated gofers at all club functions and the club bar. The striker must perform these duties willingly and without complaint—patchholders are always right. Some clubs, particularly criminal organizations, require strikers to commit criminal acts during the striking period to demonstrate commitment and eliminate the possibility of bringing an undercover cop into the club (see Veno, 2003). Others, according to biker and law enforcement sources, require that a striker must have either his sponsor's or the chapter president's permission to engage in criminal activities. This is to instill in the striker the idea that crimes are done by and for the benefit of the club, not for individual enhancement.

The interpersonal relationships between striker and club members creates a group social network in which the striker learns the accepted behavior patterns—criminal or noncriminal—and creates the basis for trust that facilitates and sustains criminal activities as a tacit supporter or participant (for social criminal organizations or criminal organizations). These interpersonal relationships among and with club members (riding, partying, working on bikes, performing club duties, and drinking and fighting together) come to dominate the striker's world.

The frequent, intense, and exclusive relations with club members leave little time for anyone else but the striker's brothers. He soon withdraws from all social contacts with non-club members and loses his other social identity. Being a brother is his whole social world. He is and always will be a club member. Family birthdays, anniversaries, births, deaths, and other special occasions come second or third in preference behind club activities or duties. The one-percent biker clubs express this theme in sayings and tattoos such as "Angels Forever, Forever Angels," "Bandidos Forever, Forever Bandidos," "Outlaws Forever, Forever Outlaws," "Pagans Forever, Forever Pagans," and so on.

Those striker/prospects that successfully progress through the prospecting stage are brought up for a vote to become members—patchholders. Depending on the club, the vote to become a member must be unanimous or have no more than two negative votes (see Lavigne, 1999; Veno, 2003; Wolf, 1991). See Box 4.8.

BOX 4.8 PAGANS MC AS A CRIMINAL ORGANIZATION

CHARLESTON, WV October 06, 2009—[Today] the unsealing of a 44-count indictment charging a total of 55 members and associates of the Pagans Motorcycle Club (PMC) with numerous violent crimes such as kidnapping, racketeering, robbery, extortion, and conspiracy to commit murder.

As alleged in the indictment, PMC chapters in multiple states including: West Virginia, Kentucky, Virginia, Pennsylvania, New York, New Jersey, Delaware, and Florida. The indictment charges five PMC officers, including national president, David Keith Barbeito, also known as "Bart," of Myersville, Md., and the national vice president, Floyd B. Moore, also known as "Jesse" and "Diamond Jesse," of St. Albans, W.V., with Racketeering Influenced and Corrupt Organizations (RICO) violations, conspiracy to commit RICO, and other charges.

… The indictment alleges that PMC members and associates have engaged in racketeering activities since March 2003. According to the indictment, in March 2003, PMC members, at the direction of Moore, traveled to Huntington, W.V., and restrained and beat a member of another motorcycle gang, the Road Disciples Motorcycle Club (RDMC) in an attempt to extract information from the victim in order to find the RDMC president. Moore ordered the PMC members to find the RDMC president to collect money and to threaten to shut down the RDMC if the president failed to comply with Moore's orders. The indictment also alleges that in September 2005, Moore and other PMC members and associates conspired with a prison guard to kill an inmate suspected of cooperating with law enforcement. Further, according to the indictment, Moore ordered another PMC member to commit a murder to help out the president of a local chapter of the Avengers Motorcycle Club.

Source: *FBI-Pittsburgh Division. Press Release.* October 06, 2009.

Fourth Stage—Initiation Patchholder

The actual initiation ritual varies with the club and has been the subject of controversy and myth since the 1950s. The accounts, appearing primarily in the popular literature, describe activities ranging from sexual depravity to murder. Some law enforcement authorities repeat these accounts as fact in their training seminars as they attempt to portray one-percent bikers as demonic sex perverts. Hells Angels authors, such as the late Dr. Maz Harris [Ph.D. in Sociology], Sonny Barger, and Chuck Zito, dismiss these accounts as myths at least for the Hells Angels (Barger et al., 2000; Harris, 1985; Zito & Layden, 2002). Both Barger and Zito say that there is no initiation beyond that of serving as a prospect. However, they do not describe the actual ceremony when the prospect is given his colors. Veno speculates that the clubs themselves may be the source of these initiation myths, in order to cause "in your face" outrage among outsiders (2003:59). Wolf (1991) says that the Canadian clubs he was familiar with held "initiation nights," "color parties," or "initiation runs" when the prospect was given his colors.

Some bizarre initiation rites have occurred. A video of a late 1960s or early 1970s Hessians MC initiation shows initiates lying on the ground while others urinate on them, and it appears that one or more of the initiates engaged in oral sex with a young woman (Centaur Productions, 2005). Quinn (1983) reported that initiates "may be forced to cook and eat excrement or drink from a boot filled with urine, vomit and beer." Wolf describes an initiation he attended where two Rebel prospects were roughed up, stripped, and then staked, spread-eagle, to the ground. They were then smeared with a concoction of "engine oil and transmission fluid, grease and urine, STP and shit" (Wolf, 1991:113). The members then stood around them, drinking beer and urinating on them before throwing them in a lake. He also relates the account of a Satans Choice MC prospect that engaged in a gang sodomy of a woman during his initiation. Other Satans Choice members told of being thrown in a frozen lake, passing out, and being dragged back and forth by a rope tied around them or having to fight another member. Recall ATF Special Agent Billy Queen, who working undercover, became a patched member of the Mongols Motorcycle Club. He says that the night he was initiated the president handed him his rocker, and the rest of the members poured 50-weight motorcycle oil and beer all over him. He says "It was a mess, but I was happy I made it" (Queen, 2000). It is instructive to observe that even an undercover law enforcement officer felt a certain elation after progressing though the rigorous selection and socializing process of an outlaw motorcycle gang.

The nature of the rituals is not as important as the process they represent, as shown by Queen's comments. The initiation process is important to the club and the striker. For the striker, it is the end of a series of transformations in his personal status and identity. He began as a citizen, then separated himself emotionally and symbolically when he became a righteous biker. From there, the righteous biker became a friend of the club, was invited to become a striker, and now he will be initiated into the "club and the lives of his brothers as a patchholder" (Wolf, 1991:110). It is important for the club members because it reaffirms their identity as patchholders, clearly identifies the boundaries between the club and the outside world, and ensures that the club perpetuates. When the club loses its identity—its patch—it ceases to exist. One-percent bikers are aware of clubs that have forcibly lost their patches or have been assimilated—"patched over"—by other clubs. As mentioned earlier, the Hells Angels assimilated the Rebels MC (with whom Wolf rode). See Box 4.9.

BOX 4.9 SONS OF SILENCE MC AS A CRIMINAL ORGANIZATION

INDIANAPOLIS-April 8, 2012—Phillip Mannebach, age 47, a member of the Sons of Silence Motorcycle Club was found guilty of participating in a local methamphetamine organization, as well as helping to orchestrate the abduction of an individual. His sentencing is the culmination of a multiyear investigation and prosecution of a drug trafficking organization that operated in Indianapolis, and had extensive connections to a motorcycle club operating in Terre Haute [Sons of Silence]. The methamphetamine operation operated from approximately May 2010 until the arrests of most of the members of the organization on August 6, 2011.

Mannebach, a member of the Sons of Silence Motorcycle Club in Terre Haute, was convicted of operating a methamphetamine distribution ring in Terre Haute along with co-defendant Michael Pitts, age 51, also of Terre Haute. They would receive the drugs from James Taylor, a previously prosecuted member of the Sons of Silence motorcycle gang of Indianapolis.

In addition, co-defendants Travis Umphries and Dustin Coffey, "hangarounds" with the Sons of Silence Motorcycle Club in Terre Haute assisted Mannebach with the abduction of Mannebach's stepson in Terre Haute on November 1, 2010...

Source: *Department of Justice. Southern District of Indiana. Press Release.* April 8, 2013.

Leaving a One-Percent Club

Short of dying, there are only two ways to leave a one-percent club—**out in bad standing** or **out in good standing**.

Out in Bad Standing

A member leaves the club "out in bad standing," when he is thrown out because of a serious violation of the club's rules; discovered to be a "snitch" or informant (in which case he is lucky to be alive to leave); misuses his office if an officer; sponsors a prospect who turns out to be a snitch, informer, or undercover police officer (again he is lucky to be alive); or commits any other infraction that the membership thinks brings discredit to the club. This is a very serious event in the life of a patchholder and has dire consequences for the biker deemed out in bad standing. He is normally ostracized by the patchholders of all clubs and must surrender any personal items deemed to be club property, such as his motorcycle and anything with the club name or logo on it. The pariah surrenders his motorcycle because most clubs require that a prospect must sign over the title to his bike to the club during his prospecting period. Any club tattoo must be removed or covered over. Depending on how serious his exit was, the removal of tattoos can be horrendous—there are examples of hot spoons, irons, or other metal objects being applied to the skin. Other examples of removal have included cutting off the skin containing the tattoos or the tattoo being burned off. One member of a Canadian Hells Angels chapter had a tattoo (complete top and bottom rocker with logo in the middle) on his back burned off with a blowtorch. He was hung from the ceiling and tied spread-eagle as the burning took place, with his "brothers" laughing and high-fiving each other to his screams. His violent actions while high on meth, shooting a girlfriend in public, and shooting and killing a citizen who came to her aid, brought serious discredit and adverse publicity on the club.

Out in Good Standing

A member leaves the club in "good standing" because of illness or an accident or injury that prevents him from riding his motorcycle—you cannot be a member of a bike club if you cannot ride a bike. On occasion, well-respected members who have served the club faithfully for a number of years are allowed to retire. These "retired" individuals will, depending on the club, wear a patch on their "cut" (vest) that says retired". If a member leaves in good standing, he can keep any tattoos with the logo or name of the club, but usually there must be a "date in" tattooed above the logo and a "date out" below the logo. These former members, again depending on the club, can attend all club functions, attend meetings (but not vote), and ride with the club on runs, but in the back of the pack.

Members' Criminal Behavior

OMG Members' Biographies

As we have seen in the boxes in this chapter, outlaw motorcycle clubs' qua outlaw motorcycle gangs' members and leaders acting as members of a criminal organization have been indicted, convicted, and sentenced for numerous federal racketeering offenses. Five of the boxes discussed the criminal organizations Hells Angels, Outlaws, Bandidos, Pagans, and the Sons of Silence, which shall be discussed later as the "Big Five Motorcycle Gangs." Box 4.10 describes the criminal actions of members and leaders of the Mongols Motorcycle Club, a club we will categorize as an Independent Motorcycle Club that is not a part of or under the influence of one of the Big Five Motorcycle Gangs. All six will be among those outlaw motorcycle clubs we place on the extreme right side of the Criminal Organization Continuum of outlaw motorcycle clubs, that is, gangs. In addition to indictment and conviction in court, it is possible to get a measure of the extent of OMG members' criminal activity from the autobiographies of past and present members. In recent years, following the success of Sonny Barger's autobiography, these **"crooks' books"** have flooded the popular market. They all have the same common themes: the member's criminal activity, including multiple convictions and prison sentences by the authors; drug taking; extreme violence; and pride in living their lives outside the restrictions of law and society. As a group, the majority of these one-percenter authors revel in the camaraderie and brotherhood of the one-percenters, while at the same time they describe the bashing, maiming, and murder of "brothers" over territory, colors, and perceived or real acts of disrespect. This violence, as we shall see, extends to patched members of the same club. Several one-percent bikers with best-selling autobiographies have pop-culture celebrity status, including Hells Angels' Sonny Barger, former chapter, national, and international president and ex-con; Chuck Zito, former chapter president, ex-con, TV star, and bodyguard to the stars; and former Devils Diciples MC member Duane "Dog" Chapman, ex-con, bounty-hunter extraordinaire, and star of his own dramatic TV series. All three are convicted felons who have served long prison sentences. These celebrities also have their own websites. Barger, who markets himself as an "American legend," sells Hells Angels support merchandise, ranging from calendars, souvenirs, and beer to barbecue sauce (www.sonnybarger.net/main.html). Zito's website and the dust cover of his book have a picture of him and former President Bill Clinton. The smiling former president has his arm around Zito's shoulder (www.chuckzito.com/default2.htm). "Dog" Chapman's autobiography is a bizarre book—the list of crimes this former outlaw biker alleges to have committed are astronomical, and his conversations with, and sightings of, his deceased mother are eerie (Chapman & Morton, 2007).

BOX 4.10 ORGANIZED CRIME ACTIVITIES BY SELECTED ONE-PERCENT OUTLAW MOTORCYCLE GANGS/CLUBS 1995-2006

Avengers MC

Now, here's the deal, gentlemen. I'm gonna tell you guys flat out. Anybody in this room that doesn't want to be involved in criminal activity, you can be excused.

I'm serious. You're excused because our backs are against the...wall, man. If we have to start doing felonious... stealing motorcycles, dealing dope, or whatever the...that we got to do. (Statement made by **Avenger Chapter President** Thomas Khalil, Elyria, Ohio, 199 *US v Kahlil*, No. 00-3636. 2002 FED App.0048P (6th Cir).

In 1999, Tom Hakaim, a prominent South Lorain, Ohio, businessman and **treasurer and road captain** of the Avengers MC, pleaded guilty to charges of racketeering and attempting to commit a violent crime on behalf of an enterprise. Hakaim testified against fellow members to have several charges dropped (emphasis added) Anon. 12, 1999).

In 2001, a member of the Avengers MC was convicted of interstate commerce facilitation in the commission of the murder for hire, interstate travel in aid of crime of violence, and conspiracy to distribute cocaine. The cocaine supplier was the Medellin Cartel in Colombia (*Wright v. United States*, Civil Case No. 05-71569. Crim. Case No. 96-80876).

Bandidos MC

In 2006, George Wagers, the **International President and Chapter President** of the Bellingham, Washington, chapter of the Bandidos, pleaded guilty to federal racketeering and conspiracy charges.

Breed and Pennsylvania Warlocks MC

The Breed and the Pennsylvania-based Warlocks MC were once bitter enemies but in 2006 members and leaders in both biker gangs were arrested and charged with cooperative crimes of meth and crystal meth (ice) distribution. Arrested were the **presidents** of the Pennsylvania chapter of the

Continued

BOX 4.10 ORGANIZED CRIME ACTIVITIES BY SELECTED ONE-PERCENT OUTLAW MOTORCYCLE GANGS/CLUBS 1995-2006—cont'd

Warlocks and the Breeds New Jersey Mother Club. Also arrested were five of the seven-member Pennsylvania Breed's **executive board and two executive members** of the New Jersey Breed MC. Seized were 22 pounds of crystal meth; $500,000; 44 firearms, including a submachine gun; ten explosive devices; numerous vehicles; and 24 motorcycles (Anon. 13, 2006).

Diablos MC

In 1998, the **president** of the Connecticut chapter of the Diablos MC and 12 other members of the Connecticut and Massachusetts chapters were charged with RICO and racketeering charges. The **president** of the Connecticut chapter was convicted of the 26 charges, including RICO, murder for hire, narcotics, and auto theft violations. (*U.S. District Court for the District of Massachusetts,* 145 E. Supp. 2d 111; 2001 U.S. Dist. Lexis 5362).

Freelancers MC

Following the 2004 arrest and seizure of "substantial quantities of methamphetamine and cocaine," the founding member and former **vice-president** of the New Hampshire MC was found guilty of possession with intent to distribute dangerous drugs (*United States v. Belton,* No. 04-cr-192-01-JD).

Hells Angels MC

On August 12, 1986, members of the Outlaws motorcycle club shot and killed John Cleve Webb, a member of the Anchorage Alaska chapter of the Hells Angels, in Louisville, Kentucky. Shortly thereafter, Barger, **[International President]** a member of the Oakland chapter of the Hells Angels, said it's time to start killing Outlaws again. [Barger was later convicted of conspiracy charges related to attempts at revenge.] (*United States v. Barger,* Nos. 89-5606, 89-5607, 1990).

A defense attorney and three Hells Angels members of the Troy, New York, chapter pleaded guilty to being part of a drug ring that distributed methamphetamines in central New York (*New York Lawyer,* April 29, 2004).

The **president** of the San Diego chapter of the Hells Angels pleaded guilty to racketeering charges, distributing methamphetamine, and conspiracy to kill members of the Mongols MC. Nine other members also pleaded guilty to racketeering charges (Soto, 2005).

The former **president** of the Chicago chapter of the Hells Angels pleaded guilty to federal racketeering charges related to the sale of cocaine and methamphetamine (Anon. 13, 2006).

Two officers **(president and former president)** of the Spring Valley, Illinois, chapter of the Hells Angels pleaded guilty to selling drugs, to intimidation, and to robbery charges (Kravetz, 2006).

Iron Horsemen

In 2002, two members of the Maine Iron Horsemen MC were charged and subsequently found guilty of possession with intent to distribute a controlled substance (oxycodone and methamphetamine) (*United States v. Fournier,* Crim. No. 02-57-B-S, U.S. District Court for the District Court of Maine 2002 US Dist. Lexis 20732).

Loners MC

A 1999 arrest led to the conviction of two Loners MC officers (former **president** of the Quapaw, Oklahoma, chapter and the **president** of the Kentucky chapter) for the production and distribution of methamphetamine (*United States v. Cervine,* No. 00-40024-21-SAC).

Outlaws MC

Harry "Taco" Bowman served as **international president** for 13 years, until 1997. As international president, Bowman handled matters large and small, from setting the Outlaws' policies regarding other gangs to monitoring the activities of members. In the early 1990s, the Warlocks, another Florida club, allied with the Hells Angels and began selling drugs on their behalf. This ignited a war between the Outlaws and the Warlocks. When the Outlaws learned that Raymond "Bear" Chafin, a former member [of the Outlaws], was the leader of a Warlocks chapter in Edgewater, Bowman told

BOX 4.10 ORGANIZED CRIME ACTIVITIES BY SELECTED ONE-PERCENT OUTLAW MOTORCYCLE GANGS/CLUBS 1995-2006—cont'd

Hicks to find Chafin and kill him. [Chafin was later killed by an Outlaws prospect that received his patch and lightning bolts—literally a patch for killing for the club].

On New Year's Eve 1993, Bowman announced a meeting of all Outlaws at a party in Fort Lauderdale. During the meeting, Bowman announced that the Outlaws would escalate their hostilities in 1994, showing no tolerance for Hells Angels or their sympathizers. [The Outlaws' national president has final authority over all club activities.]

…At a meeting near Chicago, Bowman told Hicks [Wayne "Joe Black" Hicks, Bowman's "right hand man"] and others that an Outlaw had become a snitch. Bowman said that the snitch would be killed and explained that the killing would be made to look like an enemy had done it. He also said that the murdered snitch would be given an Outlaws funeral. [The Outlaw snitch was later killed and received an Outlaws funeral.]

…At a meeting near the end of 1994, Bowman…announced that the Outlaws would take the war against the Hells Angels to California. Bowman planned to send a group of trustworthy Outlaws to California to conduct surveillance on, and possibly assassinate, either Sonny Barger, the international president of the Hells Angels, or George Christie, a national officer [Outlaws went to California but no one was assassinated]. (*United States v. Bowman*, No. 01-14305).

Pagans MC
The 1998 arrests and subsequent convictions of 27 Pagans for conspiracy to commit murder, extortion, arson, weapons violations, and assault eliminated four Pagans chapters on Long Island, New York (MAGLOCLEN Assessment, 2003:43).

Renegades MC
In November 1999, 28 members of the Virginia Chapter of the Renegades MC were convicted of distributing methamphetamines in the Tidewater area. The drug trafficking had gone on for several years (MAGLOCLEN Assessment, 2003:43).

Road Saints MC
In 1996, the **President** of the Columbus, Ohio, chapter of the Road Saints MC was charged and convicted of possession of a firearm by a person convicted of a crime punishable for a term exceeding one year (*United States v. Scarberry*, No. CR2-98-00008).

Sons of Silence MC
In 1995, 13 Sons of Silence MC members were charged and subsequently found guilty of conspiracy to commit racketeering: conspiracy to distribute and possession to distribute methamphetamine; obstruction of justice; possessing with intent to sell a motor vehicle part knowing that the vehicle identification number of the part had been removed, obliterated, tampered with, and altered; money laundering; the commission of violent crimes in aid of racketeering activity; and engaging in a continuing enterprise (*United States v. Gruber et al.*, No. CR (4-MJM), 1998).

Sundowners MC
In 1998, several members of the Sundowners MC were tried and convicted of conspiracy to sell narcotics, conspiracy to distribute methamphetamine, and use of the telephone in the commission of a drug offense (*United States v. Johnson*, No. 99. CR-23B).

Warlocks MC
In 2005, the **"enforcer"** for the Shenandoah County, Virginia, chapter of the Warlocks MC [Florida-based Warlocks] pleaded guilty to numerous charges related to the distribution of drugs (*U.S. v. Dezzutti*, No. 5-05CR00005-1).

Related to the case above, the **acting enforcer** of the Brevard County, Florida, chapter of the Warlocks MC pleaded guilty to numerous charges related to the distribution of drugs (*U.S. v. Framelli*, No. 5-05CR00005-2).

In recent years there has been a plethora of popular literature from a variety of sources of "crooks' books"—current and former biker autobiographies, undercover agents, informants-rats, and journalists describing the criminal and violent behavior of one-percent bikers in the United States and Canada. Some of these include Martineau (2003), *I Was a Killer for the Hells Angels: The True Story of Serge Quesnel* (autobiography of a paid Hells Angels "rat" who was also a merciless killer for the Canadian Hells Angels); Sanger (2005), *Hell's Witness* (the story of a Canadian Hells Angels hit man and police informant, this book documents the viciousness and thoroughly criminal nature of the Canadian Hells Angels); Queen (2005), *Under and Alone: The True Story of the Undercover Agent Who Infiltrated America's Most Violent Outlaw Motorcycle Gang* (autobiography of an ATF Special Agent who became the Secretary Treasurer of a Mongols chapter; Langton (2006), *The Unlikely Rise of Walter Stadnick in the Canadian Hells Angels* (the story of the Canadian National Hells Angels President responsible for the spread of the gang throughout Canada; the diminutive Stadnick is the "poster child" of biker criminals and thugs); Droban (2007), *Running with the Devils: The True Story of the ATF's Infiltration of the Hells Angels* (criminal defense attorney and writer who describes the Hells Angels infiltration by Dobyns and his fellow agent); Caine (2008), *Befriend and Betray: Infiltrating the Hells Angels, Bandidos and Other Criminal Brotherhoods* (describes the infiltration of the U.S. Hells Angels and Bandidos by a contract informant); Hayes and Gardner (2008), *Outlaw Biker: My Life at Full Throttle* (autobiography of a member of the Los Valientes MC in Saint Paul, Minnesota); Cavazos (2008), *Honor Few, Fear None: The Life and Times of a Mongol* (autobiography of the International President of the Mongols MC, who led the gang during it most criminally active period [he later "ratted" out his fellow brothers for a lesser sentence]); Hall (2008), *Riding on the Edge: A Motorcycle Outlaw's Tale* (autobiography of one of the early members of the Pagans MC in the 1960s who became a chapter president, was sent to prison, and then became a college professor); Dobyns and Johnson-Shelton (2009a, 2009b), *No Angels: My Harrowing Undercover Journey to the Inner Circle of the Hells Angels* (about an ATF Special Agent who infiltrated the Arizona Hells Angels [anyone who believes there are no outlaw motorcycle gangs, only clubs, should read this book]); Caine (2009), *The Fat Mexican: The Bloody Rise of the Bandidos Motorcycle Club* (based on his contract infiltration of the Bandidos MC in the United States and Canada); Aguilar (2010), *Forgive Me Father for I Have Sinned* (self-published autobiography of Pastor Phil Aguilar, a convicted felon and ex-con, the founder of the Set Free Soldiers, a supposedly Christian outlaw motorcycle gang); Ball (2011), *Terry the Tramp: The Life and Times of a One Percenter* (autobiography of the legendary Vagos MC leader, Terry the Tramp); Hall (2011), *Hell to Pay: Hells Angels vs. The Million-Dollar Rat* (describes the trial and tribulations of a member of the Vancouver, Canada, Hells Angel who became a paid police "rat" [shows the Vancouver Hells Angels chapter as a true economic criminal organization from its forming]); Menginie and Droban (2011), *Prodigal Son, Pagan Son: Growing Up Inside the Dangerous World of the Pagans Motorcycle Club* (autobiography of the son of a Pagan MC leader that describes just how dangerous this biker gang is [again, those who believe there are no outlaw motorcycle gangs should read this book]); Spurgeon (2011), *Bikin' and Brotherhood: My Journey* (a self-published surreal account of his 15 years as a 1% outlaw biker, including being a chapter and regional president of the Outlaws MC, before he "found Jesus" and supposedly turned his life around [this work is a vivid account of the biker lifestyle best described as one of violence, death, and betrayal]); Caine (2012), *Charlie and the Angels: The Outlaws, The Hells Angels and the 60 Years War* (based on the author's contract infiltration of both the Outlaws and the Hells Angels, and describing their violent behavior to each other in the United States and Canada); Falco and Droban (2013), *Vagos, Mongols and Outlaws: My Infiltration of America's Deadliest Biker Gangs* (autobiography of an informant who infiltrated the Vagos, Mongols, and Outlaws MC, eventually becoming the vice-president of the Petersburg, Virginia, Outlaws chapter); and Rowe (2013), *Gods of Mischief: My Undercover Vendetta to Take Down the Vagos Outlaw Motorcycle Gang* (describing the author's joining of the Vagos MC as a police informant to avenge the brutal death of a friend [again this work is a description of the abject violence and criminal behavior of outlaw motorcycle gangs]). *Gypsy Joker to a Hells Angel,* by Phil Cross and Meg Cross, is a recent crooks' book and describes an unbelievable 43-year membership in the Hells Angels. In the epilogue, Phil Cross says that: "I have been hospitalized at least 20 times and had ten surgeries (most of them from fights and accidents); I have been in so many hundreds of fights that I couldn't even begin to guess the number. I have been arrested 14 times (that I can count), but I was always innocent…honest." Cross was also on the FBI's Ten Most Wanted List in 1986. No doubt, he was innocent and being "picked on" by federal authorities.

In addition to these popular literature works, there have been at least two attempts to gather empirical data on the criminal activity of OMG members: Barker and Human's (2009) study and an earlier law enforcement survey (2003). Barker and Human (2009), using Quinn and Koch's (2003) *Typology of Biker Criminal Activity,* conducted a content analysis of newspaper articles in the LexisNexis database in a 25-year period (1980-2005). What were known at the time as the Big Four OMGs—the Hells Angels MC, the Outlaws MC, the Bandidos MC, and the Pagans MC—because of their criminal behavior and violence—were selected for analysis. The first three OMGs, although U.S.-based, have international chapters and are the largest motorcycle gangs in the world. All four OMGs are known for their criminal activity and violence toward others and each other. The Pagans are also known for their ties with white supremacist prison gangs, a topic that will be examined later. See Table 4.2 for a typology of OMG criminality.

The study found that 301 of the 631 articles (48%) contained 89 separate accounts of criminal incidents in which a member or members of the four motorcycle clubs committed an illegal act. The most common illegal acts involved ongoing instrumental enterprises common to economic criminal organizations such as drug trafficking, racketeering, various weapons charges, and murder. One incident noted in 77 articles was a 2,000 Milwaukee, Wisconsin, racketeering trial of 17 members of the Outlaws Motorcycle Club. In this trial, there were several regional leaders as well as members, indicating full "club" involvement.

Table 4.2   Typology of OMG Criminality

Typology of OMG Criminality

Spontaneous expressive acts: usually involve one or a few members in violent crimes directed at rivals or other actors from within the saloon society milieu (i.e., bar fights)

Planned aggressive acts: are usually directed at rival groups and are either planned by established cliques, chapters/regional/national officers, or tacitly reflect the priorities of the chapter or club

Short-time instrumental acts: usually involve one or a very few members in thefts that take advantage of unique opportunities or are designed as a response to the particular needs of one of the involved members (e.g., motorcycle thefts, prostitution). They may vary along the continuum from planned to spontaneous

Ongoing instrumental enterprises: involving the fairly consistent attention of one or more cliques and designed to supply large amounts of money to the members; these are usually planned well in advance of their execution (drug production/distribution)

Source: Quinn & Koch, 2003. The nature of criminality within one-percent motorcycle clubs. Deviant Behavior, 24, 296.

The Outlaws members were charged with several offenses, ranging from murder to bombing the clubhouses of rival OMGs, to narcotics trafficking, racketeering, attempted arson, and dealing in stolen motorcycles. There were numerous victims, most of whom were unnamed. The investigations that led to this large number of indictments were precipitated by a gang war between the Outlaws MC and the HAMC.

There were 25 articles related to the Pagans Motorcycle Club. Thirteen articles were crime-related and dealt with six crime incidents, with four classified as ongoing instrumental enterprises (1:distributing methamphetamines, marijuana, and firearms; 2:selling cocaine to Amish youths; 3:large-scale drug trafficking ring; 4:drug and racketeering charges). There was one incident classified as a planned aggressive act (brawl at a tattoo expo with a rival biker club) and one spontaneous expressive act (murder in a sports bar brawl).

The Bandidos Motorcycle Club had a total of 50 articles, with 25 on criminal acts involving 16 different criminal incidents. Twelve of the articles covered four planned aggressive acts: three in Australia (1:drive-by shooting of rival gang member; 2:murder of club rival; 3:shoot-out known as the Father's Day Milperra Massacre) and one in Canada (murder of infringing drug dealer). Seven articles were found on six **spontaneous expressive acts**: five in Australia (ranging from a brawl with police to a brawl in a pub) and one in Texas (knife murder during a brawl). Five articles reported on five **ongoing instrumental enterprises**: three in Australia (drug charges, trafficking in LSD, drug and weapons charges), one each in Texas (drug possession) and Colorado (drug and conspiracy charges). One article dealt with a short-term instrumental act (possession of illegal weapons).

The Outlaws Motorcycle Club had 347 total articles with a majority (204 or 59%) related to 26 criminal incidents. The most articles (176 or 51%) were on 13 ongoing instrumental enterprises: six in Canada, two in Australia, and five in the United States. As we shall see, for the most part, Canadian one-percent outlaw motorcycle clubs, both indigenous and U.S.-based, operate as adult criminal gangs, not clubs. This is especially true for the U.S.-based clubs—the Hells Angels, Bandidos, and Outlaws—who are considered by Canadian law enforcement authorities to be the number-one organized crime threat in Canada. The next category with the most articles was spontaneous expressive acts, with 17 articles reporting on six criminal incidents: three in Australia and three in the United States (hate crime against an African American in Massachusetts, fatal stabbing in a party setting, attempted murder in clubhouse). There were three planned aggressive acts: two in Australia and one in Massachusetts, and there were six articles on three short-term instrumental acts: two in Australia and one in Canada.

The HAMC had a total of 209 articles, with 59 that pertained to 40 criminal incidents. The most articles (37) dealt with 23 ongoing instrumental enterprises: 12 U.S. incidents (most racketeering and drug charges), six in Australia (most drug- and weapons-related), and five in Canada (most drug-related). There were 14 planned aggressive acts articles reporting on ten criminal incidents: five U.S. incidents, four in Canada, and one in Australia. The eight-year Canadian biker war (1994-2001) during the period under study between the indigenous drug trafficking Rock Machine Motorcycle Club (later patched over to the Bandidos) and the Hells Angels over drug-trafficking territory was the worst organized crime war in history in terms of dead and wounded. The war resulted in 160 murders, including an innocent 11-year-old boy, 175 attempted murders; 200 people wounded; and the disappearance of 15 bikers (Roslin, 2002). Four articles discussed four spontaneous expressive acts that occurred in the United States. Four articles reported on four short-term instrumental acts: two in Canada and two in Australia.

Table 4.3 identifies the type of criminal activity by club/gang. As one can see, the data showed that the HAMC had the highest number of ongoing instrumental enterprises (23 of 49, or 47% of the criminal incidents). This was as expected, as the Hells Angels here and abroad have the reputation as being the most criminally oriented economic criminal organization in the outlaw motorcycle club world. The Outlaws had 13 incidents and the Bandidos had five incidents of ongoing instrumental enterprises. The Pagans, the smallest gang, had the lowest number of ongoing instrument enterprises reported (four), but that was 67% of their total number of criminal incidents reported in the newspaper articles. The Hells Angels also had ten of the 18 (56%) reported incidents of planned aggressive acts. Again, this was expected because the HAMC has been in violent wars with other OMGs over territory and criminal markets since Ralph "Sonny" Barger and his gangs of young toughs formed the present-day Hells Angels in Oakland, California, in 1957. The reported incidents of spontaneous expressive acts and short-term instrumental acts were fairly evenly divided among the three largest gangs.

Table 4.3 *Types of Criminal Activity by Outlaw Motorcycle Gangs*

Category	Hells Angels	Outlaws	Bandidos	Pagans	Total
Ongoing Instrumental Enterprises	23	13	5	4	45
Planned Aggressive Acts	10	3	4	1	18
Spontaneous Expressive Acts	4	6	6	1	17
Short-term Instrumental Acts	4	4	1	0	9

Source: Barker & Human, 2009.

The MAGLOCLEN (Middle Atlantic Great Lakes Organized Crime Law Enforcement Network), a regional information sharing system (RISS), as part of government efforts to address gang violence surveyed 1,061 law enforcement agencies in 2003 on the criminal activities of OMGs in the region. Eight hundred and nineteen (77%) of the agencies responded. Thirty percent of the agencies reported OMG activity in their areas from 2000 to 2003. Sixty-two percent of the agencies had arrested OMG members during the prior four years. There were 201 agencies that reported that investigations (undercover, task force, and informant) and intelligence were the leading cause of OMG arrests, but the single leading cause was routine traffic arrests, in 74 agencies. The survey found that OMGs in their area had associations with other organized crime groups. The OMGs were most likely to be associated with traditional organized crime groups such as the Mafia/Cosa Nostra (41 agencies). A disturbing finding was the number of agencies responding that OMGs in their jurisdictions had associations with white supremacist groups (22) and street gangs (23). We will see that OMG associations with white supremacist groups continue today. The report also stated that OMGs use street gangs in their narcotics distribution activities to isolate club members from law enforcement scrutiny, a common technique for organized crime groups. In these cases, one or two club members controlled the illegal activities of the street gangs, further isolating the club and making the prosecution of members more difficult. We will see that national and international OMGs use their puppet/support clubs for the same purpose.

Survey respondents reported that the primary source of income for OMGs in their area was the manufacture and distribution of illegal narcotics. When asked about crimes committed by OMG members in their jurisdiction, some interesting results were obtained (see Table 4.4).

Even though the agencies reported that 90% of the OMG members in their area had engaged in narcotics distribution frequently or occasionally, some responded that 10% of the members had never done so. Seventy-six percent of the OMG members were reported to be involved in narcotics manufacturing, but 24% had never committed this organized crime activity. Moreover, large numbers of OMG members, according to the law enforcement respondents, never engaged in the organized crime activities of money laundering (47%), fencing stolen property (31%), and firearms trafficking (33%). The law enforcement respondents also reported that 28% of the OMG members had never engaged in automobile theft, a crime typically associated with outlaw motorcycle gangs. Furthermore, although gang rapes created the original moral panic associated with biker gangs, respondents reported that 61% of the OMG members never committed rapes. However, only 12% of the members had never committed an assault, which serves as evidence of the violent nature of these gangs/clubs.

Table 4.4   Crimes Committed by OMG Members
Agencies were asked whether they experienced OMG members committing these crimes

Crime	Frequently	Occasionally	Never
Narcotics Distribution	49%	41%	10%
Narcotics Manufacturing	29%	47%	24%
Assault	24%	64%	12%
Motorcycle Theft	21%	51%	28%
Money Laundering	17%	36%	47%
Witness Intimidation	16%	57%	27%
Fencing Stolen Property	15%	54%	31%
Prostitution	14%	39%	47%
Firearms Trafficking	12%	55%	33%
DL/Registration/Title Fraud	11%	38%	51%
Extortion	9%	48%	43%
Automobile Theft	8%	49%	43%
Gambling	7%	34%	59%
Rape	4%	34%	61%
Attempted Homicide	3%	53%	44%
Robbery	3%	45%	52%
Arson	3%	38%	59%
Home Invasion	2%	25%	73%
Homicide	2%	50%	48%
Counterfeit	1%	19%	80%
Bombings	1%	25%	74%
Other	2%	11%	47%

These results indicate that although the law enforcement respondents believe a majority of the members of these clubs/gangs are involved in serious and organized criminal activities, they also believe that some members are not. These results indicate that group dynamics and social structure appear to be a factor, as Quinn and Koch opined, and raises the possibility of clubs that do not engage in organized criminal activity. How important group dynamics and social structure are in determining if and when an outlaw motorcycle club becomes an outlaw motorcycle gang is an empirical question worthy of study. In any case, the diametrically opposed positions suggested by "club" spokesmen (i.e., there are no one-percent outlaw motorcycle gangs) and the opposite law enforcement position (i.e., all outlaw motorcycle clubs are outlaw motorcycle gangs) appear to be deviant points on a Criminal Organization Continuum by outlaw motorcycle clubs.

Focus: Club/Gang Criminal Activity

There have been very little data gathered on the criminal activities of one-percent biker clubs/gangs using club affiliation as the focus of analysis. However, the **National Alliance of Gang Investigators Association (NAGIA)** in their *2005 National Gang Threat Assessment* reports that a compilation of information from the FBI, the National Drug Intelligence Center (NDIC), and the International Outlaw Motorcycle Gang Investigators Association (IOMGIA) reveals that four of the major U.S. outlaw motorcycle gangs—Hells Angels, Bandidos, Outlaws, and Pagans—have been involved in a variety of criminal activities (see Table 4.5).

Drug trafficking is generally considered to be the number-one crimal activity engaged in by organized crime groups. According to the NAGIA report, all of the OMGs examined were involved in some form of drug trafficking. The Pagans MC was reported to be engaged in the distribution of drugs but not the production, smuggling, and transportation of drugs. All the gangs were involved in the organized crime activities of weapons trafficking, motorcycle and motorcycle parts theft, extortion, counterfeiting, and insurance fraud. The four gangs were also involved in the violent activities of murder, explosive violations, bombings, and arson, all crimes that typically accompany or facilitate organized crime activities. Surprisingly, according to the NAGIA report, the Pagans were not involved in money laundering, or prostitution, both typical organized crime activities.

Also using gangs/clubs as the unit of analysis, Box 4.10 is a compilation of organized crime activities by U.S. biker gangs/clubs, large and small, taken from a variety of sources, newspapers, court cases, and so on, in the 11-year period between 1995 and 2006. It is not exhaustive, but instead meant to be illustrative of the extent of the criminal activities of U.S. OMGs.

Emphasis was added by using boldface type in Box 4.10 whenever an officer of an outlaw motorcycle club was involved because officer involvement in criminal activities is an important factor in determining gang status; it goes right to the point of indicating the level of organized "club" involvement. Historically, the established leaders of many outlaw motorcycle clubs are or have been involved in criminal activities. The former National HAMC President George Christie Jr. and his son, George Christie III, former **Vice** President of the Ventura chapter of the Hells Angels, were sentenced to three years' probation for conspiracy to sell drugs (www.gligic.org/00000007.htm). The elder Christie's ex-wife was also convicted. Father-son involvement in OMGs and criminal activity is not uncommon. In 2007, the son of the Vancouver, Canada, East End Hells Angels chapter president was sentenced to six years in prison for cocaine trafficking and extortion (Hall, 2007). The son was also a patched member of the chapter. In addition to the officers emphasized in **bold** in the box, there have been officers from the following outlaw motorcycle clubs indicted, arrested, or convicted in recent years: Pagans MC (in 2010), Wheels of Soul MC (in 2012 and 2013), Hells Angels MC (in 2013); Bandidos MC and two of their support clubs—Los Homeboys MC and Rebel Riders MC (in 2011); Outlaws MC (in 2010 and 2011), Sons of Silence MC (in 2013), and the Mongols MC (in 2008).

Table 4.5   Criminal Activities of Four Outlaw Motorcycle Gangs

Criminal Activities	Hells Angels	Bandidos	Outlaws	Pagans
Drugs				
Production	X	X	X	
Smuggling	X	X	X	
Transportation	X	X	X	
Distribution	X	X	X	X
Weapons Trafficking	X	X	X	X
Murder	X	X	X	X
Prostitution	X	X	X	
Money Laundering	X	X	X	
Explosives Violations	X	X	X	X
Bombings	X	X	X	X
Motorcycle and Motorcycle Parts Thefts	X	X	X	X
Intimidation	X	X	X	X
Extortion	X	X	X	X
Arson	X	X	X	X
Assault	X	X	X	X
Insurance Fraud	X	X	X	
Kidnapping	X	X	X	
Robbery	X	X	X	
Theft	X	X	X	
Stolen Property	X	X	X	
Counterfeiting	X	X	X	

Source: Modified from National Alliance of Gang Investigators, 2005 National Gang Threat Assessment, p. 14. The number of times each gang was involved in the criminal activities is not shown. The time period for gathering the information is also not shown.

DIMENSION: LEADERS' INVOLVEMENT IN THE PLANNING AND EXECUTION OF CRIMINAL ACTIVITIES

In Box 4.10, we emphasized when the leaders were identified as being involved in the criminal activities. We did so because outlaw motorcycle clubs can be described as quasi-formal organizations with the following characteristics (Wolf, 1991; Barker, 2007). They have (1) a club name that becomes a shorthand statement of corporate identity (in recent years, most of the large clubs/gangs have registered their names as trademarks), (2) a written mandate stating the purpose of association, (3) written statutes outlining criteria of membership, and (4) formal regulatory mechanisms for enforcing those statutes. In combination, these characteristics result in a degree of autonomy and a sense of exclusivity. In addition, outlaw motorcycle clubs follow the Hells Angels Model, known as such because it was transported throughout the world by the spectacular and oversaturation of media attention on the HAMC in the early 1960s and thus used as a model for the formation of indigenous motorcycle clubs that sprang up in other countries (see Harris, 1985, for the imitation in England and Europe; Wolf, 1991, for Canada; Veno, 2003, for emulation in Australia; and Gilbert, 2013, for clubs in New Zealand). The basic organizational structure of biker clubs following the Hells Angels Model consists of a president, vice president, sergeant at arms, secretary-treasurer, road captain, and patched members (see Box 4.11). These officers fill the typical roles found in formal organizations, except sergeant at arms and road captain. Therefore, all motorcycle clubs, here and abroad, are structurally organized for decision-making with a multilevel chain of command, making a demonstration of leaders' involvement in the planning and execution of organized criminal activities a key element in determining whether any club or chapter of a club is a criminal organization acting as a criminal gang. The officer positions are usually elective positions, with new officers elected when the current officeholder is unable to carry out the job, usually due to imprisonment, death, illness, or accident.

BOX 4.11 BIKER CLUB/CHAPTER ORGANIZATIONAL STRUCTURE

President
The president has claimed the position through force or fear or has been voted in. He has final authority in the club. He has veto power over decisions voted upon by that chapter. The president is usually the club spokesman in dealing with the press or law enforcement authorities. He chairs the clubs' meetings and represents the club at regional, national, or international meetings.

Vice President
The vice president is second in command and acts for the president in his absence. He often has been handpicked by the president. He may be heir apparent but not always. It is his job to make sure that matters decided on in meetings are carried out.

Secretary-Treasurer
This officer is responsible for the club's paperwork. Keeps the chapter roster, maintains their accounting system, takes the minutes, collects dues and fines, pays bills, and collects profits—legal and illegal. He corresponds with other clubs and keeps members informed of upcoming events, such as mandatory runs.

BOX 4.11 BIKER CLUB/CHAPTER ORGANIZATIONAL STRUCTURE—cont'd

Sergeant at Arms

Although all formal organizations might have someone to maintain order during the meetings, it is largely a ceremonial role. Not so in biker clubs. The sergeant at arms, also known as the enforcer, is often the strongest or most violent member. He is completely loyal to the president and will administer beatings or worse for violations of club rules. He is the enforcer for the club, often having killed for the club. He is in charge of security at meetings and on runs. He oversees the club's weapons and is responsible for attacks on rival clubs.

Road Captain

The road captain, unique to biker clubs, is the logistician and security officer for the club on runs and outings. He maps out the route, arranges for fuel and food stops, and often carries money for bail. He rides in front and leads the pack with the president. On occasion, he liaisons with local police to prevent unnecessary stops and harassment.

Patchholders

Patchholders are members who have earned the right to wear the club's colors and have gone through the prospecting process. They take an active part in participating in church meetings and running the club.

Others—Important to the club but have no vote and cannot attend meetings

Prospects

These are prospective members who have earned their patch. They do what they are told and follow the orders of patchholders. They have no voting rights and do not attend meetings unless asked to.

Hangarounds

The purpose of this position is to allow a "righteous" biker to become known to all members prior to becoming a prospect.

Friends of the Club

Supporters of the club. They are often regulars at the clubhouse, but not at meetings, attending functions and taking part in events. Some will become hangarounds and begin the process of becoming patchholders.

Associates

They are linked to the club in some way, persons who are connected through criminal activity, drugs, family or friends, sports, legitimate business interests, social, or other interests.

The gangs usually hold regular meetings called church, which all members must attend unless they are ill or in jail. Discussion of club business is recorded in minutes, except business dealing with criminal matters. Missing church meetings is a serious offense that often leads to expulsion or making the transgressor go through the prospecting process again. Each chapter has its own set of officers, with varying autonomy to conduct club business. Many clubs, such as the Outlaws and Mongols, have national officers who decide issues for the clubs. Some, such as the Pagans and the Warlocks [Florida-based], have a defined group (Pagans Mother Group; Warlocks Counsel) who make all important decisions affecting the club. Other clubs, such as the Hells Angels, allow for more chapter autonomy, with important decisions made at regional, national, and international meetings. Nevertheless, no outlaw motorcycle club allows a chapter to operate without some control and coordination from national and/or international officers. The organizational structure and the decision-making process are often denied by club leaders in order to prevent them from being declared criminal enterprises at trial, particularly when faced with RICO (Racketeer Influenced and Corrupt Organizations) prosecution. However, it is well known in the one-percent world that senior officers of biker gangs coordinate the distribution of drugs among chapters for sale by members. The Hells Angels and other U.S.-based OMGs and their international networks created by expansion have made it easier to arrange deals crossing borders for drug smuggling, importation and exportation of precursor chemicals necessary for the manufacturing of methamphetamine, and trafficking guns and military-grade weapons.

The organizational structure, including written constitution and by-laws, can be helpful to the club as they conduct their affairs and can be used to argue that they are voluntary associations united by their love of biking and brotherhood. Why would members of a criminal organization wear a patch on their backs making them a target for law enforcement and have a written constitution and by-laws proclaiming their existence and operation, they ask. A very good question, but the truth is that some prison gangs, such as the Aryan Brotherhood, and criminal street gangs, such as the Vice Lords, do the same thing (Barker, 2012). Whatever the reasons for criminal gangs promulgating and producing these trappings of formal organizations, they are useful in prosecutions against them as criminal organizations. Billy Queen, who became secretary-treasurer of a Mongols MC chapter, used the chapter books as a crucial piece of evidence to show that the club was an ongoing criminal enterprise (Queen, 2005).

CRIMINAL ORGANIZATION CONTINUUM OF OUTLAW MOTORCYCLE CLUBS

As stated, determination of whether any particular one-percent outlaw motorcycle club or chapter of a club is considered an adult criminal gang lies along a Criminal Organization Continuum depending on the members' involvement [individual, group, club] in organized crime or whether the officers and leadership are involved (see Figure 4.1). Therefore, we can infer that on a Criminal Organization Continuum, any outlaw motorcycle club can vary. On one end are OMGs where criminal activities are a product of the deviant individuals who are members and individual criminal behavior is neither known or of concern to other club members nor structured or organized. Members in these clubs or chapters of clubs live the deviant lifestyle common to the saloon society milieu observed in biker bars and rallies, but they do not engage in serious criminal behavior. In some of these clubs, members who do engage in serious crime risk losing their patch and membership, especially when their behavior brings unwanted attention to the club. Clubs of this nature are true motorcycle clubs, even though they identify themselves as one-percenters and outlaws. Because of the confusing nature of the existing literature and sparse data on one-percent clubs with some saying that all clubs fit this category and others saying that no clubs fit this category, it is virtually impossible to find a "real world" example.

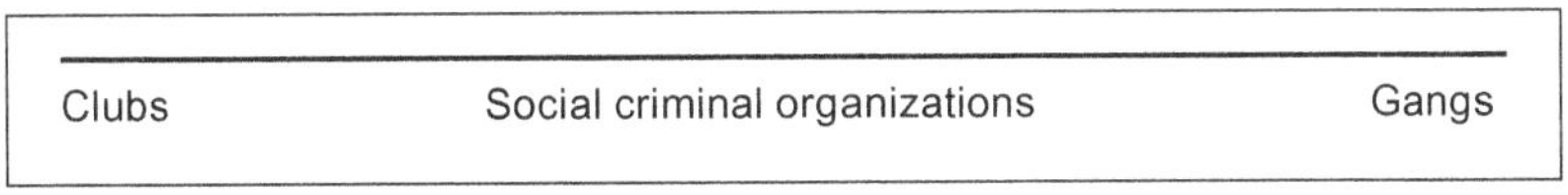

| Clubs | Social criminal organizations | Gangs |

FIGURE 4.1

Criminal Organization Continuum of One-Percent Motorcycle Clubs.

Moving along the continuum of criminal organization, we encounter clubs where a small group or groups of members engage in criminal behavior, including some that is organized and structured. Other club members know what is going on but do not engage in these organized criminal activities; however, their silence and inaction gives tacit support and increases the likelihood that criminal behavior will continue and progress. Complicating the existence of small groups of criminals operating with tacit support is the supposed Biker's Code of Brotherhood that is analogous to the purported Code of Silence in police agencies. However, we will see that this Biker Code of Brotherhood is more rhetoric than reality, especially in "clubs" that become gangs. The same thing is true in police agencies that become criminal organizations (Barker, 2011). The advent of RICO prosecutions has shown that the old saw of "honor among thieves" is a myth. "Clubs" become social criminal organizations through the selection and socialization process and in all likelihood will evolve into criminal organizations unless the members or agents of law enforcement take some action. Their number in the world of outlaw motorcycle clubs is an empirical question; however, social criminal organizations provide the basis for evolution into adult criminal gangs.

Those clubs or chapters of clubs in which all, or the majority, are involved in organized criminal activity at the direction of the leadership coalition are examples of criminal organizations and adult criminal gangs organized for profit through crime. They are "clubs" in name only. Daniel "Snake Dog" Boone describes in detail how the Warwickshire (England)-based Pagans MC [no relationship to U.S.-based Pagans MC] became a criminal organization selling drugs (Thompson, 2011:77-78). In the 1970s, the club's leadership decided that the club would begin selling drugs. At a club meeting, a small bag containing five grams of amphetamine was set in front of each member. Each member was told the street value of the drugs and told that at next week's meeting he had to return with that sum of money. Members were told that they could use it themselves or share it with others if they wanted to—no one was going to stop them. All the leaders wanted was the money—the club was now a criminal organization. The British-based Pagans MC later became a chapter of the U.S.-based Outlaws MC. Several outlaw motorcycle gangs have become worldwide leaders in the drug and gun trade in all stages of manufacture, importation, and street sales. Many one-percent outlaw motorcycle clubs of all sizes, based on their history of involvement in criminal behavior as indicated by published autobiographies, members' criminal histories, indictments and court decisions, limited research, and media reports, fit in this category. Some examples are the Big Five Motorcycle Gangs—the Hells Angels, Bandidos, Outlaws, Pagans, and Sons of Silence—and their puppet or support clubs; the Avengers, the Breed, the Devils Diciples, Dirty Dozen, Galloping Goose, Iron Horsemen, Mongols, Vagos, Warlocks

(Florida and Pennsylvania-based), and the Wheels of Soul. See Box 4.12 for other examples of motorcycle clubs that have been declared criminal organizations (motorcycle gangs) in recent years. Again, this is an illustrative, not exhaustive list.) Once the leadership and the majority of any one chapter or club decide to engage in organized criminal behavior, they can ensure the safe operation of their criminal activities through the membership by selecting only those prospects who have engaged in or will engage in crime and screening out all cops and snitches. As we saw earlier, this screening process is not always successful; law enforcement officers and special agents have infiltrated and will continue to infiltrate outlaw motorcycle gangs up to the point of becoming patched members and even officers.

BOX 4.12 SELECTED MOTORCYCLE CLUBS AS CRIMINAL ORGANIZATIONS

Phantom MC

Nine members of the Phantom MC were indicted and arrested on November 4, 2013, for a variety of charges including murder and attempted murder, narcotics trafficking, the possession and sale of stolen motor vehicles and motorcycles, and witness intimidation. The Phantom MC is headquartered in northwest Detroit and has chapters in Michigan, Ohio, and Kentucky.

Source: *FBI Press Release. Detroit Division. November 4, 2013.*

Saddle Tramps MC

St. Louis, Missouri, September 10, 2013—25 people were arrested on federal indictments alleging drug and weapons charges involving the distribution of large amounts of methamphetamine in the Eastern District of Missouri from October 2010 to September 2013. Several of those arrested were members of the Saddle Tramps Motorcycle Club, including the club's president.

Source: *FBI Press Release. St. Louis Division. November 10, 2013.*

Barbarian Brotherhood MC

San Francisco, CA. August 9, 2013—The Vice President of the Barbarian Brotherhood MC was sentenced to six years in prison after pleading guilty to being a felon in possession of a weapon.

Source: *FBI Press Release. San Francisco Division. August 9, 2013.*

Devils Diciples MC

Detroit, Michigan, July 13, 2013—Forty-one members and associates of the Devils Diciples MC were indicted, including the National President and Vice President. Thirty-one of those indicted were arrested in Michigan and Alabama. The charges included participation in various criminal acts, including violent crimes in aid of racketeering, drug trafficking, illegal firearms offenses, obstruction of justice, illegal gambling, and other federal offenses. Eighteen of those arrested, including the National President and Vice President, were charged with violations of the Racketeer Influenced and Corrupt Organization (RICO) Act by conducting their illegal enterprise through a pattern of racketeering activity which included murder, robbery, extortion, drug trafficking, obstruction of justice, and other federal and state offenses.

Source: *FBI Press Release. Detroit Division. July 13, 2013.*

Demon Knights MC

New York, November 27, 2012—A member of the Demon Knights MC, a puppet/support club of the Hells Angels, was arrested along with a member of the Gambino crime family of La Cosa Nostra, and a member of the Westies street gang. The three gangsters were charged with extortionate extension of credit, extortionate collection of credit, and conspiracy to do the same. These three members of different crime groups banded together to commit their criminal acts.

Source: *FBI Press Release. New York Field Office. November 27, 2012.*

United States Outlaw Motorcycle Gangs: Big Five, Major Independents, and Others

KEY TERMS

The Big Five biker gangs

"Charlie"

La Eme

Loki

major independent outlaw motorcycle gangs

patched over

puppet/support gangs

INTRODUCTION

As previously stated, there is no accurate count on the number of one-percent biker gangs or the number of members of such gangs in the United States or in the world. Law enforcement authorities have made club and membership estimates in reports or when they have prosecuted the gangs and/or the members in affidavits, indictments, and testimony. The official estimates appear accurate for some gangs and not others. A problem for the scientific study of OMGs, or for that matter all criminal organizations, is that law enforcement estimates are made based on confidential government sources; therefore, we do not know how the calculations were made. Some gangs maintain national and chapter websites that include a listing of chapters, but this is subject to their control, and many chapters are not listed. It is difficult for academic criminologists to estimate the true numbers because of the limited scholarly research on these deviant, secret, and dangerous groups. In spite of the vagueness of the club and member numbers, there is agreement among the authorities and biker experts that five gangs—Hells Angels, Bandidos, Outlaws, Pagans, and the Sons of Silence—are the largest in membership and numbers of chapters in the United States. This is also subject to debate, as some gangs such as the Mongols and Vagos expand. Rightly or wrongly, **The Big Five biker gangs** are considered to be the most dangerous and most likely to engage in violence and criminal activities in a structured and organized manner. Based on their past and present violent and criminal behavior, this reputation is well earned. These gangs, except for the Pagans MC, have expanded outside the United States and become a serious international crime problem; this point is examined later. Figure 5.1 shows the United States.

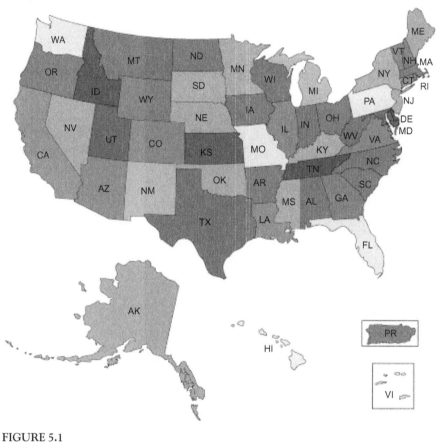

FIGURE 5.1

The United States.

Map courtesy of Bruce Jones Design Inc.

THE BIG FIVE ONE-PERCENT BIKER GANGS

Hells Angels Motorcycle Club/Gang (HAMC)

The Hells Angels MC (HAMC) is by all accounts the most prominent and numerous national and international motorcycle gang. This gang is also the most violent and crime-prone outlaw motorcycle gang. Law enforcement estimates put their membership at 2,000 worldwide and 700 in the United States (unnamed ATF Special Agent). The gang is also known as "Local 81," after the placement of the letters H (8) and A (1) in the alphabet, and "The Big Red Machine" and the "Red and White," after the colors of their patches. Supporters and associates are allowed to wear Local 81, Big Red Machine, and Red and White patches and other support gear, but not the Hells Angels (without the apostrophe) patch, which is a registered trademark worn only by patched members. Their puppet/support clubs (discussed later) are the only one-percent biker clubs/gangs allowed to wear red and white patches; anyone else caught wearing the same color patch is subject to losing it after a stomping or sometimes a killing. Wearing red and white colors is considered to be a serious transgression and act of disrespect to the gang. The gang's logos, the winged "death's head" (seen below) is also protected by copyright and can only be worn by patchholders. The HAMC will sue, and has sued, to protect its copyrights.

IDENTIFY THE COLORS

The Hells Angels Insignia

Photo courtesy of U.S. Department of Justice. See www.justice.gov/criminal/ocgs/gangs/motorcycle.html.

Sonny Barger has a personal attorney who is also a Hells Angels intellectual property lawyer. It is this attorney's job to protect the club's two registered trademarks. In doing so, he has sued or threatened to sue Gotcha Sportswear, Marvel Comics, and a pornography producer who made a film titled *Hell's Angels: Demon of Lust* (McKee, 2001). Marvel Comics published a comic book titled *Hells Angels* and ignored the cease-and-desist letter. The Angels filed a lawsuit in federal court, and the federal mediator sided with the Hells Angels. The comic book's name was changed to *Dark Angel*, and Marvel gave the Hells Angels $35,000, which was donated to Ronald McDonald House Charities. Gotcha Sportswear was sued for putting a death's head logo on surfer hats. As this book is being written, the Hells Angels are suing Walt Disney Corporation, claiming that their logo and name have been used in a film script without permission.

As detailed earlier, World War II veterans who were former members of the Pissed Off Bastards of Bloomington (POBOB) formed the first Hells Angels chapter in San Bernardino, California, on March 17, 1948. The present-day Hells Angels Motorcycle Club was formed in Oakland, California, in 1957 by Ralph "Sonny"

Barger and his gang of young toughs, without them knowing that other Hells Angels chapters existed. Within the next ten years, the Oakland chapter became the mother chapter, disbanding or taking in other Hells Angels chapters. San Bernardino is now the mother chapter. In 1966, the Hells Angels incorporated as a club "dedicated to the promotion and advancement of motorcycling riding, motorcycle clubs, motorcycle highway safety, and all phases of motorcycling and motorcycle driving" (Lavigne, 1987:1). After its incorporation, the HAMC began moving out of California. Today, it is the largest one-percent biker club qua gang in the world.

The actual number of Hells Angels charters [chapters] is unknown and probably unknowable by anyone outside the gang. The official HAMC website—www.hells -angels.com/?HA=charters—lists 353 charters worldwide, with 286 charters in 40 countries outside the United States and 67 charters in the United States (see Box 5.1).

BOX 5.1 COUNTRIES OUTSIDE THE UNITED STATES WITH HELLS ANGELS CHARTERS

Canada, Brazil, Argentina, Australia, South Africa, New Zealand, Spain, France, Belgium, Holland, Germany, Italy, Switzerland, Liechtenstein, Austria, England/Wales, Finland, Norway, Sweden, Denmark, Greece, Russia, Bohemia, Portugal, Chile, Croatia, Luxembourg, N. Ireland, Hungary, Dominican Republic, Turkey, Poland, Iceland, Ireland, Malta, Thailand, Latvia, Lithuania, Caribbean, and Serbia.

Prospects—Romania, Slovakia, Japan, Estonia, and Ukraine.

Source: *www.hells-angels.com/?ha=charters*, accessed June 29, 2013.

The official website also lists 21 hangaround and prospect charters and adds that not all charters are listed. In 2002, the Australian expert on outlaw motorcycle clubs, Arthur Veno, said that there were 100 HAMC charters in the world, with 65 in North America and 35 in others countries (Veno, 2003). If his 2003 calculations were accurate, the HAMC has grown phenomenally since then, especially outside North America.

The HAMC's first expansion outside the United States occurred in 1961 when a charter was established in Auckland, Australia. The first European charter was established in London in 1969, followed by Zurich, Switzerland, in 1970; Hamburg, Germany, in 1973; and Paris, France, in 1981 (Haut, 1988). At the present time, HAMC has more charters outside the United States than within the country. Accompanying its international expansion has been the creation of criminal networks with other transnational organized crime groups such as the Colombian cartels, the Italian mafia, and Asian-based drug trafficking organizations (Nicaso & Lamonthe, 2006). It is alleged that the Canadian Hells Angels have been importing hashish and heroin from the U.K. since the 1980s (Nicaso & Lamonthe, 2006).

The Canadian and Australian HAMC charters are particularly problematic in terms of crime. Canadian authorities consider the Hells Angels Motorcycle Gang to be one of the most powerful and well-structured criminal organizations in Canada (CICS, 2000). There were organized biker gangs in Canada since the early 1930s, but biker gangs were not a problem until the Hells Angels arrived (Alain, 1995).

Since their arrival, the Angels have increased their criminal activities from the usual OMG crimes of extortion, prostitution, and drug trafficking to criminal ventures into the stock market, real estate, and control of the west coast docks. Nicaso and Lamonthe (2006) opine that on the west coast of Canada some Hells Angels chapters are "fully operational criminal syndicate[s] with influence and control in every segment of society" (p. 222). Lavigne (1987:235) says that the "Quebec Angels are the most vicious and conscienceless bikers in the world." The 1980s Quebec biker war between the Hells Angels and the Rock Machine was the bloodiest organized crime war in history. In Australia, the Hells Angels have been a crime problem for over 20 years, engaging in narcotics trafficking, prostitution, major armed robberies, movement of arms and explosives, fencing, assaults, and murders since their formation. Figure 5.2 shows a HAMC New York City clubhouse.

FIGURE 5.2

A HAMC New York City clubhouse with many security cameras and floodlights on the front of the building.

Photo courtesy of David Shankbone, en.wikipedia.org.

Bandidos Motorcycle Club/Gang

There are conflicting versions concerning the formation of the Bandidos Motorcycle Club/Gang. The most often quoted version, following the disillusioned veterans theme, says that former Marine and Vietnam veteran Donald Eugene Chambers formed the Bandidos somewhere in Texas in 1966 and chose the Marine Corps colors of red and gold and the "Fat Mexican" logo (Hayes, 2011).

A second version is offered by biker and former Bandidos leader, media celebrity, and authors Winterhalder and De Clercq (2008). Winterhalder and De Clercq accept that Chambers is a former U.S. Marine but states, "[Chambers] was anything but a disillusioned Vietnam vet. The closest he got to Vietnam was watching the news. Whether he [Chambers] was disillusioned or not is a moot point; it sounds good in print and gels with the clichéd portrayal of bikers. In society's collective consciousness, anybody who starts or joins an outlaw motorcycle club must be disillusioned, disturbed, antisocial, or rebelling against something—perhaps all of the above" (Winterhalder & De Clercq, 2008:xiv). Winterhalder and De Clercq also dispute the selection of colors by Chambers. He says that the original colors were red and yellow inspired by the poisonous coral snake and the Southern expression "red and yellow, kill a fellow." The colors were changed to red and gold years later. The official Bandidos website has a totally different version of the Bandidos formation (see Box 5.2)

IDENTIFY THE COLORS

The Bandidos Insignia

Photo courtesy of U.S. Department of Justice. See www.justice.gov/criminal/ocgs/gangs/motorcycle.html.

BOX 5.2 FORMATION OF THE BANDIDOS MOTORCYCLE CLUB

It was 1965, headed back to the United States from an annual trip to the bullfights in Sonora, Mexico, Don Chambers and his friends stopped at a local cantina. When they entered, a patron asked the waitress, "Who are those guys?" The waitress answered, "That's DC and his American Bandidos"—hence the name. In March of 1966, The Bandidos Motorcycle Club was born. The Southwest Houston chapter soon followed the Houston chapter or "Mother Chapter." A year later, riding back from that annual trip as full patch Bandidos, a problem occurred with the Federales in Mexico and Bandido Sunshine was killed, and that was the last time the Bandidos went to Mexico. With hundreds of chapters across the United States, and Central and South America, and thousands of members with a worldwide following, the Bandido Nation is strong and thriving.

Source: *www.bandidostexas.com/index_more.html.*

Another area of controversy concerning the founding of the Bandidos is their original purpose. Law enforcement sources allege that the Bandidos MC was formed as an outlaw motorcycle gang, not a club, to control drug trafficking and prostitution in Texas. Winterhalder and De Clercq dispute this explanation; however, they acknowledge that Chambers was convicted and sentenced to life for a drug-related double homicide in 1972. Chambers and two other Bandidos kidnapped two drug dealers from El Paso, Texas (one was twenty-two and the other seventeen), who had attempted to rip the gang off on a drug deal. They tortured the two men for several days then drove them out into the desert, forced them to dig their own graves, and then executed them. Ronnie Hodges took over as president and expanded the criminal activities of the Bandidos. Hodges forged links with Colombian and Cuban drug dealers who supplied them with cocaine and perfected the manufacturing of high-quality methamphetamine. Chambers was paroled in 1983, retired from the gang, and was not involved in Bandidos activities after this until his death from cancer in 1999. Whatever the original purpose for forming the Bandidos MC, there is ample evidence to support the suspicion that the Bandidos is a criminal organization. As a testament to the criminal nature of the Bandidos Motorcycle Gang, starting with Chambers, every national president of the Bandidos MC has been convicted of a felony, usually drug trafficking, and been sentenced to prison. This is one of the dimensions of the Continuum of Criminal Organization of One-Percent Motorcycle Clubs—involvement of leaders in the planning and execution of organized criminal activities. The other dimension, the extent of the members' involvement in organized criminal activities, is demonstrated by the numerous federal and state indictments and convictions of Bandidos members. Internationally, the Bandidos MC has been heavily involved in criminal activities, including the internecine murder of eight fellow Bandidos, one a chapter president, outside a hamlet of Shedden, Ontario, Canada, on April 8, 2006. The so far–unproven allegation is that this incident was an internal cleansing ordered by the Bandidos International President in Texas.

Since the group's founding in 1966, the Bandidos have expanded throughout the United States and internationally. The gang's first European expansion was in 1989 when the Bandidos "**patched over**" (that is, assimilated) the Club de Clichy in Marseille, France, igniting a war with the Hells Angels. The Department of Justice (2011) estimates that there are 2,000-2,500 Bandidos members in the United States and 13 other countries. The official Bandidos MC lists chapters in 23 different countries but does not list the chapters in each country (see Box 5.3). According to law enforcement authorities, the Bandidos MC is involved in the transportation and distribution of cocaine and marijuana as well as the production, transportation, and distribution of methamphetamine. This fast-growing outlaw motorcycle gang is most active in the Pacific, Southeastern, Southwestern, and West Central regions of the United States.

BOX 5.3 BANDIDOS MOTORCYCLE GANG: WORLDWIDE LOCATIONS

The United States, Germany, France, Belgium, Thailand, Spain, Australia, Norway, Italy, Sweden, Finland, Indonesia, Channel Islands, Ukraine, Denmark, Malaysia, Russia, Serbia, Costa Rica, Singapore, Estonia, Romania, and Bosnia.

Source: *www.bandidostexas.com/index_more.html, accessed on June 30, 2013.*

Outlaws Motorcycle Club/Gang

According to their national website, www.outlawsmc.com/, the Outlaws MC is the oldest outlaw motorcycle club, having been established in 1935 as the McCook Outlaws Motorcycle Club "out of Matilda's Bar on old Route 66 in McCook, Illinois just out of Chicago." This motorcycle club was quite different from the Outlaws motorcycle gang of today. A picture of the original McCook Outlaws Motorcycle Club appearing on the Outlaws MC national website shows a benign group of young men and women, none of whom appear to be wearing colors. Danny Lyons, a famous photographer of the 1960 civil rights movement, joined the Chicago Outlaws in 1965 and rode with them until 1967. The photographs he took while riding with the Chicago Outlaws were published in *The Bikeriders*, first published in 1968 and republished in 2003 (Lyons, 2005). Lyons's account of the Outlaws MC history is quite different from what appears on the national website. Lyons says that the original 1930s McCook Outlaws disbanded in 1947 "when most of its surviving members became policemen in Chicago and it suburbs" (Lyons, 2005:6). In the early 1950s, according to Lyons, a new club, the Chicago Outlaws Motorcycle Club, was formed, and in 1968 this club split with half the members, going with Johnny Davis, a transit truck driver. It is this group that evolved into the present one-percent Outlaws Motorcycle Club (Lyons, 2003). During this same period, the skull and crossed pistons, affectionately called "Charlie," was chosen as the club's logo. Supposedly, this logo was inspired by the logo worn by Marlon Brando in the first biker movie, *The Wild One*. By the late 1960s, the outlaws motorcycle club, like the Hells Angels, had evolved into the Outlaws Motorcycle Gang. The last three national/international presidents are currently serving life sentences for their RICO convictions, again satisfying the second dimension of the Criminal Organization Continuum.

IDENTIFY THE COLORS

The Outlaws Insignia: Charlie

Photo courtesy of Bill Hayes.

The U.S. Department of Justice (2011) estimates that this OMG is slightly smaller than the HAMC and the Bandidos MC, with an estimated 1,700 members in 20 U.S. states and 12 foreign countries. A check of their website, www .outlawsmcworld.com/, on June 30, 2013, lists 108 chapters in 24 states. That is larger than the 67 charters [chapters] listed by the HAMC. The website lists 124 chapters in 23 countries, not as many as the HAMC with 286 charters in 40 countries, although the Outlaws claim on their website that they are the largest outlaw motorcycle club in the world. It is interesting to note that both the HAMC and the Outlaws MC have more chapters outside the United States than in the United States.

The Outlaws MC also identifies itself as the American Outlaws Association (AOA) and the Outlaws Nation. This criminal motorcycle gang is the dominant OMG in the Great Lakes region. As is common with all OMGs, the Outlaws are involved in the production, transportation, and distribution of methamphetamine. They are also involved in the transportation and distribution of cocaine, marijuana, and to a lesser extent, ecstasy. The HAMC and the Outlaws are bitter enemies and have a long history of violence toward each other. This was not always so. Lyons (2003:53) has a picture of a Chicago Outlaw riding his bike with a smiling Hells Angel on the back. They would be shooting each other today.

Pagans Motorcycle Club/Gang

The Pagans MC, a fierce one-percent biker gang with ties to organized crime groups in Philadelphia, Pittsburgh, and New York, did not start out as a one-percent club, and disillusioned veterans have no place in its early history—once again evidence discounting the myth of disillusioned veterans in the formation of outlaw motorcycle clubs. Lou Dobkins, a biochemist at the National Institutes of Health, established the club in 1959 in Prince George's County, Maryland. Tradition says that the original 13 members wore white denim jackets with Surt, the pagan fire giant, carrying a flaming sword logo on the back. The original members rode Triumph motorcycles. Their benign beginning did not foreshadow what the club would evolve into. According to an early member and Long Island Pagans chapter president who earned his college degree in prison and went on to become a journalist and college professor, by the late 1960s the Pagans had become "the baddest of the ass-kicking, beer drinking, hell-raising, gang-banging, grease-covered, roadkill-eating 1960s motorcycle clubs…" (Hall, 2008:7). During the 1970s, the fierce fighting club became an extremely violent criminal organization under the leadership of John Vernon "Satan" Marron. Whenever a man has the nickname "Satan" or a dog named "Devil," he and his dog are to be avoided. The club expanded in the 1980s into 900 members in 44 chapters from New York to Florida (Southeastern Connecticut Gang Activities Group, 2000; Jenkins, 1992; Lavigne, 1987). With their expansion came increased criminal activities.

IDENTIFY THE COLORS

The Pagans Insignia

Photo courtesy of U.S. Department of Justice. See www.justice.gov/criminal/ocgs/gangs/motorcycle.html.

In June 2005, 125 federal and local law enforcement officers raided six houses in northeastern Ohio belonging to the Order of the Blood, a criminal network financed by the notorious white supremacists, the Aryan Brotherhood, and the Pagans Motorcycle Gang (Holthouse, 1992). This is just one more indication of the close ties between outlaw motorcycle gangs and white supremacist groups here and overseas. In the 1990s, New Zealand indigenous outlaw motorcycle clubs had close ties with "white power" skinhead gangs (Gilbert, 2013). There have always been ties between white supremacist groups and outlaw motorcycle gangs in Germany. The raid seized 60 weapons, including 13 fully automatic machine guns and large quantities of methamphetamines, cocaine, heroin, and oxycodone.

Pagans membership appears to be dropping since its high point in the 1970s, as a result of law enforcement pressure, competition from other biker gangs (particularly the Hells Angels), and internal dissension. Seventy-three Pagans MC members, most in leadership positions throughout the Northeast, were arrested after a bloody battle between them and the HAMC at a bike show in Plainview, New York (Kessler, 2002). The battle left one dead, three wounded by gunfire, and seven stabbed and beaten. Three of the Pagans' national leaders, members of the Pagans Mother Club national leadership group, were arrested and later pleaded guilty to several federal charges. In all, 73 Pagans were convicted or pleaded guilty to several federal charges and received sentences ranging from 27 to 63 months (Kessler, 2002). The fight was in retaliation for the HAMC patching-over Pagans in New York. The battle and the depletion of Pagans members and leaders led to an infusion of Hells Angels into the Delaware Valley, particularly Philadelphia. The Hells Angels moved into Philadelphia and patched-over Pagans in this traditional Pagans stronghold, setting off a war between the two clubs.

Three high-ranking Pagans defected and patched-over to the Hells Angels when the South Philadelphia chapter president was in prison, but this was short-lived. At the present time, the Philadelphia Hells Angels chapter has been disbanded, and all three members have turned in their colors, leaving the appearance that for now, the Pagans have won the war. The Pagans are also having trouble with the Outlaws moving in on their territory. Several members of the Breed—tolerated by the Pagans—patched-over to the Outlaws and established a chapter in the Philadelphia suburb of Kensington (Caparella, 2006). New Jersey authorities say that the Pagans are building up their membership by patching-over members of their puppet gangs and establishing a Central Jersey chapter (State of New Jersey, 2004:88). The Outlaws MC, in an obvious attempt to counter the expansion of the HAMC, has established five chapters in Pennsylvania. The Pennsylvania-based Warlocks, reacting to a perceived Pagans weakness, have established two chapters in South Jersey. Nevertheless, the Pagans remain one of the largest one-percent biker gangs in the United States. New Jersey law enforcement authorities estimate that there are 300-400 Pagans, with 40-60 members in three New Jersey chapters (www.mafianj.com/mc/pagans.html.).

The Pagans have the general reputation among bikers as being very reclusive and having little to do with other clubs. Their proclivity for violence reinforces this reputation. In addition, their heavy involvement in criminal activities, particularly organized crime, places them in the criminal organization–gang category. The Pagans MC does not have a national website, although there is a website for Jailed Pagans MC New York (www.hometown.aol.com/JAILEDPAGANS/). The website contains several pictures of burly, thick-armed Pagans covered with tattoos. The website also lists e-mail and conventional mail prison addresses. One, Conan, states that he was the National Sergeant at Arms of the Pagans Motorcycle Club and is in his seventh year of a 16-year sentence at the federal penitentiary in Lewisburg, Pennsylvania. The "13" he wears and uses in his name may signal that he was a member of the Pagans Mother Club.

The Department of Justice reports that the Pagans are the most prominent OMG in the Mid-Atlantic region and are involved in distribution of cocaine, methamphetamine, and PCP (Department of Justice, 2011). Most of the 11 Pagans chapters are in the Northeast United States—New Jersey, New York, Pennsylvania, Delaware, and Maryland. The Pagans MC is the only Big Five Motorcycle Gang that does not have any chapters outside the United States, although there are rumors that it is attempting to establish a presence in Canada.

Sons of Silence Motorcycle Club/Gang

The Sons of Silence MC (SOS MC) did not start out as a one-percent biker gang either. Bruce "The Dude" Richardson in Niwot, Colorado, founded the club in 1966. As was common in the 1960s during the time of the military draft and the Vietnam War, Richardson was in the military (U.S. Navy); however, there is no evidence that he had been to Vietnam or was a disillusioned veteran. The club appears to have been formed as a "drinking" social club. As the club evolved into a criminal gang, Richardson left the club. Today, the Department of Justice (2011) reports that the SOS MC is an outlaw motorcycle gang with 30 U.S. chapters and five chapters in Germany. Club members, according to the Department of Justice, have been involved in a wide range of criminal activities, including drugs and weapons trafficking.

IDENTIFY THE COLORS

The Sons of Silence Insignia

Photo courtesy of U.S. Department of Justice. See www.justice.gov/criminal/ocgs/gangs/motorcycle.html.

The SOS MC patch is unique and different from the traditional one-percent three-piece patch. The patch itself is one big center patch with the Latin saying *"Donnec Mors Non Separate"*—Until Death Separates Us—appearing on the bottom of the center patch.

The SOS MC have tenuous relationships with several of the other Big Five clubs. The Bandidos have had a chapter in Denver since the early 1990s. The clubs are on "friendly terms" and list each other on their websites, but the Hells Angels—enemies to both clubs—patched over a local Denver motorcycle club and established a chapter in Denver, causing concern about a biker war (Foster, 1999). In 1980, the national vice president of the Sons of Silence killed the national vice president of the Outlaws MC in Indianapolis (Foster, 1999). In an interesting turn of events, on June 19, 2003, members of the Hells Angels, Outlaws, and Bandidos attended the funeral of Leonard "JR" Reed, who was the Sons of Silence president for 22 years (www.bikerlife.com/notices.html). According to the article (posted on bikerlife.com), Reed was well respected by other clubs and had been seen as a peacekeeper (see Box 5.4).

BOX 5.4 PROMISE TO MOMMA

One of the hardest things for undercover officers to do is to avoid taking drugs during the infiltration of a biker gang without raising suspicion that they are cops. In the late 1990s two ATF special agents infiltrated the Sons of Silence, eventually becoming patched members. One of the agents told the bikers that he had been an addict and his mother saved him and made him swear that he would never use drugs again. She died shortly after he made the promise, and he had "Never Forget" tattooed on his arm as a reminder of the promise to his mother. The bikers believed him.

Source: *McPhee* (1999, November 20).

PUPPET/SUPPORT GANGS

Puppet/support gangs are outlaw motorcycle clubs affiliated with a dominant outlaw motorcycle gang (see Boxes 5.5 and 5.6). The puppet/support clubs do the bidding, including criminal activities, of the dominant gang, serve as potential recruitment sources, and provide cannon fodder in the wars between clubs/gangs. As is common with prison gangs, the outlaw motorcycle gangs acting as puppet/support gangs give a portion of their illicit gains to the dominant OMG. For example, the Nomads chapter of the Quebec Hells Angels required each member of their puppet club, the Rockers, to give a ten-percent tithing or a minimum of $500 (Sanger, 2005). The larger or dominant OMGs handle the wholesale distribution of drugs, and the puppet clubs handle the dangerous retail sale, thereby insulating the dominant club members from prosecution. On occasion, if the subordinate club member is caught committing a crime and demonstrates that he "has class" (keeps his mouth shut and takes the fall), he will be rewarded by becoming a "prospect" for the club.

BOX 5.5 PUPPET/SUPPORT OMGs IN CANADA

…outlaw motorcycle gangs for example do have a formalized structure for dealing with its support crime groups [puppet clubs]. Essentially these supportive crime groups are used to train the younger generation, identify those candidates with the potential to become full-fledged members, as well as exclude undesirables. In this kind of relationship, the advantage for the dominant is that the subordinate one further insulates the dominant group's members from the day-to-day criminal activities that would bring them into direct contact with the authorities or their rivals. Other benefits for the dominant group include the payment of money, goods, and services they receive from members of the subordinate group.

Source: *CICS* (2000).

BOX 5.6 PAGANS MC RETALIATION AGAINST TITANS MC (HELLS ANGELS PUPPET CLUB)

A Pagans MC member was indicted for arson after allegedly burning down Bad Water Bill's Barbeque Barn in Strasburg, Virginia. The Pagan member from Florida allegedly torched the restaurant because the Titans Motorcycle Club was scheduled to host a bike show at Bad Water Bill's. The HAMC and the Pagans MC were at war because of the Hells Angels move into an area considered Pagan territory.

Source: *DOJ 9* (2009, June 11).

The Caribbean Brotherhood MC is a HAMC puppet club in Curaçao that supplies cocaine from the FARC (Revolutionary Armed Forces of Colombia) to the Hells Angels in Europe (Sher & Marsden, 2006). The Red Devils MC (see Box 5.7) proudly announce on their website that they are an "Official 81 support club." The Red Devils list 121 chapters in 16 different countries—Germany (59), Australia (2), Belgium (10), Brazil (3), Bosnia Herzegovina (4), Chile (1), China (1), England (2), Italy (3), Luxembourg (2), New Zealand (1), Singapore (1), South Africa (5), Sweden (6), Turkey (8), and the United States (8) (reddevilsmccom/main/).

BOX 5.7 RED DEVILS MC

CW (confidential informant) stated that the Red Devils' continued and sole purpose is to support the HAMC through several facets, including increased membership, collecting drug and prostitution debts, extorting jobs and acquiring and maintaining weaponry and narcotics on behalf of HAMC members.

Source: BATF Search Warrant Affidavit, 2003.

The Black Pistons MC is the largest puppet/support club for the Outlaws MC. It is estimated that the Black Pistons MC has 70 U.S. chapters and an unknown number of chapters in Canada, Belgium, Germany, Great Britain, and Norway. The website for the Black Pistons Great Britain (www.blackpistons.co.uk/history.php) reports that the Black Pistons MC was first established in Germany in 2002; then at the Daytona Bike Week in March 2002 the Satan's Syndicate MC of Columbus, Ohio, patched over to the Black Pistons MC, becoming the first Black Pistons MC chapter in the United States. This is an example of an OMG formed overseas and expanding to the United States, even though it is a puppet club for a U.S.-based OMG. There is an unknown number of additional Outlaws MC puppet/support clubs, including the Foresaken Few MC and the small local Undertakers MC of Lexington, Kentucky. The Undertakers MC post on their website "We are a motorcycle club and are **PROUD SUPPORTERS OF THE OUTLAWS MC AND THE BLACK AND WHITE WORLD... IF IT AIN'T BLACK AND WHITE. IT JUST AIN'T RIGHT!**" (emphasis in the original).

IDENTIFY THE COLORS

The Black Pistons Insignia

Photo courtesy of U.S. Department of Justice. See www.justice.gov/criminal/ocgs/gangs/motorcycle.html.

The Bandidos Nation lists their puppet/support clubs on their national website. There are 22 puppet clubs listed on the Bandidos website in the "Red and Gold" section (see Table 5.1); however, Winterhalder (2005), the only former Bandidos author, at this time, lists 47 Bandidos "support clubs in 13 states with 929 members." In August 2012, the founder and president of Los Homeboys, a Bandidos support gang, was found guilty of conspiracy with intent to distribute heroin. He was part of a drug-trafficking organization between the Bandidos MC and the Medellin drug organization throughout the Dallas–Fort Worth metroplex (DOJ 8, 2012, August 24).

Table 5.1 Red and Gold World—Bandidos Puppet Clubs		
Amigos MC	Asgard MC	Bandaleros MC
Blazes MC	Campesinos MC	Commancheros MC
Compadres Mc	Companeros MC	Destralos MC
Diablos MC	Gringos MC	Guardian MC
Guerrillos MC	Hermanos MC	Hombres MC
LA Riders MC	Lones MC	Los Mados MC
OK Riders MC	Pistoleros MC	Regulators MC
Zapata MC		

The puppet/support clubs of the Pagans include the Tribe MC, the Last Rebels MC, and the Shore Dogs MC. All of the Pagans MC subordinate clubs are easily identifiable because they wear a "16" on their cut (the 16th letter in the alphabet is P). Support clubs for the SOS MC are reportedly the Silent Few MC (Arkansas), the Silent Rebels MC (Louisiana), the Silent Thunder MC (North Dakota), the American Iron MC (Denver, Colorado), and the Deuce's Wild MC (Greely, Colorado).

MAJOR INDEPENDENTS

Major independent outlaw motorcycle gangs are considered to be those that are not listed in the Big Five and are not puppet/support clubs of a Big Five club. Because of the jealousy of their territory by Big Five clubs, it is not easy to be an independent club. Independent clubs operate in areas where there are no Big Five clubs, or in the same area as a Big Five club with the permission of the dominant club, but this is often a tenuous relationship. Outlaw motorcycle gangs must maintain complete dominance over their territory or disband—take their colors off. There is no other option. Big Five clubs have been known to challenge all clubs wearing a three-piece patch in their dominant territory, even law enforcement officer's motorcycle clubs (LEO MCs), which often act and behave more like outlaw bikers than cops. On this point, most outlaw clubs feel that if LEO clubs want to dress and behave like outlaw bikers, they should be treated appropriately. This challenge extends to wearing "protected" color combinations on patches. All bikers know that red-on-white is the Hells Angels "protected" color combination, as is black-on-white for the Outlaws MC and red-on-yellow for the Bandidos. The Big Five clubs and the major independents control their territory and claim oversight of all other clubs, especially one-percent biker clubs. They take it very seriously when an individual or a club challenges their perceived superiority. The majority of biker wars occur because of territory issues or access to crime markets, particularly drugs. Independent clubs are often on friendly or tolerant terms with a dominant club; however, they may be at war with another club. For example, in Virginia, the Florida-based Warlocks, an independent club, are on "friendly" terms with the Hells Angels but at war with the Pagans. The Mongols are on friendly terms with the Pagans, Bandidos, and Outlaws throughout the United States but are at war with the Hells Angels everywhere. The Hells Angels, being the largest outlaw motorcycle club and the one with the most publicity, and whose members display what is considered by the other clubs to be arrogant and have a bad attitude, are continually at war with other clubs.

The Mongols MC is an example of an independent club that operates in the same area as clubs that claim dominant status, but they do so because of their ferocity and willingness to use violence. The Hells Angels and the Mongols MC fought a 17-year war over the wearing of the California bottom rocker. The Hells Angels said that they were the only motorcycle club who could wear the California rocker because they were the dominant California club. The Mongols objected and went to war. After 17 years of murder and mayhem between the clubs, a truce was signed in 1977. Under the terms of the truce, the HAMC retained their Southern California chapters (Monterey, Orange County, Riverside, Fresno, Ventura, San Diego [Dago], and the original chapter and now mother chapter, San Bernardino [Berdoo]), and the Mongols MC promised not to establish chapters in Northern California. The Mongols MC were granted a free reign over the rest of Southern California and "allowed" to wear the California rocker. The truce has not stopped the violence between the gangs, however. An altercation took place at Harrah's Casino in Laughlin, Nevada, on April 27, 2002, resulting in the deaths of one Mongols member and two Hells Angels, as well as numerous injuries. In May 2005, the president of the Hells Angels San Diego chapter was sentenced to 57 months in federal prison after pleading guilty to racketeering charges for conspiring with other HAMC members to kill Mongols (AP, 2005). Other clubs challenge the Hells Angels. The longtime California independent club, the Vagos, is challenging the HAMC in California, Nevada, and Arizona. The Vagos are also challenging the Bandidos in New Mexico.

The major independent clubs, in terms of chapters, membership, and geographical expansion are the Warlocks (national and international), Mongols (national and international), Vagos (national and international), and the Wheels of Soul (national). Other smaller independent clubs, such as the Avengers MC, the Breed MC, the Devils Diciples MC, and the Iron Horsemen, operate in limited geographical areas.

The Mongols MC

The Mongols MC started as a Chicano prison gang in East Los Angeles in 1969 [Mongols website says December 15, 1979, in the city of Montebello, California] and formed an alliance with **La Eme**, the Mexican Mafia. Many of these early members had never owned or ridden a motorcycle. It appears that the Mongols MC was formed to be, and still is, a criminal organization for profit through criminal activities. The Mongols MC official website makes the following statement:

He [Reuben "Doc" Cavazos, former National and International President] has been blamed for turning the club into one of the largest criminal organizations on the West Coast of the United States during his time as president. In order to bolster the gang's ranks, he also recruited members of street gangs [Cavazos, himself, had been a member of the notorious LA street gang, the Avenues] into the club, much to the disgust of the old school bikers. He was voted out of the club on August 30, 2008 during a meeting in Vernon, California, due to the majority of the membership believing that he was stealing from the club and provoking a war with the Mexican Mafia (Out Bad—www.mongolsmc.com/chapters/usa.)

[An alternative explanation for the expulsion of "Doc" Cavazos from the Mongols MC is that he "flipped" on the Mongols and pleaded guilty at trial and admitted that the Mongols MC was a drug-dealing enterprise.]

IDENTIFY THE COLORS

The Mongols Insignia

Photo courtesy of U.S. Department of Justice. See www.justice.gov/criminal/ocgs/gangs/motorcycle.html.

The gang is still predominately Hispanic, especially in California, with a large number of street gang members, according to Queen (2005). The Mongols are a particularly violent motorcycle gang due to the large number of former gangbangers in their chapters. Former Minnesota Governor, Navy Seal, and media celebrity Jesse Ventura was a member of the Mongols MC in the early 1970s when he was stationed at the naval facility at San Diego but claims that he did not participate in or hear of their criminal activities (Queen, 2005).

In addition to the 17-year war they fought over the bottom California rocker mentioned earlier, the Mongols and the Hells Angels have been bitter enemies for decades, but nothing happened that compared to the events that took place in Harrah's Laughlin Casino, at about 2 A.M. on April 27, 2002. Both gangs were in Laughlin, Nevada, for the annual River Run when a contingent of 80 Hells Angels staying at one casino invaded the Harrah's casino and engaged about 40 Mongols on the casino floor among numerous citizens shooting craps, playing slot machines, and having a good time.

The entire vicious melee was recorded on security cameras, showing a scene of chaos, murder, and senseless violence that became a national and international spectacle. When it was all over, one Mongol and two Angels were dead. There were about a dozen bikers and innocent citizens treated in the hospital. Six guns and 50 knives of all descriptions were recovered from the floor of the casino. The heroic actions of the first two responding police officers brought most of the violence under control until reinforcements poured in. Six members of each gang were convicted for their part in the riot, but most of the more serious offenses were reduced, and 35 participants had their charges dismissed for a variety of legal errors. The security tape is now part of training tapes shown at police conferences and police academies.

The official website of the Mongols MC lists 106 chapters in 14 U.S. states and eight countries outside the United States—United States: Arizona (2), Arkansas (1), California (49), Colorado (4), Florida (3), Montana (1), Nevada (2), New York (1), Oklahoma (6), Oregon (6), Pennsylvania (2), Utah (5), Virginia (1), and Washington (1); Outside the United States: Australia (8), Mexico (1), Norway (4), Spain (1), Germany (4), Thailand (2), Malaysia (1), and Israel (1) (www.mongolsmc.com/chapters/usa). Queen claims that there is also a chapter in Georgia.

Doc Cavazos, the national Mongols MC president mentioned earlier, was convicted as a result of an investigation known as Operation Black Rain. On October 21, 2008, Mongols President Cavazos and 79 other Mongols were arrested after a three-year investigation in which four undercover officers infiltrated the gang. The indictment alleged 86 counts of murder, attempted murder, assaults, hate crimes, gun violations, and drug trafficking. It was alleged that Mongols members in continuing the war with the Hells Angels had killed and assaulted numerous Hells Angels in California. It was alleged that senior Mongols members, including the national president, traveled to Atlantic City, New Jersey, to meet with Pagans members (the Pagans are considered to be the dominant club in the area) to form an alliance to allow for expansion into the Northeast. The hate crime allegation asserted, according to the indictment, that the Mongols MC is … "racist and hostile to the presence of African-Americans in bars or clubs where Mongols are present, or African-Americans in the presence of females associated with Mongols or Mongols members." See the Mongols Fight Song in Box 5.8.

BOX 5.8 MONGOLS FIGHT SONG

We are Mongol raiders, we're raiders of the night
We're dirty sons of bitches, we'd rather fuck and fight
Hidy, hidy, Christ Almighty, who the fuck are we
Shit, fuck, cunt, Mongols MC!

Warlocks MC

There are at least two one-percent biker gangs with the name Warlocks. There is also a Warlocks MC in Detroit that is not a one-percent biker club. In the United States, there is a Florida-based Warlocks MC and a Pennsylvania-based Warlocks MC. They are not affiliated with each other.

Pennsylvania Warlocks MC

This one-percent biker gang is clearly proud of its racist nature and touts on its website that the club is "ALL WHITE! RED AND WHITE." They go on to say "…the club is now probably the only one-percent club in America that retains a membership which is, racially, identical to its original members…we have in the past experimented with token non-white, but found it unproductive and self-destructive" (www.theoriginalwarlocksmc.com/allwhite.htm). Bowe (1994:21-22) says that the Pennsylvania-based Warlocks came into being in the summer of 1967 when a group of Philadelphia "young toughs" formed the club and elected a president, vice president, secretary, treasurer, and sergeant at arms. They formulated rules and chose as their insignia a multicolored caricature of a harpy—a mythical minister of divine vengeance. They declared themselves to be a one-percent club and wore the one-percent diamond on their denim vest. Three tattoos were mandatory—a swastika, a naked lady, and the words "BORN TO LOSE." Members had to be male, between 18 and 35, own a Harley, and have committed a felony—theft, rape, or murder—to be considered for membership. The last criterion makes the Pennsylvania-based Warlocks MC a criminal organization at formation. Membership was confined to those with identifiable criminal exploitable ties.

The gang has been a significant crime problem in the Delaware Valley since the 1970s. The Pennsylvania Crime Commission (1980) reported that the regional Warlocks and the regional Pagans were the major motorcycle clubs in the southeast region of Pennsylvania. Both clubs were known for their violence and acted as enforcers for La Costa Nostra families. The report listed 22 Warlocks members by name. One of those listed, Bobby Nauss, was a 1970s serial killer, drug dealer, and the subject of a book and an HBO movie (Bowe, 1994). In 1995, Franklin County, New Jersey, Police Sgt. Ippolito Gonzalez pulled over two Warlocks members on a traffic stop just after the two had committed a burglary. One of the two Warlocks, Robert "Mudman" Simon, shot the police sergeant twice because he did not want to go back to prison. Mudman was quickly arrested, pleaded guilty, and sentenced to death (Anon. 15, 1997, April 3). He was later stomped to death by a fellow prisoner who claimed self-defense and was acquitted. In 2008, the Warlocks were alleged to be involved in a methamphetamine manufacturing operation in Berks County, Pennsylvania.

The Pennsylvania-based Warlocks also have several chapters in New Jersey (State of New Jersey, 2004). A 1989 New Jersey Commission of Investigation report put the membership range from 60 to 136 with chapters in Philadelphia (the mother club), southern New Jersey, and Delaware County, Pennsylvania. The latest information reports that the Pennsylvania-based Warlocks have five chapters in Pennsylvania and additional chapters in South Jersey, Delaware, and Maryland.

Florida-Based Warlocks MC

According to their national website, the Florida-based Warlocks MC was founded aboard the aircraft carrier *USS Shangri-La* in the Mediterranean Sea in the summer of 1966 (www.warlocksmc.net/about.html). The 13 original members, all "fanatic motorcycle enthusiasts, who liked to party," chose the orange Phoenix bird as their logo. Each of the 13 members was to establish a chapter in his hometown when they retired from the Navy. Only one of the sailors made good on the promise to establish a chapter, Grub from Orlando, Florida. He founded the first chapter in Jacksonville Beach, Florida, and soon moved it to Orlando, where it is now the mother chapter.

The official website lists 38 chapters, 31 in the United States: Florida (11), South Carolina (7), Virginia (4), West Virginia (4), New York (1), Ohio (2), Minnesota (1), and Georgia (1); and seven outside the United States: Germany (2), England (3), and Canada (2). In the United States, the chapters are divided into three regions—Northern, Central, and Southern. The Northern Region chapters are located in Brooklyn, New York; Martinsburg, West Virginia; Mt. Jackson, Virginia; and Charlottesville, Virginia. Central Region chapters are in Florence, Columbia, and Greenwood, South Carolina. The Southern Region chapters are located in Cocoa, Orlando, Seminole, Brooksville, and Melbourne, Florida (ATF Search Warrant Affidavit, 2003).

The Warlocks, even though they have extensive membership applications and background checks and a membership process of hangaround, probate, and then membership, have been penetrated several times by law enforcement officers. In 2003, two ATF special agents became patched members; one became his chapter's road captain, an appointed officer position (ATF Search Warrant, 2003). In 1991 during an investigation dubbed Operation Easy Rider, four undercover federal agents (ATF) and a Volusia County, Florida, deputy sheriff became patched members. One of the special agents became president of the Fort Lauderdale Warlocks chapter, which he set up on instructions from the Warlock national president. The special agent recruited the other undercover agents to join him. They became an all-police one-percent biker club. This was not the first all-cop one-percent biker club. In the early 1970s, the Long Beach, California, Widow Makers Motorcycle Club was made up of six undercover ATF agents (Queen, 2005). This was the first undercover operation on biker gangs on the West Coast.

The Warlocks, the Pagans, and the Outlaws are bitter enemies of each other. In 1991, the International Outlaws President, Harry "Taco" Bowman, murdered the National Warlocks President.

Vagos Motorcycle Club

The Vagos Motorcycle Club/Gang, aka The Green Nation, was formed in 1965 in San Bernardino, California, which is also where the modern-day Hells Angels came into being. Allegedly, Hispanics who were refused membership in the Hells Angels because of their ethnicity formed this gang.

The gang was originally called the "Psychos." According to the official website (vagosmcworld.com/), the name Vagos comes from the Spanish term meaning "traveling gypsy" or a "street-wise person that's always up to something." The club insignia, "Loki," is the Norse god of mischief. The website says that it was designed by an incarcerated member.

IDENTIFY THE COLORS

The Vagos Insignia: Loki

Photo courtesy of U.S. Department of Justice. See www.justice.gov/criminal/ocgs/gangs/motorcycle.html.

The Vagos MC is one of the few motorcycle gangs/clubs that publishes mission statements (see Box 5.9).

BOX 5.9 VAGOS MISSION STATEMENTS

Experience and share brotherhood.
Share our passion for riding motorcycles.
Protect and promote our way of life.
Motorcycling. Brotherhood. Loyalty. Friendship.

The website reports that there are chapters in 10 U.S. states: Missouri, Nevada, New York, Pennsylvania, California, Arizona, Hawaii, Utah, Oregon, and Idaho; and international chapters in Sweden, Germany, Mexico, Canada, Costa Rica, and Nicaragua. The former president of the Nicaragua chapter, Ernesto Gonzalez, was convicted of murdering the President of the San Jose chapter of the Hells Angels during a fight at a Sparks, Nevada, casino September 23, 2011 (Newton, 2013, July 24). The Vagos MC has been involved in criminal activities since its formation, and this has increased in recent years. In 2006, 700 agents from the Bureau of Alcohol, Tobacco, Firearms, and Explosives (ATF) and local law enforcement officers began making arrests for federal and state firearms and drug violations in five Southern California counties following a three-year investigation of the Vagos MC. The operation, called Operation 22 Green—green is the gang's color and 22 corresponds to the letter V in the alphabet—was, at that time, the largest law enforcement–coordinated action ever conducted in Southern California. Among those arrested were seven chapter presidents, one secretary, one treasurer, and seven sergeants at arms (Anon. 16, 2006, March 10). Ninety-five weapons were seized along with some illegal drugs, $6,000 in cash, and two stolen motorcycles. Law enforcement spokespersons claimed that the Vagos MC had been dismantled, a claim often made after large operations against OMGs. As usual, this claim was soon found to be premature and erroneous.

One of the characteristics of criminal organizations is that they can, in time, replace the absent leaders and continue.

Operation Pure Luck: This four-year multistate and multiagency federal, state, and local law enforcement operation was named Pure Luck because an undercover infiltration of the Vagos MC by Las Vegas police officers expanded beyond all expectations and led to arrests in Nevada, California, Utah, Arizona, Texas, New York, and Hawaii (Blasky, 2013, June 27; Synder & Taylor, 2013, June 27). Before it was all over, law enforcement officers from the following agencies: Las Vegas, ATF, U.S. Marshals Henderson, Nevada; North Las Vegas, Nevada; Los Angeles County Sheriff's office, and the Montebello, California were involved in the arrests and investigation. Outlaw bikers, including high officers, from the following gangs were taken into custody: the Vagos, Bandidos, Green Machine, Wicked Riderz, and the Chosen Few. The 32 bikers indicted were charged with a variety of state and local charges ranging from drug trafficking to theft and insurance fraud.

Wheels of Soul

The Wheels of Soul Motorcycle Club/Gang (WOS), although predominately black, is a multiracial national motorcycle club that was established in Philadelphia, Pennsylvania, in 1967 (www.wheelsofsoul.wordpress.com/). The website says that they have a four-piece patch made up of three "rockers" (Wheels, Of Soul, Location) and the "wing and wheel" center patch. This national outlaw motorcycle gang has chapters in at least 20 states. The gang has a violent and criminal reputation. A coordinated federal and state investigation into the criminal activities of the Wheels of Soul MC began in 2009 after a robbery and murder in St. Louis, Missouri, by members of the gang. The investigation led to a number of arrests and convictions:

1. Eighteen members of the Wheels of Soul outlaw motorcycle gang were indicted and arrested and it was alleged that "…between 2009 and the present time, the Wheels of Soul Outlaw Motorcycle constituted an 'enterprise' engaged in racketeering activity as defined by the federal RICO statute, and that the eighteen charged current and former members conspired to commit racketeering acts in furtherance of that 'enterprise'" (DOJ 9, 2009, June 11). The list of the 18 included national and regional officers of the Pennsylvania-based gang.
2. Two WOS members were convicted and sentenced to prison. One, a former WOS vice president, admitted to attempting to kill two different individuals in separate incidents in Chicago, Illinois, in 2009. He admitted that he committed the offenses to increase his status in the Wheels of Soul Motorcycle Club, a criminal enterprise (DOJ 10, 2012, January 23).
3. Three members of the WOS (two from Chicago and one from Denver) pleaded guilty to racketeering conspiracy charges in the U.S. District Court in St. Louis. The two WOS members from Chicago admitted to trafficking in crack in furtherance of the Wheels of Soul criminal enterprise (DOJ 11, 2009, April 4).

4. A former president of the Midwest Region of the Wheels of Soul admitted to engaging in numerous acts (distributing crack, attempting to kill members of rival motorcycle clubs, and transporting pipe bombs from Kentucky to Chicago) in furtherance of the Wheels of Soul criminal enterprise (DOJ 12, 2009, June 3).

5. The president of the Kentucky chapter of the Wheels of Soul, a correctional officer at the Kentucky State Reformatory in LaGrange, Kentucky, admitted that he agreed to manufacture pipe bombs, which he knew would be used against rival motorcycle clubs in the Chicago area (DOJ 13, 2009, November 25).

BLACK OR INTERRACIAL ONE-PERCENT OUTLAW MOTORCYCLE CLUBS

We have just discussed the multiracial Wheels of Soul outlaw motorcycle club/gang, which has been classified as a criminal organization or gang. Black or multiracial outlaw motorcycle clubs are an anomaly among the predominately white male, often predominately racist or white supremacist, outlaw motorcycle clubs. In fact, there have been numerous one-percent bikers (some to me personally) that vehemently insist that there are no black one-percent bikers, insisting that, like women, blacks are not welcome in the one-percent subculture. It is true that the one-percent subculture is basically sexist (women cannot be patchholders in any one-percent club), with some clubs/gangs more racist than others; however, it is also true that there are black or multiracial biker clubs.

Blacks in the One-Percent Biker Subculture

With a few exceptions to be discussed later, blacks are excluded from membership or from riding with one-percent biker clubs. A possible explanation for the exclusion of blacks is that one-percent bikers are white supremacists or racists (see Box 5.11). Lavigne (1987) claims that the Hells Angels are white supremacists and Hells Angels chapters in the southern United States are allied with the Ku Klux Klan. He cites as evidence of the latter statement the involvement of North Carolina Hells Angels chapters with the Klan. The National Gang Crime Research Center (NGCRC) includes motorcycle gang members among the category "White Racist Extremist Gang Members" (WREGs), along with groups such as the Aryan Brotherhood, Aryan Nation, Ku Klux Klan, neo-Nazis, and Skinheads. One law enforcement source says that outlaw motorcycle gang members have performed security details at Klan rallies (MAGLOCLEN, 2003:18). The same source said that 22% of their members reported that there is a relationship between outlaw and white supremacist groups. Skinhead groups were the most often mentioned. In an early study, Hopper and Moore (1990) reported that the white motorcycle gang members they encountered in the 1980s were members of the Aryan Brotherhood. They had become members of the Aryan Brotherhood while serving time in prison. Outlaw motorcycle gang members in California have been found to have ties to PEN1 (Public Enemy Number 1), a skinhead group, and the Aryan Brotherhood (California Department of Justice, 2004). A publication by Paladin Press says that the white supremacy beliefs of outlaw motorcycle gangs parallel those of the Ku Klux Klan and the Nazis (Anon. 17, 1992). They report that these same beliefs can be seen in the tattoos, patches, and pins—Nazi swastikas, white-power fists, and white supremacist pins. Michael Upright, a professional photographer, took black-and-white pictures of outlaw motorcycle clubs in various locations throughout the United States from 1992 to 1995. Among his photographs are pictures of 19 Outlaws with a patch containing a swastika (Upright, 1999). Upright's photos also show women wearing shirts stating "Property of Outlaws."

All members of one-percent biker clubs may not be racists and white supremacists, but some outlaw motorcycle clubs qua gangs have a long history of racism and racial statements in their by-laws. In his classic work on the early Oakland Hells Angels, Hunter S. Thompson explained why blacks did not become members (Thompson, 1966). He observed a "Negro named Charley," who had been riding with the Oakland Angels for some time, and asked several members if Charley would ever get in the club.

> "Hell I admire the little bastard," said one, "but he'll never get in. He thinks he will, but he won't… shit, all it takes is two blackballs (votes), and I could tell you who they'd be by just looking around the room."
>
> (Thompson, 1966:304)

The Hells Angels have a long history of excluding blacks and other groups from membership. The San Francisco Hells Angels chapter's rules and by-laws for the 1960s had the following membership restrictions: "No niggers, no cops, or ex-cops" (Lavigne, 1999:491). According to Lavigne (1999), more recent Hells Angels' rules also restrict membership:

Proposed United States Rules Update:
25. No niggers in the club. Cops or ex-cops (p. 500).

Hells Angels Canadian By-laws:
No member of African descent (p. 501).

Hells Angels World Rules (revision date for the following new rules):
Revised March 11, 1998
August 3, 1986—No cops or ex-cops in the club.
August 3, 1986—No niggers in the club.
August 3, 1986—No snitches in the club (p. 506).

There has been at least one black Canadian who was a member of the Hells Angels organization—a member of a puppet gang—because of his drug-dealing abilities and usefulness as a hit man, but he was not allowed to become a patched member or ride with the club in the United States (Sher & Marsden, 2006). In addition, the traditionally homophobic Hells Angels had a homosexual member (Sher & Marsden, 2006).

Other biker gangs, particularly the Big Five—Hells Angels, Outlaws, Bandidos, Pagans, and Sons of Silence—have similar membership restrictions in their constitutions and by-laws. During the trial of Harry "Taco" Bowman, former regional president and national vice president before becoming the international president of the Outlaws Motorcycle Club (1984-1997), the Outlaws Constitution was admitted into evidence. The constitution stated that only white males ("no niggers") could become members (*United States v. Harry Bowman*, 2002). The Bandidos Motorcycle Club/gang has had at least one black member in the past. Betsy Guisto (1997) documents the case of "Spook," the only black to become a member of the club. A musician who played in a band that performed at a Houston, Texas, Bandidos club bar told me the story of the reception they received when a black musician temporarily replaced one of the members of the band. They were told in no uncertain terms that a "nigger" was not allowed in the bar.

Black Outlaw Motorcycle Gangs

In addition to the Wheels of Soul MC discussed above, there are several black or multiracial OMGs that can be classified as outlaw motorcycle gangs. The Hell's Lovers is a multiracial Chicago-based OMG formed by a Mexican American who was not accepted into the motorcycle clubs in the area (see Box 5.10). It is reported to be the first integrated biker organization in the Chicago area. Former Bandidos leader Ed Winterhalder, reports that they have chapters nationwide. In 2012, 19 members of the Hell's Lovers from Denver, Colorado, were indicted and arrested for a number of RICO offenses, including possessing stolen explosive materials; possession of a prohibited weapon; possessing, making, and transferring prohibited weapons; and possession of body armor by a prohibited person (Roberts, 2012).

BOX 5.10 HELL'S LOVERS AS A CRIMINAL ORGANIZATION

Sixteen Hell's Lovers MC members of the Commerce City and Denver chapters were indicted for various offenses, including maintaining a drug involved premise, possession with intent to distribute crack cocaine, prohibited person in possession of a firearm, possession of a firearm in furtherance of a drug trafficking felony, possession with intent to distribute marijuana, conspiracy to distribute cocaine, conspiracy to maintain a drug-involved premise, and aiding and abetting.

Source: *DOJ 10 (2012, January 23)*.

The Chosen Few Motorcycle Club started out in 1959 in Los Angeles as an all-black motorcycle club, then in the 1960s became multiracial with chapters that were "all Black, all White, half White and Mexican, half Black and half White, all Mexican, half Mexican and Indian with a few Asians and one Iranian" (www.chosenfewmc.org/). The Los Angeles police department calls them a violent criminal gang (LAPD, 2011). The LAPD says that this primarily black gang was involved in three shootings and one homicide during the first four months of 2010. In 2010, a combined federal, state, and local task force was created whose primary purpose was to reduce the criminal activities of the Chosen Few MC.

The Anti-Defamation League (ADL) has released a comprehensive report of the links between white supremacist groups and biker gangs. The ties are substantial and represent a direct threat to minority groups and law enforcement authorities (see Box 5.11). The report is one more indication that one-percent biker gangs and the one-percent subculture are more dangerous than the one-percent spokesmen would have us believe.

BOX 5.11 BIGOTS ON BIKES: LINKS BETWEEN WHITE SUPREMACISTS AND BIKER GANGS

Introduction

According to the ADL, there has been an increase in links between white supremacists and outlaw motorcycle clubs/gangs in the United States. The ADL reports that all five of the major U.S. white supremacist movements (neo-Nazis, racist skinheads, Ku Klux Klan groups, racist prison gangs, and Christian Identity) have developed ties to the biker subculture. Many bikers hold dual membership in biker clubs and white supremacist groups. Biker gangs co-sponsor white power events and allow white supremacists to meet at their clubhouses. In recent years, a number of explicit white supremacist outlaw motorcycle clubs/gangs have been formed.

Cultural Overlaps Between Bikers and White Supremacists

Symbolic Overlaps

Biker gangs and white supremacists share the use of symbols from Nazi Germany and the German military of the Nazi era: Iron Crosses, swastikas, the Totenkopf death's head image, SS lightning bolts, Nazi war eagles, and German army helmets. The early outlaw bikers, even World War II veterans, began their use to show their nonconformist nature and "shock and awe" as part of their "in your face" ideology. However, the common use of these symbols today can be interpreted as prima facie evidence of white supremacist beliefs or leanings.

Linguistic Overlaps

The underground nature of both biker and white supremacist subcultures and common prison experiences promotes the sharing of similar terms, slogans, and phrases. Most of these shared phrases pledge loyalty to the group. For example, OMGs, racist skinhead groups and prison gangs alike often use the phrase 'X Forever, Forever X' where 'X' is the name of the group. Members of the Hammerskins racist gang often use the phrase 'Hammerskin Forever, Forever Hammerskin,' while members of the outlaw biker club Hells Angels use 'Angels Forever, Forever Angels.' Often these phrases are turned into acronyms, such as OFFO for 'Outlaws Forever, Forever Outlaws,' or CFFC for '[Aryan] Circle Forever, Forever [Aryan] Circle.'

Both groups (biker gangs and white supremacists) share a penchant for alphanumerically coded phrases. A common white supremacist symbol is the number 88, which stands for "Heil Hitler" (H is the eighth letter of the alphabet). HAMC members refer to the club by the number 81 (H is the eighth letter and A is the first letter in the alphabet). Members of the White Knights of America, a racist and street gang in Arizona and Texas, display the numbers 23 and 11 (an alphanumeric representation of W and K).

Both groups (biker gangs and white supremacists) also share the expression of a common value of Brotherhood and refer to each other as brothers or family. The members speak of "love, loyalty, honor, and respect" for their fellow members. They each have phrases that reference group loyalty and the dangers of snitching—snitches are a dying breed, snitches get stitches, your brother may be wrong, but he is always your brother, etc. Those familiar with both groups know that these lofty statements of loyalty and brotherhood are more rhetoric than reality.

BOX 5.11 BIGOTS ON BIKES: LINKS BETWEEN WHITE SUPREMACISTS AND BIKER GANGS—cont'd

Shared Practices

The recruitment, indoctrination, and organization of both groups are often similar. The "practice of prospecting" where the group has a chance to examine the potential recruit and socialize him into group loyalty is similar. To become a member of the Hammerskins, a potential recruit has to "prospect" for 1 year and then serve as a "probate" for six months. Almost all racist prison gangs such as the Aryan Brotherhood, Texas Aryan Brotherhood, and the Aryan Circle use the prospect system.

Another shared practice between OMGs and white supremacist groups is the exclusion of women as members.

Shared Interests

The most common shared interests between outlaw bikers and white supremacists are motorcycles, bike accessories, the apparel bikers wear, and business interests related to motorcycles (motorcycle dealers and repair shops, etc.). The ADL provides the example of a former member of the Confederate Cavalry Corps, a small Alabama white supremacist motorcycle club. This owner of a motorcycle repair shop recently left the Calvary and joined the Pistelero MC, an **Outlaws MC puppet club** (emphasis added).

Cross-Membership Between OMGs and White Supremacist Groups

The ADL report provides examples of cross-membership (names have been redacted).

_____, a Mongols MC member from El Cajon, California, was convicted in 2004 for the murder of a rival motorcycle gang member. At trial, it was revealed that he was a member of the racist prison gang, the Nazi Low Riders.

_____, a Mongols MC member, was convicted in 2008 of menacing, reckless endangering, and reckless driving after a run-in with Oregon police. Evidence at trial revealed that he was affiliated with racist skinhead groups and motorcycle gangs.

_____ is the president of the Redding, California, Vagos MC, uses the nicknames "nocalSS" and "Mysterious Psychobilly Skinhead" and is also a Hammerskin. Law enforcement authorities revealed that the Hemet, California, Vagos chapter had a high proportion of racist skinheads as members.

_____, a Christian Identity preacher, created the Riding for the Firstborn Motorcycle Ministry in Georgia. Christian Identity is a racist and anti-Semitic religious sect.

_____ was an admitted outlaw biker who became a white supremacist and was anointed to the Christian Identity ministry.

_____, a prominent white supremacist and antigovernment extremist in the 1990s and early 2000s, is now the president of the Sierra Casters MC of Mariposa, California.

_____, the leader of the Florida Outlaws MC was a Confederate Hammerskin in the 1990s.

Group Associations

In June 2006, members of the Imperial Klans of America attended the Barbarians MC Annual Biker Reunion in Ohio.

In March 2008, the Outlaws MC, Black Pistons MC, and Cobras MC participated in a St. Patrick's Day event sponsored by the Confederate Hammerskins and Blood and Honor (a racist skinhead group) in Central Florida. The event was held at the Outlaws clubhouse and attended by members of white supremacist groups such as Volksfront, White Revolution, Aryan Nations, and the Nationalist Coalition.

In September 2008, the Death's Head Hooligans, a neo-Nazi skinhead group, organized a white power music concert in Tonopah, Arizona. The event was co-sponsored by the Sons of Aesir MC, a white supremacist motorcycle club and the White Knights of America, a racist prison gang.

The White Pride Internet users group has over a 100 members including members from outlaw motorcycle clubs such as the Pagans, Hell's Angels, and Sons of Aesir.

Continued

BOX 5.11 BIGOTS ON BIKES: LINKS BETWEEN WHITE SUPREMACISTS AND BIKER GANGS—cont'd

Criminal Connections

In 2008 and 2009, nearly 30 members of the White Boys Posse, a Canadian white supremacist street gang that is also a HAMC puppet club, were arrested for drug trafficking. Canadian authorities say that the Hells Angels created the White Boys Posse to do their dirty work and insulate them from prosecution.

An Aryan Brotherhood member formed the outlaw motorcycle gang, The Order of the Blood MC, after his release from prison. The gang was formed as a criminal organization, and its criminal networks were financed and managed by the Aryan Brotherhood and the Pagans Motorcycle Gang.

Operation Silent Thunder was an 18-month investigation into a large meth ring linked to white supremacists and biker gangs in Lancaster County, California. The 2001 operation led to the arrests of prison, street, and motorcycle gang members such as the Peckerwoods, Nazi Low Riders, and the Vagos MC.

Examples of White Supremacist Biker Gangs

First Kavallerie Brigade of Aryan Nations
Supposedly have three units in Florida and Tennessee with close ties to the Florida chapter of the Outlaws MC.

Southern Brotherhood Motorcycle Club
The largest white supremacist prison gang in the Alabama Department of Corrections.

Iron Circle Motorcycle Club
This motorcycle gang is an offshoot of the Aryan Circle white supremacist prison and street gang.

Schutzstaffet Motorcycle Club
A former Klansman for Florida formed this white supremacist motorcycle club/gang. According to the ADL, the following statement appears on their website:

"We are an elite organization whose members include Germans and Aryans as Waffen—SS members and Officers. We are a regional office of the Worldwide SS and we seek to return National Socialism as the dominion of the world. Jews, Negros, White Negroes (wiggers), Gypsies, Freemasons and Homosexuals are not allowed for any reason."

Berserker Brotherhood
The Berserker Brotherhood is a relatively new motorcycle division of Temple 88, a white supremacist group that describes itself as a brotherhood of "white separatists."

Their colors have a skull in the middle of an Iron Cross, flanked on the right by the number 88.

Sons of Aesir MC
The Arizona-based Sons of Aesir (SOA) is a white supremacist biker club created in 2005. They are known to associate with the HAMC.

Confederate Calvary Corps MC
Membership is primarily from small Alabama towns and some in Missouri and Mississippi.

5150 Crew
This is a small white supremacist outlaw motorcycle gang operating in Phoenix, Arizona. 5150 is from the California legal code provision referring to people who can be involuntarily committed to a psychiatric institution—gangs adopted it as a shorthand term for "crazy." Law enforcement sources consider them to be a **Hells Angels puppet club** (emphasis added).

White Boy Society
An Illinois-based, loosely organized white supremacist biker group.

Peckerwoods MC
A small outlaw motorcycle club/gang of California white supremacists operating in the towns of Santee, Lakeside, La Mesa, and El Cajon.

Source: *Adapted from ADL (2011, September).*

BASIC ORGANIZATIONAL STRUCTURE OF OUTLAW MOTORCYCLE GANGS

Even though we can divide outlaw motorcycle gangs into the Big Five, independent, and puppet clubs, the basic organization is the same or similar. Common to almost all OMGs is the structure of laws and regulations that define their organization and administration. These laws and regulations apply at the local, national, and transnational level (see Appendix A—Bandidos By-Laws).

The most sacred rule is loyalty to the club and fellow brothers. Loyalty includes fighting for the club and for brothers, and facilitating the criminal activities of members and the club. The security review and prospecting process emphasize the value of loyalty and brotherhood. Most, particularly those who operate transnationally, have an identified body or meeting that brings together high-ranking officers to discuss rules and other matters. For the Hells Angels, it is the "world rally," others may have an international president who meets with or confers, at least through social media. The clubs maintain websites that allow for restricted use by members.

At the international or transnational level, all outlaw motorcycle gangs are organized into chapters. Each chapter is organized along a hierarchical structure often known as the "Hells Angels Model" [discussed in Chapter 4]. The model provides for a president, vice president, sergeant at arms, secretary/treasurer, and road captain. Most members belong to a chapter from a defined geographic area where they conduct their criminal activities, except for nomads chapters. Nomads chapters do not have a defined geographic area, and are usually composed of the most experienced members. However, in some gangs the nomads are the toughest or most vicious members who act as enforcers at the direction of high-ranking members. Chapters have a minimum of five or six members on the ground and riding to sustain itself as a viable chapter. If the membership falls below the minimum for any reason (arrests, resignation, death, or injury), the chapter can be frozen or disbanded.

U.S.-Based OMGs: Criminals Without Borders

KEY TERMS

Europol
Interpol
Operation DE-BADS
Operation Rocker
Project Monitor

INTERNATIONAL EXPANSION

> Italy gave the world the Mafia; Asia spawned the triads; Russia and the collapsing Soviet empire gave birth to the new eastern mob. But America gave the world the bikers.
>
> (Sher and Marsden, *Angels of Death*)

Outlaw motorcycle gangs (OMGs) have been called the "only organized crime group developed in the United States (without ethnic ties) that is being exported around the world" (Smith, 1998:54). One law enforcement expert on OMGs says that "Biker gangs are the only sophisticated organized crime groups that we export from the United States" (Trethewy & Katz, 1998). To add credence to this statement, many biker gangs have established ties and working relationships with international organized crime groups such as La Cosa Nostra, Colombian cartels, and even the Chinese triads.

As one experienced prosecutor of biker gangs put it:

> Biker gangs like the Hells Angels are nothing more than multinational corporations— and they're certainly interested in pursuing business opportunities around the world....
>
> (Pat Schneider, Assistant U.S. District Attorney, Phoenix, Arizona, quoted in Sher & Marsden, 2006:421)

The business opportunities for these biker gangs are crimes for profit. Interlocking networks with indigenous OMGs in other countries allowed U.S.-based OMGs to link common criminal enterprises and the benefits derived from these, allowing these gangs to enter the global marketplace of crime. Although exported U.S.-based OMGs are a major crime threat worldwide, indigenous OMGs from Australia, Canada, and Europe are also crime threats within their own boundaries and transnationally—they are "criminals Without borders."

INTERNATIONAL ORGANIZATIONS: INTERPOL AND EUROPOL

Organized criminal networks have become more complex, diverse, and international in recent years, requiring new approaches and coordination and cooperation between and among law enforcement throughout the world. **Interpol** and **Europol** are the keys to this coordination and cooperation and the disruption of international organized criminal networks, including OMGs. International organizations such as Interpol, Europol, and the United Nations recognize the criminal potential of U.S.-based OMGs. Interpol includes OMGs with Mafia-type organized crime organizations exhibiting highly structured hierarchies, internal rules of discipline, codes of ethics [sic], and diversity of illegal and legitimate affairs (Kendall, 1998). Interpol (see Box 6.1) recognized the international expansion of U.S.-based outlaw motorcycle clubs in the early 1980s and declared them to be international crime threats, that is, OMGs.

BOX 6.1 INTERPOL

Interpol is the world's largest international police organization, with 184 member countries. Created in 1923, it facilitates cross-border police cooperation and supports and assists all organizations, authorities, and services whose mission is to prevent or combat international crime.

Interpol's Three Core Functions
Secure Global Police Communications Services
Interpol runs a global police communication system called I-24/7, which provides police around the world with a common platform through which they can share information about criminals and criminality.

Operational Data Services and Databases for Police
Interpol's databases and services ensure that police worldwide have access to the information and services they need to prevent and investigate crime. Databases include data on criminals such as names, fingerprints, and DNA profiles, and stolen property such as passports, vehicles, and works of art.

Operational Police Support Services
Interpol supports law enforcement officials in the field with emergency support and operational activities, especially in its priority crime areas of fugitives, public safety and terrorism, drugs, organized crime, trafficking in human beings, and financial and high-tech crime. A Command and Coordination Center operates 24 h, seven days a week.

Source: *Interpol. See www.interpol.int/Public/icpo/about.asp.*

Interpol

In May 1984, Interpol convened a meeting on motorcycle gangs in St. Cloud, France. Law enforcement authorities from eight countries (Canada, Denmark, France, West Germany, the Netherlands, Switzerland, the United Kingdom, and the United States) attended this meeting (Interpol, 1984). A 1984 report from the General Secretariat of Interpol reported that the Hells Angels MC and the Outlaws MC had chapters in Canada and were involved in organized crime activities (Interpol, 1984). The report stated that the Hells Angels were the only motorcycle gang with chapters in 11 countries (seven Western European countries), Great Britain, West Germany, the Netherlands, Denmark, Switzerland, France, Austria, Australia, New Zealand, Canada, and the United States. Since that time, the Angels have expanded internationally, and other U.S. OMGs have established chapters in numerous countries outside the United States. Furthermore, indigenous OMGs from Australia, Canada, and Europe have now expanded outside their home countries, even into the United States.

Operation Rocker

In 1991, Interpol created **Operation Rocker** to deal with the rapid expansion of U.S.-based OMGs throughout the world (Smith, 1998). Named after the banner on the top and bottom of the club's colors, Project Rocker (no longer in existence) had the following objectives:

- to identify motorcycle gangs that are engaged in continuous criminal activity
- to identify each gang's membership, hierarchy, modus operandi, and specific criminal activity
- to correlate the information for analysis and dissemination
- to assist member countries in the exchange of criminal intelligence information, and
- to identify specific contact officers within the NCBs [Interpol's National Central Bureau in member countries] and law enforcement agencies having expertise with OMGs.

In 2000, in addition to the United States, there were 28 countries cooperating in Operation Rocker. These countries included all those with Hells Angels chapters. A *Project Rocker Newsletter* was initiated in 1998 (McClure, 2000). The newsletter contained international OMG activities from NCB reports and other intelligence sources. There was also a yearly meeting of those involved in the effort. Operation Rocker had some success in dealing with OMGs, but it did not stop their expansion.

Europol

Europol, the European Union's law enforcement organization that handles criminal intelligence, in its 2005 *EU Organized Crime Report*, states that the three main OMGs throughout Europe are the Hells Angels, the Bandidos, and the Outlaws (Europol, 2005; see Boxes 6.2 and 6.3). A 2010 policy brief reports that outlaw motorcycle club gangs (OMCGs—EU term) have been detected across the entire European continent, except in Cyprus (OC-Scan Policy Brief for Threat Notice: 002-2010). The EU report says that members of these gangs are involved in drugs (cocaine, synthetic drugs, and cannabis), stolen vehicle trafficking, and exploitation of prostitutes. Finland and Sweden also reported OMGs were involved in firearms trafficking. Europol says that these gangs use extreme violence, including intergroup violence, as the gangs battle each other for territory, as well as intraclub violence used to maintain discipline and compliance from club members and associates. The use of violence also expands outside the gangs in their extortion operations. Europol reported that the use of violence and intimidation against law enforcement agents by OMGs is a serious problem in Sweden.

BOX 6.2 EUROPOL

Mission

Europol is the European law enforcement organization that handles criminal intelligence. Its aim is to improve the effectiveness and cooperation between the competent authorities of the member states in preventing and combating serious international organized crime and terrorism. Its role is to help achieve a safer Europe for the benefit of all EU citizens by supporting EU law enforcement authorities through the exchange and analysis of criminal intelligence.

Mandate

Europol supports the law enforcement activities of the member states mainly against:

Drugs

Support includes the coordination and initiation of criminal drug investigations as well as on-the-spot assistance to EU law enforcement agencies during the dismantling of illicit drug producing facilities and collation of evidence.

Operation DE-BADS

Scope Belgium police started an investigation into a Belgium-Dutch criminal group who were very active in producing and trafficking synthetic drugs. After police seized 62 kg of amphetamine in the Ghent area of Belgium, it became clear that those drugs were destined for a local organized criminal motorcycle gang. In close cooperation with the Dutch police, the two forces then identified a possible production site in Tilburg, the Netherlands. As a result of the cooperation, arrests were made and substantial quantities of drugs were seized.

Results

- Twelve arrests were made: nine in Belgium and three in the Netherlands for extradition to Belgium.
- Houses were searched in Belgium, and 36 kg of amphetamines found.
- Ten more house searches resulted in the dismantling and seizure of two cannabis nurseries, 1 kg of amphetamine, 100 ecstasy tablets, and 5 liters of amphetamine oil.
- Dutch police seized half a kilo of cocaine, 30 kg of ecstasy tablets (150,000 tablets), 5 kg of ecstasy powder, and 720 lbs of chemicals for the production of ecstasy tablets.

Trafficking in Human Beings

In 2011, Europol actively supported 22 high-level human trafficking investigations. In some of these cases, on-the-spot operational support was provided via the mobile office.

BOX 6.2 EUROPOL—cont'd

Facilitated Illegal Immigration
Europol supported nine major European operations targeting criminal networks facilitating illegal immigration in 2011.

Europol Cyber Crime Centre
Europol's High Tech Crime Centre was established in 2002 and was broadened to incorporate expertise in further specialist areas within the Europol Cyber Crime Centre in 2011. This move enables online crime specialists to provide more targeted and effective countermeasures in the areas of child sexual exploitation, payment card fraud, and cybercrime—crime areas in which the Internet plays a key role.

Intellectual Property Crime
Europol is involved in support, training, and awareness for the member states in the field of intellectual property rights (IPR) infringement that covers such areas as counterfeit food and pesticides.

Cigarette Smuggling
Europol supports law enforcement agencies in the struggle against the illegal manufacture and distribution of cigarettes and tobacco products, which costs the EU about ten billion Euros annually in lost revenues.

Euro Counterfeiting
VAT Fraud
It is estimated that value-added tax (VAT) fraud costs EU member states approximately 60 billion Euros annually.

Money Laundering and Asset Tracking
Organized crime generates massive illicit revenues, and Europol provides support to member states in the areas of preventing and combating money laundering, as well as tracking criminal assets.

Mobile Organized Crime Groups
Mobile organized crime groups (MOCGs) have increasingly come to the public attention, and they are primarily involved in property crime and fraud.

Outlaw Motorcycle Gangs
Europol's specialist Project Monitor helps prevent and combat the criminal activities of outlaw motorcycle gangs (OMCGs). The U.S.-based Hells Angels MC has become a worldwide crime problem and the number one criminal organization among all European outlaw motorcycle gangs (European Police Office, 2012).

HAMC Expansion by Continent 2005-2011

North America	
2005—108 chapters	2011—103 chapters
Central/South America	
2005—6	2011—18
Europe	
2005—120	2011—209

Continued

BOX 6.2 EUROPOL—cont'd

South Africa

2005—5	2011—6

Asia

2011—1

Australia and New Zealand

2005—12	2011—17

HAMC Worldwide Expansion 1940-2011

1940—1 chapter
1950—3
1960—16
1970—20
1980—66
1990—153
2000—288
2011—351

Project Monitor

To counter the threat presented by outlaw motorcycle gangs (OMCGs), Europol's **Project Monitor** helps prevent and combat the criminal activities of OMCGs such as the Hells Angels MC, Bandidos MC, Outlaws MC, and their support motorcycle clubs. There are 15 member states participating in this project who view OMCGS as a national threat and a policing priority. The project follows a multidisciplinary and horizontal approach, focusing on the organized crime groups rather than just on the crime phenomena inherent to OMCGs by:

- Identifying the structures and members of these OMCGs
- Revealing the meaning of new phenomena within this subculture and detecting new trends through strategic analysis
- Initiating, promoting, and coordinating new operational activities with operational analysis
- Supporting partners in policing major biker events, such as the 2011 HAMC World Run in Laconia, USA, and other operational activities through the use of Europol's mobile office
- Organizing OMCGs training courses throughout Europe
- Providing high-level support to law enforcement management, and judicial and government authorities
- Supporting the European Platform for Gang Experts, which is a unique environment for sharing strategic information, best practices, expertise, and knowledge amongst law enforcement officers who are active in combating outlaw motorcycle, street, and other similar gangs

Terrorism

In 2011, Europol continued to assist member states in their fight against terrorism by providing them with a range of products and services.

Source: *Adapted from www.europa.eu and European Police Office, 2012.*

BOX 6.3 BASIC FACTS ABOUT EUROPOL (2011)

Headquarters
The Hague
The Netherlands
Staff
777 personnel at headquarters
including 145 Europol liaison officers

Every member state seconds at least one liaison officer to Europol, who is hosted at the headquarters in their own liaison bureau. The liaison bureau represents the interests of their country at Europol. These liaison officers play a role in law enforcement activities by the exchange of information, as well as providing support and coordination for ongoing operations. Europol has established channels of communication with Interpol. Europol has two liaison officers seconded to Washington, D.C., and one to Interpol's headquarters in Lyon, France. Europol also hosts liaison officers from ten non-EU countries and has cooperative relationships with U.S. law enforcement agencies—Albania, Australia, Colombia, Croatia, Iceland, Norway, Switzerland, Interpol, and the United States of America. U.S. law enforcement agencies—Bureau of Alcohol, Tobacco, Firearms and Explosives (ATF), Drug Enforcement Administration (DEA), Secret Service (USSS), Federal Bureau of Investigation (FBI), Immigration and Customs Enforcement (ICE), and Internal Revenue Service (IRS).

Budget
EUR 84.8 million
Servicing
27 EU member states, 500 million EU citizens

Europol has a live 24/7 connection with the Europol national units in all 27 EU member states and organizes regular awareness and training events, road shows, and seminars to enhance knowledge of its services and expertise. All Europol databases and services are available 24 hours a day, seven days a week.

Supporting
13,697 cross-border law enforcement cases

Source: *European Police Office, 2012.*

As in the United States, the European OMGs use legitimate means to mask the criminal nature of their groups. They register their clubs as legal associations or even foundations; they protect their "colors" as registered trademarks, and sue companies that misuse them. The gangs sell support merchandise and engage in legitimate businesses. The Europol report concludes with the statement:

> Outlaw motorcycle gangs are present in force in the Nordic countries, Germany, and Belgium, but they are expanding their activities to the new member states with the support of existing gangs in Russia and Eastern Europe. They are involved in a variety of crimes such as drug trafficking, smuggling of commodities and illegal prostitution. They have no scruples about using violence.
>
> (Europol, 2005:31)

The 2010 Threat Notice mentioned earlier reported that the HAMC has expanded significantly into Eastern Europe, including Bulgaria, Croatia, Czech Republic, Greece, Hungary, Poland, and Turkey.

Europol Information System (EIS)

The main objective of the Europol Information System (EIS) is to be a reference system for offenses, involved individuals, and other data to support member states, Europol, and cooperating partners in their fight against organized crime, terrorism, and other forms of serious crime. In 2011, Germany provided the most data into the EIS, followed by Belgium, France, Spain, and Europol (on behalf of third parties) (see Box 6.4).

BOX 6.4 EUROPOL INFORMATION SYSTEM (EIS) 2011

Content
183,240 objects
41,193 "persons" entities
(An increase of 5% on 2010)
Major crime areas
Drug trafficking (25% of all objects)
Trafficking in human beings (23%)
Forgery of money (18%)
Robbery (10%)
Fraud and swindling (5%)
Usage
111,110 searches were run through the system

Source: *European Police Office, 2012.*

U.S.-BASED BIKER GANGS WITH CHAPTERS OUTSIDE THE CONTINENTAL UNITED STATES

According to the official club/gang 2010 websites, there are seven U.S.-based biker gangs with 484 chapters located in countries outside the United States (see Table 6.1). They are the Hells Angels, Bandidos, Outlaws, Mongols, Vagos, Warlocks, and the Sons of Silence. As testament to their international expansion, the Hells Angels, Bandidos, and Outlaws now have more chapters outside the United States than inside—Hells Angels: 64 U.S. chapters, 183 outside the United States; Outlaws: 93 U.S. chapters, 161 outside the United States; Bandidos: 102 U.S. chapters, 125 outside the United States (see Tables 6.1 and 6.2).

These chapters are located in 41 countries around the globe. Germany, with 116 chapters, has the largest U.S.-based biker gang presence, with chapters of the Hells Angels, Bandidos, Outlaws, Sons of Silence, and the Warlocks (see Table 6.1). England/Wales is next, with 40 chapters of Hells Angels and Outlaws and one Warlocks chapter. Canada has 37 chapters of Hells Angels and Outlaws. There were two Bandidos chapters until one chapter killed eight members of the other chapter and the U.S. Bandidos disbanded the surviving chapter members after they were convicted of the murders. The Mongols claim to have a chapter in Canada, but there is no evidence to support the claim. It appears to be a ploy to rattle the Canadian

Hells Angels, the dominant biker gang in Canada. France has 36 chapters of Hells Angels, Outlaws, and Bandidos. Australia has 30 chapters of Hells Angels, Bandidos, and Outlaws. The remaining chapters are spread throughout Europe and Asia with a concentration of U.S.-based biker gangs in the Nordic countries of Denmark, Finland, Sweden, and Norway (see Table 6.2).

Table 6.1 U.S.-Based Biker Gangs Outside the Continental United States by Country—2010

1. Argentina 3	22. Italy 6
2. Australia 30	23. Japan (Okinawa) 1
3. Austria 7	24. Liechtenstein 1
4. Belgium 20	25. Luxembourg 1
5. Bohemia 2	26. Malaysia 1
6. Brazil 3	27. Mexico 4
7. Canada 37	28. Northern Ireland 1
8. Channel Islands 2	29. New Zealand 2
9. Chile 1	30. Norway 24
10. Costa Rica 1	31. Portugal 3
11. Croatia 1	32. Philippines 1
12. Denmark 23	33. Poland 7
13. Dominican Rep. 1	34. Russia 13
14. England/Wales 40	35. Singapore 1
15. Finland 10	36. South Africa 5
16. France 36	37. Spain 7
17. Germany 116	38. Sweden 25
18. Greece 1	39. Switzerland 6
19. Hungary 1	40. Thailand 7
20. Holland 9	41. Turkey 1
21. Ireland 9	Total—484

Table 6.2 U.S.-Based Gangs by Chapters—U.S. and Outside Continental United States (CONUS)

Gang	United States	Outside CONUS
Hells Angels	64	183
Outlaws	93	161
Bandidos	102	125
Mongols	76	3
Vagos	24	3
Sons of Silence	13	6
Warlocks	13	2
Total	385	484

U.S.-based outlaw motorcycle clubs have evolved into OMGs and have expanded their reach and criminal activities outside the United States (see Figures 6.1 and 6.2). The international expansion of the U.S.-based biker gangs has had a profound effect on the nature and composition of many clubs, particularly the Hells Angels, Bandidos, and the Outlaws. Each of these gangs has more chapters and members outside the United States than it does inside the United States. Often, new international members do not meet the established criteria for membership; for example, there are instances where some members do not even own motorcycles or are former police officers. The international chapters have gained in influence and power. All new Hells Angels full-patch members must be approved by the Hells Angels council meeting at the yearly international run. The U.S. Bandidos only approved the Canadian Bandidos chapters that were to cause the Bandido Nation so much grief after pressure from their European allies. The gangs hold regional, national, and international meetings attended by the key officers—presidents, vice-presidents, sergeants at arms, and secretary/treasurers. At these meetings, major policies and procedures are set, and chapters are approved or disbanded, members are approved, and criminal activities are planned.

FIGURE 6.1

"1%er" symbol shown at a clubhouse of the Bandidos MC chapter in Berlin, Germany.

Photo courtesy of Oliver Wolters, en.wikipedia.org.

FIGURE 6.2

"1%er" symbol shown at a clubhouse of the Hells Angels MC chapter in Karlsruhe, Germany.

Photo courtesy of Michael Kaufmann, en.wikipedia.org.

U.S.-based biker gangs have become more criminal as they and their drug links as they have expanded beyond U.S. borders. They have become more violent toward each other as they fight over territory and drug markets, and have become serious organized crime threats in their new host countries. This expansion and spread of organized crime activities and violence is ongoing and leading other U.S.-based OMGs to consider establishing chapters outside the United States.

The Hells Are No Angels: Organized Crime, Death, and Mayhem in Canada

KEY TERMS

Bandidos Massacre

Bill C-95

Canadian Biker War

Criminal Intelligence Service Canada (CISC)

No Surrender Crew

Operation SPRINGTIME

OPP (Ontario Provincial Police) Biker Enforcement Unit

INTRODUCTION

Motorcycle gangs in Canada (see Figure 7.1)—indigenous and U.S.-based—are extremely violent, engaging in intergang, intragang, and gratuitous violence on nongang members, including criminal justice officials, reporters, and, on occasion, innocent civilians. For the most part, Canadian one-percent motorcycle clubs are criminal gangs and not clubs. This is especially true for the U.S.-based clubs—Hells Angels, Bandidos, and Outlaws—that have established chapters in Canada.

> I am satisfied beyond a reasonable doubt that one of the main purposes or activities of the Hells Angels Motorcycle Club in Canada is the facilitation of serious offences including trafficking in cocaine and other drugs, extortion and trafficking in firearms.
>
> Ontario Superior Court Justice John McMahon in sentencing the president of the Ontario Hells Angels (Edwards, 2008, December 26)

In Canada, the Hells Angels MC (HAMC) is the supreme biker gang and without a doubt an extremely violent criminal organization. One diminutive Hells Angels killing machine, Yves "Apache" Trudeau, murdered 43 persons and was involved in the murders of 40 others. The Hells Angels are the number-one organized crime threat in the country. They are also the most criminal motorcycle gang in the world. They are a criminal organization engaged in a variety of organized criminal activities. As an indication of the criminal activity of the Canadian Hells Angels and other Canadian motorcycle clubs/gangs, the Sûreté du Quebec determined that

Quebec Hells Angels had $18 million in drug sales from November 10 to December 19, 2000 (Cherry, 2005:168). The sales included 1916 kg of cocaine for a profit of more than $8 million. They also moved 838 kg of hashish during that period for a profit of $680,000. The largest North American police force devoted exclusively to outlaw motorcycle gangs is the hundred-officer Ontario Biker Enforcement Unit.

FIGURE 7.1

Canada.

Map courtesy of Bruce Jones Design Inc.

The United States' neighbor to the north saw the first expansion of U.S.-based biker gangs when the Hells Angels established a chapter outside Montreal on December 5, 1977. The first 17 members of this new Hells Angels chapter came from a violent Montreal motorcycle gang, Popeyes, who were on friendly terms with the New York Hells Angels (Cherry, 2005). Apache Trudeau, a five-foot-six, 145-pound psychopathic drug addict, was a co-founder of this chapter. Looking into his soulless eyes one can see that no one is home.

It is possible to trace the growth and activities of the U.S.-based OMGs through the annual reports of the Criminal Intelligence Service Canada.

CRIMINAL INTELLIGENCE SERVICE CANADA

The **Criminal Intelligence Service Canada (CISC)** unites "the criminal intelligence units of Canadian law enforcement agencies in the fight against organized crime and other serious crime in Canada" (www.cisc.gc.ca). The CISC is composed of a Central Bureau, located in the capital of Ottawa, and a system of nine Provincial

Bureaus located in each of the Canadian provinces of Alberta, British Columbia, Manitoba, New Brunswick, Newfoundland and Labrador, Nova Scotia, Ontario, Quebec, and Saskatchewan. The Province of Prince Edward Island is served by the Criminal Intelligence Service Nova Scotia; and the territories of Yukon, Northwest, and Nunavut are served by Criminal Intelligence Service Alberta and Criminal Intelligence Service Ontario, respectively (CISC, 2005:i).

There are two levels of membership in the CISC. Level I members are federal, provincial, regional, or municipal police services and agencies that are responsible for the enforcement of federal and provincial statutes and have a permanent criminal intelligence unit. Level II members are agencies who are responsible for the enforcement of federal or provincial statutes but cannot meet other qualifications (e.g., they may not have a permanent intelligence unit). The intelligence units "supply their Provincial Bureaus with criminal intelligence and raw data related to organized and serious crime... for further analysis and dissemination" (www.cisc.gc.ca).

Every year the CISC issues an Annual Report on Organized Crime "to inform and educate the public." The CISC seeks to elicit the public's help in partnership with law enforcement agencies. The CISC believes that: "One of the keys to success in the fight against organized crime is a partnership between law enforcement agencies as well as with policy makers and the public" (CISC, 2005:iii). The reports provide information on a number of organized crime groups in Canada (aboriginal-based, Asian-based, Eastern European, outlaw motorcycle gangs, and Italian-based). The annual reports for 1997 through 2005 are summarized here. The format for the CISC reports was changed with the 2005 annual report.

CISC Annual Report—1997

In 1996, there were 38 OMGs in Canada with the Hells Angels being the largest and best organized. They were in every province, except Ontario. This was surprising because Ontario had the largest number of OMGs (13) and a lucrative drug trade. Law enforcement authorities said that the Angels were too busy fighting with the Rock Machine, an indigenous motorcycle gang, in Quebec to set up a chapter in Ontario. The war with the Rock Machine had started over drug-trafficking markets in Montreal and other parts of the Province of Quebec. The Biker War that started in 1994 had so far claimed 50 victims. There were 57 attempts, or conspiracies, to commit murder and 40 bombings and/or cases of arson. The highlights of the CISC 1997 annual report are listed in Box 7.1.

CISC Annual Report—1998

There were still 38 known OMGs in Canada, with the Hells Angels being the most powerful and well organized. The Biker War was still going on in Quebec with 68 dead thus far. In a move to find allies in their battle with the Angels, members of the Rock Machine had contacted both the Bandidos and the Outlaws about possible membership and it was believed that the Bandidos had granted hangaround status to the Rock Machine. The OMGs were still heavily involved in drug trafficking. In the spring of 1997, the Sûreté du Quebec [Quebec Provincial Police] disrupted three marijuana hydroponic operations in Montreal. The Hells Angels ran one, and an Angel puppet club, the Death Riders, ran the other two.

BOX 7.1 1997 CISC HIGHLIGHTS

Highlights

- The Hells Angels remain one of the most powerful and organized criminal groups in Canada.
- Drug trafficking is the most lucrative activity of outlaw motorcycle gangs. This is especially true of the Hells Angels who, with the support of their affiliated clubs [puppet clubs] have taken over the distribution and sale of drugs such as cocaine, cannabis, LSD, and PCP. Furthermore, the Hells Angels are involved in the hydroponic cultivation of marijuana.
- The armed conflict between the Hells Angels and the Rock Machine still rages in the province of Quebec.
- The Hells Angels have moved into Alberta and forged ahead with their plans for expansion into the provinces of Saskatchewan, Manitoba, and Ontario.

Source: *CISC Annual Report on Organized Crime in Canada—1997.*

The Quebec Hells Angels began a campaign of intimidation against the provincial criminal justice system resulting in the destruction of 13 police vehicles and the murder of two correctional officers. The president of the Nomads chapter of the Quebec Hells Angels, Maurice "Mom" Boucher, was arrested and charged with the murder of the two correctional officers.

Law enforcement authorities moved against Satan's Choice MC, an indigenous OMG, arresting 135 members and associates on more than 1,085 charges. Authorities also investigated the St. Catherine's chapter of the Outlaws MC, arresting the chapter president and former national president, eventually bringing drug trafficking and weapons charges. Several indigenous OMGs, Winnipeg-based Los Bravos MC, the Saskatoon-based Alberta Rebels MC, and the Alberta Grim Reapers MC, patched over to the HAMC.

The five British Columbia (BC) Hells Angels chapters—the wealthiest Angels' chapters in the world—controlled the drug trade in the province, particularly the hydroponic cultivation of marijuana. This marijuana, known as "BC Bud," was exported to the United States, where it is sold and swapped for cocaine, crystal meth, and firearms. The BC Angels were also in the production of live sex (pornography) over the Internet. The highlights of the 1998 CISC annual report are listed in Box 7.2.

CISC Annual Report—1999

As a result of patching over (the process of inviting OMG members to give up their patch/club and accept a new one/club) indigenous motorcycle gangs by U.S.-based OMGs—Hells Angels, Bandidos, and Outlaws—there were now 30 [sic] known OMGs in Canada. CISC reports that the Hells Angels have 214 patched members and 35 prospects. Of these members, 205 had criminal records; 105 of the records were for drug-related offenses. The B.C. Angels created a new chapter and increased their hydroponic marijuana trade. The Alberta HAs disbanded the indigenous King's Crew MC (only two members were allowed to patch over to the Angels) and took over all biker-related criminal activities in Alberta. Forty-five of the 46 members of the Alberta Hells Angels had criminal records, with 25 of them having been convicted of serious crimes.

BOX 7.2 1998 CISC HIGHLIGHTS

Highlights

- The Hells Angels are still one of the most powerful and well-structured criminal organizations in Canada. In 1997, they continued to grow and added three new chapters to the 11 that already existed across the country.
- Drug trafficking remains their primary and most lucrative criminal activity.
- The armed conflict between the Hells Angels and the Rock Machine still rages in the province of Quebec.

Source: *CISC Annual Report on Organized Crime—1998.*

The Manitoba Los Bravos MC had been in existence for 30 years and was expected to become a Hells Angels club during the year. Ontario still had the most OMGs: nine, down from 13 in 1997. The Angels still had the goal of establishing a chapter in the province once the Biker War was over. In Ontario, the indigenous Para-Dice Riders MC were the most prosperous, and the Satan's Choice MC were most involved in criminal activities—fencing stolen goods, auto theft, insurance and credit card fraud, tractor trailer thefts, and smuggling. CISC also reported that Satan's Choice members worked with traditional organized crime (Italian-based) members in extortion and debt collection as well as firearms and narcotics distribution. In London, Ontario, indigenous OMG members killed two prominent members of the Outlaws MC in turf wars.

In the province of Quebec, the Hells Angels now had six chapters and a vicious Nomads chapter and seven puppet clubs. The Biker War between the Angels and the Rock Machine still continuied. There were now 103 homicides, 124 murder attempts, nine missing persons, 84 bombings, and 130 incidents of arson, for a total of 450 violent incidents since 1994. The 1999 CISC annual report highlights are listed in Box 7.3.

BOX 7.3 1999 CISC HIGHLIGHTS

Highlights

- The Hells Angels are one of the most powerful and well-structured criminal organizations in Canada. In 1998, they formed two new chapters: one in British Columbia and one in Saskatchewan, for a national total of 16 chapters.
- The armed conflict between the Hells Angels and the Rock Machine is still raging in Quebec. In 1998, there were 27 related homicides and 27 murder attempts.

Source: *1999 Annual Report on Organized Crime—1999.*

CISC Annual Report—2000

OMGs, especially the Hells Angels MC, were a national priority for Canadian law enforcement during the year. OMGs were reported to be involved in a long list of crimes: importation and distribution of cocaine, the production and distribution of methamphetamines, the cultivation and exportation of high-grade marijuana, illegal trafficking of firearms and explosives, the collection of protection money from both legitimate and illegitimate business operations, fraud, money laundering, and prostitution.

There were a number of significant law enforcement actions against OMGs during the year. In British Columbia, there were two trials going on against HA members. One involved Haney chapter members charged with three counts of cocaine trafficking. The other trial involved East End HA chapter members charged with conspiracy to traffic cocaine, trafficking cocaine, and laundering proceeds of crime. Members and associates of the Edmonton Rebels MC pleaded guilty to drug-trafficking offenses. In Quebec, the police dismantled a Hells Angels drug ring with the arrest of 34 members and associates. Quebec police arrested ten of the 11 members of a Hells Angels puppet club, Blatnois Maurice MC, and they were going to use this arrest to test the new **Bill C-95** anti-gang legislation (see Box 7.4). A Calgary Hells Angels MC member was charged with a plot to cause serious harm to a Calgary alderman, a city hall staff member, and a member of a community association. The latter charges arose out of the destruction of the HA Calgary clubhouse for noncompliance with local building codes.

BOX 7.4 BILL C-95—ANTI-GANG LEGISLATION

Canadian police agencies, pointing to the United States RICO (Racketeer Influenced and Corrupt Organizations) law pressured Parliament for a similar law. In April 1997, Parliament amended the Criminal Code to prevent and deter the commission of criminal activity by criminal organizations and their members, such as outlaw motorcycle gangs.

The Act defines a "criminal organization" as any group, association, or other body consisting of five or more persons whether formally or informally organized (later changed to three or more members)

(a) having as one of its primary activities the commission of an indictable offense under this or any other Acts of Parliament for which the punishment is for five years or more, and

(b) any or all members of which engage in, or have within the preceding five years engaged in, the commission of a serious offense.

The Act does not make membership in a criminal organization a criminal offense in Canadian law, but rather, the commission of crimes within a criminal organization framework.

The new amendments include:

- A new offense—participation in a criminal organization with a penalty of up to 14 years in jail
- Greater police discretion in using electronic surveillance against gangs for up to a year compared with the previous 60 days
- Expanded proceeds of crime laws to allow seizure of all proceeds from gang-related offenses
- Additions to the Criminal Code concerning the use of explosives in criminal gang activity

BOX 7.4 BILL C-95—ANTI-GANG LEGISLATION—cont'd

- A new peace bond, designed to target gang leadership, would allow a judge to prohibit associating or communicating with other gang members
- A change in bail provisions; anyone charged with a gang-related offense would be held without bail until trial, unless he/she could show why detention was not justified
- Tougher sentencing
- New sentencing provisions in the Criminal Code aimed at delaying parole eligibility for certain organized gang offenses.

Source: RCMP (1999).

Although the Hells Angels still did not have a chapter in Ontario, the CISC reported that the majority of the OMGs in the province did business with the Angels, though, of course, the Rock Machine did not do business with them. Ontario now had 11 OMGs—up two from the year before—including the Para-Dice Riders MC, Outlaws MC, Satan's Choice MC, and the Rock Machine MC. It appeared that the Hells Angels were trying to patch over the Para-Dice Riders MC to form the first HA chapter in Ontario. Box 7.5 presents the 2000 CISC highlights.

BOX 7.5 2000 CISC HIGHLIGHTS

Highlights
- The Hells Angels remain one of the most powerful and well-structured criminal organizations in Canada. In 1999, they formed two new chapters, bringing the total to 18 chapters nationally.
- The armed conflict, which started in 1994 between the Hells Angels and the Rock Machine in Quebec, continues.

Source: CISC Annual Report on Organized Crime—2000.

CISC Annual Report—2001

The Hells Angels retained their status as the largest and most criminally active OMG in Canada. The Angels finally established a chapter in the Province of Ontario by patching over the Satan's Choice MC and the Last Chance MC. The Angels also patched over the Edmonton Rebels MC and the Winnipeg-based Los Bravos MC. The Bandidos countered the expansion of the Hells Angels in Ontario by making the Rock Machine probationary Bandidos on December 1, 2000, and patching over the Loners MC. They also established two probationary Bandidos chapters in Montreal and Quebec City. The Outlaws retained their seven chapters in Ontario.

In 2001, members of the British Columbia Hells Angels were convicted for the first time for a serious crime: trafficking in cocaine. Two members of the Vancouver Hells Angels chapter were convicted of conspiring with four other men to traffic in cocaine, trafficking in cocaine, and possession of the proceeds of crime. In a test of the Bill C-95 Anti-Gang Law, four members of the Rock Machine were found guilty of gangsterism.

The Hells Angels continued their intimidation of nongang members and threats of violence. A prosecutor in the British Columbia Angels case was approached by two men and had his life threatened. The ex-president of the Calgary Hells Angels was found guilty of two counts of counseling mischief and two counts of common assault in the 1999 plot to bomb the homes of an alderman and a community activist. A crime reporter for the *Journal de Montreal* was shot five times but survived. He had just completed a series of stories on the deaths and disappearances of Hells Angels and Mafia members as a result of drug-trafficking conflicts. The Edmonton police discovered that the Hells Angels were conducting counter-surveillance and intelligence on them.

It appeared that the Biker War was over in Quebec when Hells Angels and Rock Machine leaders and their lawyers met at the Quebec City courthouse and declared a public truce in October 2001. The truce lasted two months, until the Rock Machine became probationary Bandidos, bitter enemies of the Angels. Sporadic violence broke out again. See Box 7.6 for the 2001 CISC highlights.

BOX 7.6 2001 CISC HIGHLIGHTS

Highlights

- The year 2000 saw dramatic growth for the Hells Angels as chapters were formed in Manitoba and Ontario. The Bandidos patched over the Rock Machine as probationary members (one step below full membership) in December 2000.
- OMGs in Canada continue to use violence, ranging from intimidation and assault to attempted murder and murder.
- OMGs continue to associate with street gangs and other organized groups at the regional, national, and international levels.

Source: *CISC Annual Report on Organized Crime—2001.*

CISC Annual Report—2002

The CISC reports that OMGs, particularly the Hells Angels, are engaged in a wide variety of criminal activities: money laundering, intimidation, assaults, attempted murder, murder, fraud, theft, counterfeiting, extortion, prostitution, escort agencies/strip clubs, after-hours clubs (selling alcohol illegally), and the possessing and trafficking of illegal-weapons, stolen goods, and contraband.

The Hells Angels remained the largest and most criminally active OMG in Canada. Through the patching over of indigenous biker gangs and active expansion, the Angels had 35 chapters, up from 14 in 1998. CISC reports the gang continues to be involved in the importation and trafficking of cocaine, the cultivation and exportation of high-grade marijuana, and, to a lesser extent, the production and trafficking of methamphetamine, and the trafficking of ecstasy and other illicit synthetic drugs. The British Columbia Angels were criminally active in the province's marine ports and smuggling contraband, including drugs, into and out of Canada through the ports. They had developed criminal alliances with Italian crime families and were forming alliances with Asian-based crime groups.

In Quebec, the Hells Angels continued their intimidation of witnesses and criminal justice officials. One witness home was firebombed, and the home of another witness was fired on with a shotgun. A former gang unit police officer had her vehicle torched and her residence firebombed twice. Members and associates appeared in court in "colors" in an attempt to intimidate witnesses, police officers, and members of the justice system.

The U.S.-based motorcycle gangs took over the province of Ontario by patching over the indigenous OMGs, violently disbanding others, and establishing new chapters. The Hells Angels had 14 chapters in 2001 and one prospect chapter in Ontario, up from zero in 1996. The Outlaws MC had 10 chapters, and the Bandidos MC had formed two chapters in Ontario. There were several incidents of violence between the Angels and the other two gangs. The CISC also reported that the three gangs had formed alliances with street gangs to perform lower-level criminal activities and security duties.

The Biker War continued between the Hells Angels and the Bandidos (Rock Machine patched over in 2001) with two civilian deaths, in addition to seven biker murders. A teenager was killed when he was caught in the crossfire outside a bar, and an innocent man was killed when his car was bombed after being confused with that of a Bandidos member. There were also 26 arsons in bars and clubs associated with the Angels.

Mom Boucher, the infamous leader of the Quebec Hells Angels Nomads, was retried on charges of ordering the murders of two prison guards as well as the attempted murder of another in 1997. In his first trial, Boucher was acquitted, but the prosecution appealed and was allowed to retry him, a move allowed in Canada but not in the United States. Boucher was found guilty on all three counts and must serve 25 years before being eligible for parole. He is currently appealing this conviction.

There were several important law enforcement actions against OMGs throughout the provinces. Operation SHADOW shut down seven methamphetamine labs in Calgary, Alberta; Kelowna, Vancouver; and the Fraser Valley in British Columbia. In Ontario, Operation WOLF against the Bandidos resulted in 149 charges against 27 members and associates for hijacking and stealing cargo truckloads of merchandise. Drugs, weapons, and $3 million in stolen property were recovered. Project AMIGO targeted the Bandidos in Ontario and Quebec. Sixty-two arrest warrants were issued for offenses ranging from conspiracy to commit murder to trafficking in drugs (cocaine, heroin, ecstasy, and marijuana). CISC reports that the entire Bandidos Montreal chapter and half of the Bandidos Quebec City chapter were arrested. The Bandidos national president was also arrested. Operation 4-H resulted in the arrests of 55 members and associates of the Quebec City Hells Angels and the New Brunswick Dammers MC (puppet club). The charges were conspiracy to traffic in cocaine, ecstasy, and marijuana, and conspiracy to launder the proceeds of crime. The operation identified a national drug network with drugs imported from British Columbia and Quebec into Atlantic Canada. Operation HAMMER led to the arrests of 20 individuals with ties to the Halifax Hells Angels. See Box 7.7 for the 2002 CISC highlights.

BOX 7.7 2002 CISC HIGHLIGHTS

Highlights

- Across Canada, there have been a number of incidents of intimidation by OMGs and their affiliates against victims, witnesses, and law enforcement.
- Violence continues in Quebec between the Hells Angels and Bandidos over the protection and expansion of drug trafficking networks. There have also been a number of violent incidents between the Outlaws and the Hells Angels in Ontario.
- OMGs, particularly the Hells Angels, continue to form and maintain associations with street gangs.

Source: *CISC Annual Report on Organized Crime—2002.*

CISC Annual Report—2003

The CISC reported that U.S.-based OMGs—Hells Angels, Outlaws, and Bandidos—were the most influential OMGs in Canada, with the Angels being the most powerful with 34 chapters. The Outlaws were concentrated in Ontario with nine chapters. The Bandidos did not have any Canadian clubhouses, but they still had a small number of members and probationary members in Ontario. Law enforcement authorities continued to hammer the OMGs, particularly the Outlaws and the Bandidos.

In Ontario, Project RETIRE, a three-year operation against the Outlaws, resulted in the arrests of 60 members and associates, including two U.S.-based members, the Outlaws U.S. national vice-president, and the international president. Five Outlaw clubhouses in Ontario were seized, and according to authorities, they were in disarray and their criminal influence diminished. Project AMIGO against the Bandidos in Ontario and Quebec ended in June 2002. Authorities said that the operation ended the criminal influence of the organization in both provinces. Megatrials against the Hells Angels as a result of the 2001 **Operation SPRINGTIME** were also in progress. See Box 7.8 for the 2003 CISC highlights.

BOX 7.8 2003 CISC HIGHLIGHTS

Highlights

- Outlaw motorcycle gangs (OMGs) remain a serious criminal threat in Canada. They are involved in an array of criminal activities such as murder, drug trafficking, prostitution, illegal gambling, extortion, intimidation, fraud, and theft.
- Successful law enforcement action within the last two years has had an impact on the degree of criminal influence of OMGs in Central and Atlantic Canada.

Source: *CISC Annual Report on Organized Crime—2003.*

CISC Annual Report—2004

The Hells Angels remained the largest and most powerful Canadian OMG, with 34 chapters and 500 members. However, they were facing pressure from law enforcement authorities and other OMGs. CISC reported that the Outlaws and the Bandidos were maintaining a low profile following the 2002 law enforcement actions. The Outlaws had seven chapters in Ontario, but CISC reported that only three operated with any degree of stability. The Bandidos had a chapter in Ontario and established a probationary chapter in Alberta. CISC reported that the Alberta chapter might pose a challenge to the drug activities of the Hells Angels in western Canada.

The Canadian Hells Angels were reported to have significant links to other organized crime groups, particularly the British Columbia Angels and Italian-based groups. These criminal networks were used to facilitate the importation/exportation of illicit commodities, especially drugs. See Box 7.9 for the 2004 CISC highlights.

BOX 7.9 2004 CISC HIGHLIGHTS

Highlights

- The Hells Angels remain the largest OMG in Canada; however, this group is experiencing varying degrees of weakness in Alberta, Manitoba, Quebec, and Atlantic Canada due to law enforcement operations, internal conflict, and increased competition from other criminal organizations.
- Drug trafficking remains the primary source of illicit income for the Hells Angels in Canada, though the group is also involved in a variety of other criminal activities.

Source: CISC Annual Report on Organized Crime—2004.

CISC Annual Report—2005 and Beyond

As noted earlier, the format for the CISC reports was changed with the 2005 annual report. There was no longer a separate section on each of the organized crime groups in Canada, and highlights were no longer listed. Nevertheless, the report said that OMGs were still involved in marijuana growth operations (Hells Angels), cocaine trafficking, and methamphetamine production and distribution. OMGs were also reported to be involved in motor vehicle thefts.

THE END OF THE CANADIAN BIKER WAR

The **Canadian Biker War** between the Hells Angels and the Rock Machine, later the Bandidos, was the worst organized crime war in history in terms of the number of dead and injured. The war raged on for eight years (1994-2001), resulting in 160 murders (including an innocent 11-year-old boy), 175 attempted murders, 200 people wounded, and the disappearance of 15 bikers (Roslin, 2002). It began in 1994 when the Quebec Hells Angels, led by Maurice "Mom" Boucher, attempted to take over control of the province's cocaine, hash, and marijuana markets from a coalition of the rival Rock Machine, independent dealers, and some Mafia elements. The war ended with Operation SPRINGTIME.

Operation SPRINGTIME 2001 is described as the largest one-day police operation in Canadian history (CISC, 2001). On March 28, 2001, 2,000 police officers from the Quebec Police Force, the Royal Canadian Mounted Police, Montreal

Urban Community Police Department, and 23 municipal police forces spread out throughout Quebec and carried out simultaneous raids in 77 Quebec municipalities. They executed more than 130 arrest warrants and seizures of gang assets, including 20 buildings, 70 firearms, 120 kg of hash, 10 kg of cocaine, as well as $8.6 million Canadian and $2.7 million U.S. (Cherry, 2005). In addition, arrests also took place in Ontario, Manitoba, and British Columbia. Two suspects were also arrested and deported from Jamaica and Mexico. The targets for these raids and arrests were the Hells Angels, and their puppet clubs, the Rockers MC and Evil Ones MC. The operation may have ended the Quebec Biker War, but it did not end the violence associated with Canadian OMGs. The largest mass murder in Ontario's history would involve the Bandidos in 2006.

CONTINUED EFFORTS AGAINST CANADIAN OMGs

Canadian authorities continue to apply pressure on one-percent biker gangs. The 2001 anti-gang law, outlined earlier, allows the Crown to charge the group as a criminal organization if one of three offenses is committed: (1) participating in the activities of a criminal organization to enhance the ability to commit offenses; (2) committing an offense for the benefit of a criminal organization; or (3) instructing someone to commit an offense for the benefit of a criminal organization (McKnight, 2009). The law defines a criminal organization as a group of three or more people that has as one of the main activities the commission of serious offenses for material benefit. The Crown has been successful in prosecuting OMGs in some provinces and unsuccessful in others. Many of the Hells Angels brought to trial under the anti-gang law were found guilty of the offenses but not guilty of committing the offenses for the benefit of a criminal organization. One of the Angels was convicted of having illegal grenades and six weapons—a Colt .45 semiautomatic pistol, an Intratec 9-mm semiautomatic pistol, a sawed-off Ruger .22-calibre semiautomatic rifle, a Franchi .22-calibre semiautomatic rifle, a Voere bolt-action rifle, and a .44 Ruger revolver, and four silencers. The main witness in this case was a friend of the club who turned informant for $1 million. In addition to this fee, the Royal Canadian Mounted Police (RCMP) also bought him a Harley-Davidson motorcycle and paid for riding lessons.

The Canadian authorities are keeping up the pressure on the HAMC. A 2006 police operation named Project Tandem resulted in 24 arrests in the Toronto, Oshawa, Windsor, and Niagara regions. A member of the Oshawa chapter, acting as a police agent, was paid hundreds of thousands of dollars. In 2008, two high-ranking HAMC members, a 60-year-old founding member and president of the Niagara chapter and the president of the Simcoe chapter, pleaded guilty to trafficking in cocaine and possession of the proceeds of a crime. However, they claimed that their criminal activities were not for the club. The judge, disagreeing with them, stated that the HAMC was a "criminal organization that is dedicated to the facilitation and commission of serious criminal offenses that benefit the members of the HAMC" (Hammer, 2008, December 13). The judge found him guilty of instructing others to commit a criminal offense—trafficking in cocaine. The judge pointed out that 75 percent of Canada's HAMC members have been convicted of criminal offenses, the club maintains a defense fund, and members in prison are referred to as the Big House Crew. Furthermore, the judge, in pointing out that internal documents were found in the Niagara chapter clubhouse, stated "One cannot but question the need for a legitimate motorcycle club to be involved in endeavours such as counter-surveillance and theft of sensitive police intelligence…. The purpose of obtaining the material is to allow the club to know what the police are up to and thereby protect the club's criminal enterprises" (Anon. e, 2008, December 13).

In April 2007, a raid in the Greater Toronto area by the Provincial Biker Enforcement Unit, a task force composed of Toronto police, provincial police, and the RCMP, served warrants on 12 locations, including the Hells Angels clubhouse, arresting 30 bikers (Nguyen, 2007, April 4). The police seized weapons and drugs as well as the HAMC clubhouse, the largest in Canada. The authorities also arrested a police officer for leaking police information to gang members. The authorities used a full-patched Angel as a mole to infiltrate the gang. The Code of Brotherhood among Canadian biker gang members is eroding under intense police pressure. This was the third time in two years that Canadian police were able to use full patched members as police informants.

The oft-repeated saying "Three can keep a secret if two of them are dead" may be a truism, even for Angels brothers. The same seems to apply to the Canadian Bandidos. The main witness in the trial of the "Bandidos Massacre" (to be discussed in more detail later) was an eyewitness and a full-patched Bandido. The biker code of brotherhood cracks under the weight of long prison sentences and the knowledge that the first "rat" gets the best deal. The best deal often includes immunity from prosecution and large sums of money. A former 20-year Canadian Hells Angel, Sylvain Boulanger, "ratted out" his brothers for immunity for various crimes, including murder, and $3 million. A 2009 police sting action against the Winnipeg Hells Angels involved an Angel-turned-police-informant in exchange for $450,000 and witness protection. Thirty-four suspects were arrested in the year-long undercover operation, and 165 ounces of cocaine, 12 ounces of methamphetamines, 12,000 ecstasy pills, an ounce of heroin, seven pounds of marijuana, cash, and firearms were seized (McIntyre, 2010a, 2010b). Making the operation easier for police surveillance and recording, the drug deals took place in public places. Some of Winnipeg's most popular restaurants, shopping malls, and entertainment outlets were the backdrop for the drug and weapons deals.

The head of the **OPP (Ontario Provincial Police) Biker Enforcement Unit** said that the raid proved that the gangs claim that they were a group of motorcycle enthusiasts is "misleading propaganda" (Vallis, 2007, April 5). He further stated that:

> The goals of outlaw motorcycle gangs are to create criminal enterprises in Ontario and Canada for financial gain through violence, threats and attempts to control various criminal activities focusing on drug trafficking.

The president of the Niagara Falls Hells Angels chapter was found guilty in December 2008 of instructing others to commit offenses on behalf of a criminal organization, the Hells Angels. Nevertheless, all Canadian courts do not view biker gang members as criminals. A Hells Angel convicted of assaulting a Canadian police officer, leaving him with a split lip, was given a 30-day sentence even though the Crown asked for four months. The Justice said that the Angel had been a contributing member of society for a decade, and his offense was spontaneous and out of character (www.theglobeandmail.com).

Canadian authorities are going after OMG clubhouses under the Civil Remedies Act, which allows the attorney general to seize property if it can be proved that the property is a proceed or instrument of unlawful activity (Anon. 1, 2009). Two HAMC biker clubhouses have been seized, and six other biker clubhouses have been frozen and are in the process of forfeiture. The Canadian Parliament in Ottawa is also considering whether the government should create a list of banned criminal organizations, starting with OMGs, just as terrorist organizations such as al-Qaeda, Hezbollah, and the Colombian rebel group FARC are officially blacklisted. If this were enacted, the Crown would not have to prove in each case that the banned group meets Canada's definition of a criminal organization. It is costly and time consuming for Canadian authorities to have to continually present the same evidence to the court on each case. Support is growing for this legislation, but its detractors worry that such a list will infringe on people's rights to associate under the Canadian Charter of Rights and Freedoms.

On January 28, 2009, the sergeant at arms of the Simcoe County, Canada, Hells Angels chapter was sentenced to five years in prison for trafficking 4 kg of cocaine and four years for doing so for the benefit of a criminal organization (Pazzano, 2009, January 29). He had pleaded guilty to the trafficking charge but not guilty to the criminal organization charge. The sentenced Angel was a tow truck supervisor with a $500,000 home. His dated criminal record and testimony saying he was a good family man with a history of steady employment did not impress the judge, who said that his cocaine sales were certain to "cause havoc" in other families. A 20-year veteran Montreal lawyer was found guilty of gangsterism (committing a crime for the benefit of a criminal organization) and two counts of drug possession with the intent to traffic (CBC News, 2009a, 2009b, 2009c). He was acting as the liaison between the leader of a Hells Angels drug gang and an airplane pilot who had ties with the HAMC in British Columbia. This was the first time a Canadian lawyer had been convicted of being a gangster. In order not to raise issues of lawyer-client privilege, a judge listened to thousands of wiretaps and selected 229 that did not involve privilege issues.

In Operation SharQc (Strategic Hells Angels Region Quebec), Canadian authorities arrested nearly every Hells Angel in the gang's five Quebec clubs (Cherry, 2009). Raids on April 15, 2009, led to the arrests of 123 Angels in Canada, Mexico, France, and the Dominican Republic; several of those who were arrested were retired. Forty-five HA associates were also arrested, and five HA clubhouses were seized. They were charged with drug trafficking, 22 murders, and conspiracy to commit the murder of rival gang members. A full-patched member told authorities that a membership vote was taken in 1994 across the Quebec Province to go to war against the Rock Machine. That led to 160 deaths from 1994 to 2002. The blanket action against the HAMC was based on Canada's anti-gang law, new in 2009. The theory behind the arrests was that for 20 years every member of the Quebec Hells Angels had been involved in drug dealing and had been committed to use violence to control the market. The police informant was given a contract worth $2.9 million to "rat out" his former brothers. He received $300,000 at signing and was promised the remainder in increments after the arrests and trials. Operation SharQc led some to speculate that the Hells Angels were finished in Quebec. That remains to be seen. Twenty-four HA members and associates evaded capture, but the most wanted, Michael Smith, aka "L'Animal," accused of 22 murders, was captured in 2012 in Panama (Ravensbergen, 2012, March 13). Still on the loose is David MacDonald Carroll, the only Canadian to be listed by Interpol on its "most wanted" website (Godfrey, 2012, March 13). Carroll is wanted for 13 murders.

There are allegations that the Hells Angels Sherbrook chapter was involved in manipulating the election of Quebec's largest and most powerful construction union (CBC News, 2009c, September 23). Allegedly, the Hells Angels, at the behest of the eventual winner of the election, convinced a rival to pull out of the election at the last moment. This is not the first allegation that the Angels have been involved in Canadian unions.

Project Divide, a 13-month operation against the Manitoba and British Columbia Hells Angels, ended in December 2009 with the arrest of 35 Angels and associates. The operation has been a huge success. As of August 2010, 23 of those arrested have pleaded guilty, including the vice president of the Zig Zag Crew MC, a puppet club of the Manitoba Hells Angels. All those who pleaded guilty received prison sentences of varying lengths. As is becoming the most frequent police tactic against Canadian biker gangs, the authorities paid $450,000 to a Zig Zag member for his cooperation. He secretly recorded drug and weapons deals with his former "brothers."

DRUG SMUGGLING INTO THE UNITED STATES FROM CANADA

Drug smuggling across the Canadian border into the United States is increasing. Law enforcement efforts against the manufacturing and smuggling of ecstasy in Europe have dramatically reduced the amount coming from the predominant sources in Belgium and the Netherlands but led to a tenfold increase from Canada between 2003 and 2008 (Silverman, 2008, December 7). Outlaw motorcycle gangs, particularly the Hells Angels and Asian gangs, are blamed for this increase in manufacturing and smuggling. Ecstasy, a synthetic drug that produces euphoria and breaks down inhibitions, can also lead to a shutdown of vital organs and death when the heart rate and body temperature increase with its use. In 2010, a Washington state man was sentenced to 14 years in prison for smuggling ecstasy from the British Columbia

Hells Angels into the United States (Ivens, 2010). The drugs, for which he was paid $30,000 per load, were transported by jet ski from British Columbia to an isolated cove in the San Juan Islands.

In 2007, two Canadian citizens were indicted for smuggling high-powered marijuana ("BC Bud") and cocaine into the United States. The sophisticated smuggling operation involved drugs hidden in hollowed-out logs on trucks, within the false walls of cargo containers and vehicles, within loads of commercial lumber, inside large PVC pipes, and in the interior of a propane tanker. According to the indictment, the two men worked "to facilitate the distribution of controlled substances on behalf of the Hells Angels Motorcycle Club and others" (Bolan, 2008, December 2). The indictment also says that the two men "discussed their ongoing criminal enterprise and pledged to work with the undercover agent toward greater cooperation in smuggling thousands of pounds of BC Bud into the United States." The 2008 arrests did not stop the smuggling of BC Bud into the United States. In 2012, three U.S. citizens with ties to the BC Hells Angels were convicted of running a multinational drug smuggling ring (Raptis, 2012, March 24). One of those convicted was a pilot who distributed the BC-grown marijuana to Chicago, St. Louis, and Atlanta. The co-conspirators would collect the money from the sale of marijuana and use it to buy cocaine to smuggle into Canada.

CANADIAN OMG VIOLENCE

OMG violence continues unabated in Canada. A murdered man found in the Fraser River in Vancouver (Bolan, 2009) was once a member of the "The Crew," a violent street gang that served as the enforcers for the Hells Angels puppet club, the Renegades. Crew members cut off the fingers and hands of those behind on their drug debts. However, the internecine warfare between OMG brothers resulted in the worst case of violence in Canadian history: The Bandidos Massacre.

Canadian Bandidos Massacre

On Sunday April 8, 2006, the police were called to a rural farmhouse in Shedden, Ontario. The farm owners had discovered a minivan and a tow truck with a car hooked to the back. A fourth car was found about 100 meters down a dirt road. The police found eight bodies inside the two vehicles and began an investigation into the worst mass murder in Ontario's history. The massacre is also considered the largest biker massacre in world history. Within days, the eight men, all from the Toronto area, were connected to the Bandidos Motorcycle Club. One victim, John "Boxer" Muscedere, was the national president of the Bandidos MC Canada. He had eight criminal convictions since 1996, including assault with a weapon, breaking and entering, resisting arrest, and escaping custody. Three MCs, the Loners, Bandidos, and Hells Angels, were all reported to be, or have been, active in the area. By Monday, the police had arrested and charged five people with first-degree murder. One of the five was a 46-year-old woman charged with helping in the killings. After being held for six weeks, the charges were dropped, but her common-law husband was sentenced to two years in prison after pleading guilty to being an accessory after the fact in the murders.

Also charged was Wayne Kellestine, a Bandidos-patched member from the Toronto chapter who was the former leader of the St. Thomas Annihilators MC and the St. Thomas Loners MC. Speculation about the reason for the murders came fast and furious in the first days after the massacre. Julian Sher, journalist, biker expert, and the author of two books on Canadian biker gangs, said that the slayings were the result of a turf war between the Hells Angels and the Bandidos (Anon. n, 2006, April 11). The police, on the other hand, said that it was "internal cleansing" and no other criminal organization was involved. The police said that six of the dead were full-patched Bandidos members, one was a prospect member, and the other was an associate. Ed Winterhalder, former president of the Oklahoma Bandidos and author of what was at that time the only book on the Bandidos, indicated that the murders had to be fueled by methamphetamine. He went on to say that when the St. Thomas Loners MC disbanded, half the members became Hells Angels and the other half, including Kellestine and most of those who were murdered, became Bandidos. The Bandidos needed quantity, not quality, to block the expansion of the Angels. Kellestine, contrary to all biker club rules, did not even own a functioning motorcycle, let alone a Harley-Davidson. Another theory said that Kellestine was a "loose cannon" who had a swastika cut into his lawn, was a known white supremacist, and had become a problem for the Bandidos. As testimony to Kellestine's irascibility, he was rejected as a possible member of the Outlaws when the biker gang established a chapter in Canada (Edwards, 2010). According to this account, they felt he was too bizarre and unruly, especially when he was high on cocaine and methamphetamine. He once introduced himself to a fellow biker by proclaiming, "I sell drugs and I kill people." Because of his bizarre behavior, which drew police attention to himself and the Bandidos, the theory goes that 10 bikers were on their way to pull Kellestine's "patch" when they stopped for coffee, and two of the bikers called Kellestine and alerted him. Allegedly, the two that ratted out their brothers are among those arrested for the murders (Robertson, 2006, April 13). There was also speculation that the victims had announced plans to "patch over" to the Hells Angels, further angering the U.S. and Canadian Bandidos. Fueled by all the speculation and competing theories, the preliminary investigation spread to other parts of Canada and the United States.

In June 2006, three Winnipeg Bandidos, two full-patched members and a prospect, were charged with the eight murders (Lambert, 2006, June 16). One of those arrested was the Winnipeg Bandidos chapter president and a former police officer, Michael Sandham, who was also turned down for membership by the Outlaws. Ex-cops are persona non grata in most one-percent clubs. Six Bandidos, five from the Winnipeg chapter and a traitor from the Toronto chapter, would eventually be charged and go to trial for murder.

Court testimony from a police informant, called M.H. (currently in the witness protection program), who was the sergeant at arms of the Manitoba chapter and a cocaine dealer and was present when the massacre occurred, revealed the events leading up to the killings and how they were carried out. The victims were members of the Toronto Bandidos, also known as the **No Surrender Crew**, after a branch of the Irish Republican Army (IRA), and the five of those on trial for their murders were members of the probationary Winnipeg chapter and one was a member of the Toronto chapter. The Toronto traitor, Wayne Kellestine, appeared to be the main conspirator of the murderous plot against his fellow "brothers." He invited his former brothers to come to his farm for a "church" meeting.

Testimony from M.H. alleged that the U.S. Bandidos were deeply involved in the events leading up to the massacre (Anon. p, 2009). The Bandidos International President, Jeff Pike, reportedly told the Winnipeg chapter to pull the patches of the Toronto chapter because they were not following Bandidos rules or paying required dues. Whatever took place between the Texas Bandidos and the Canadians may never be known. However, it is known that the No Surrender Crew was a "motorcycle club that wasn't"; they had allowed members in who were not approved by Texas, they were not paying their dues, and most were bikers without bikes, a most egregious violation in the world of bikers. Pike allegedly told Michael Sandham, Winnipeg Chapter president, that after the Toronto chapter was dissolved the Winnipeg chapter would get full status. In addition, Kellestine would become national president, Sandham would become national secretary/treasurer, and Kellestine would also set up a chapter in London, Ontario. At trial, Sandham took the stand and testified that the International Bandidos changed their mind and the world sergeant at arms said that El Presidente Jeff Pike wanted Bandidos Canada president John "Boxer" Muscedere and Toronto chapter president Frank "Bam Bam" Salerno killed (Sims & Dubinski, 2009). Sandham also testified that he met face-to-face with El Presidente Pike one month after the murders in Houston, Texas, and Pike told him that he had ordered the murders (Anon. u, 2009). This is probably fiction invented by Sandham, who has been known to be a pathological liar. Sandham offered to testify against his fellow conspirators but was turned down by the authorities because he could not be believed. At trial, he took the stand and claimed that he was never an outlaw biker but was instead working deep undercover against one-percent bikers, although he could not name any police officers or agencies he worked for (Edwards, 2010). His tale was such an obvious fabrication that no one believed him.

The possibility that methamphetamine, first mentioned by Ed Winterhalder, may have played a role in the murders is revealed in court testimony by the girlfriend of one of the victims. She testified that a call to Kellestine the morning after the murders elicited the following statement: "He said 'I got (expletive) up and (expletive) up" (Sims, 2009a). Kellestine appears to have difficulty keeping his mouth shut. He told the Ontario Provincial Police (OPP) officer taking him to headquarters after his arrest: "I wish that they would have put a gun to my head and killed me, too." Several of the victims were shot with guns pressed to their heads, but Kellestine had not been told that at the time (Edwards, 2009). In the interview at police headquarters, "motor mouth" Kellestine told the police that he was invincible and untouchable, but police officers know that most of those in prison are there because they talked themselves into prison.

According to M.H., the conspirators opened fire on their former colleagues when they entered the barn, wounding several and killing one. M.H. testified that Sandham, a former police officer, claimed to his fellow assassins that the dead Toronto member, Luis Raposo, had fired first. Testimony and autopsy results suggest that Raposo was shot through the right middle finger, shearing it off. The bullet broke apart and hit Raposo's neck and lung (Sims, 2009c). The vulgar one-finger salute was Raposo's trademark, appearing in all his photos. The one-finger salute to his killer was Raposo's last gesture of contempt. After Raposo was killed, each of the surviving Toronto Bandidos was led outside and executed. During the executions, one of the victims chastised his fellow bikers waiting to die for their praying and whining. He told them:

> "Keep your mouth shut. We are bikers. We're not the f____in' Boy Scouts. We know how the game is played."
>
> (Shannon, 2009)

> The turncoat Kellestine killed the first four. M.H.'s testimony portrays Kellestine's bizarre behavior during the massacre, most likely methamphetamine induced.
>
> (Sims, 2009b)

> "I'm here to pull your patches," he [Kellestine] told them and that they were "done by orders of the States."

> "He sang a German anthem, he did a jig. He said the Lord's Prayer on one knee with the Toronto victims as they prayed over Raposo's body [the first killed]."

> "He saved his most savage ridicule for Jamie Flanz [victim]—calling him a 'f____ king Jew,' 'a police informant' and promised to 'save you for last.'"

After the killings, the murderers faced the dilemma faced by all murderers, especially those who act without planning: that is, what to do with the body or in this case the bodies. The murderers stuffed the bodies in the victims' cars and drove them to a rural road 14 kilometers away and left them in plain view where they were discovered the next morning. This amateurish disposal of the bodies fuels speculation that the murderers were "methed up" at the time. Testimony reveals that there was not a prior plan to kill the victims. Events probably spiraled out of hand after Sandham fired the first shots and the drugged-up killers were never able to think rationally after that.

There were no letters of condolence from the Bandidos Nation, and no U.S. Bandidos attended any of the funerals. After all, the No Surrender Crew had died during a patch-pulling session by their brothers in the Winnipeg chapter. They would soon suffer the same indignity from their Texas brothers. According to a senior Texas Department of Public Safety investigator, the Bandidos international president revoked the Winnipeg Bandidos' membership and barred them from wearing Bandidos colors (Appleby, 2006, June 22). Evidently, the "last straw" was when the U.S. Bandidos learned that their Canadian brothers had allowed a former police officer to become a member—a fact that, if the police informant is believed, they knew for some time before the massacre. No doubt the revocation was a move on the part of the U.S. Bandidos to distance themselves from what they possibly set in motion. A recent check of the Bandidos website has no Canadian chapters listed (www.bandidosmc.com/).

A bizarre aspect of the massacre is the tie that three of the six murderers had to other competing/enemy motorcycle clubs/gangs. The informant, M.H., testified that he had been a member of an unnamed Hells Angels puppet club, although he did not own a motorcycle or have a license to drive one, and decided to join the Bandidos when that club dissolved. M.H. testified that he had at one time been a personal bodyguard for the notorious Hells Angels leader Maurice "Mom" Boucher, now serving two life sentences for ordering the murders of two corrections officers, and the Canadian Hells Angels national leader Walter Stadnick. The Hells Angels and the Bandidos are bitter enemies, and it is surprising to learn that M.H. would be welcome in the Bandidos unless it was his skills as a drug dealer (often earning $25,000 a day selling cocaine and collecting welfare at the same time) or his reputation for violence that was attractive to his new "brothers." He also testified that Michael Sandham, the president of the Winnipeg Bandidos, had been an Outlaw and ran the Black Piston chapter, a puppet club of the Outlaws MC (Sims & Miner, 2009). Allegedly, Sandham had joined the Bandidos after a police crackdown on the Outlaws. The only surviving member of the Toronto chapter, Robert "Peterborough Bob" Pammett, appears to have been aiding the Outlaws" expansion into Peterborough, Ontario. Pammett was invited to the meeting that resulted in the massacre, but for some reason did not attend, prompting speculation that he, like Kellestine, was a turncoat. Whatever the reason for not attending, it was lucky for him. It appears that being a member of a motorcycle gang for these Bandidos was more a matter of expediency and opportunity rather than any sense of brotherhood and commitment to the Bandidos way. Once again, this is evidence that the supposed Code of Brotherhood among biker clubs/gangs is more rhetoric than reality.

Further confusion comes from testimony by M.H. that he became involved in the Bandidos because it offered brotherhood and a chance to ride with friends, even though he *did not actually own a motorcycle* (Anon. q, 2009). M.H. would later testify that the Winnipeg Bandidos chapter was "pretty much" a bike club with no bikes. A police biker expert testified that two of the six club members accused of slaughtering their eight fellow Bandidos did not meet the basic criteria for membership in an outlaw motorcycle club (Miner, 2009); that is, they did not own motorcycles. The Winnipeg prospects also did not spend the minimum six months probationary period before getting their patches. These two Bandidos chapters, as with most one-percent biker clubs, were more criminal gangs than motorcycle clubs.

The trial went on for seven months, with testimony from 70 witnesses, but it only took a little more than a day for the jury to return 44 counts of first-degree murder and four counts of manslaughter (Kari, 2009). This was an anticlimatic ending to a highly charged trial of internecine murder among supposed "brothers" that began with a "patch-pulling" conspiracy with alleged roots at the highest levels of the international Bandidos leadership. The Crown, in its closing, argued that the killings were the result of orders from U.S. Bandidos to "pull the patches of the Toronto Bandidos."

The trial's outcome reinforces the common knowledge among criminals that when the sentences are long and the evidence is overwhelming "the first rat gets the best deal." The prosecutor told the jury in closing that M.H. would have been charged with eight counts of first-degree murder if he had not agreed to testify and tell the truth. He knew of the plan to kill his Winnipeg brothers, and he held them at gunpoint until each was led one by one to their execution. M.H., although armed, never once voiced any opposition to this "march to the death." He witnessed the shooting of one of the bikers and aided in dumping the bodies and destroying evidence. As a reward for his testimony, M.H. received full immunity and a new identity. One can only speculate as to how long it will be before M.H. returns to a life of crime, if he has not already. The deal M.H. received points out that the criminal justice system often has "to shake hands with the devil" to secure convictions. M.H. was an admitted drug dealer, biker enforcer, and sergeant at arms of the Winnipeg Bandidos. M.H.'s Bandidos brothers were not so fortunate. All the defendants were convicted of at least six counts of first-degree murder. Three defendants—Kellestine, Mushey, and Sandham—were convicted of eight counts of first-degree murder, which carries a sentence of life in prison with no chance of parole for 25 years. These three defendants were the only ones charged with killing anyone. The others were charged with intentional aiding in the murders. First-degree murder, according to the Crown, occurs when the killing is planned and deliberate or when an intentional killing occurs during a forcible confinement, clearly what happened in this case. Two others were convicted of six counts of first-degree murder and one count of manslaughter. The last defendant was convicted of six counts of first-degree murder and two counts of manslaughter.

The **Bandidos Massacre** may be an aberration when examining biker gang violence; however, association with outlaw motorcycle gangs (as a member or not) is a magnet for violence. A Nova Scotia judge stated as he sentenced a Hells Angels hit man for murdering a man and his wife: "They [people who have ties to the Hells Angels] live their lives in fear of people they associate with," he said. "They do terrible things to one another. The lifestyles they lead must be as close to hell as anyone can imagine" (Delaney, 2012, May 9). The couple was murdered with their 18-month-old baby in the next room. The victim, a long-time drug dealer, had close ties to the Hells Angels. The murderer, who was sentenced to life in prison with no hope for parole for 25 years, killed the couple to erase a $28,500 drug debt owed to the Hells Angels. The same day as the double murder, the assassin killed a man who picked him up hitchhiking. He wanted the man's truck to commit a robbery. His accomplice in the crime (who pleaded guilty) said he would kill anyone to feed his crazed $400-a-day cocaine and marijuana habit. The Hells Angels member who ordered the hit was found dead of an apparent suicide before the trial started.

MORE RECENT ACTIONS AGAINST BIKER GANGS

Canadian law enforcement authorities continue their efforts against biker gangs and their puppet/support clubs (see Box 7.10). Project Flatlined, a Winnipeg operation begun in September 2011, focused on the Hells Angels and their Redlined MC puppet club (Anon. 4, 2012, April 21). From September 2011 until February 2012, numerous search warrants were executed and 23 people were arrested. Then, on March 16, 2012, 150 Winnipeg officers arrested 11 more bikers, including three full-patched Hells Angels and eight Redlined members. One of those arrested was the Manitoba Hells Angels president. An outgrowth of the operation was the implementation of a rarely used law to arrest Hells Angels not charged with an offense. Section 810 of the Criminal Code allows for an arrest under a peace bond of someone likely "to commit a criminal act for the benefit of an organization" (McIntyre, 2012b, April 4). Seven Manitoba Hells Angels have been arrested under this peace bond statute. The terms of the peace bond state that the gang members cannot have any contact with a Hells Angel member or associate in the Province of Winnipeg. The list of those the seven cannot contact is three pages long and includes more than 50 names. There are 13 other terms, including a midnight curfew and no wearing or possession of any gang clothing or paraphernalia. One of the Hells Angels members agreed to leave the gang in order to be released from custody. Law enforcement authorities submitted verbatim transcripts of taped phone calls to support the peace bonds. The use of the peace bonds in this manner, if it stands, is a powerful weapon against the Manitoba Hells Angels, a gang with a history of criminal activities. In effect, almost every Manitoba Hells Angel is either in custody as a result of Project Flatlined or barred under the peace bonds from having contact with any other Hells Angel or associate. Several members have agreed to the peace bonds, but one prospect, who has no criminal record and is not facing any criminal allegations, is mounting a court challenge (Turner, 2012, April 18).

Even though the Canadian police have maintained constant pressure on their outlaw motorcycle gangs, they have never totally eliminated them. The profits involved in supplying illegal goods and services to a willing clientele insure that organized crime is seldom eliminated. However, the desire to commit crime for profit is not the only incentive to join and remain in an outlaw motorcycle gang. Outlaw motorcycle gangs also provide a sense of power and prestige to the wearer of the gang's colors, which appeals to the members of the social milieu from which outlaw bikers are recruited. The lure of a supposed brotherhood living the lifestyle characterized by the ideals of independence, solidarity, and freedom masks the violence and treachery common in biker gangs. The long membership process, with its demands and uncertainties, creates in the prospective member a sense of motivation and commitment to the gang. As a result of these factors, even those bikers who join the gangs and do not commit serious organized crimes, provide tacit support for their criminal brothers. The best that can be hoped for by law enforcement and the criminal justice system is a series of wins and losses while maintaining constant pressure and vigilance. An example of this ebb and flow of wins, losses, and stalemates against Canadian biker gangs is demonstrated by the events that occurred in Niagara, Canada, from 1998 to 2013 (see Box 7.11).

BOX 7.10 BACCHUS MOTORCYCLE CLUB

According to the CISC, the New Brunswick–based Bacchus Motorcycle Club is a one-percent club and a puppet/support club for the Hells Angels and is involved in drug trafficking and moving stolen goods (Cunningham, 2012, July 30). The estimated 100-member gang has chapters in every province in Atlantic Canada with three in New Brunswick, two in Newfoundland and Labrador, and one each in Nova Scotia and Prince Edward Island (Ross, 2012, August 1). The president of the Saint John, New Brunswick, Bacchus MC chapter pled guilty to manslaughter in a shooting outside the gang's clubhouse. In a bizarre twist to this unprovoked fatal shooting, it was caught on camera from the clubhouse's security camera and introduced as evidence. The chapter president is seen standing outside the clubhouse with fellow members as the victim walks by. The Bacchus president is seen handing his drink to a member, pulling his gun, then walking out of camera range, and then returning and reloading his weapon (Mantle, 2012, July 26).

BOX 7.11 KEY EVENTS IN NIAGARA BIKER GANG HISTORY

The following key events in Niagara biker gang history are adapted from Sawchuk (2013, November 7).

1998-1999: Former Hells Angels national president Walter Stadnick, a member of the Quebec Nomads chapter of the Hells Angels with ties to Hamilton, makes frequent trips to Niagara. Police say at the time they believe he is laying the foundation for an Angels takeover of the region by 2000. This sparks fears of a gang war between the Angels and their longtime rivals, the Outlaws, long established in St. Catharines, Ontario.

July 1999: The Sherbrooke, Quebec, chapter of the Hells Angels arrives in Niagara Falls. It's the first time the Angels have visited in such large numbers. They are in the Falls for an annual ride—essentially a big party. However, Stadnick meets with Welland resident and convicted criminal Gerald Ward during the Angels' weeklong stay.

2000: The much-touted arrival of a Niagara Hells Angels chapter and an ensuing turf war with the Outlaws never happens.

December 2000: In a massive ceremony in Sorel, Quebec, nearly all of Ontario's 13 biker gangs adopt the colors and name of the Hells Angels. The move shocks police who expected a bloody turf war with the province's biker gangs. The Outlaws remain independent of the Angels.

(Continued)

BOX 7.11 KEY EVENTS IN NIAGARA BIKER GANG HISTORY—cont'd

2001: Stadnick's handpicked men become probationary members of the Hells Angels. None of them have a previous history of being bikers, including Ward, who will become the club president. They start up shop in a clubhouse on Darby Road in Welland. (For the most part, these new Hells Angels are examples of bikers without bikes. A common occurrence as some motorcycle clubs evolve into criminal gangs. They were chosen for Hells Angels membership because of their known reputation as thugs and criminals.)

May 2001: The new Niagara chapter hosts Angels from across Canada for the first time in Welland.

September 2002: A joint-police task force operation breaks the back of the Outlaws. The Outlaws clubhouse in St. Catharines is seized and most of the gang members are arrested on charges from attempted murder to drug trafficking.

September 2004: Stannick is convicted in a Quebec court of drug trafficking and conspiracy to commit murder. He is sentenced to 20 years in prison.

September 28, 2006: Project Tandem, a joint-forces OPP-led operation, cracks down on Hells Angels across the province. The Welland clubhouse and at least one Hells Angels residence is raided. Ward is arrested.

March 2010: Eight years after police broke the club, the Outlaws clubhouse in Oakdale is demolished. It takes two days to finally bring down the fortified building.

November 6, 2013: Project Resurgence, a nine-month investigation of the Outlaws motorcycle gang's activities, resulted in the NRP [Niagara Regional Police] executing 30 search warrants on the Black Pistons [Outlaws Puppet club] clubhouse in St. Catharines. (The Outlaws established the Black Pistons chapter to reestablish an Outlaws presence in Niagara. In time, the Outlaws intended to "patch over" the Black Pistons chapter.)

A more recent event that has Canadian law enforcement reeling is the arrest of the most prominent Montreal biker cop. Organized crime seldom exists without some cooperation between thugs and cops, but this arrest was totally unexpected. The subsequent trail should provide an interesting look into Canadian biker gangs.

Source: *Adapted from Sawchuk, November 7, 2013.*

Whoever fights monsters should see to it that in the process he does not become a monster.

And if you gaze long enough into an abyss, the abyss will gaze back at you.

Friedrich Nietzsche

If Detective Sergeant Benoit Roberge of the Montreal police would have heeded to the words of the German philosopher Nietzsche, he might have avoided his current predicament. Roberge, now retired, was the lead detective for the Montreal police during the Montreal biker wars and is considered the primary officer behind the efforts to stop the war, break up the Nomads Hells Angels, and put Hells Angels leader "Mom" Boucher in prison. He is currently charged with two counts of gangsterism, one count of obstruction of justice, and one count of breach of trust (Scott, 2013, October 8). The allegations against Roberge include selling police secrets to the Hells Angels.

Bikies Down Under— OMGs in Australia and New Zealand

KEY TERMS

Australian Crime Commission

bikies

milk-bar cowboys

Milperra Massacre

Notorious MC

OMCG (Outlaw Motorcycle Gang)

Organized and Financial Crime Agency New Zealand (OFCANZ)

Panzer Task Force

AUSTRALIA

Australia is a commonwealth federation consisting of six states (Queensland, New South Wales [NSW], Victoria, Tasmania, South Australia, and Western Australia) and two territories (Australian Capital Territory and Northern Territory) (see Figure 8.1).

The country has two levels of law enforcement agencies: state police and the Australian Federal Police (AFP). Each state and the Northern Territory have their own police force; the Australian Capital Territory is under the jurisdiction of the AFP. Since 1992, these forces have come together in five National Task Forces coordinated as national responses to particular complex organized crime activities (National Crime Authority: www.nca.gov.au). The first of these was the Panzer Task Force created in 1995 to deal with outlaw motorcycle gangs (OMGs) (see Box 8.1).

Australian Outlaw Motorcycle Gangs

Australian "homegrown" and U.S.-based outlaw motorcycle gangs, or **bikies**, as they are called in Australia, have been a serious crime problem for decades (see Figure 8.2). Australian bikies have a reputation for quick and intemperate violence. U.S.-based OMGs first expanded to Australia in 1961. In a curious twist on OMG expansion, Australian homegrown bikie gangs are now expanding outside their

FIGURE 8.1

Australia.

Map courtesy of Bruce Jones Design Inc.

borders. Since 1961, Australian bikie gangs have gone through major changes as they evolved into a national crime threat; the government approach to this threat at the national and state level has changed in response to this evolution. We will begin our discussion with the current status of Australian bikie gangs and then review the evolution of these gangs. The best source for the current state of Australian outlaw motorcycle gangs is contained in Annual Reports issued by the **Australian Crime Commission** (ACC).

Australian Outlaw Motorcycle Gangs: Bikies
AUSTRALIAN CRIME COMMISSION

The ACC was created by Parliament in 2002 as a statutory authority to combat serious and organized crime. The ACC reports directly to the Minister for Home Affairs for Australia.

BOX 8.1 PANZER TASK FORCE—1995

Mission

Targets the organized criminal activities of outlaw motorcycle gangs, especially those related to the cultivation and supply of cannabis, the manufacture and supply of amphetamines, and organized violence.

Agencies

New South Wales Police	New South Wales Crime Commission
Victoria Police	Queensland Crime Commission
Queensland Police	Tasmania Police
South Australia Police	Northern Territory Police
Western Australia Police	Australia Federal Police—ACT Region
Australian Federal Police	Australian Bureau of Criminal Investigation
Australian Customs Service	
AUSTRAC [Australian Transaction Reports and Analysis Centre—Money Laundering]	Australian Securities and Investment National Crime Authority
Department of Immigration and Multicultural Affairs	Australian Taxation Office

Activities

More than 1,800 Task Force members have participated in the investigation of OMG criminal activities. Each agency has a representative on the Panzer Coordination Committee, and this committee meets three times a year to coordinate and monitor the progress of the Panzer Task Force. In addition to drug activities, Panzer investigations have revealed that OMG members have been involved in the organized theft of motor vehicles and motorcycles, currency counterfeiting, and fraud.

Source: *Modified from National Crime Authority www.nca.gov.au/html/pg_TskFce.htm.*

The purpose of the Commission is to unite the fight against nationally significant crime. Commission goals are:

- Shape the national agenda on fighting serious crime.
- Provide solutions for national serious crime priorities.
- Maintain a leading-edge capability on national criminal intelligence and information service.
- Maximize the potential of the Commission's people.
- Build highly effective business practices that support the Commission's strategy.

OMGs, known as Mocks and bikies in Australia and New Zealand, are a national organized crime threat in Australia and come under the purview of the ACC. The ACC publishes a fact sheet on Australian outlaw motorcycle gangs (Australian Crime Commission, 2011) (see Box 8.2). They use the initials **OMCG** to refer to an outlaw motorcycle gang.

BOX 8.2 NATURE OF AUSTRALIAN OUTLAW MOTORCYCLE GANGS—ACCs

1. Almost 40 motorcycle clubs linked to criminal activities in Australia describe themselves as outlaw motorcycle gangs.
2. The reference to "outlaw" is not a legal definition; rather it refers to their view as operating outside the law. Specifically, OMCGs describe themselves as the "one-percenters." If 99% of motorcyclists operate within the law and society's convention, they see themselves as the 1% who don't.
3. The criminal activities of OMCGs distinguish them from many recreational motorcycle riding clubs comprised of people who get together solely for the purpose of riding their motorcycles and socializing (although some OMCGs claim to be simply recreational riding clubs).
4. While they have become one of the more identifiable and high profile groups in Australia's crime landscape, OMCGs are not typical of organized crime entities in Australia and their members do not pose more or less of an organized crime threat than many other groups and individuals. Other syndicates or networks rarely aim for public identification. In contrast, OMCGs maintain websites, identify themselves through patches and tattoos, have written constitutions and by-laws, trademark their club names and logos, and have publicity campaigns.
5. Australian OMCGs evolved from core groups of males who shared common interests, came from working class backgrounds, were Caucasian and sought to mirror the activities of OMCGs which were established overseas (originally in the United States) after the Second World War. Club members were expected to obey strict rules and a militaristic hierarchy that levied harsh and sometimes violent retribution for disobedience.
6. Admission to groups was once formally regulated by strict internal procedures, although this has been relaxed to counter declining membership and to strengthen positions against rival OMCGs. This, combined with Australia's increasing multicultural population and a desire to broaden spheres of interests, means the traditional Caucasian makeup of biker gangs has changed. There is now a strong Middle Eastern presence in a number of OMCGs. Some gangs do not work to a constitution and others include members who do not even ride motorcycles.
7. OMCGs are characterized by a hierarchy divided into several regions, each with some autonomy, also referred to as chapters. Each chapter is headed by a president who has absolute rule and oversees the principles of brotherhood, loyalty, and an enforced code of silence.
8. The criminal activities of OMCG members range from social nuisance in residential communities to their involvement in some of the most significant criminal syndicates in Australia today. *There has always been a criminal element within OMCGs but in the majority of cases OMCG chapters do not engage in organized crime as a group. Rather, individual members may leverage off the OMCG to aid their criminal activity. This may include enlisting the support of fellow members to recover debts or dissuade potential competitors; enhancing their status in criminal circles; or using the existence of chapters in different states, territories, and sometimes other countries to exploit criminal opportunities* (Emphasis added. The Continuum of Criminal Organization in action).
9. OMCG chapters do however, pose a serious (if sporadic) risk to the public safety because they are liable to react violently to attempts by rival OMCGs to poach their members or encroach on their "territory." In these circumstances, OMCG members have, on a number of occasions (notably on the Gold Coast and at Sydney Airport), paid scant attention to the safety of innocent members of the public.
10. OMCGs are also no longer isolationist groups. They may provide their "expertise" or "services" to traditional organized crime groups on a contractual basis in order to establish a presence in a crime market or to facilitate the commission of a crime. This might include debt collection, extortion, blackmail, intimidation, and violence.

BOX 8.2 NATURE OF AUSTRALIAN OUTLAW MOTORCYCLE GANGS—ACCs—cont'd

11. They [OMCGs] often recruit street gangs to undertake the higher risk of their criminal enterprise, and to distribute drugs or commit other crimes. These connections with more traditional crime groups appear more prevalent and reflect the more diverse ethnic composition of some OMCGs. [An unintended consequence of the current crackdown on criminal motorcycle gangs in Australia's Gold Coast is the recruitment of teenagers to fill the void in the bikie underworld (Wuth, 2013, November 13). Teenagers, some as young as 16, are trafficking drugs and extorting money as the bikies go underground. The Gold Coast Brotherhood is allied with the Nomads MC, and the Mexican Soldiers are working for the Bandidos MC.]

12. Members of OMCGs are involved in many aspects of serious crime in Australia. These include:
    * production and distribution of drugs
    * vehicle rebirthing
    * serious assault
    * use and trafficking of illegal firearms
    * serious frauds
    * money laundering
    * extortion
    * prostitution
    * robbery
    * organized theft
    * property crime
    * bribing and corrupting officials [The latest incident of this occurred when a Victoria Senior Constable was arrested after a probe of police leaks to outlaw motorcycle gangs (Deery, 2013, November 7). The Senior Constable was the epitome of a rogue police officer. It is alleged that he had links to outlaw motorcycle gangs, stole drugs from the police station and sold them, ran a large-scale drug operation from his home, and was behind an amphetamine operation.]
    * tax evasion
    * arson

Source: *Adapted from Australian Crime Commission, 2011.*

Australian OMGs

Among the 40 bikie gangs alluded to in the ACC report are indigenous (home-grown) and U.S.-based outlaw motorcycle gangs. The indigenous gangs include the Coffin Cheaters, Comancheros, Gypsy Jokers, Finks, and the Rebels (Australia's largest 1% club with 63 chapters), and the U.S.-based OMGs (Hells Angels, Bandidos, and Outlaws). The Rebels MC was founded in 1969 in Brisbane, Queensland, Australia. They originally called themselves the Confederates after the South in the American Civil War. The Rebels MC logo is a Confederate battle flag with a gray cap–wearing skull with a 1% patch in the middle. They have begun to expand nationally by establishing a chapter in New Zealand, and it is reported that they have chapters in Thailand, Spain, and Malta (Edwards, 2012, November 7). It has recently been reported that the Rebels have opened chapters in six Asian countries—Indonesia, Singapore, the Philippines, Thailand, Laos, and Cambodia (Downsley, 2013, November 23). This would mean that the Australian-based Rebels MC is the outlaw motorcycle gang with the largest presence in Asia.

In addition to the Rebels expansion, the Australian-based Coffin Cheaters MC has expanded internationally and patched over the Forbidden Few MC in Norway. There are now five Coffin Cheaters MC chapters in Norway (see Box 8.3). Lastly, the Australian-based Gypsy Jokers MC is now affiliated with the U.S.-based Gypsy Jokers. This demonstrates that the transnational expansion of biker gangs that began with U.S.-based OMGs has become a worldwide phenomenon in the biker world of organized crime. The first move in this worldwide expansion began with the HAMC.

BOX 8.3 COFFIN CHEATERS MC—NORWAY

Coffin Cheaters: The History of the Club
Coffin Cheaters MC Norway began as Craftsman MC.
"In 1994, we joined up with Wild Wheels MC and started Forbidden Few MC in 1997.
It was in the year 2000 that we seriously began to work at getting into Coffin Cheaters MC.
We went from being [sic] Forbidden Few MC Lillestom to become Coffin Cheaters MC Norway, March 9, 2004."
This happened after four years of hard work and traveling back and forth to Australia.

Source: Adapted from www.coffincheatersmc.org.

HELLS ANGELS ARRIVE DOWN UNDER

The Hells Angels MC's first expansion outside the United States occurred in 1961 when a chapter was established in Auckland, Australia. Although the Hells Angels have had a chapter in Auckland since that year, the real expansion of the Angels and other U.S. gangs did not start in earnest until 1972 with an atypical biker recruit into the Melbourne Hells Angels (Sher & Marsden, 2006). Peter John Hill, known as the "Original Australian Speed King," one of the founding members of the Melbourne chapter, was a rich, private-schooled, upper-class kid. However, the words of a tattoo on his left arm reveal how similar he is to the biker culture:

> "Yea, though I walk through the valley of death I fear no evil because I am the evilest mother fucker who has ever walked through the valley."

Hill and the other members of the Melbourne chapter wanted to make the Hells Angels the dominant motorcycle gang in Australia, and their plan to do so included introducing methamphetamine to Australia. Hill made several trips to Oakland, California, and learned how to manufacture methamphetamine from the experts at that time: the Oakland Hells Angels, led by Sonny Barger. In return, Hill agreed to supply the Oakland Angels with P2P (phenyl-2-propanone), a major ingredient in the manufacture of meth that was illegal in the United States but not in Australia. Hill and the other members of the Melbourne chapter were highly successful and grew rich. This stimulated the overseas expansion of first the Bandidos and later the Outlaws. Hill's activities and growing wealth resulted in tension among his patched brothers, leading to betrayals and eventually to Hill being thrown out of the gang. Hill later turned police informer and ratted out his brothers, but the expansion of U.S. biker gangs continued. Old-time bikers continually complain that drugs and drug trafficking destroyed the Code of Brotherhood. That may be true if the supposed Code ever existed in more than talk. Probably more to the issue is that "there is no honor among thieves," and there is ample evidence to support that in the history of Outlaw Motorcycle Gangs.

Australian Bikies: 1% Bikers and 100% Violent Criminals

The Australian OMGs have a history of violence, as shown in Box 8.4. In 1984, in what is known as the **Milperra Massacre**, seven people (six bikers—two Bandidos and four Comancheros—and a 14-year-old girl) were killed in a shootout between the Comancheros and the Bandidos over a drug-selling disagreement (Stephenson, 2004). The Australian Bandidos were originally Comancheros who left the club because they were not allowed to sell drugs. Eight Comancheros received life sentences, and 16 Bandidos received 14 years for manslaughter. As reflected in Box 8.4, 1999 was an especially violent year for Australia's bikie gangs. In 1999, a Victoria Comanchero was tortured and beaten to death, and the clubhouses of the Bandidos, Comancheros, and Rebels were bombed. The two bombs that exploded outside the Brompton Rebel clubhouse did $500,000 in damage.

The year 2001 was also a violent one for Australian bikie gangs. Three members of the Rebels MC were murdered in South Australia in 2001. The most notorious biker gang murder since the Milperra Massacre occurred in 2001 when members of the indigenous outlaw motorcycle gang, the Gypsy Jokers, set off a car bomb killing Don Hancock, the retired chief of Western Australia's criminal investigations branch (CIB) and his best friend Lou Lewis, a former bookmaker. The bombing, called the worst criminal assassination in West Australia's history, was done out of revenge for the sniper killing of a Gypsy Joker member near Kalgoorlie, West Australia, a year earlier. After his retirement, Hancock moved to Ora Banda, a small mining community near Kalgoorlie where he owned a pub. Several Gypsy Joker members on a run stopped at the pub and insulted the bar tender, Hancock's daughter. Hancock threw the bikers out of the pub. An hour later, when the bikers were sitting around a campfire, a sniper, believed to be Hancock, shot and killed one of them with a high-powered rifle. Two weeks later, Joker members, blaming Hancock for the murder, bombed his hotel. They later bombed a general store adjoining the hotel and burned Hancock's house down. Hancock moved to Perth, refused to cooperate with the investigation, and turned down police protection. A year after the Joker was killed, a bomb planted in Lewis's car went off, killing both Lewis and Hancock.

The reaction to the assassination was immediate and vociferous. Public outcry led to the appointment of a Task Force—Operation Zircon—to find the killers. There was also a clamor for new laws against bikie gangs. A Gypsy Joker who was present at the campfire and planted the bomb in Lewis's car confessed and turned against his fellow members. He was convicted of murder and sentenced to life in prison. However, the alleged mastermind of the attack was acquitted, and four other members were found not guilty for the destruction of Hancock's property. Operation Zircon received an international award from the International Motorcycle Gang Investigators Association in 2004 (Media Release—Western Australia Police Service, September 16, 2004). Bikie violence is still continuing unabated, as seen in Box 8.5.

BOX 8.4 OMG VIOLENCE IN AUSTRALIA (1984-2001)

September 2, 1984: Milperra Massacre: Seven people killed in battle between Comancheros and Bandidos.

August 31, 1998: Six people wounded when 85 warring Outlaws and Odin's Warriors MC fought in the Queensland city of Mackay.

October 14, 1998: Coffin Cheater member shot to death at the wheel of his car in Perth.

November 9, 1998: Bandidos president and two other gang members shot dead at Sydney's Blackmarket nightclub.

May 1, 1999: Arson attack on the Bandidos clubhouse in Adelaide's northwest.

May 1999: Violent clashes between Rebels and Black Uhlans MC in Gladstone, Queensland.

July 13, 1999: Police use a bulldozer to raid the Melbourne headquarters of the Hells Angels as part of a murder investigation.

July 15, 1999: A bomb blast demolishes a building in Adelaide that was to be the Rebel's new clubhouse, causing damage to nearby homes and businesses.

August 1, 1999: Three biker club members charged after a shootout in Adelaide's northern suburbs, shots also fired the next day when the men were due to appear in court.

August 3, 1999: Federal and state police meet in Adelaide, form special operation code-named AVATAR to crack down on bikie violence.

August 4, 1999: Comanchero beaten to death and his body dumped outside his ex-wife's western Sydney home.

August 5, 1999: Disused (abandoned) house firebombed on the Rebels' Bringley-based western Sydney chapter property.

August 6, 1999: One-time Rebels president disappears from outside a hotel in Queanbeyan, NSW.

August 8, 1999: Bomb attack on Bandidos clubhouse in Geelong, Victoria.

September 20, 1999: Homemade bomb attack on Bandidos clubhouse in Gosford, NSW.

September 22, 1999: Rebels member shot dead in drive-by attack on the gang's central NSW coast chapters' headquarters at west Gosford.

September 28, 1999: Finks member shot in the head and arm by unidentified sniper in Coffs Harbour on NSW mid-north coast.

October 8, 1999: Police detonate a device outside the Bandidos Ballarat, Victoria, clubhouse.

October 8, 1999: Three Rebels gunned down outside the club's Adelaide headquarters.

September 2, 2001: Former Western Australian detective Don Hancock and his friend killed in car-bomb by Gypsy Jokers.

This list is illustrative of early bikie violence and not exhaustive.

Australian bikie violence is often indiscriminate, and no one is safe from bikie violence, not even one's fellow patchholding "Brothers." In 2002, a New South Wales Comanchero sergeant at arms received 10 years for manslaughter after the beating death of another Comanchero while administering discipline for violating club rules. The Bandidos have also engaged in intragang violence. The Australian Bandidos' national sergeant at arms, on parole after the 1998 manslaughter of two men, killed the Australian Bandidos national president following an argument at dinner. He later committed suicide (Braithwaite, 2006, May 12). At times, the gangs have cooperated with each other in criminal activities, but this does not assure that they will discontinue their violent attacks on one another in battles over turf and "showing class." A 2004 operation by New South Wales police authorities led to the arrest of members of the Rebels, Nomads, Gypsy Jokers, Hells Angels, and Finks who had formed a network to produce cannabis and methamphetamines (Anon. 18, 2004, May 26). Within two years, the former partners in crime were shooting, stabbing, and bashing each other. In 2006, the Finks and the Hells Angels fought at a surfer's convention, resulting in five persons—one a bystander—being shot and stabbed (Anon. 19, 2006). In the same year, the Rebels and the Hells Angels were involved in turf battles over the drug trade (Anon. 20, 2006, May 20). On occasion, bikie violence is directed at non-members for revenge. In 2004, the ex-wife of a Hells Angel member was murdered because she testified against him and other HA members, connecting them to a gun used in a 1996 South Australian double murder (McAloon, 2004, January 29).

BOX 8.5 AUSTRALIAN BIKIE VIOLENCE IN THE NEWS APRIL 2012 BY STATE

Adelaide (Capital South Australia)

- An internal feud between Hells Angels bikies led to one member being shot by another four times.
  - Eight shots were fired into a family house while a man with links to the Comancheros was on the verandah. His wife and three children were just meters away in the family car.

Melbourne (Victoria)

- A Finks MC sergeant at arms was jailed for assaulting a car dealer and driving away in a $400,000 Lamborghini and demanding $50,000 for its return.

Sydney (Capital New South Wales)

- Two suspected Hells Angels bikie gang associates were charged with firing into a house.
  - Comanchero boss Mahmoud "Mick" Hawi jailed for 21 years for the murder of Hells Angels member's brother at Sydney airport.
  - Hells Angels member accused of burning police patrol car outside his tattoo parlor.

Perth (Western)

- Rock Machine MC member found guilty of shooting Western Australia Rebels president.

Queensland (Queensland)

- Hells Angels member evicted from pub near Bandidos clubhouse on the Gold Coast a day after a Bandidos-protected tattoo parlor was shot up.

Source: Adapted from Farquhar, 2012, April 27.

Australian Bikies by State

Queensland

OMGs operate throughout Australia; however, gang activity is a serious crime problem in the eastern state of Queensland. Queensland is considered Australia's Gold Coast and is the center of large casino operations and an international tourist market with an increasing methamphetamine market. In its 2004 report on organized crime, the

Queensland Crime and Misconduct Commission states, "Members of outlaw motorcycle gangs (OMCGs) have a significant involvement in organized crime in Queensland" (Queensland Crime and Misconduct Commission, 2004:4). These OMGs [we will continue to use the term "OMG," even though Australian authorities use "OMCG"] are primarily involved in the manufacturing and distribution of amphetamines. Members are, to a lesser extent, involved in the distribution of Ecstasy, cannabis, and occasionally heroin. Gang members have also been involved in fraud, identity crimes, motor vehicle thefts, firearms trafficking, extortion, loan sharking, and prostitution. A key finding was that criminal activity more often consisted of members acting as a part of a criminal network with non-OMG criminals or members from other OMGs, often competing with each other, rather than as a club/gang (Queensland Crime and Misconduct Commission, 2004:36). This finding would put the OMGs found in the Australian State of Queensland in the category of Social Criminal Organizations on the **Criminal Organizations Continuum of One-Percent Motorcycle Clubs.**

The authorities expect the violence between bikie gangs in Queensland to escalate. The competition over drug markets has expanded to violence between bikie gangs and street gangs. A member of a street gang, the JJs, was shot in the head, execution-style, outside a shopping center, allegedly by two members of the Brisbane Bandidos Centro chapter in April 2012 (Robertson & Baskin, 2012, June 12). The street gang was reported to be "muscling in on" the Bandidos drug-running business on Brisbane's southside.

Brisbane is the home of the Rebels "mother" chapter, and they have engaged in a bloody war with the Bandidos. Bikie gangs exist all throughout Queensland, but the Gold Coast is the major hub for the gangs, with traditional gangs such as the Finks, Bandidos, Black Uhlans, and the Nomads joined by new clubs such as the Brotherhood and the Cruisers (Sutton, 2013).

Victoria

The Hells Angels and the Bandidos have been recruiting members of rival Middle-Eastern families who have members inside and outside of prisons (Sutton, 2013). It is estimated that Victoria has 1,200 bikies belonging to gangs such as the Hells Angels, Bandidos, Rebels, Vikings, Immortals, and two Hells Angels puppet clubs, the Red Devils and the Tramps.

New South Wales

The State of New South Wales and Sydney, the most populous city in Australia, are the sites of violent criminal behavior by Australian bikie gangs. The Australian Hells Angels announced their move into Sydney, Australia, with the shooting of a local bouncer (Gibbs, 2006). The shooting was meant to be a signal to Sydney's other biker gangs—the Rebels, Bandidos, Nomads, Finks, Comancheros, and Gypsy Jokers—that the Angels wanted a part of the lucrative drug trade. In addition, the Rebels moved into territories controlled by the Outlaws and the Bandidos, spurring turf wars with these gangs. Five Bandidos were charged with arson for setting fire to the Brisbane clubhouse of the Rebels (Sid, 2007, April 16). The clubhouse was demolished because of fire damage. In April 2008, the Hells Angels and the Finks brawled in the Adelaide (Australia) Airport, when they met by chance while waiting for members on different flights. A war between the Australia-based Rebels MC and the Bandidos was linked to 13 shootings in Sydney in a two-week period during December 2008. Two Rebel members went on trial in August 2009 for a drive-by shooting in front of a Bandidos clubhouse that killed a Bandidos enforcer. There was a shooting war between the Hells Angels and the Nomads MC in Sydney and the Hells Angels and Bandidos bikie gangs at this time. The authorities expect the violence between bikie gangs to escalate. The competition over drug markets has also expanded to violence between bikie gangs and street gangs.

During the tit-for-tat shootouts between the Hells Angels and Nomads MC in Sydney, Australia, an innocent couple "took evasive action by diving on the floor and crawling into a hallway to take shelter behind a double-brick wall," as 13 shots were fired into their apartment by Hells Angels associates (Anon. 2, 2012, April 24). The lady in the apartment above them had to seek cover on the floor during the drive-by shooting. The previous tenant of the couple's apartment was a member of the Nomads motorcycle gang. There were 23 shootings in April 2012, most of which were attributed to the biker war. On one Monday night in April 2012, there were five random shootings into houses and businesses and a machine gun spraying of bullets into the street. Police believe that gang associates are carrying out the shootings to protect the patchholders from prosecution. The Sydney police, under tremendous public pressure, have formed a task force to curb the escalating turf war between the motorcycle gangs. These random shootings will undoubtedly lead to innocent deaths and injuries if they continue. Bullets meant for someone else can kill anyone with whom they come into contact; there is no "oops" in random shootings.

South Australia

The ACC reported in January 2008 that 10 of the nation's bikie gangs had added 26 new chapters (www.news.com.au/adelaidenow/story). Three of the new chapters were added in the State of South Australia which already had eight bikie gangs: Bandidos, Descendants, Finks, Gypsy Jokers, Hells Angels, Mobshitters, Rebels, and Red Devils. This expansion only added to the tension between gangs and led to territorial disputes and violence.

Western Australia

The Coffin Cheaters and the Gypsy Jokers are the major motorcycle gangs in Western Australia. These two gangs are bitter enemies and have been involved in violent clashes with each other for years.

Northern Territory

According to the ACC report, the Hells Angels, in an expansion move, patched over the Blonks MC in the Northern Territory. All but two members were patched in. An interesting aspect of this move was that all the members of the Blonks had criminal records that prevented them from incorporating.

IMPLICATIONS OF BIKIE EXPANSION

The Commission estimates that there are 3,500 "full-patched" members in these new gangs. One of these new bikie gangs, the **Notorious MC**, composed of former Nomads members and men of Middle East or Pacific Island descent, was formed and is staking out territory in other bikie areas. The Notorious MC is a curious group who are more criminals than bikers. They sport a vest with a three-piece patch, but most do not own or ride motorcycles. The president of Notorious is quoted as saying that the bike club "was formed as a motorcycle club to not be undermined and not to be dictated to by existing clubs" (www.news.com.au/story/0,25252114-421,00.html). One of those dictated rules they will not accept is that "new age" motorcycle club members must have motorcycles.

Tasmania

Six major motorcycle gangs (Rebels, Satan's Riders, Devil's Henchmen, Outlaws, the Finks, and the Black Uhlans) and several offshoot gangs operate in Tasmania (Sutton, 2013). In July, 2013, the former Rebels state president was convicted of trafficking in methamphetamine.

Official Response to Australian Bikie Gangs

We have already examined the creation of the Panzer Task Force in 1995, a cooperative effort between federal and state agencies. Individual states have also acted against bikie gangs. South Australia passed legislation, the Serious and Organized Crime (Control) Act, 2008, that would allow bikie gangs to be banned from public places and their members to be prosecuted for criminal association. The law would allow the police to ban, on public safety grounds, after an 72 hour notice, individuals or group members going to a public place or event. The law would allow the government to declare bikie gangs prohibited criminal groups and arrest members for criminal association. This would be a powerful weapon against the gangs, as the police could arrest members without having to go through the difficulty of infiltrating the group. A case against the Finks MC was the first test of the legislation in 2009. The court declared the Finks a criminal organization, but an appeal to the Supreme Court was successful and the court ruled the law was invalid. The decision was appealed to the High Court, which scrapped the law, claiming it would impinge on individual freedom. Several states are proposing that the federal government step in and introduce national anti-bikie laws that cannot be challenged in the High Court (Farquhar, 2012, April 27). If the Australian laws are ultimately successful, New Zealand plans to follow suit (Grover, 2009, January 14). There is growing concern in New Zealand as gang violence escalates between biker gangs over control of the drug markets (Anon. d, 2007, April 5). A raid on the Bandidos across New Zealand seized drugs and weapons. Several cities in New Zealand have passed laws to ban the wearing of gang patches in public.

In May 2012, New South Wales passed a ban on the wearing of gang regalia in Sydney's King's Cross district—a late-night, "sleazy" district (Shand, 2012, May 5). The list of banned gang regalia includes any article of clothing or jewelry displaying club names, color schemes, the club patch, insignia, and the "1%" or "1%er" symbol. Authorities in New South Wales have taken a unique step against the Sydney chapter of the Hells Angels. The state's Supreme Court has ruled that the police do not need a warrant to raid the Sydney Hells Angels clubhouse. The court decided that the clubhouse falls under the Restricted Premises Act of 1943, which holds that a restricted premise can be raided without a warrant if there is suspicion that drunken, disorderly, or indecent conduct is occurring, or if drugs or liquor are being unlawfully sold or supplied (Anon. g, 2009, January 28).

An Outlaw Motor Cycle Gang Squad was formed in Queensland, Australia, "to fight against bikie gangs who are involved in drug dealing, extortion and violence" (Wilson, 2006). The impetus for this bikie squad was a shoot-out between the Hells Angels and the Finks motorcycle gangs. In that shoot-out at a kickboxing tournament, three people were shot and two people stabbed. Operation Ranmore, a 2008-2009 police operation against the Hells Angels, Rebels, Bandidos, Lone Wolf, Finks, Fourth Reich, and Nomads in Queensland resulted in 811 arrests for 1,838 charges ranging from drug offenses to affray [fighting], assault, weapons offenses, and participation in a criminal group. However, the bikie violence has not abated in Queensland. Three days after the police applied to the Queensland Supreme Court to have the Gold Coast chapter of the Finks MC declared a criminal organization, there were two early morning shootings into Bandidos properties, a Brisbane Clubhouse and a tattoo parlor (Barrett, 2012, June 5). One of the five shots sprayed at the reinforced clubhouse ricocheted off a metal wall that had been put over the front window evidently in anticipation of an attack, hit a nearby restaurant, increasing fears that innocent victims will be injured or killed in the escalating bikie violence (Robertson, Kyriacou, & Vonow, 2012, June 5).

In order to succeed, the 95-page application to the Queensland Supreme Court requires the police to prove three things: (1) there are more than three members of the group, (2) the group gathers for the purpose of crime, and (3) the group is an unacceptable risk to the community (Wordsworth, 2012, June 4). The application details that there are 48 members of the alleged criminal organization, and they have been convicted of murder, drug trafficking, extortion, robbery, grievous bodily harm, and firearms offenses. The prospects for a successful conclusion of the criminal organization application are not good. The Supreme Court has previously rejected applications from South Australia against the Finks and from New South Wales against the Hells Angels on the grounds that such declarations violate freedom of association.

A 2012 Gold Coast shooting of a senior Bandidos member by a reported Finks member at a shopping mall left an innocent woman injured. As a reaction to the shootings, the police attributed the shootings to biker gang turf rivalry and took the usual law enforcement approach to lessen tit-for-tat violence by creating a task force, Taskforce Kilo Cajun, to investigate the incidents; however, the

Queensland police already have an anti-bikie unit, Taskforce Hydra. It appears that the new Brisbane Bandidos chapter, the victims of the shootings, named the Balkan Bandidos because of members predominately from nations of the former Yugoslavia, is another example of a biker club without bikers. Newspaper sources report that some of the bikies do not have motorcycle licenses (Robertson et al., 2012, June 5).

New South Wales fighting has been in evidence between the Bandidos and the indigenous Notorious MC, a bikie gang without motorcycles, as well as between the Hells Angels and the Comancheros. New South Wales was the site of one of the most violent acts of violence by bikies in recent Australian history. The brother of a senior member of the Hells Angels Guilford chapter was stabbed with scissors and bludgeoned to death with a metal bollard found frequently in airport assembly areas on March 22, 2009, in a brawl involving at least 20 "bikies" between the Hells Angels and the Comancheros in one of the most secure areas of Sydney, the Sydney Airport, a high-security public place (Welch, Kennedy, & Harvey, 2009). The two groups were on the same flight, and the threats and insults began on the plane. Members of each bikie gang text-messaged for reinforcements to meet them in the airport. When the passengers got off the plane, the two groups began fighting. One of the passengers in the terminal, a nurse, is being recognized as a heroine during the bloody brawl because she pushed her way through the fighting bikers and attempted to save the life of the mortally wounded victim (Foy, 2009). Ironically, the victim was wanted for stabbing an off-duty police officer the Friday before he was killed (Ramachandran, 2009). The airport brawl occurred just two hours after drive-by shootings at six homes in a suburb of Sydney linked to the Bandidos and the Notorious. The brazen nature of this violence in front of 50 witnesses and four CCTV cameras caused a public outcry and demands for legislation to outlaw bikie gangs. Among the laws passed in New South Wales is one that makes it a criminal offense to recruit members to a bikie gang (Anon. k, 2009). Another new law allows the police to apply to the Supreme Court to have bikie gangs declared criminal organizations. New South Wales has also banned the wearing of colors and the bikie ownership of tattoo parlors in an attempt to end the bikie wars.

This airport incident may be a harbinger of things to come in the future. An Australian bikie expert, Arthur Veno, predicted, "Yesterday was nothing compared to what's on the scene" (Sullivan, 2009). Veno's prediction appears to be coming true. The surviving brother of the victim of the Sydney airport brawl was shot and critically wounded in his car in front of his house a week later, just three days after his brother was buried. True to the biker code, the victim refuses to cooperate with the police and will not tell them anything about the person who shot him, another example of what former HAMC president Chuck Zito called biker's "street justice." Bikers handle their own problems without resorting to the criminal justice system used by "citizens."

The leader of the Comancheros, Mahmoud "Mick" Hawi, and another member were charged with murder in the Sydney Airport shooting. Ten Comancheros and three Hells Angels have been charged in the airport incident, most for riot and affray. Hawi was convicted and sentenced to 21 years for the murder. The violence and crackdown on bikie gangs in the states of South Australia and New South Wales has the authorities in the state of Queensland fearing that the gangs will relocate there. There is some evidence to support that fear as the number of gangs in Queensland has grown from 10 to 14 since 2006, and membership in OMGs had increased from 600 to 830 patched members. Queensland is moving forward with anti-bikie laws similar to that of New South Wales and South Australia. The Queensland laws would give the Supreme Court the power to:

- Declare a bikie gang a criminal organization.
- Apply control orders against individual members of declared organizations.
- Stop members of declared organizations from associating.
- Order removal of fortifications, such as metal gates, which prevent police access (Gills, 2009).

Non-OMG members are sometimes caught up in the violence. A 53-year-old innocent woman was wounded in the shooting of a Bandidos member by a reported member of the Hells Angels during a Saturday shootout in a Queensland Gold Coast shopping center. Law enforcement authorities are worried that this shooting signals an escalation of the Queensland bikie wars. The accused shooter is a member of the Finks MC and has tattoos on his face reading "1%," "carnage," and "revenge." The Hells Angels member, also heavily tattooed, had visible tattoos on his face, neck, and arms as well. According to newspaper accounts, bikie sources say that the shooting may have been a personal matter between the two rival club members and not sanctioned by the Finks MC, who are reportedly trying to negotiate a peace pact (Stolz, 2012, May 4). Supposedly, the two had a history of bad feelings for each other and clashed after bumping into each other at the shopping center. Other versions have the Finks shooter as a hired "hit man" for the Hells Angels who are at war with the Bandidos. Time will tell what version of the shooting is accurate.

Recent Developments Down Under

In another ominous development for Australian bikie gangs, police authorities report that the Bandidos and the Outlaws often use street gang members for low-level drug distribution, car thefts, and break-ins (Miranda, 2003). The Hells Angels have allegedly used young "associates" in their Sydney turf war with the Nomads MC. In May 2012, two 18-year-old boys were charged with drive-by shootings at homes and businesses of Nomads (Ralston, 2012, May 11). This practice insulates Hells Angels members from arrest and prosecution. Young bikie "wannabes" are eager to increase their status and reputation by being linked with the Hells Angels.

A case involving extortion against the Sydney Hells Angels that was dropped by the New South Wales police has hit the headlines (Carson, 2012, May 31). Two Hells Angels charged in the extortion attempt claim that they should be compensated $45,000 in legal fees because the police prosecuted them "without reasonable cause." The police counter that the charges had to be dropped because the Hells Angels threatened the witness against them, causing the witness to refuse to testify. The Hells Angels and their lawyer rejoin that the alleged victim is an unreliable witness who has laundered money for cocaine dealers in the past. They claim that the reluctant extortion "victim" offered to "clean" drug money for a 10% fee and say the police knew or should have known of this because the allegation was made in open court the preceding year, and assert they should have also known that the "victim" had been convicted of fraud in 1995. The hearing magistrate has reserved his decision on their request. If there is merit to the Hells Angels allegation, the alleged "victim" would be an unreliable, or at least tainted, witness who would likely be loath to testify in court where he would be subjected to what surely would be an aggressive cross-examination.

Australian law enforcement authorities have stated that the six chapters of the Sydney Hells Angels have tripled in size and have been co-opted by international organized crime networks (Box & Aikman, 2012, May 18). According to the head of the New South Wales Organized Crime Directorate, the majority of the 150 Sydney Hells Angels are of Middle Eastern descent with family ties to criminal organizations in Australia and overseas. In effect, these ties mean the old image of the bikie gang is over. These are criminal gangs, first, then they are bikies. The organized crime networks are taking advantage of the bikers "power of the patch" for their criminal activities.

The Attero National Task Force, an ACC Board Task Force, has been established to target the Rebels MC, which has chapters in every state and overseas. The focus of the task force is to disrupt the business model of the Rebels MC. The task force has three phases: (1) gathering intelligence on the Rebels MC, (2) nationally coordinating disruptive activities, and (3) review of the activities and outcomes and targeting other OMCGs. Phases 1 and 2 have had the following results:

- Arrested more than 330 people;
- Laid more than 500 charges, ranging from violence-related offenses including serious assaults, kidnapping, and affray, to a range of firearms and weapons offenses, drug offenses, and property, street, and traffic offenses;
- Searched more than 300 premises;
- Seized more than 40 firearms, as well as other weapons including knuckle dusters, a set of throwing stars, machetes, illegal knives, and batons; and
- Seized drugs including amphetamines, cannabis, Ecstasy, and steroids (ACC, 2012, November 7).

Bikie violence continues unabated in Australia. The current war between the Hells Angels MC and the Comancheros MC in Sydney has led to five shootings in one two-week period, with two dead. The Prime Minister described the shootings as a case of criminals shooting criminals (Walker, Auerbac, 2013, July 24).

In a menacing twist to the international crime threat of U.S.-based OMGs, the violent and criminal biker gang, the Mongols MC, have patched over 90% of the

Australian Finks MC. This is coupled with the Mongols MC expansion to Norway where they now have four chapters (www.mongolsmc.com/chapters). According to the Mongols MC official website, they have six chapters in Australia—two in Sydney, and one each in Adelaide, Central Coast, Melbourne, and Perth. Mongols MC Australia has its own website and declares:

> Mongols Motorcycle Club [Australia] has been building brotherhood and biking worldwide for over 40 years and has built its reputation in the biker world. It has now evolved into Australia with massive support. We, as a club, have gone back to the true basic values of what a motorcycle club is and should be and that reflects on the Brotherhood that we have with our Support, Love, and Respect for one another, and our passion for Motorcycles is unheard of…
>
> (www.mongolsmcaustralia.com.au/)

In spite of the flowery proclamation above, violence will assuredly increase because of the worldwide enmity between the Mongols MC and the Hells Angels MC. Fighting each other is a natural way of life for the bitter enemies, or as the Mongols MC stated on their blog: "Off and on for the last 35 years members of the Hells Angels Motorcycle Club and the Mongols Motorcycle Club have fought when they meet. Outlaw bikers are among the last Americans honor-bound to fight duels and sometimes duels are fatal." The problem is that there is nothing honor-bound about these supposed "duels," as they shoot each other from ambush, drive-by and blast each other off their bikes, plant bombs that kill bikers and civilians, and "rat pack" enemies and beat them to death.

NEW ZEALAND

New Zealand is an island country in the southwestern Pacific Ocean (see Figure 8.2). The Criminal Investigative Branch of the New Zealand police reports that: "There are many motorcycle gangs in New Zealand and they are frequently involved in the illegal manufacture and sale of drugs, violent crime, and vice. Membership of these gangs can be of mixed race" (www.police.govt.nz). However, these gangs, even though engaged in criminal activities, are not the serious organized crime threat that OMGs are in Australia. And, as we will see, the establishment of OMGs, namely the Hells Angels, changed the gang scene in New Zealand to one not found anywhere else in the world.

The official *Te-ARA: The Encyclopedia of New Zealand* reports that there are 20 OMGs in New Zealand with 39 chapters (newzealand.gov.nz). Two gangs are not listed: the Rebels MC from Australia and the U.S.-based Bandidos that opened up a prospect chapter in 2012. As shown in Box 8.6, the Hells Angels are the only U.S.-based OMG to have a presence in New Zealand (the Bandidos chapter is a prospect chapter that may or may not become a fully recognized chapter). The majority of the New Zealand OMGs are indigenous gangs, often Maori.

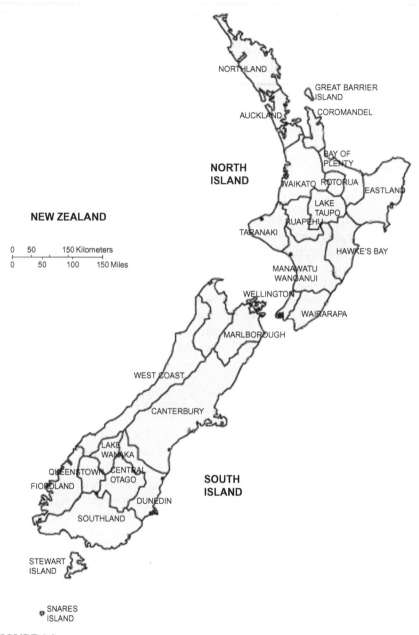

FIGURE 8.2

New Zealand.

Map courtesy of Bruce Jones Design Inc.

The Rise of the Outlaw Clubs 1960-1980

Gilbert (2013) describes the evolution of New Zealand's OMGs from "milk-bar cowboys" in the 1950s to the establishment of the first Hells Angels chapter in Auckland (1961) and its effect on the rise of New Zealand outlaw clubs. Milk bars in the 1950s, before the rise of fast food franchises and shopping malls, were places where young people could hang out and buy ready-made food and non-alcoholic drinks, and socialize. Those patrons known as **milk-bar cowboys** were unruly, disorganized groups of young "delinquent" motorcyclists with the philosophy of "do what you like when you like." No doubt these "cowboys" were influenced by the biker movies coming out of Hollywood, such as *The Wild One*, and the media given to American juvenile delinquents in the early 1950s. Crime, particularly juvenile crime, was rising in the 1950s in New Zealand, and much of it was attributed to the milk-bar cowboys by the popular media making them folk devils in the moral panic paradigm.

BOX 8.6 NEW ZEALAND OMGs

Gang (20)	Chapters (39)
Headhunters	4
Highway 61	6
Tribesmen	3
Forty Five	1
Hells Angels	2
Filthy Few	4
Outcasts	1
Greasy Dogs	1
Hu Hu	1
Magog	1
Outlaws (not U.S.-based)	1
Mothers	1
Tyrants	1
Satan's Slaves	1
Sinn Fien	1
Lost Breed	1
Red Devils	1
Epitaph Riders	2
Devil's Henchmen	2
Road Knights	3
Southern Vikings	1

Source: *www.tera.gov.nz/en/interactive/28243/motorcycle-gangs. Found October 28, 2013.*

Jim Carrico, an American claiming to be a member of the San Francisco Hells Angels, was a member of a group of milk-bar cowboys in Auckland. The small group called themselves the Auckland Outcasts. Carrico decided to turn this group into the Hells Angels, complete with patches sewn on the back of their old short-sleeved school pullovers. The three-piece patch held the words "Hells Angels" on top, an eagle and "death's head" insignia in the middle and Auckland below. The media soon learned of this new Hells Angels chapter and a reporter sought out Carrico for an interview. Carrico told the reporter: "I'm a member of the Hells Angels of San Francisco... They're a big club, you know, and they go back to a fighter squadron of World War I" (Gilbert, 2013:18). In addition to giving erroneous information about the Hells Angels' founding, Carrico went on with his exaggerated claims and said there was a Hells Angels group "in every major city in the South Western United States. Regional headquarters were established in San Francisco and Los Angeles and today there are thousands of members from Canada to Mexico and now New Zealand."

After the newspaper article appeared, Carrico sent a letter to the President of the San Francisco Hells Angels trying to explain his deception and claim of membership: "As far as me telling him [the reporter] that I was a member of your club, I extend my humblest of apologys [sic] to you and your club, but like I had to give him some sort of direct connection. And as far as there being thousands of members from Canada to Mexico, well you know how it is. I mean I get kind of carried away some times" (Gilbert, 2013:18-19). Gilbert authenticated this correspondence and reports that there are two letters from Carrico to the San Francisco Hells Angels at the Auckland HAMC clubhouse. Carrico went on to tell the San Francisco Hells Angels that the officers of the Auckland Hells Angels included a president, a vice president, a treasurer/secretary, and a road captain. Membership requirements included: a person had to pay a weekly fee for three weeks, ride with the group for a month, and be unanimously voted in by existing members—the same rules used in the United States. Carrico also set up the same system of fines for rules violation that existed in San Francisco. Carrico's familiarity of the Hells Angels organizational structure leads to the belief that he must have obtained some knowledge of the Hells Angels when he lived in the United States. The San Francisco Hells Angels agreed to officially sanction the Auckland Hells Angels as a charter [chapter], though with Pete Skinner, not Carrico, as president.

Gilbert (2013:28) opines that two "Hells Angels innovations had a particularly powerful impact on the gangs scene [youth gangs, street gangs and biker gangs] in New Zealand." The first innovation was the adoption of the patch by all New Zealand gangs, not just outlaw motorcycle gangs. This symbol and identifier gave members a sense of identity and pride. This new identifier created strong intragroup bonds within the gangs. The patch created separate groups within the previously homogeneous milk-bar cowboy subculture.

The second innovation was the establishment of a formal organizational structure and the rules that maintained it. This held true with outlaw motorcycle gangs and street gangs. Nearly all the New Zealand street gangs adopted the Hells Angels organizational model. Gilbert reports that this HA model gave the New Zealand gang scene a unique degree of structural form that eventually aided the gangs, both street and outlaw motorcycle, when they were later involved in "crime for profit" (i.e., organized crime). The organizational structure meant the gangs were not so prone to disintegrate when key members left for whatever reason. Gang leadership became a position, not a person. An identity and organizational structure supported the longevity of the gang. The gang was a separate and distinct entity that endured as members came and went. As the gangs, particularly the Hells Angels, evolved, they moved into organized crime.

Although the first Hells Angels chapter was formed in Auckland in 1961, it was not until the 1980s that the Angels became involved in organized crime (Newbold, 1997). According to Newbold, the Auckland Angels did not become involved in the manufacture and distribution of amphetamines and LSD until the California Hells Angels became their main supply source. Drug dealing allowed the New Zealand Angels to become prosperous, leading to the purchase of real estate and a home in an Auckland suburb for a clubhouse. In the 1990s, the Hells Angels were the best organized gang in New Zealand and the supplier of methamphetamines and LSD to the other gangs (Newbold, 1997). At one time, a New Zealand Angel, Andrew Sisson, was the Hells Angels world secretary. He often made trips to the United States, Canada, Europe, South Africa, and Australia to conduct Hells Angels business. Sisson and his wife were convicted in 1999 of conspiring to manufacture methamphetamine and money laundering.

New Zealand police say there are four outlaw motorcycle gangs in Christchurch: the Devil's Henchmen, Highway 61, Epitaph Riders, and the Road Knights. These indigenous OMGs have also been involved in organized crime activities. The authorities say that a prospect must commit a criminal act to become a member of these gangs. In 1999, the Hells Angels and the indigenous Headhunters MC were reportedly making millions working together in criminal activities (Manning, 1999). In previous years, there were wars between the OMGs, but now it appears that they cooperate with one another in criminal activities.

New Zealand's Actions Against Patched Gangs, Including OMGs

Governmental agencies have tried several strategies against the patched gangs of New Zealand. The New Zealand Police is a national organization with central headquarters control. It is New Zealand's primary agency dealing with organized crime. It was first established as a national force under the Police Act of 1886. From 1886 until 1958, the organization was known as the New Zealand Police Force. In 1958, the word "force" was removed from the name when the legislation was revised (www.police.net.au/new-zealand_police.htm). The New Zealand Police was established by an Act of Parliament and is under the control of a Cabinet minister responsible for policy and overall administration; however, direct control is the responsibility of a Commissioner. The New Zealand Police is divided into 12 districts: nine in the North Island (Northland, Waitematā, Auckland City, Counties Manukau, Waikato, Bay of Plenty, Eastern, Central, and Wellington) and three in the South (Tasman, Canterbury, and Southern). Each district is under the control of a commissioned officer that has the responsibility for law and order in that district. Each district has a central station from which the subsidiary and suburban stations are controlled. There are 352 police stations in New Zealand. A map with further information can be found at: www.police.govt.nz/about-us/structure/districts.

Table 8.1 Core Values of the New Zealand Police	
Intelligence-Led Policing	**Community-Focused Policing**
The New Zealand Police have built a first-class intelligence model to combat and reduce organized crime. The model gathers, analyzes, and distributes detailed and current criminal intelligence to proactively target and prosecute organized crime. Organized crime entities and individuals will be analyzed to ensure those creating harm in the community will be prioritized for targeted responses. Tasking and Coordination Groups across Areas and Districts will strengthen the police fight against organized crime by coordinating police activities.	The New Zealand Police deploy a community-focused approach to tackling organized crime. The approach involves all of their police partner agencies, non-governmental organizations, and individual citizens. Agencies, organizations, and individuals have a key understanding of what is happening in their community. They are critical eyes and ears in the prevention and disruption of organized crime and enhance the intelligence-led approach. Actively listening to local people and implementing robust, relevant, and effective responses will ensure public confidence and build resilience to organized crime.

Source: *police.govt.nz/sitesdefault/files/documents/POLICE%20SO*

The New Zealand Police follow the modern police strategies of intelligence-led policing and community-focused policing in their actions against the patched gangs and organized crime (see Table 8.1 and Box 8.7).

The Organized and Financial Crime Agency of New Zealand (OFCANZ)

The **Organized and Financial Crime Agency of New Zealand (OFCANZ)** and its task forces are the major effort against patched gangs, including Outlaw Motorcycle Gangs, in New Zealand. OFCANZ works with 22 New Zealand government agencies. According to New Zealand (NZ) Police Press Releases, the first OFCANZ action was a 100-person task force known as Operation Abyss against the Tribesmen motorcycle gang in the Northland Police District in 2008. The task force was composed of members from NZ Police, NZ Customs Service, Ministry of Fisheries, Department of Corrections, Ministry of Social Development, and the Serious Fraud Office. As a result of the action, 14 members and associates of the Tribesmen MC were arrested on charges of selling, supplying, and conspiracy to supply and manufacture methamphetamines. The Hells Angels and their puppet club also have been targets of OFCANZ operations. Four members of the Auckland Hells Angels were arrested in an OFCANZ operation targeting unlawful debt collection (Anon. 21, 2011, September 2). The Angels were charged with aggravated robbery, burglary, and theft in relation to crimes committed while collecting debts. This is another example of gang members using the "power of the patch" for illegal purposes. In the same year, an OFCANZ operation was carried out against the Red Devils MC, a Hells Angels puppet club, in the city of Nelson in the Tasman Police District (Anon. 22, 2011, March 11). The 18-month Operation Explorer resulted in 11 gang members arrested for offenses that included: participating in an organized crime group, drug supply and use, conspiracy to commit arson, assault, theft, burglary, receiving stolen property, and unlawful possession of firearms and explosives. According to the former New Zealand Police Minister Judith Collins, OFCANZ will combine with the police and other government agencies to prevent the expansion of the Australian Rebels Motorcycle Gang into New Zealand (Anon. 23, 2011, January 28). OFCANZ has already staged two operations against the Rebels MC.

BOX 8.7 ORGANIZED CRIME IN NEW ZEALAND

Organized Crime in New Zealand

Organized crime in New Zealand is perpetuated both by traditional groups with established hierarchies (patched gangs, including OMGs) and fluid criminal networks without rigid structures. Some organized criminal groups operate like sophisticated multinational businesses (Hells Angels MC). Individuals may also use membership of a criminal gang to facilitate their offending (social criminal organizations).

Organized crime networks and gangs in New Zealand are involved in:

- illicit drug trafficking, manufacturing, and distribution
- burglary and vehicle crime
- violence and intimidation
- electronic crime
- identity crime
- financial crime
- environmental crime

How Police Combat Organized Crime

New Zealand Police target, disrupt, and dismantle organized crime. Their approach is built upon first-class intelligence targeting key criminal groups and maximizing use of legislative powers. They claim to achieve this through:

- a National Organized Crime Control Strategy with concrete actions and clear measures
- a National Intelligence Centre that provides current and comprehensive organized crime intelligence
- hosting of the Organized and Financial Crime Agency of New Zealand [OFCANZ]
- dedicated district-based operational Organized Crime Units
- focused investigations cemented by first-class intelligence
- attacking the profits of crime through targeting of criminal assets [Criminal Proceeds (Recovery) Act]
- using technology and covert capability to infiltrate and gather evidence of organized crime

Source: *police.govt.nz/sitesdefault/files/documents/POLICE%20SO*.

New Zealand District Councils

As part of the democratic decision-making process, there are 54 district councils in New Zealand. Among the duties of the district councils are making by-laws and enforcing them (e.g., dog control, liquor licensing, noise control) (localcouncils.govt.nz). Some have interpreted this to also apply to "anti-patch" laws to control gang violence between rival patch wearers.

In an attempt to control gang violence, Whanganui District Council passed an anti-patch law that includes those worn by OMGs. Gangs are prohibited from wearing their insignias in a public place subject to confiscation and a $2,000 fine. The Hells Angels and their puppet club, Red Devils, are among the gangs specifically mentioned in the law. The other non-motorcycle gangs named in the by-laws are the Black Power, Magogs, Mongrel Mob, Nomads, Tribesmen, Head Hunters, and Mangu Kaha. As previously stated, these street gangs identify themselves with patches and often three-piece patches similar to those worn by biker gangs. The law was passed on the theory that the wearing of gang patches intimidates and harasses members of the public, and increases the potential for confrontation between rival gangs. For purposes of this legislation, a gang is defined as an organization, association, or group having "a common name or common identifying signs, symbols, or representations; and its members, associates, or supporters individually or collectively promote, encourage, or engage in a pattern of criminal activity." Wanganui District Council (Prohibiting of Gang Insignia) ACT 2009 defines gang insignia as:

(a) means a sign, symbol, or representation commonly displayed to denote membership of, an affiliation with, or support for a gang, not being tattoos; and
(b) includes any item of clothing to which a sign, symbol, or representation referred to in paragraph (a) is attached (www.legislation.govt.nz/local/2009).

The Hells Angels mounted a spirited effort to block the passage of the act, arguing that they are a motorcycle club and not a gang and that the act violated their rights of freedom of expression guaranteed under the New Zealand Bill of Rights Act. The act and its by-laws, which had the support of the New Zealand Police Association, had its first test in March 2010 when a Wanganui District Court judge ordered a Hells Angels member to turn in his patch to be destroyed after he was found guilty of illegally wearing it in public. This is probably not the end of challenges to the controversial law. However, one can expect other New Zealand district councils to pass anti-patch laws.

Back Patch Clubs in the United Kingdom

KEY TERMS

back patch clubs

Bulldog Bash

death's head logo

Road Rats MC

Vikings MC

UNITED KINGDOM

The United Kingdom of Great Britain and Northern Ireland, commonly known as the United Kingdom (U.K.), is a sovereign state located off the northwestern coast of continental Europe. The country includes the island of Great Britain (a term sometimes loosely applied to the whole state), the northeastern part of the island of Ireland, and many smaller islands (see Figure 9.1)

The "Big Four" **back patch clubs** (a U.K. term for OMGs in the United Kingdom) are considered to be: Hells Angels; Satans Slaves, with chapters mostly in the north and Scotland; the Outcasts, mostly in London; and the Outlaws. Two of these clubs, the Hells Angels and the Outlaws, are U.S.-based gangs that expanded to the United Kingdom. In addition, there are an unknown number of indigenous one-percent biker clubs, some with a long history, such as the Sons of Hell MC (formed in early 1970) and the Road Rats MC (see Box 9.1). The **Road Rats MC** is very proud of its British heritage and independence: "the club was formed in London and has remained in London, with no outside influences from America or Europe." Several U.K. back patch clubs have expanded internationally. The Satans Slaves list 17 chapters in England, two in Scotland, and four in Germany on their website (www.satansslavesmc.co.uk).

FIGURE 9.1

The United Kingdom (U.K.).

Map courtesy of Bruce Jones Design Inc.

In the late 1960s and early 1970s, U.K. indigenous motorcycle clubs, reacting to the international publicity of the notorious California Hells Angels, adopted the colors, red on white, name, or a variation of the Angels **death's head logo** as their own. The current **Vikings MC** England was formed in 1969 as the Hells Angels Vikings MC (HAVMC). Their colors were, and still are, blue and black, on white, with black borders, and their logo was a Vikings death's head facing forward. According to their official website (www.vikingsmc/home_html), the club was in a constant state of war with some other clubs over the back patch, most probably the London Hells Angels. The club was asked in 1980 to join with all the back patch clubs flying red and white colors or using the name Hells Angels under the banner of the U.S.-based Hells Angels. Prior to this solicitation by the Hells Angels, in 1975, four English members of the HAVMC moved to Ireland and established a new Vikings Motorcycle Club chapter in Dublin, Ireland. Their English brothers decided that now was the time to drop the Hells Angels from the back patch and simply become the Vikings Motorcycle Club, an independent club run by members with no outside interference. Therefore, they declined the offer by the Hells Angels because they knew they would come under the control of the U.S.-based Hells Angels and inherit all their enemies and troubles. The Vikings MC Ireland chapter is also proud of its independence (see Box 9.2). The Vikings MC now has chapters in England, Ireland, France, and Spain.

BOX 9.1 ROAD RATS MC—LONDON HISTORY

- Has run in an unbroken line since the early 1960s
- Has never stopped and started
- The club has never changed its name
- Never had other clubs affiliated with it and sharing its name
- Has never been part of a wider coalition of clubs
- Has always been an independent club

Source: *roadratsmc.co.U.K./history.html.*

BOX 9.2 VIKINGS MC—IRELAND: THE 1% CLUB WITH THE RIGHT ATTITUDE

The Vikings MC Ireland are proud to be members of the "Alliance Ireland" group of combined Irish MC 1% clubs, who are united to keep the Irish bike scene free of international biker politics. In the words of our Ancestors "Ireland her own, from the earth to the sky."

Source: *www.vikingsmcireland.com.*

The Sons of Hell were a red-on-white back patch club with a death's head logo from 1970 to 1990. The death's head was not the same in appearance as the Hells Angels. The Henchmen back patch club (formed in 1969 and later becoming the Outlaws North Wales) at the time were also a red-on-white club with a winged skull logo. The Devils Diciples (formed in 1965) and the Dragons (starting to ride together in 1957 but donning a back patch in 1957) also had red-on-white colors. The Outlaws MC Birmingham chapter originally started out as the Cycle Tramps MC, a red-on-white back patch club with a 1%er in a diamond patch and the number 13 in a square patch. In 1986, the Cycle Tramps changed their colors to red and yellow at the urging of the Hells Angels (www.outlawsmcbirmingham.com/history,asp). As stated earlier, at that time, it was common for U.K. back patch clubs to wear red-on-white colors and even call themselves Hells Angels, causing the London Hells Angels to "clean the mess up." The Sons of Hell changed their colors to black on white, their current colors.

HELLS ANGELS EXPANSION INTO THE U.K.

The first expansion of the U.S.-based outlaw motorcycle clubs into the U.K. came with the Hells Angels movement into London. It started with an invitation to visit England extended to the San Francisco charter (chapter) by the *Beatles* (HA members Tricky Tramp and Andy B, in Shaylor, 2004:16). The next year two British bikers were invited to travel to the United States, and they returned to England with two charters. The United Kingdom Hells Angels (HAMC) chapters were established in 1969. At the time, the two chapters, a South London chapter and an East London chapter, had different-sized logos—a big death's head insignia worn by the Oakland HAMC chapter and a small death's head insignia worn by the San Francisco chapter. In 1973, the two chapters merged, becoming one London chapter with the present large death's head logo. This expansion changed forever the nature of outlaw motorcycle gangs worldwide and their criminal activities; unfortunately, this expansion was marked by the violence and biker politics common in the United States. The newly established chapters served as a door to Europe and a bridge for the U.S.-based biker gangs that was quickly seized upon and became a road well-traveled by the Hells Angels, Outlaws, and Bandidos. Within the next 30 years, the Hells Angels granted 14 charters/chapters in England and Wales (see Box 9.3).

BOX 9.3 HAMC U.K. EXPANSION 1969-1999

London (2 chapters) July 1969

West Coast: August 1974	Wolverhampton: October 1985
Essex: August 1976	Ashfield: May 1986
Kent: December 1976	Nomads: February 1989
Wessex: January 1977	Middlesex: January 1994
South Coast: February 1977	Manchester: April 1998
Tyne and Wear: June 1979	South West (first in Wales): October 1999
Les Valley: March 1985	Northants: October 1999

Source: *Shaylor, 2004:16.*

The book, *Buttons: the Making of a President* (Mandelkau, 1971), is the autobiography of "Buttons" Peter Welsh, one of the two first English HAMC presidents. In May 1969, Buttons flew to San Francisco and "prospected" with the San Francisco chapter. He returned to England in November 1969 with the official club charter for the Hells Angels–England. The book describes the early deviant lifestyle common to the early Angels—drug taking, sex orgies, and drug dealing. Buttons also relates the account of earning his "brown wings"—the sodomy of a man observed by other Angels. He and a group of Angels sodomized a "drag queen." Others, particularly law enforcement, have alluded to "brown wings"; however, recent works by Hells Angels members say these rituals never existed. Nevertheless, according to records released under the Freedom of Information Act, FBI agents in their reports to Director J. Edgar Hoover described the Hells Angels as drug addicts and homosexuals, supposedly because of such activities.

One of the first scholarly books on bikers was *Bikers: Birth of a Modern Day Outlaw*, by Maz Harris, published in 1985. The late Maz Harris (killed in a motorcycle accident in 2000) was the president and a founding member of the Hells Angels chapter in Kent, England. The legendary Harris was a writer for most of the biker magazines and was the official Hells Angels public relations person. Harris was also a sociologist from the University of Warwick, and the book was based on his doctoral dissertation research titled "Myth and Reality in Motorcycle Subculture." In addition, he was the official tester for Harley-Davidson in the U.K. He died while testing a bike; he blew a front tire and crashed. Harris's book describes the development of the "outlaw" subculture and the Hells Angels Motorcycle Club. The 128-page book has 81 photographs, many of early English bikers. Harris says that the "tribes of the biker nation" are international, and although they do not share a common language, they share "a belief in freedom and in brotherhood" (Harris, 1985:125). His work downplays the criminal involvement of the HAMC, and it is not very objective, but it is a good sociological explanation of the subcultural development of biker clubs.

Biker violence soon followed the HAMC expansion. The HAMC is well known in the biker subculture for its arrogant attitude and feelings of superiority. The Angels want to be seen as the dominant motorcycle club in any area they occupy. Their well-recognized proclivity to disband, gobble up, or patch over any smaller or weaker clubs soon leads to trouble and violence. The Road Rats MC, mentioned earlier, started out as a London street gang before evolving into a motorcycle club, and they were very proud of their British roots and could not care less for the arrogance and reputation of the bad-assed bikers from "the Colonies." The Hells Angels offered the Road Rats the opportunity to join as a prospective chapter, thus beginning the process of becoming an official chapter, if found worthy. The Road Rats MC disrespectfully declined the invitation and would not cede domination of North London to the intruding Hell Angels. Following several months of tension, the two groups decided to meet on the Chelsea Bridge over the River Thames in West London, which connects Chelsea on the north bank to Battersea on the south bank. As they approached each other in classic "OK Corral" fashion, they were within six feet of one another when the 20-year-old president of the Road Rats pulled a sawed-off shot gun from under his jacket and shot the president of the Hells Angels in the stomach, killing him. Two dozen more bikers were injured in the following fracas, and to add insult to injury, two visiting Hells Angels from the newly charted Zurich chapter had their patches torn off, the ultimate insult for an outlaw biker. Thompson (2011) reports that the Zurich visitors complained to Sonny Barger in California. He sent two high-ranking Hells Angels to London to see if the London chapter should have its charter pulled because it could not control its territory. There has been a frosty relationship between the Road Rats and the Hells Angels ever since.

The Road Rats added to their reputation as a fierce and violent motorcycle gang when, in 1983, six Road Rats members and 24 members of the indigenous Satans Slaves made national news when the two groups battled each other in the quiet village of Cookham in the heart of the English countryside at an event sponsored by the Hells Angels (Thompson, 2011:45-46). The two groups of thugs were queued up in a line waiting to have sex with a young female splayed out spread-eagle on the ground inside a tent when someone started taking pictures, "pissing off" the queued-up rapists. They began to pummel each other with axes, knives, chairs, and anything available to use as a weapon. Two Road Rats were killed quickly with stabs to the heart, but the remaining Rats fought ferociously and soon drove the Satans Slaves to a cottage on the property. The Slaves, fearing for their lives, barricaded themselves in the cottage. Then, the attacking Rats set the cottage on fire. Finally, the Hells Angels intervened and came to the rescue of the Slaves. Later, in 1989, a member of the North London Road Rats callously and without apparent reason shot the founder of the Cycle Tramps MC in the back of the head while the two groups were drinking together in a pub (www.outlawsmcbirmingham.com//history.asp). The bonds of brotherhood among and between outlaw bikers become tenuous during drinking and other drug-taking bouts.

As the tensions increased between the indigenous back patch clubs and the Hells Angels, so did the profits from crimes, which only intensified the battle for territory and drug markets. During the 1980s, the British motorcycle gangs moved into serious organized crime. The Scorpios MC cornered the market for cannabis, amphetamines, and LSD in the London area, then began to import cannabis resin from North Africa, and arranged with Colombian cartels to have cocaine shipped directly from South Africa (Thompson, 2011). Eyeing the success and financial gain of the Scoprios, the other indigenous motorcycle gangs began to emulate their drug trafficking. The British police, in Operation Enmesh in 1986, raided the Scorpios clubhouse and made 50 arrests in London and Manchester, seizing large amounts of cash, drugs, and weapons. Ten members and associates of the Scorpios MC were convicted, but the genie was out of the bottle and more gangs moved into drug trafficking.

BIKER ALLIANCE AGAINST HAMC

In 1992, an event occurred in the U.K. biker community that would have a profound effect on that community and the relationships between gangs, particularly relations with the Hells Angels. In order to protect themselves from the Hells Angels, the U.K. clubs had a limited number of options: they could align themselves with each other and become a more formidable enemy; they could "patch over" to a larger

U.S.-based enemy of the Hells Angels, such as the Outlaws, who were just beginning to expand internationally; or the club could disband, and individual members would be free to either continue the one-percent life with another back patch club or give up the life. Seven indigenous motorcycle clubs—the Pagans, Cycle Tramps, Road Tramps, Coventry Slaves, Pariah, Wolf Outlaws, and Stafford Eagles—grew tired of being bullied and threatened with disbandment by the larger and arrogant club transported from the United States, the Hells Angels. On July 17, 1992, 122 members of these clubs tore off their old patches and replaced them with a new patch—the Midland Outlaws (Thompson, 2011:107). The new club was not only larger than the Hells Angels, but it was committed to not acting like the arrogant interlopers. One of the new club's senior leaders, marching up and down in front of the new Midland Outlaws, proclaimed "There's one thing I would like to say that I hope we can all agree on, let no man here ever act like a Hell's Angel and bring this club into disrepute" (Thompson, 2011:107).

Within days, the proverbial "shit hit the fan" in the clubhouse of the London Hells Angels, as well as in California as the word spread that a new motorcycle club was challenging the dominant status of the London Hells Angels and that the new club bore the name of the Angels, bitter enemy, the Outlaws. They wondered if this new club was affiliated with the U.S.-based Outlaws. The Hells Angels had to know the answer to that question and quickly put a stop to this effrontery. The London Hells Angels issued an order for the Midland Outlaws to appear at the Angels' clubhouse and explain their actions. The response was swift and curt: If you want to meet with us, come to our clubhouse. Thompson (2011) describes the meeting that took place. After a guarantee of safety, six Angels did come to the Midland Outlaws clubhouse, but the meeting did not proceed as the Angels expected. When the Midland Outlaws were told that they could not form a new club, the reply was: get over it, we did it. When the upstarts were told that they could not call themselves Outlaws, again, the curt answer was: we did it and we are not going to change it. Finally, the Hells Angels representatives dropped what they considered to be the most compelling argument to change the name: "But the thing is, we're at war with the Outlaws in America." Though it had not occurred to the Midland Outlaws that they were about to become namesakes of a big U.S. club of which they were not aware, the new club would not change its name. In no uncertain terms, the Midland Outlaws, were told that if they were ever to become affiliated with the U.S. Outlaws there would be war between the two clubs. That prophecy would come true later.

The Hells Angels were, true to form, having problems with other homegrown motorcycle clubs. In 1998, a bitter feud between the Outcasts, an indigenous motorcycle club, and the Hells Angels led to the murder of two Outcasts (McGrath, 1999, February 12). A partying crowd of approximately 1,700 were gathered at the Battersea Arts Centre in south London, when security guards, two of them Outcasts, noticed a Hells Angel in full colors on the dance floor. Soon there were a dozen Angels on the dance floor, and the Outcasts headed toward a side door to beat a hasty retreat. An estimated 30 Angels armed with axes, knives, metal bars, and baseball bats surrounded two Outcasts members as they arrived, unaware that trouble was brewing. An Outcasts member, wearing a prosthetic leg from a previous motorcycle accident, was attacked first with iron bars and knives. The Angels swarmed the outnumbered disabled biker. He later died in the hospital from a heart attack as a result of his injuries. An Outcasts member coming to his aid was hit repeatedly with a blunt instrument, probably a hammer or the side of an axe. He collapsed and died at the scene. A Hells Angels member was convicted of the murders and sentenced to 15 years in prison, where he died. Supposedly, the bad blood between the two back patch clubs began a year earlier when the Outcasts patched over a smaller club, an expansion move that disturbed the Hells Angels. Then 22 Outcasts members defected to the Hells Angels, disturbing the Outcasts.

OUTLAWS EXPANSION

The Hells Angels' fear that the Midland Outlaws would align themselves with the U.S.-based Outlaws MC was about to come true. In the early 1990s, an English motorcycle club called the Wolf Outlaws became friendly with a biker named Ranier, who was the sergeant at arms of the Ontario, Canada, Outlaws and also served as the enforcer for all the Ontario Outlaws chapters (Thompson, 2011). The Wolf Outlaws, seeking an ally against the powerful London Hells Angels, invited Ranier to visit them in England. During his visit, Ranier extended an invitation to join the American Outlaws Association (AOA) to both the Wolf Outlaws and the Midland Outlaws. Ranier suggested that the English clubs visit him and the Canadian Outlaws, so the Outlaws could get to know them and vice versa. Ranier's invitation was an enticing offer to motorcycle clubs seeking allies against the Hells Angels because he reportedly had killed at least six Canadian Hells Angels. He wore the neo-Nazi SS lightning bolts on his vest to signal that he was a member of the elite SS group who had killed for the club. Because of his fierce and violent reputation, Ranier was tasked by the AOA to approach clubs throughout the world with "Outlaw" in their name and ask them to join the AOA.

The Midland Outlaws decided to visit the Canadian Outlaws and determine if there were any benefits to joining the AOA. They sent a delegation to Toronto, Canada. At the Outlaws clubhouse, they came face-to-face with security precautions during a biker war. The Canadian Hells Angels and the Canadian Outlaws were shooting and bombing each other on sight. Both clubs had "greenlighted" each other, meaning permission was not needed to kill the enemy. No Outlaw could travel alone. Travel was in packs, with security vehicles in front and back. Even barhopping required a security detail. The Outlaws compound was monitored by surveillance cameras 24 hours a day. Every Outlaws clubhouse had a shooting range with mandatory practice. Thompson (2011) reports that the Midland Outlaws that returned to England were different bikers. They were more confident and understood what it would be like to be members of a powerful international biker organization. The Midland Outlaws learned to shoot and became proficient in a wide range of weapons. Even more ominous, their mentors had demonstrated that trafficking in drugs could provide the resources to compete with Hells Angels and make them individually rich. They also were keenly aware that visiting the Ontario Outlaws was an in-your-face insult to the Hells Angels. The Midland Outlaws had committed a disrespectful act that would forever change their tenuous relationship with the Hells Angels and have consequences. The Midland Outlaws were also cognizant that continued association and affiliation with the AOA would eventually lead to involvement in international organized crime, but they continued on the path to perdition.

In 1994, Ranier suggested to the Midland Outlaws that they visit the Florida Outlaws and attend the Daytona Beach Bike Week (Thompson, 2011). There they met Harry "Taco" Bowman, the notorious international president of the Outlaws MC. The Midland Outlaws delegation stayed in Florida after the Daytona bike rally ended and traveled the state visiting other Outlaw chapters. A visit to Australia, where they met with Bandidos and Outlaws, soon followed, and the Midland Outlaws moved closer to aligning themselves with a U.S.-based motorcycle gang, knowing that such a move would make their motorcycle club a motorcycle gang. In 2000, the Midland Outlaws voted to become a member of the AOA and inherited all the perks and problems associated with membership. Their newfound relationships with Outlaws brothers in other countries made it easier to cross international borders and acquire drugs and weapons; however, they were now implicated in the internecine warfare common among the U.S.-based outlaw motorcycle gangs. Violence between bitter enemies would soon be exported to England.

Within the space of four years, two Outlaws international presidents were convicted of racketeering offenses and sentenced to long prison terms, leaving Jack "Milwaukee Jack" Rosga at the helm of the AOA. Then, in June 2007, a member of a support club for the Hells Angels shot an Outlaws member dead in the parking lot of the Crazy Horse Saloon in Forrest Park, Georgia (Thompson, 2011). Rosga, reacting to this slaying and other Hells Angels attacks on Outlaws throughout the United States, issued what is known in gang parlance as a "green light" on all Hells Angels. This authorized all Outlaw MC members or their support clubs to seek out and kill any Hells Angels member. Back in England, the Midland Outlaws had split into two chapters: The North Warwickshire Outlaws and the South Warwickshire Outlaws. Simon Turner, the president of the newly formed South Warwickshire Outlaws chapter, who was well-known for his propensity for violence, believed that the "green light" to kill Outlaws applied to him also, and he set about plans to kill a Hells Angels member—any Hells Angels member.

Thompson (2011) recounts the plans Turner and his equally volatile and violent sergeant at arms made to execute a Hells Angel. Turner and his colleague believed that the best option was to shoot an Angel from a moving car. They had a ready-made opportunity in the **Bulldog Bash**, an annual motorcycle rally the Hells Angels had organized in 1987, which was to be held in August at the Shakespeare County Raceway. The Bulldog Bash, which drew upwards of 50,000 bikers from all over England and Europe, took place in territory now claimed by the South Warwickshire Outlaws chapter. Turner decided to kill a patched Hells Angels member returning from the Bulldog Bash. Each of the chapter's seven members was given an assignment for the ambush. Turner, his sergeant at arms, and another Outlaw would ride in the ambush vehicle, and the other four Outlaws members were given back-up duties in the area. On August 12, 2007, the bushwhackers spotted a three-motorcycle convoy traveling down the M40 highway with a full-patched Hells Angels member riding the lead motorcycle. The ambush car followed the unsuspecting victims until they were able to pull alongside the lead rider and fire two shots at him, killing him.

Gary Tobin, a Hells Angels member known to his friends as "Gentlemen Gerry," had the misfortune of being the lead rider of the three-motorcycle convoy. He was born in England, brought up in Alberta, Canada, and had been working as a mechanic in a London Harley-Davidson dealership for the eight years prior to his assassination. He had no criminal record in England or Canada, and his only "crime" that fateful August afternoon was riding a motorcycle and wearing his Hells Angels colors. Within days, the entire biker community knew who the killers were, and surveillance cameras from a nearby gas station led the police to execute search warrants on the South Warwickshire Outlaws clubhouse, revealing further evidence. Within 13 days, the entire membership of the South Warwickshire Outlaws was arrested and charged with Tobin's murder. All seven Outlaw members were convicted of murder and are currently serving life sentences.

Bad blood and retaliatory actions continued between the English Outlaws and the Hells Angels and erupted in bizarre fashion a year later at the Birmingham Airport terminal (Anon. 12, 2009). On January 20, 2008, in a curious twist of fate, members of the Outlaws and Hells Angels found themselves on the same flight back from a holiday in Alicante, Spain. Both groups called for "brothers" to meet them at the terminal when the plane landed. What followed was described by the police as "horrendous" violence unprecedented in the history of the airport. Up to 30 gang members assaulted each other with knives, a machete, a club, knuckle-dusters (brass knuckles), three hammers, and a meat cleaver as terrified travelers raced for safety. Three gang members were injured, and one suffered a serious head injury. Four Outlaws and three Hells Angels were later found guilty of rioting and sentenced to six years each in prison.

The potential for biker gang violence still exists in the United Kingdom as indigenous and U.S.-based clubs jockey for territory and drug markets. Complicating this arrangement are the expansion plans for the Hells Angels and the Bandidos.

Outlaw Motorcycle Gangs in Europe

10

KEY TERMS

Coffin Cheaters MC

Great Nordic Biker War

Hells Angels World Runs

"mafia paragraph" (Norway)

Satudarah MC

INTRODUCTION

As noted earlier in the text, Europol is the European law enforcement agency that coordinates the activities of member states in the prevention and combating of terrorism and organized crime. Europol reports that the continent of Europe has seen the largest increase of the U.S.-based outlaw motorcycle gangs in the five-year period of 2005-2010. Since 2002, the U.S.-based Hells Angels, Bandidos, and Outlaws have added 120 European chapters, for a total of 425 chapters in Europe (Europol, 2010, October 8). This overshadows the number of these clubs in the United States. These three gangs (HAMC, Bandidos, and Outlaws) have around 300 chapters in North America.

The Hells Angels have expanded into southeast Europe, particularly in Turkey and Albania (Europol, 2010, July 30). Turkey has become the anchor point for the distribution of drugs through the "Balkan route." Turkish members of the Bandidos have "patched over" to the Turkey Hells Angels chapter, setting the stage for a war over territory in the future. The HAMC has established close relationships with indigenous biker gangs in Albania, Bulgaria, and the former Yugoslav Republic of Macedonia. The Bandidos already have chapters in Serbia and Bosnia, increasing the likelihood that any move in this area will lead to violence. Further complicating the HAMC expansion in southeast Europe is the Outlaws presence there (Montenegro). See a general map of Europe in Figure 10.1.

The 2005 and 2010 **Hells Angels World Runs** were held in Prague, Czech Republic. Fourteen hundred and 85 Angels attended the 2005 World Run. However, 100 HAMC members were refused entry into the Czech Republic because of their criminal history and missed the World Run. Four of the seven Hells Angels World

FIGURE 10.1

Europe.

Map courtesy of Bruce Jones Design Inc.

Runs from 2005 to 2012 were held in Europe, a significant occurrence for a motorcycle club that had its beginnings in the United States (see Box 10.1).

BOX 10.1 HELLS ANGELS WORLD RUNS 2005-2012

2012—Austria
2011—Laconia, New Hampshire, United States
2010—Prague, Czech Republic
2009—Rio de Janeiro, Brazil
2008—South Africa
2007—Portugal
2006—Cody, Wyoming, United States
2005—Prague, Czech Republic

The European expansion of U.S. OMGs continues. As of 2010, U.S.-based outlaw motorcycle gangs, primarily the Hells Angels, Outlaws, and Bandidos, had one or more chapters in 20 European countries. The European countries with the largest number of U.S.-based OMGs are Germany (116), France (36), Sweden (25), Norway (24), Denmark (23), Belgium (20), Russia (13), Holland (9), Ireland (9), Austria (7), Poland (7), Spain (7), and Switzerland (6) (see Chapter 5). The criminal activities of these gangs vary with the presence of drug markets and conduits for drug trafficking in each of the countries they occupy. Violence associated with these U.S.-based OMGs also varies with the presence of competing motorcycle gangs, whether indigenous or U.S.-based, over territory, markets, or drug routes. As we saw in England, bitter enemies in the United States are bitter enemies wherever they meet throughout the world.

GERMANY

The U.S.-based Hells Angels, Outlaws, Bandidos, and Sons of Silence motorcycle clubs have chapters in Germany, but the Hells Angels appear to be the greatest problem for the German authorities. They are involved in organized crime activities and several charters/chapters, particularly the Hanover charter/chapter, have close ties with right-wing groups such as the militant neo-Nazis (Spiegel Online, 2009, January 5). The Hells Angels have been banned for 20 years in Hamburg because of their criminal activities. The Bandidos, the Angels' bitter enemy, have had a significant presence in Germany since the first three probationary chapters were established in 1999. According to their 2009 official website, there are 46 Bandidos chapters, three prospect chapters, and 50 support clubs (Bandidos MC Worldwide, 2009). The other bitter enemy of the HAMC, the Outlaws MC, have 40 chapters and eight prospective chapters (www.outlawsmcworld.com accessed September 4, 2013).

In Germany as throughout the world, tension is high and violence erupts between the HAMC and the Bandidos wherever they compete for territory, criminal markets, or drug routes. In 2008, two Bandidos were sentenced to life in prison for the murder of a Hells Angels member. Fourteen members of the HAMC were put on trial for grievous bodily harm and theft arising from a raid on a Bandidos clubhouse where five Bandidos were brutally beaten and money, insignias, and a laptop were stolen (DW Staff, 2008, December 15). Two members of the Hells Angels have been accused and put on trial for stabbing to death an officer of the Outlaws. The Outlaw had been one of a group of bikers that had beaten one of the defendants days earlier. At the trial site, the police had to separate 1,000 bikers showing contempt for, and throwing lumps of asphalt at, each other. One police officer was injured, and several cars were damaged during the clash that forced the postponement of the trial.

German authorities recently said that the northern German state Schleswig-Holstein is in the midst of a biker war as the Bandidos move into what has been a HAMC stronghold (Anon. j, 2009). The German police allege that the motorcycle gangs are criminal gangs with ties to other organized crime groups and neo-Nazis. They point out that the vice president of the Potsdam Hells Angels chapter is a convicted felon. His crime was the brutal beating of a French police officer during the 1998 World Cup (Anon. u, 2009). In that event, he and four other soccer hooligans left the officer for dead. The officer was in a coma for days and left unable to work, blind in one eye, and with difficulty in speaking. One of the other hooligans involved in the attack has also joined the Hells Angels. An Angels spokesman asked to comment on this said they were not interested in a person's past: "In the Hells Angels we look at a person's character and not at what is in his police file" (Diehl, 2009). That statement is certainly a truism. This author is not aware of any outlaw motorcycle gang turning down a prospective member because of his prior criminal acts. A criminal past is generally a plus and rather than negative mark when being considered for membership in the Hells Angels in Germany or anywhere else. The German state recently issued a ban against the Hells Angels and the Bandidos (Crime, 2010). The interior minister of Schleswig-Holstein said the ban "isn't about harmless motorcycle clubs whose members meet each other for friendly trips on the weekend." Under the ban the police can confiscate the "colors" worn and arrest any person publically displaying allegiance to either group.

A recent surprise defection of 76 members of the Bandidos Berlin chapter to the Hells Angels has escalated the tension between the two gangs and has the German authorities bracing for violence (Diehl, 2010). Thompson (2011) reports that all the defectors were of ethnic Turkish background, and the group is known as Hells Angels Nomads Turkiye. So far there has been no explanation or reaction from either gang. It would be totally out of character for the two bitter enemies to embrace and let bygones be bygones or for the Bandidos to refrain from retaliating. At stake for both gangs is control over the drug and vice activities in Germany's major cities.

There is now a Mongols chapter in Bremen, Germany (Thompson, 2011). This Mongols chapter is actually a motorcycle gang in name only because it is entirely composed of local Kurdish immigrants called the Miri clan. When it was founded, only one member possessed a motorcycle, a Honda Fireblade. He was killed when he lost control of his bike, and now the chapter is a motorcycle club without motorcycles. The affiliation with the U.S.-based Mongols MC provides this group of thugs with the infrastructure and trading channels for drug trafficking.

FIGURE 10.2

The Nordic Countries.

Map courtesy of Bruce Jones Design Inc.

NORDIC COUNTRIES: THE GREAT NORDIC BIKER WAR

In 1994 what was known as the **Great Nordic Biker War** between the Hells Angels and Bandidos erupted in Scandinavia, the Nordic countries of Denmark, Finland, Norway, and Sweden (see Figure 10.2). Law enforcement authorities say the gangs were fighting over the lucrative drug markets. During the period 1994-1997, in the Nordic countries 11 bikers were murdered and there were 74 attempted murders (see Box 10.2). Five of the murders and 40 attempted murders occurred in Denmark

(National Commissioner of Police, 2002, September 25). Some of these acts of violence displayed a total disregard for law enforcement authorities and the consequences for their actions. In 1996, Bandidos members broke into the minimum-security prison where Hells Angel Jorn Nielsen was being held (Neely, 1996, August 28). They blew open his cell with a grenade and shot him four times. Nielsen survived, but the attack created a national outcry. Following this attack and the outrage that followed, Denmark passed a temporary "Biker Law" (now permanent) that allowed the police to prohibit certain people from gathering in residential areas if it presents a danger to the residents. Ultimately, 650 bans were issued against 200 bikers.

The two gangs committed to a 1997 "peace agreement" which is still, more or less, in effect in the Nordic countries. The National Police claim that after the "peace agreement" the two gangs divided the country into regions of organized crime autonomy, with several towns declared "open" where both gangs can operate.

BOX 10.2 GREAT NORDIC WAR CASUALTIES

- February 13, 1994: During a shootout at the Roof Top Club in Helsingborg, Sweden, a 23-year-old Hells Angels supporter was shot and killed.
- June 22, 1994: The president of Klan C, a biker club that supports Bandidos, was murdered by a Hells Angel.
- July 17, 1995: The president of the Swedish chapter of Bandidos was shot on his way home from a meeting in Finland.
- March 1, 1996: Two Finnish Bandidos were shot outside their clubhouse in Helsinki. One died on the spot, the other died later in the hospital.
- March 10, 1996: A young Bandidos member was killed during a shootout at Copenhagen's Kaastrup.
- July 15, 1996: A Danish member of the Swedish chapter of Bandidos was shot in Norway.
- October 5, 1996: Two people died and 18 were seriously injured when a missile was fired at the Hells Angels clubhouse in Titangade, Copenhagen.
- January 10, 1997: A 26-year-old Hells Angel was shot dead in his car in Aalborg, Denmark.
- June 4, 1997: A car bomb exploded outside the Bandidos clubhouse in Drammen, Norway. A female passer-by became the first civilian causality when she was killed as she drove by in her car.
- June 7, 1997: A young Bandidos "trainee" was shot dead as he left a café in Liseleje in Northern Zealand, Denmark.

Source: *Anon. v, 1998, May 28.*

Denmark

The Hells Angels were the first U.S.-based motorcycle club to establish a Danish chapter in 1980. The Bandidos joined them in 1993. Both gangs are involved in criminal activities. The Danish National Police, in their report *Organized Crime in Denmark in 2004*, states: "members of biker groups [are involved] in forms of organized crime such as robbery and narcotics smuggling" (p. 8). They are also involved in homicides, violence, smuggling of goods subject to high levels of tax, intimidation, and various forms of financial crime. The National Police also report that Serbian criminal networks have links with biker groups. According to the National

Police, Danish biker groups have "special connections" with North American biker groups. Biker groups dominate the amphetamine market in Denmark. They are also involved in the distribution of ecstasy. The Danish police report that the Hells Angels have formed their own youth gangs to help them in their illegal activities. The Danish Hells Angels has recently established the Vikings Defence League, to allow those under 18 to join and support the Angels. Supporters under 18 are not eligible to join the support club AK81. Biker groups operate legitimate businesses as "fronts" for their illegal activities and the laundering of money. In 2003, a Copenhagen Angel was arrested in a bankruptcy fraud case involving 57 companies who had been cheated out of millions.

Denmark is considered one of the safest and most crime-free nations in the world. The Economics Intelligence Unit that ranks 140 countries ranks Denmark as the world's second-most peaceful country right behind Iceland (Nielsen & Wienberg, 2009). However, there have been several biker wars in Denmark. The first occurred in the early 1980s as two indigenous Denmark motorcycle gangs, the Galloping Ghosts and Bullshit, fought over who would become the Danish Hells Angels chapter. Eight bikers were killed during the war. Bullshit lost the war after its leader was machine-gunned down (Neely, 1996, August 28). The leader of the Angels, Jorn "Jonke" Nielsen, who killed the Bullshit leader, became a national celebrity, publishing two books and appearing on television. Former Bullshit members patched over to the Bandidos in 1993.

As stated, Denmark was the center of the Great Nordic War between biker gangs, which left 11 bikers murdered. Now, the war is between Denmark's biker gangs, particularly the Hells Angels, and immigrant groups in Copenhagen. Some have reported that it is a cultural war between native Danes and immigrant groups who will not accept the Danish way of life. However, Danish law enforcement authorities claim that the war is over control of the drug market, prostitution, and human trafficking (Fisher, 2009, February 27). There are also claims that violent crimes in Denmark are the result of attacks by Muslim immigrants, and Angels and their support clubs are retaliating. The trouble between the two groups reportedly started when two members of an immigrant gang beat an AK81 member with a baseball bat. Then, members of the Black Cobras, who are composed of largely Middle Eastern immigrants, killed a member of the mostly ethnic Danish Hells Angels. The HAMC website has posted the following on their website according to one source:

> HAMC is made up of proud men with their honor intact, which is why we have the current situation. If what is going on is to be stopped, responsible immigrants and their descendants must clean up their own ranks.
>
> (www.zimbio.com)

The Danish Hells Angels added fuel to the fire when they published what they called their "Jackal Manifesto," using "jackal" as a term that describes Muslims or others of Arab background who supposedly hate the Danes and their mentality, lifestyle, Christianity, and symbols (Anon. i, 2009).

The escalating violence has left three dead and 23 injured, many of whom are innocent parties. This has led to the introduction of strict anti-crime measures that would double maximum sentences for gang-related crimes. Denmark has raised the penalty for gun possession to allow for deportation of foreigners found guilty of weapons crimes. Amnesty International has called this discriminatory legislation because it provides for different measures depending on whether or not you are a Danish citizen (Anon. h, 2009). The Danish police have also increased police patrols in a country where police patrols are rare.

The Danish biker gangs may be expanding their influence outside of the country as well. Three members of the Denmark Bandidos were recently charged with extortion, money laundering, and six counts of illegal sale of public land in Thailand.

Norway

In 2010, the Norwegian National Police Directorate issued a 22-page report, *The Norwegian Police Force's Efforts to Combat Outlaw Motorcycle Gangs, 2011 to 2015*. The report opens with the statement: "Policing biker gangs has been and remains a top priority" for the Norwegian police forces (National Police Directorate, 2010:3). The report goes on to say that, in spite of their efforts, "…there has been a substantial growth among motorcycle gangs since they were first established in Norway around the start of the 1990s." As was mentioned in Chapter 7, this is a common occurrence when dealing with biker gangs, given that they have been resilient in resisting law enforcement efforts, but there have been successes. Furthermore, the efforts to eliminate the criminal element in outlaw motorcycle gangs will continue.

There are four outlaw motorcycle gangs that represent the largest crime problem in Norway. They are the U.S.-based biker gangs, the Hells Angels, Bandidos, and Outlaws, and the Australian-based biker gang, the **Coffin Cheaters MC**. Each of these biker gangs has spread its crime tendrils transnationally from its home base. The Hells Angels have 113 members in seven member chapters and one prospect chapter (see Table 10.1).

Table 10.1 Hells Angels Chapters in Norway

Location	Date Established
Trondheim	February 1, 1997
Oslo	September 14, 1996
Stavanger	September 14, 1996
Hamar	May 8, 1999
Skein	November 30, 2002
Troms	September 20, 2006
Drammen	September 1, 2007

Table 10.2 Bandidos Chapters in Norway	
Location	**Date Established**
Oslo	February 1, 1997
Drammen	February 1, 1997
Fredikstad	1998
Stavanger	November 9, 2002
Kristiansand	July 5, 2003 [frozen at this time]
Lillestom	No date given

The Norwegian police report that the Hells Angels are the dominant biker gang, with more than 90% of the Norwegian one-percent clubs supporting them. Obviously, one of the one-percent clubs not supporting the Hells Angels is their bitter enemy, the Bandidos. The U.S.-based Bandidos have 48 members in six established chapters and one prospect chapter (see Table 10.2).

The Bandidos have reinforced their numbers by establishing support groups such as the Red and Gold Crew and Support X-team. Some of these support groups are young criminals who are not bikers, another example of "biker" gangs recruiting non-bikers into their ranks when reinforcement is needed.

The U.S.-based Outlaws MC share the bitter hatred of the Hells Angels with the Bandidos. They have 70 patched members in nine full-fledged chapters and two prospective chapters in Norway (see Table 10.3).

Table 10.3 Outlaws Chapters in Norway	
Location	**Date Established**
Oslo	2000
Nomads	February 1, 1997
Drammen	No Date
Fredikstad	No Date
Jessheim	No Date
Stavanger	No Date
Trondheim	No Date
Sarpsborg	September 8, 2003
Eldsvoil	January 2010

In a surprising twist to the transnational expansion of U.S. biker gangs, biker gangs from other countries have begun to establish chapters outside their home boundaries. The Australian-based Coffin Cheaters MC now has 25 members in three chapters in Norway, Lillestrom, Stjodal, and Gjevik. According to the Norwegian police, the Hells Angels were forced to accept this expansion into Norway because the Coffin Cheaters are larger in Australia than the Hells Angels.

Any effort to thwart the Coffin Cheaters' expansion to Norway would have started a war in Australia, one that the Hells Angels would likely lose.

The Norwegian police cooperate with three international projects and groups in their efforts against outlaw motorcycle gangs:

- *The PTN-collaboration:* The collaboration of police and customs in the Nordic countries is an important tool for cooperation among the Nordic countries. Norway is in charge of the PTN Rocker project. The goal of this project is to collect, process, analyze, and communicate relevant information on crimes committed by members of outlaw motorcycle clubs.
- *Europol* includes outlaw motorcycle clubs as one of its main target areas. Norway is part of the Europol project called Monitor.
- *International Outlaw Motorcycle Gang Investigators Association (IOMGIA)* is a worldwide association and organizes an annual conference for the police.

According to the 2010 report, the Norwegian police have set three goals for the future in dealing with outlaw motorcycle gangs: (1) to reduce the number of existing outlaw motorcycle gangs, (2) to prevent recruitment, and (3) to prevent the establishment of new outlaw motorcycle gangs. A 2013 case against eight Hells Angels members and associates provides evidence to support the successful efforts against Norway's outlaw motorcycle gangs. Norway has a "**mafia paragraph**" in their law that allows for the conviction of an organization as a criminal organization, if it exhibits a social network and structure similar to a Mafia organization for the commission of criminal acts. The Hells Angels and associates were tried under this "mafia paragraph." The hierarchical structure and the social networks between and among members and evidence of a network relationship existing between the Hells Angels in Norway and the United States were introduced at trial. Eight defendants, including the leader of the Hells Angels in Norway, were found guilty, and the Hells Angels MC of Norway was for the first time recognized as a Mafia organization (Berglund, 2013, June 18). The court said that there was no doubt the defendants' Hells Angels membership had considerable impact on their criminal acts involving the planning and execution of drug trafficking. The court found that the structure and hierarchy of a president, enlisted members (patched members), prospects, and hangarounds determined who carried out specific tasks and who makes decisions within the club. On November 15, 2013, an appeals court in northern Norway affirmed the convictions for seven of the eight defendants (Staff, 2013, November 15). This is a significant victory against the Norway Hells Angels and we will likely see similar actions against the Bandidos, Outlaws, and Coffin Cheaters in the future.

Sweden

Biker gangs are expanding in Sweden, especially the Hells Angels, Bandidos, and Outlaws. The Hells Angels are the largest gang, with 12 chapters, five established since 2010, as they have acted to counter the Outlaws expansion (www.thelocal.se). Swedish biker experts report that the Hells Angels are the best organized and engage in the most sophisticated criminal activities such as employing illegal construction workers, drug trafficking, money laundering, and extortion. Swedish motorcycle gangs are turning to the sale of Viagra because it is more profitable than the sale of cocaine, and the risks are less than smuggling and selling cocaine (Anon. w, 2012, May 21). Also, making it easier to traffic in Viagra is a loophole in the law that forbids Swedish customs officers from inspecting packages from within the European Union. The newspaper reports the annual trade in impotency and diet pills at about 900 million kronors ($126 million).

The Bandidos have eight or nine chapters and engage in the most violent crimes. The leader of the Swedish Bandidos was recently sentenced to prison for his part in two bombings aimed at witnesses. Fortunately, the two victims survived with minor injuries (Anon. f, 2009, January 14). The gang members attached hand grenades to the victim's cars, which detonated when the vehicles were put in reverse. The authorities used a former Bandidos member as a witness. The Swedish Outlaws list seven chapters on their website and three chapters of the Troopers, a support club.

Finland

The Great Nordic War ended on September 25, 1997, and was marked in Finland on October 14, 1997, when members of the Hells Angels and the Bandidos had their pictures taken together in front of the Finnish Parliament in Helsinki. The Hells Angels and their bitter enemies, the Bandidos, did not clash until three years later, although members of both gangs regularly wore bulletproof vests in public, anticipating the resumption of hostilities. In 2000, members of an Angels puppet club killed three Bandidos in a Helsinki fast food restaurant, wounding three innocent citizens caught in the crossfire.

THE NETHERLANDS

In 2004, the Dutch Hells Angels were involved in a bizarre multiple intraclub/gang murder with international connections. According to newspaper accounts and the recently published book *Angels of Death* (Sher & Marsden, 2006:260-278), the vicious leader of the Amsterdam Nomads chapter of the Hells Angels, Paul "The Butcher" de Vries, decided to "rip off" a Colombian drug cartel. The Hells Angels Curaçao chapter had arranged the drug deal. Drug deal "rip-offs" are forbidden by Hells Angels rules. When other members of the Nomads chapter learned of the "rip-off," they decided to take retribution. Paul de Vries was hated by the other members and was called by one "the most evil man on the planet" (Amoruso, no date). He was alleged to have committed 11-15 murders. His "brothers" tortured and killed de Vries and two other HA members and dumped their bodies in a nearby stream. Two members of the Curaçao-based Hells Angels were sent to Amsterdam as part of the Angels' international internal investigation and were rescued by the police just before their murders. Twelve Nomads were sentenced to six years in prison for the manslaughter of de Vries. The court said that there was no premeditated decision to kill the three Angels. Based on this event and other drug deals by Dutch Hells Angels, it appears that they are more gangs than clubs. In spite of this, it has been reported that several dozen soldiers in the Dutch army are also members of the Hells Angels (www.dutchnews.nl/news/archives, February 3, 2007).

The Netherlands public prosecutor's office attempted to have the Hells Angels banned nationwide as a criminal organization. The prosecutors filed seven cases against all seven HA chapters (Amsterdam, Haarlem, Alkmaar, Ijmuiden, Rotterdam, Kampen, and Harlingen) declaring that they were criminal organizations united in crime efforts. However, Dutch judges in the first case agreed that Hells Angels were involved in crime, but there was insufficient evidence to suggest that the biker gang "threatens public order to the extent it should be banned" (Associated Press/AP Online, 2007, March 6). The judges in the case involving the Harlingen chapter said that members of other chapters could not hold them responsible for criminal acts. They also said that the criminal records of some members did not prove that the chapter was a criminal organization. The prosecutor's office said it would appeal; therefore, their efforts to ban the gang were not over.

In October 2007, 22 members of the Hells Angels went on trial for a variety of criminal offenses: illegal weapons possession, violence, and drug possession. The charges are the result of raids on six clubhouses throughout the country and the arrests of 47 current and former Angels. Among those charged were a former chapter president, his successor, and other influential Angels. The public prosecution's office again attempted to have the Hells Angels Motorcycle Club declared a criminal organization under Dutch law that would effectively ban the organization in the Netherlands. This effort failed, and the public prosecution's office abandoned its efforts.

There are other efforts against the Hells Angels in the Netherlands. The Dutch Council of State Rules recently shut down one of Amsterdam's luxurious brothels, the Yab Yum club, because authorities said it was being used for criminal conduct and had been taken over by a chapter of the Hells Angels. The biker gang was running the club with someone else's name on the license. The Council said that the Angels had taken over the club by extortion.

The Dutch gang, **Satudarah MC**, was established in 1990 by several Dutch bikers of Asian descent and is reported to be larger than the Dutch Hells Angels with 400 members in 20 different chapters (Anon. x, 2012, April 30). The official black-and-yellow Satudarah MC website lists 18 chapters in the Netherlands and a chapter in Belgium and Germany (www.satudarahmc.ni). Most members are known criminals according to law enforcement sources. The website for the Midlands chapter contains the following statement:

> We are a mulitcultural motorcycle club where every motorcycle enthusiast is welcome regardless of race or religion and we go our own way. Everyone who treats us with respect and friendship will be treated with respect.

> Respect—Brotherhood—Motorcyclying

It appears that this one-percent biker club is truly multicultural, with a diverse ethnic representation: Malukin, Dutch, Manush, Surinamese, Dutch Antillean, Moroccan, and Turkish. The Satudarah MC is on friendly terms with the Bandidos and bitter enemies of the Hells Angels. The members are reported to engage in drug trafficking and blackmail.

The international links between outlaw motorcycle gangs and drug trafficking can be seen in a recent Australian drug bust (ABC News, 2013, September 25). The president of the Chinatown Chapter of the Hells Angels in Sydney was arrested in a plot to import more than half a ton of pseudoephedrine, used to make methamphetamine, from the Netherlands. Three other gang members were arrested: a 43-year-old Australian man living in the Netherlands, a 65-year-old man living in New South Wales, and a 38-year-old U.S. citizen in central Sydney.

OTHER EUROPEAN COUNTRIES

France

The first expansion of the Bandidos occurred in 1989 when they patched over the Club de Clichy in Marseille, France, igniting a war with the Hells Angels. Two years after its founding, the vice-president of the new chapter was killed in a drive-by shooting by four men on motorcycles (Caine, 2009). Two other Bandidos were wounded in the attack. Eight members of the Grenoble, France, Hells Angels chapter were charged with the murders. The Bandidos chapter survived and celebrated its 20th anniversary in 2009. There are reports that the U.S.-based Mongols MC has established one or more chapters in France. The author has seen a photograph of a Mongols member wearing a "cut" with France on the bottom rocker. If this is true, we can expect more warfare between the Mongols and their bitter enemy, the Hells Angels.

Spain

In April 2009, the Spanish Civil Guard, the Spanish gendarmerie, arrested 22 Hells Angels in a nationwide sweep. The Angels were arrested for drug trafficking, racketeering, and other charges. The raids took place in San Pedro del Pinatar, Madrid, Valencia, and Las Palmas in the Canary Islands. The biggest bust took place in Barcelona, where the Civil Guard seized a kilo of cocaine, firearms, and ammunition. The Spanish Hells Angels have a reputation for violence and drug and weapons trafficking as well as robbery and other criminal activities. In March 2010, three Hells Angels were arrested for the murder of a lawyer during a daytime robbery at his office.

In a classic case of criminal displacement because of increased law enforcement pressure, 25 Hells Angels were arrested on the Spanish island of Mallorca on July 24, 2013. The charges included trafficking in drugs and human beings, extortion, and money laundering. The majority of the Hells Angels members were

German, including Frank Hanebuth, the head of the Hanover, Germany, chapter, who was also the leader of the Hells Angels in Germany (Burgen, 2013, July 24). A local police officer was also arrested. Hells Angels from Germany have been migrating to Mallorca since 2009 because of police pressure in Germany. Hanebuth had a $3.3 million estate on the island where the gang planned to build a Formula One racetrack. The track was going to be used to launder money made by Hells Angels criminal activities in Germany and Turkey. Most of their illegal gains came from forcing women into prostitution and extortion. The two-year investigation, code named Operation Casablanca, involved Interpol, Europol, and law enforcement authorities from Germany, Spain, Luxembourg, Austria, and the Netherlands, a truly international operation. In September 2013, two full-patched British Columbia, Canada, Hells Angels members and two associate members were arrested in Spain for smuggling 500 kg of cocaine into the country (Bolan, 2013, September 16). The Angels smuggled the cocaine from Colombia to the Galician coast of Spain and intended to distribute it throughout Europe. One of the Canadian Hells Angels had been a member of the San Diego Hells Angels chapter. The investigation was an international law enforcement effort with the involvement of the Royal Canadian Mounted Police, Spain's National Police, the U.S. Drug Enforcement Administration, and Europol.

Southeast Europe

The Hells Angels have expanded into southeast Europe, particularly in Turkey and Albania (Europol, 2010, July 30). Turkey has become the anchor point for the distribution of drugs through the "Balkan route." Turkish members of the Bandidos have "patched over" to the Turkey Hells Angels chapter, setting the stage for a war over territory in the future. The HAMC has established close relationships with indigenous biker gangs in Albania, Bulgaria, and the former Yugoslav Republic of Macedonia.

THE REST OF THE WORLD

In 1998, Hells Angels leader Sonny Barger moved from California to Arizona and immediately began setting up HAMC chapters in that state. It did not take long for the Arizona Angels to become involved in international drug trafficking. In 2002, the Hells Angels Nomads South Africa chapter and the Hells Angels Nomads Arizona chapter entered into an international meth ring that trafficked drugs from South Africa to both coasts of the United States (Sher & Marsden, 2006). South African "brown" methamphetamines were transported and distributed from New Mexico and Massachusetts. The vice president of the Arizona Nomads and six other Angels were convicted and sentenced to prison.

The Bandidos have expanded into Southeastern Asia with a Singapore chapter and two support clubs, the Iron Chariot and the Ghostriders. The Ghostriders and one Bandidos chapter are in Malaysia. The Bandidos have seven chapters and two support chapters in Thailand. Authorities report that Hells Angels clubs, in an attempt to consolidate their grip on drug smuggling via the "Balkan route," are moving into Bulgaria and the former Yugoslavia Republic of Macedonia (Beesley, 2010). In true biker gang fashion, the Angels are building close relationships with local biker gangs. The next move will be to "patch over" these local gangs. This move will lead to tension with the Bandidos, who certainly will try to counter this expansion.

Conclusions

CHAPTER

11

KEY TERMS

Jay Dobyns v. United States of America
Operation Sport Track

We began with the number-one controversy in any discussion of one-percent clubs (outlaw motorcycle clubs): Are they motorcycle clubs, that is, voluntary social organizations built around the love of motorcycles, or criminal gangs whose members happen to ride motorcycles? In providing an answer to that question, we have seen that motorcycle clubs in the United States and internationally can be placed along a continuum with motorcycle clubs on one end and criminal gangs on the other. The criminal gangs labeled outlaw motorcycle gangs (OMGs) in the United States and internationally are on the extreme left end of the continuum. They are groups of one-percent bikers who have a common culture, identifying signs and symbols, and engage in crime for profit on a continuing basis. Many of them, particularly those U.S.-based OMGs known as the Big Five—the Hells Angels, Bandidos, Outlaws, Pagans, and Sons of Silence—are engaged in national and international organized criminal activities.

We then confronted two more question. First: Are all members of OMGs involved in criminal behavior? Yes, if one includes the illegal behaviors common to their deviant life style, such as using and abusing illegal drugs and barroom fights common to the saloon society milieu. Second: Are all members of OMGs involved in organized crime? Probably not. However, even if individual members are not directly involved, they indirectly support the organized criminal activities of their "brothers" through a false sense of a common brotherhood, contributing to the defense funds of those on trial, paying dues that often support criminal activities, and turning a blind eye to the crimes of their supposed brothers.

We supplied numerous examples of the violent nature of this Brotherhood of Bikers. Australian biker experts Veno and Gannon (2009) opine. "Violence is central to club life. It's implicit in the rules, the way members live, and their interactions with other clubs" (p. 139, 2009). Violent, or potentially violent men, are selected from a pool of "righteous" bikers already known for violence and then the gang facilitates their violence. After selection, the prospective biker club member is observed and scrutinized through a long probationary period to ensure that he embodies gang values, including the readiness to use violence. If the member at any time shows fear or a reluctance to engage in violence when called upon, he will be cast out of the gang, often violently. The biker gang members' world is a dangerous world for them and the others who live in it. Violence and victimization is a normal part of all gang members' lives (see Melde, Taylor, & Esbensen, 2009). This applies to street gangs, prison gangs, and OMGs (Barker, 2012). Gang members are at increased risk of being a target for robbers while engaging in trafficking crimes, retaliatory attacks from rival gangs, defending turf, and protecting the gang against disrespect from other members in their unique social milieu. Gang members become victims of violence from fellow gang members when discipline is meted out, and when they try to leave the gang. This potential for violence is enhanced by the possession of weapons at all times. There is no "brotherhood" of outlaw bikers as they claim. The truth is that one-percent bikers actually have more to fear from their supposed brothers than from anyone else. If an outlaw biker is killed or injured, his assailant is most likely a fellow brother from his "club" or another brother from the biker subculture. There is a legacy of violence associated with the world of one-percent bikers and OMGs.

Since the evolution of the Hells Angels Motorcycle Club into criminal activities under the leadership of Ralph "Sonny" Barger and the club/gangs' expansion outside the United States, there has been a steady history of violence accompanying the one-percenter's lifestyle and OMGs in the United States and overseas. The following is not an exhaustive list of all the violent acts attributed to OMGs; it is only for illustrative purposes. The brief references, many which have been mentioned throughout the book, show a history of violence against each other, other clubs, and innocent victims throughout the world.

1968: First Club-Sanctioned Execution of Another Club Member. Twenty-one-year-old Hells Angels member is force-fed barbiturates after being convicted of stealing HA President Sonny Barger's coin collection in a "kangaroo court" made up of fellow Hells Angels "brothers."

1969: Altamont Race Track. A young black man is viciously beaten, stomped, and stabbed to death by a Hells Angels member during a Rolling Stones concert.

March 7, 1971: Cleveland, Ohio, Battle Between the Breed MC and the New York Hells Angels. A battle between the Breed MC of Akron, Ohio, and the New York Hells Angels at a motorcycle show held at the Polish Women's Hall resulted in five bikers dead (four Breed and one HA) and 20 injured. The bikers went after each other with knives, clubs, and chains. There were 84 bikers arrested.

1972: El Paso, Texas. Donald Eugene Chambers, the founder of the Bandidos MC, and two other Bandidos kill two El Paso dig dealers for selling them bad dope.

November 2, 1973: Three Bodies Found in Ukiah, California. The police, working on a tip from a Hells Angels member, dig up three bodies (two men and a woman) on the property of former Oakland, California, Hells Angels Vice President George Wethern. The two men had been shot and the women died from an overdose. Three Hells Angels were arrested and tried, but only one was found guilty of the murder of one of the men.

August 7, 1977: Margo Compton Massacre. Margo Compton, a prostitute working in a San Francisco brothel, The Love Nest, run by the Hells Angels, agrees to testify against a Hells Angels chapter president, Otis "Buck" Garrett. In retaliation, a HAMC prospect, Robert "Bug Eye Bob" McClure was offered his patch (full member status) for tracking down and killing Compton. One stipulation was that Compton's twin six-year-old girls be killed while the mother watched. McClure and his fellow hit man, Benjamin "Psycho" Silva, found them in Laurelwood, Oregon, and killed Margo Compton, the two girls, and the 17-year-old son of Compton's boyfriend. In prison on an unrelated charge, the now full-patched Hells Angel bragged that he had killed the girls while they held their teddy bears. In 1994, 17 years after the murders, McClure and Garrett were convicted and sentenced to four consecutive life sentences. Silva was not charged because he was already on death row for the 1981 kidnapping, rape, and torture murders of two college students. An interesting twist to these murders is the fact that the notorious prison gang, the Aryan Brotherhood, was reportedly first offered the contract for the murders, but turned it down because they "don't kill children" (Valdemar, 2009). Michael "Iron Mike" Thompson, a former Aryan Brotherhood leader, was brought from a California prison to testify against the men (Fagan, 1995). Thompson testified that he considered having Garrett and McClure killed because of the repulsion he felt for them killing children and bragging about it. He testified: "If they [child killers] are not locked up [segregation], they're killed. And that's simply the way it is."

Early 1980s: Denmark. Two indigenous biker gangs go to war over who will be the Danish Hells Angels chapter. Eight bikers are killed.

1983: U.K. Six members of the Road Rats MC and 24 members of the Satans Slaves MC battle each other at an event sponsored by the Hells Angels.

September 2 (Father's Day), 1984: Milperra Massacre. On September 2 (Father's Day), 1984, in a suburb of Sydney, Australia, heavily armed members of the Bandidos and the Comancheros fight at a swap meet, leaving seven dead: six bikers and a 14-year-old female bystander.

March 24, 1984: Lennoxville, Canada, Massacre. Five members of Canada's Hells Angels North chapter are killed by brother Angels.

August 12, 1986: Louisville, Kentucky. Two members of the Louisville Outlaws kill a Hells Angels member from the Anchorage, Alaska, chapter in Louisville.

1986: Grondalski Family Massacre. Two Hells Angels kill Billy Grondalski (who had quit the club), his wife, and two children. One of the children, a five-year old girl, had her throat slit by a Hells Angel she called "Uncle Chuck." Hells Angels and associates burn the house down and cut the death's head tattoo off Billy's arm.

1989: U.K. A member of the North London Road Rats MC callously and without apparent reason shoot the founder of the Cycle Tramps MC in the back of the head while the two groups are drinking together in a pub.

1989: Marseilles, France. In a brutal attempt to establish a chapter, Bandidos kill the president of the Club de Clichy, igniting a war with the Hells Angels. Two years later, the vice president of the new Bandidos chapter was killed by Hells Angels.

1991: Florida. The International Outlaws MC President Harry "Taco" Bowman kills the National Warlocks MC President.

1994-1997: The Great Nordic Biker War. The Hells Angels and Bandidos fight each other for the Scandinavian drug market. The war takes place in Denmark, Finland, Norway, and Sweden. The gangs use machine guns, hand grenades, rocket launchers, and car bombs, resulting in 11 murders, 74 attempted murders, and leaving 96 wounded.

1994-2001: Canadian Biker War, Montreal. This biker war is the worst, in terms of dead and injured, in organized crime war history and results in 160 killed, 175 attempted murders, 200 wounded, and 15 disappearances. The war is between the Rock Machine MC and the Hells Angels for domination of the drug trade. The war is brought to an end after a public outcry over an 11-year-old playing in a schoolyard is struck in the head and killed by shrapnel from a nearby car bomb. Gerald Gallant admitted to 27 murders during this period, while working as a hit man. Hells Angels leader Maurice "Mom" Boucher was convicted of two counts of first-degree murder for the killing of two Canadian prison guards, one the mother of two children, on their way home from work. Yves Trudeau, a founding member of the Hells Angels in Quebec, kills 43 people during this war.

1995: Franklin County, New Jersey. A New Jersey Police sergeant pulls over two Pennsylvania Warlock MC members and is murdered by one of them.

1996: Denmark. The leader of the Danish Hells Angels kills the leader of the indigenous Bullshit MC.

August 31, 1997: Queensland, Australia. Six people are wounded when warring members of the Outlaws and the Odin's Warriors MC fight in the Queensland city of Mackay.

November 9, 1997: Sydney, Australia. The Bandidos president and two other members are murdered in a Sydney nightclub.

1998: U.K. A battle between the Outcasts MC and the Hells Angels results in the murder of two Outcasts.

1998: World Cup Games, France. The Potsdam, Germany, Hells Angels vice president and four other soccer hooligans beat a French police officer unconscious and leave him for dead. The officer was in a coma for days and left unable to work, blind in one eye, and with difficulty speaking.

September 22, 1999: New South Wales, Australia. A Rebels MC member is shot dead in a drive-by shooting.

October 1999: Adelaide, Australia. Three Rebels MC members are murdered in front of their clubhouse.

2000: Helsinki, Finland. Members of a Hells Angels puppet club kill three Bandidos in a fast food restaurant and wound three civilians.

January 19, 2000: Lahti, Finland. Three members of the Bandidos MC are killed when three cars loaded with Cannonballs MC, an indigenous motorcycle gang, drive up to a pizzeria at lunch time and open fire. There were other diners in the restaurant when the shooting started; they were not injured or killed. Six

Bandidos were shot, two died on the scene, and one died later in the hospital. Reportedly, the shooting was in retaliation for an earlier shooting of a Cannonball member.

2002: Laughlin, Nevada. On April 27, 2002, at the Harrah's Casino in Laughlin, Nevada, members of the Hells Angels and the Mongols participate in a brawl, leaving a Mongol stabbed to death and two Angels shot to death.

2002: Plainview, New York. Seventy-three Pagans MC members are arrested after a bloody battle between them and the Hells Angels at a bike show. The battle leaves one dead and three wounded.

2004: San Antonio, Texas. A Bandidos sergeant at arms, known for his bad temper and violence, stabs to death a former International Boxing Federation Super Flyweight Champion after an all-night drinking session. The Bandido said the former boxer disrespected him and "nobody disrespects a Bandido."

2004: Internecine Hells Angels Murder in the Netherlands. The president of the Amsterdam Hells Angels, alleged to have committed 11-15 murders, is tortured and killed by his "brothers" after a "drug rip-off" of a Colombian drug cartel. Drug rip-offs are forbidden by Hells Angels rules. Two other Hells Angels members are also killed.

May 2005: San Diego, CA. The president of the Hells Angels San Diego chapter is sentenced to 57 months in federal prison after pleading guilty to conspiring with other HA members to kill Mongols.

April 8, 2006: Shedden, Ontario, Canada. In the world's largest known biker murder, six Bandido brothers kill eight Bandidos brothers.

June 2006: New Hampshire. A self-employed contractor wears a Hells Angels support T-shirt into an Outlaws MC hangout and is shot to death by the sergeant at arms of the New Hampshire Outlaws.

June 2007: Georgia. A member of a Hells Angels support club shoots and kills an Outlaws member in the parking lot of the Crazy Horse Saloon in Forrest Park, Georgia.

August 2007: U.K. Hells Angels member Gerry Tobin, returning from the Bulldog Bash, is shot off his bike and killed by members of the Outlaws. Seven Outlaws, an entire chapter, were sentenced to life in prison for the murder of a man they had never met.

2008: Germany. Two Bandidos are sentenced to life in prison for the murder of a Hells Angels member. Fourteen Hells Angels members were put on trial for grievous bodily harm and theft arising from a raid on a Bandidos clubhouse where five Bandidos were brutally beaten and money, insignias, and a laptop were stolen.

January 20, 2008: Birmingham International Airport, U.K. Members of the Hells Angels and the Outlaws fight with each other in the airport. Up to 30 gang members assault each other as terrified travelers raced for safety. Four bikers are injured. Four Outlaws and three Hells Angels were found guilty of rioting and sentenced to six years in prison.

December 2008: Las Vegas. Members of the Hells Angels and the Mongols fight in a wedding chapel, after both groups showed up at separate weddings. Two members of the Mongols are stabbed, and the chapel was trashed.

2009: Victoria, Australia. There is a bomb attack on Bandidos clubhouse in Geelong, Victoria.

January 2009: Sweden. The leader of the Swedish Bandidos is sentenced to prison for his part in two bombings aimed at witnesses against the gang.

March 22, 2009: Sydney, Australia, Airport Brawl. Members of the Hells Angels and the Comancheros battle in the Sydney Airport, leaving one dead and several injured. They flew into Sydney on the same airplane and called for reinforcements prior to landing.

2009: Riihimaki, Finland. One man is killed and another injured in a firefight between the Bandidos and an unnamed local motorcycle gang. The dead and injured were from the local group.

October 8, 2009: Maine. Two members of the Maine Outlaws shoot a member of the Hells Angels on orders from the Outlaws National President, Jack "Milwaukee Jack" Rosga (Staff Writer, 2010, October 9). The attempted murder was in retaliation for an assault and robbery of two Outlaws by members of the Hells Angels. One of the men involved in this assault had also been involved in a 2005 assault on a Diablo member, a support club for the Hells Angels. In the latter act of violence, an Outlaws vehicle struck the Diablo's motorcycle. As the unconscious biker lay on the ground, the Outlaws stripped him of his colors, the ultimate insult in the biker culture.

September 23, 2011: Sparks, Nevada. The president of the Nicaragua Vagos MC chapter kills the president of the San Jose Hells Angels chapter in a casino.

April 2012: Brisbane, Australia. A member of the street gang, the JJs, is shot and killed by two Bandidos members. The street gang was reported to be "muscling in on" the Bandidos' drug running business.

April 2012: Queensland, Australia. A 53-year-old innocent women is wounded in a shootout between a Bandido and a Hells Angel in a shopping center.

May 9, 2012: Nova Scotia, Canada. A Hells Angels hit man kills an elderly couple who were HA associates to erase a drug debt. At his sentencing, the judge remarked: "They [people who have ties to the Hells Angels] live in fear of people they associate with. They do terrible things to one another. The lifestyle they lead must be as close to hell as anyone can imagine." The same day as the double murder, the Hells Angel killed a man who picked him up hitchhiking. He wanted the man's truck to commit a robbery.

OMGs, once considered a U.S. invention, have become a real transnational organized crime threat as they have expanded overseas. U.S. OMGs who have expanded outside the boundaries of the United States have become crime problems for the countries in which they are located, and interlocking networks with other indigenous OMGs have led to these gangs entering the global marketplace of crime. At the present time, seven U.S.-based OMGs—the Hells Angels, Bandidos, Mongols,

Outlaws, Sons of Silence, Vagos, and Warlocks—have established chapters outside the United States. As a testament to their transnational expansion, the Hell Angels, Bandidos, and Outlaws have more chapters outside the United States than they do within U.S. borders. This international expansion has not gone unnoticed by indigenous OMGs. Biker gangs from Australia (Coffin Cheaters, Gypsy Jokers, Rebels), Canada (Rock Machine), and Europe (including those from U.K. and the Netherlands) have expanded beyond their borders. This expansion has increased the violence associated with biker crimes as they have battled each other over territory and crime markets. To deny that OMGs are gangs and claim that they are really motorcycle clubs of men united by their love of biking and brotherhood is turning a blind eye to the extreme violence, murder, drug and weapons trafficking, and other organized crime activities committed by OMGs.

In 1994, the U.S. Congress passed the Communications Assistance for Law Enforcement Act to foil the use of communications by organized crime networks (Nolin, 2006). This act authorizes and compels the telecommunication industry to cooperate with the law enforcement agencies in electronic surveillance while assuring the privacy rights of citizens. The police can intercept virtually any cellular or Internet communications as long as they follow accepted procedural law. Electronic surveillance has been and will continue to be an important tool in law enforcement actions against biker gangs engaged in criminal activities. The OMGs are also involved in intelligence activities directed at law enforcement.

A search of a high-ranking Hells Angels home found Corrections Department profiles of Angels and associates, internal police memos, and secret road block plans (Pritchard, 2007). Canadian police authorities were disturbed but not surprised by the finding. The Winnipeg Police Chief said: "it's no secret organized crime groups like the Hells Angels conduct intelligence-gathering and counter-surveillance on police and justice officials" (McIntyre, 2007). Additionally, among the items found were names and phone numbers of Angels and associates around the world, including Canada, the United States, Denmark, South Africa, Germany, England, Portugal, France, Brazil, Australia, Italy, and the Netherlands. This is a coup for police intelligence efforts. Because of the fear of infiltration by OMG members, the OMG sessions at the Annual Meeting of the National Gang Research Center are restricted to badge-carrying police officers.

An excellent example of the use of high-tech equipment and good police tactics occurred in the recent **Operation Sport Track**, conducted by the Winnipeg, Canada, police authorities against the resurgent Rock Machine MC. The police, suspecting drug-trafficking activities at a specific location, put the location under surveillance. It was not long before the police had enough concrete evidence to obtain a warrant that allowed them to sneak into the location and plant video cameras and tap the telephones. The video cameras filmed 91 cocaine-processing incidents. On several occasions the police "sneaked" into the location and got samples of the cocaine for testing. The wiretaps recorded future drug deals. The tailing of several suspects leaving the location led to other warrants to enter homes and seize drugs. The police also pulled over a BMW and seized $463,000. The year-long operation led to the arrest of six persons and the seizure of an undisclosed amount of cocaine, nine kilograms of hash, seven kilograms of marijuana, $500,000 in cash, $40,000 worth of jewelry, and a half dozen vehicles (McIntyre, 2010a, 2010b).

Police undercover operations, although difficult and dangerous, have been used against motorcycle gangs with mixed results. Moral, psychological, and physical danger always attaches to associating with criminals and those with questionable character in order to capture them and other criminals. The gang/club structure requires long periods of time to become a member, and the prospecting period may call for the undercover officer to engage in some criminal activities, including engaging in drug activities or witnessing violent acts, to prove he is worthy. A development that could have implications for police intelligence gathering and the use of undercover police officers against biker gangs has recently come to light. In *Jay Dobyns v. United States of America* (Case Number 08-700C, U.S. Federal Court of Claims, Washington, D.C.), ATF Special Agent Jay Dobyns, who spent three years investigating the Arizona Hells Angels, has sued the Department of Alcohol, Tobacco, Firearms and Explosives (ATF), claiming that his agency has failed to provide protection to him and his family following his undercover work (Shannon, 2007, February 5). He holds that the agency said it would be too expensive. Dobyns also claims that once he filed suit, the ATF began spreading allegations that he is mentally unfit to serve as a Special Agent. Reading Dobyns's book, *No Angel*, lends support to these allegations, as it appears that he more often acted, thought, and identified himself as Jay "Bird" Davis, the outlaw biker, than as an ATF special agent (Dobyns & Johnson-Shelton, 2009a, 2009b). He was close to going "native," if in fact he did not, and becoming a real outlaw biker. In the end, Dobyns was not the same man, a fact recognized by himself, his family, and his ATF handlers. Obviously, undercover law enforcement officers are important in the investigation of biker gangs; therefore, this suit, the publicity surrounding it, and the effect the undercover assignment had on Dobyns could have a dampening effect on the willingness of ATF agents to volunteer for these assignments.

The police will continue to use confidential informants and members who have "flipped" for various reasons to prosecute cases on biker gangs. The Canadian authorities in Operation Baladeur used a 58-year-old hit man, Gerald Gallant, for the Rock Machine MC, the Mafia, the West End Gang, enemies of the Hells Angels, and several smaller gangs to solve cold case murders in the Quebec biker wars from 1994 to 2002, which left 160 persons dead (CBC News, 2009b, March 26). The self-confessed hit man who admits to 26 murders in Quebec from 1978 to 2003, has implicated 11 persons in 28 murders, including biker gang murders and 13 attempted murders. The freelance assassin, who is not a biker, killed bikers, street gangsters, and Italian mobsters. Six innocent victims were shot (one died) during the brazen assassinations in public places. One victim, a waitress, was shot four times when one of Gallant's targets grabbed her and used her as a shield. Nothing was sacred to this callous hit man who received his contracts in a pew in the basilica at Ste-Anne-de-Beaupre. Another Canadian police informant who killed even more people—43—was Hells Angels hit man Yves "Apache" Trudeau.

RESPONDING TO OMG EXPANSION

In the future we can expect law enforcement authorities in the United States and around the world to expand their intelligence activities on OMGs. This includes the expanded use of biker informants, undercover operations, high-tech equipment, and electronic surveillance.

By-Laws—Bandidos
Motorcycle Club, 1999

Note: These by-laws have been reproduced with the original capitalization, misspellings, and punctuation errors.

1: Requirements for a Chapter:

Five (5) member minimum—One (1) "Charter Member".
Charter Member = 10 years.
Keep pictures and information on all members.
Hold weekly meetings.
$25.00 per month, per member to National treasury (by the 1st of each month).
Probationary Chapters (new) will pay a one-time donation of $1000.00 to National Treasury.
Probationary Chapter members bikes and titles will be pledged to National Chapter for the first year.

2: Patches:

Only a Top and Bottom rocker, Fat Mexican, 1% diamond and MC patch should be on the back of your cut-off, It should be visible from 150 ft.
A 1%er diamond will be worn over the heart.
Anything else is up to the individual.
Year patches and buckles are not to be given early.
National can grant a "Lifer" patch or membership on a person to person basis.
One Property Patch per member. If she rides her own bike it is NOT to be worn while riding with or around Patcholders or Prospects. It should not be worn in public without her old man in view.
There is no limit on Property Belts.

3: Do's:

Labor Day and Memorial Day are MANDATORY RUNS.
A Chapter may leave one (1) member behind from a mandatory run. A member on medical leave or a Life Member is that member. This is for security

reasons, that person should have access to a phone as much as possible.

When you are traveling you should attend your host chapter's meetings. You must abide by those chapters [sic] By-Laws and policies.

4: Don'ts:

Things that will cost you your patch:

You don't lie.

You don't steal.

This includes OL' Ladies as well.

Needle use will not be tolerated.

Neither will smoking of any chemicals—coke, speed, mandrax…if it didn't grow, don't smoke it!

5: Motorcycles:

Each member will OWN at least one (1) Harley Davidson or facsimile of at least 750cc.

No more than 30 days a year down time.

After 30 days that members Chapter will pay National $500.00.

Have a good reason? Ask for more time.

Road Captains should inspect all bikes regularly.

6: Membership:

* Hangaround period to be determined by chapter President.
* Harley Davidson Motorcycle or facsimile capable of meeting the demands of Pledge period.
* Members must be at least 21 years of age
* Sponsor—May be individual (preferably charter member) or may be Sponsored by chapter as a hole.

Sponsor,

Do not turn your Pledge loose without help. If you think enough of him to sponsor him into this club, it's up to you to teach him the right way, the BANDIDO WAY. If you're not ready to sacrifice your time and share your knowledge. Don't do it. The simple things—Who's the neatest M.F. in the world? Or don't wear your Patch in a vehicle. Trivial things that will get a Prospective BROTHER run off.

- Pay $275.00 to National Treasury.
- Pledge bike and title.
- Be voted in as Pledge by Chapter (100% vote).
- Receive your Patch or Rocker.

- DO YOUR TIME.
    Prospect 6 months MINMUM.
    Probationary 1 year MINIMUM.
    This man is pledged to the whole BANDIDO
    NATION, not just one Chapter or area, City or
    State. He will attend every meeting, party,
    bike event or gathering of any kind in his area
    where Bandido Patcholders will be present.
    He will not miss any National or Regional
    runs, especially Funerals.
    This club is about sacrifice, get used to it!
    His motorcycle should be in up and running
    condition his whole Pledge period, ready to go
    anywhere. In other words, NO DOWN TIME.
- Pledge is not eligible for vote if there are any
  outstanding debts, Chapter, National or Private
  (inside club), he should start into this club on
  a level playing field.
- After the mandatory time period has passed,
  and the Sponsor feels the Pledge is ready, a
  meeting should be called. All surrounding Chapter
  Secretaries should also be notified (in advance).
- The Pledge should be voted in by a 100% Chapter
  vote. Club members outside the chapter should
  have a chance to voice their opinions. The
  Pledges Sponsor should base his decision on these
  things, for he is the One whom will have to fade
  it if things go foul.
    It is a lifelong commitment, DON'T RUSH IT.

* Charter Member is 10 years of unbroken service.
* National may grant Leave of absence—this is not
  automatic.
* Two (2) year members are eligible for transfer,
  only if both Presidents involved have agreed and a
  $50.00 fee is paid to National Treasury.

Other National Fees
New Patch Fee $275.00
Transfers $50.00
New Charter $1000.00
30 Day Downtime rule $500.00

References

AAP (2010, March 28). Police bikie strike force arrests 724. *AAP.*

ABC News (2013, September 25). Dutch court delays Hells Angels Sydney drug importation case. *ABC News.*

ACC (2012, November 7). *Attero national task force targets the Rebels.* Australian Crime Commission.

Adam, B. A. (2009, June 10). Gang colours form of intimidation: Crown. *The Star-Phoenix,* www.thestarphoenix.com.

ADL (2011, September). *Bigots on bikes: The growing links between White Supremacists and Biker Gangs.* New York: Anti-Defamation League.

Aguilar, P. (2010). *Forgive me father for I have sinned.* Lexington, KY: Author.

Alain, M. (1995). The rise and fall of motorcycle gangs in Quebec. *Federal Probation,* 59(2), 54–57.

Albanese, J. (2004). North American organized crime. *Global Crime,* 6(1), 8–18.

Anon (2006, July 8). Former Hells Angels member gets 14 years. www.signonsandiego.com.

Anon. b (2007, February 3). *Biker rivalry murder trial starts outlaws, Hells Angels feud seen as motive.* The Associated Press, www.concordmonitor.com.

Anon. c (2007). Hells Angel got state gambling license: "Full-patch" member hired for security at Valley Casino. *The Spokesman-Review,* www.highbeam.com/DocPrint .aspx?DocId=1Y1:104515487.

Anon. d (2007, April 5). Gang violence escalates in Wanganui. www.stuff.co.nz.

Anon. e (2008, December 13). Gerald Ward found guilty. *The Tribune,* www .wellandtribune.ca.

Anon. f (2009, January 14). Bandidos leader gets nine years in jail. www.local.se/article .php?ID.

Anon. g (2009, January 28). Legal first: No warrant needed to raid Sydney Hells Angels. *The Sydney Morning Herald,* www.smh.com.au/cgi.

Anon. h (2009, March 5). *Denmark moves to combat new wave of gang violence.* The Associated Press, www.msnbc.msn.com.

Anon. i (2009, July 1). Hells Angels take a stand against "jackals." *The Copenhagen Post Online,* www.chpost.dk/news/crime/155-crime.

Anon. j (2009, July 1). "Explosive" biker gang war grips Germany. *The Local Germany's News,* www.thelocal.de/national (in English).

Anon. k (2009, May 13). Bikie recruitment laws passed in NSW. http://news.theage .com.au.

Anon. l (2009). Forfeiture proceedings for the Hells Angels clubhouse begin this month. *The Tribune,* www.welllandtribune.ca.

Anon. m (2009, April 24). Hell's Angels arrested. *Costa Blanca,* www.theleader.info/ article.

Anon. n (2006, April 11). Mass Killings mean Angels win biker turf war: Expert. CBC *News,* www.cbc.ca.

Anon. o (2009, July 20). Police call for ban on Bulldog Bash biker festival. *The Times,* www.timesonline.co.uk.

Anon. p (2009). *Key witness at Bandidos trial says internal gang tensions preceded mass killing.* The Canadian Press, www.google.com/hostednews/canadianpress.

Anon. q (2009, July 14). Biker-gang rivalry preceded 8 murders. *CBC News*, www .cbc.ca.canada/story/2009/7/14.

Anon. r (2009, July 9). Two tied to Pagan motorcycle gang to go to trial. www.post -gazette.com.

Anon. s (2009). Hells Angels resurface. *The Gazette (Montreal)*, www.canada.com.

Anon. t (2009, February 12). Gangsters among 47 arrested in Operation Axe raids, police allege. *CBC News*, www.cbc.ca/canada/montreal.

Anon. u (2009, September 12). World boss ordered hits on Canadians, trial told. *The Globe and Mail*.

Anon. v (1998, May 28). Biker gangs here to stay? *The Copenhagen Post Online*.

Anon. w (2012, May 21). Viagra helps Swedish gangs get credit up. http://www.thelocal .se/40944/20120521/.

Anon. x (2012, April 30). Dutch bikers' gang expands to Belgium. *Radio Netherlands Worldwide*.

Anon. y (2012, May 11). Dutch police target Hells Angels. *Radio Netherlands Worldwide*.

Anon. z (2012, May 30). Berlin bans Hells Angels, raid details leaked. *National*.

Anon. 1 (2012, June 1). Danish biker gangs setting up in Thailand. *IceNews*.

Anon. 2 (2012, April 24). Two in court over drive-by shootings. skyNews.com.au.

Anon. 3 (2012, April 25). German courts ban Hell's Angels biker jackets. *Reuters*.

Anon. 4 (2012, April 21). Police issue arrest warrants for four men in connection with Hells Angels bust. Ctvwinnipeg.ca.

Anon. 5 (2012, April 11). Biker boss pleads guilty to cocaine possession. Canada.com.

Anon. 6 (2012, April 15). Hells Angels hides drugs in gnomes. skyNews.com.au.

Anon. 7 (2012, April 5). Fairfield officer pleads not guilty in bar brawl case. *New Jersey Hills Newspaper*.

Anon. 8 (2008, December 22). Mongol member says he was attacked at his own wedding. *KTNV ABC, Channel 13, Las Vegas*.

Anon. 9 (2008, September 12). Drug dealers sentenced to jail time. *The Kingston Whig Standard*.

Anon. 10 (2012, June 7). Police raid more than 70 biker gang addresses. *Society*.

Anon. 11 (2012, August 1). Arrests hint hike in biker gang violence. *UPI*.

Anon. 12 (1999, October 6). *Organized Crime Digest*.

Anon. 13 (2006, July 7). Meth arrests Hurt 2 motorcycle clubs: Breed and Warlock ties. *The Philadelphia Daily News*.

Anon. 14 (2005, January 21). 15 Hells Angels on trial for triple murders. *Expatica News*, http://www.expatica.com/source/site_article.asp?.

Anon. 15 (1997, April 3). Biker is sentenced to death for killing officer. *The New York Times*.

Anon. 16 (2006, March 10). *LE arrests 25 Calif. motorcycle gang leaders and associates*. The Associated Press.

Anon. 17 (1992). *An inside look at Outlaw motorcycle gangs*. Boulder, CO: Paladin Press.

Anon. 18 (2004, May 26). Raids expose alleged drug ring. *The Age*, http://www.theage .com.au/articles/2004.

Anon. 19 (2006). Man in Fort Case at brawl. *The Advertiser*, http://www.theadvertiser .news.com.au.

Anon. 20 (2006, May 20). Time for these men to explain themselves. *The Sydney Morning Advertiser*.

Anon. 21 (2011, September 2). OFCANZ targets illegal debt collection by gangs. *National News*.

Anon. 22 (2011, March 11). Enforcement agencies end 18 month operation today. *National News*.

Anon. 23 (2011, January 28). Kiwi police ready to fight Aussie gangs. *The New Zealand Herald*.

Anon. 24 (2013, November 16). Bikies thrown out of casino—For good. Thetelegraph.com.au.

AP (2005). *Local Hells Angels leader gets prison*. The Associated Press, NBCSandiego.com Accessed August 16, 2005.

AP (2012, May 30). Colors banned at NV biker rally after gang killing. MercuryNew.com.

AP 1 (2013, September 26). *Gang-color ban at Reno bike fest after shootout*. The Associated Press.

AP a (2012, May 31). *Murder charged upped in NV casino gang shooting*. The Associated Press.

Appleby, T. (2006, June 22). "It's the end of the Bandidos in Canada": Murder charges leave biker gang's membership depleted, police say. *The Globe and Mail*, www.theglobeandmail.com.

Associated Press/AP Online (2007, March 6). Dutch judges refuse to ban Hells Angels. http://highbeam.com.

Australian Crime Commission (2011). *Organized crime in Australia*. Australian Crime Commission.

Baers, M. J. (2002). Altamont. *St. James Encyclopedia of Popular Culture*, www.findarticles.com Accessed August 11, 2003.

Ball, R. (2011). *Terry the Tramp: The life and dangerous times of a one percenter*. Minneapolis, MN: Motorbooks.

Bandidos MC Worldwide (2009, December 17). www.bandidosmc.dk/.

Barger, R., Zimmerman, K., & Zimmerman, K. (2000). *Hell's Angels: The life and times of Sonny Barger and the Hell's Angels motorcycle club*. New York: William Morrow.

Barker, T. (2007). *Biker gangs and organized crime*. Newark, N.J.: Anderson Press.

Barker, T. (2011). *Police ethics: Crisis in law enforcement*. Springfield, Illinois: Charles C. Thomas.

Barker, T. (2012). *North American criminal gangs: Street, prison and Outlaw motorcycle gangs*. Durham, NC: Carolina Academic Press.

Barker, T., & Human, K. M. (2009). Crimes of the big four motorcycle gangs. *Journal of Criminal Justice, 37*, 174–179.

Barrett, R. (2012, June 5). Bandidos shootings inflame bikie war. *The Australian*.

Bashen, Y. (2012, May 20). Bikie trial fails after fire bomb. *The Sunday Telegraph*.

Beardsley, C. (2013, July 10). Severely beaten at local bar in Hollister during motorcycle rally weekend. *WorldNow*.

Beesley, A. (2010, July 31). Hell's Angels hit the road as wheeler dealers in Balkans drug smuggling. *The Irish Times*.

Berglund, N. (2013, June 18). Mafia law snares Hells Angels biker. www.newsinenglish.no.

Bibby, P. (2012, April 11). Bikie boss jailed but may not have struck murdered man. Smh.com.au.

Bland, T. (2012, September 14). Third person faces charges related to Devils Diciples gang member's death. Al.com.

Blasky, M. (2013, June 27). Investigation of motorcycle gang lead to 32 indictments. *Las Vegas Review-Journal*.

Block, A. (1983). *East Side-West Side: Organizaing Crime in New York 1930-1950*. New Brunswick, NJ: Transaction Publishers.

Bolan, K. (2008, December 2). Drug ring charges ties to Langley trucking company. *Vancouver Sun*, www.canada.com.

Bolan, K. (2009, September 1). Man found in Fraser river part of Prince George gang. *Vancouver Sun*, www.vancouver.com.

Bolan, K. (2012, June 1). Reprisals aimed at settling gang scores. *Vancouver Sun*.

Bolan, K. (2013, September 16). Four B.C. Hells Angels arrested for cocaine smuggling in Spain. *Vancouver Sun*.

Bowe, B. (1994). *Born to be wild*. New York: Warner Books.

Bowermaster, D. (2007, February 28). Hell's Angels case going to court. *Seattle Times*, http://seattletimes.nwsource.com.

Box, D., & Aikman, A. (2012, May 18). Criminal networks co-opt Hells Angels. *The Australian*.

Braithwaite, D. (2006, May 12). Fugitive Bandidos shoots himself. *The Sydney Morning Herald*.

Brenner, S. W. (2002). Organized cybercrime? How cyberspace may effect the structure of criminal relationships. *North Carolina Journal of Law and Technology*, 4(1), 1–50.

Burgen, S. (2013, July 24). 25 Hells Angels members arrested in Mallorca. Theguardian.com.

Caine, A. (2008). *Befriend and betray: Infiltrating the Hells Angels, Bandidos and other criminal brotherhoods*. Canada: Random House.

Caine, A. (2009). *The fat Mexican: The bloody rise of the Bandidos motorcycle club*. Toronto, Canada: Random House.

Caine, A. (2012). *Charlie and the Angels*. Toronto, Canada: Random House.

California Department of Justice (2004). Organized crime in California: Annual report to the California legislature 2004.

Canigilia, J. (1999, September 2). Avengers leader admits his guilt: Biker club recruited to steal, deal drugs. *Plain Dealer*.

Caparella, K. (2006, May 8). Turf wars recycled: Now it's Pagans vs. Outlaws. *Philadelphia Daily News*.

Carson, V. (2012, May 31). Hells Angels bikies want law bill paid—Witness threatened, court told. *The Daily Telegraph*.

Carty, L. (2009, June 29). International hunt for bikers wanted for murder. www.theage.com.au/action.

Cavazos, R. (2008). *Honor few, fear none: The life & times of a Mongol*. New York: Harper Collins.

CBC News (2009a, March 5). Montreal lawyer guilty of gangsterism.

CBC News (2009b, March 26). Hit man helps police make 10 arrests in dozens of biker war cold cases. www.ca/canada/montreal.

CBC News (2009c, September 23). Quebec union denies Hells Angels link.

Centaur Productions (2005). *Hessians MC*. Documentary.

Chapman, D., & Morton, L. (2007). *You can run, but you can't hide*. New York: Hyperion.

Cherry, P. (2005). *The biker trials: Bringing down the Hells Angels*. Toronto: ECW Press.

Cherry, P. (2009, April 15). Full-patch member turned. *The Gazette*, www.montrealgazette.com.

CICS (2000). *Outlaw motorcycle gangs.* Criminal Intelligence Service Canada.

CICS (2001). *Annual report on organized crime.* Criminal Intelligence Service Canada.

CICS (2005). *Outlaw motorcycle gangs.* Criminal Intelligence Service Canada

Clevenger, A. (2010, April 14). Va. Contractor gets 38 months for turning to Pagans for muscle. *Charleston Gazette.*

Cohen, S. (1972). *Folk devils and moral panics: The creation of the Mods and Rockers.* Oxford: Martin Robertson.

Crime (2010, April 29). Hell's Angels ride no more in German state. DW-World.DE.

Cross, P., & Cross, M. (2013). *Gypsy Joker to a Hells Angel.* Minneapolis, MN: Motorbooks.

CTV (2013, September 14). Spain arrests 4 Hells Angels in large cocaine bust.

Cunningham, A. (2012, July 30). About 100 members of Bacchus club are meeting in the city. *Telegraph Journal.*

Daily Mail Reporter (2012, April 10). Australian Hells Angel [sic] sentenced to 28 years in jail for killing brother of rival gang in Sydney airport. *Mailonline.*

Davidson, W. G. (2002). *100 Years of HARLEY-DAVIDSON.* Boston: Bulfinch Press.

Davis, R. H. (1982). Outlaw motorcyclists: A problem for law enforcement. *FBI Law Enforcement Bulletin, 51,* 13–22.

Davis, D. C. (2011). *Out bad: A true story about motorcycle outlaws.* Lexington, KY: CreateSpace.

DeCegile, A. (2012, June 2). Outlaw Australian Bikie gangs target Bali. *The Sunday Times.*

Deery, S. (2013, November 7). Cop said to have bikie links accused of selling seized drugs. *Herald Sun.*

Deggerich, M., Gude, H., & Ulrich, A. (2012, June 5). German Hells Angels face massive criminal probe. *Spiegel Online.*

Delaney, G. (2012, May 9). Greenwood found guilty in double murder. *Valley Bureau. The Chronicle Herald.*

DeLisi, M., Barnes, J. C., Beaver, K. M., & Gibson, C. L. (2009). Delinquent gangs and adolescent victimization revisited. *Criminal Justice and Behavior, 36,* 808–823.

Department of Justice (2011). www.justice.gov/criminal/ocjs/gangs/motorcycle.

Desroches, F. J. (2005). *The crime that pays: Drug trafficking and organized crime in Canada.* Toronto: Canadian Scholar's Press.

Detroit, M. (1994). *Chain of evidence: A true story of law enforcement and one women's bravery.* New York: Penguin Books.

Diehl, J. (2009, September 3). Convicted World Cup Hooligan becomes a Hells Angels leader. *Spiegel Online International.*

Diehl, J. (2010, February 4). Mass Biker defection has Berlin bracing for violence. *Spiegel Online.*

Dobyns, J., & Johnson-Shelton, N. (2009a). *No Angel.* New York: Crown Publishers.

Dobyns, J., & Johnson-Shelton, N. (2009b). *No Angel: My harrowing undercover journey to the inner circle of the Hells Angels.* New York: Crown Publishers.

DOJ 1 (2007, August 15). Members of "Outlaws motorcycle club" indicted in Detroit on violent crime, drug and gun charges. http://detroit.fbi.gov/dojpressrel/pressrel07.

DOJ 2 (2009, July 30). Fourteen motorcycle gang leaders and members plead/guilty in Detroit to violent crime, drug and firearms charges. http://detroit.fbi/govdojpressrel/pressrel09.

DOJ 3 (2009, July 29). Outlaw motorcycle member sentenced. http://boston.fbi.gov/pressrel?pressrel09.

DOJ 4 (2009, October 6). Federal grand jury indicts fifty-five members and associates of the Pagans motorcycle club. www.atf.gov/2009press.

DOJ 5 (2010, June 15). Twenty-seven members of American Outlaw Association motorcycle gang indicted. www.justice.gov/usao/vae.

DOJ 6 (2012, July 31). Hogsett announces sentencing of Indianapolis vigilantes motorcycle member. U.S. Attorney's Office. Southern District of Indiana. Press Release.

DOJ 7 (2013, April 23). Final members of Outlaw motorcycle gang sentenced on racketeering conspiracy charges. U.S. Attorney's Office. Eastern District of Missouri. Press Release.

DOJ 8 (2012, August 24). Federal jury convicts drug trafficking organization leader in heroin distribution conspiracy. U.S. Attorney's Office. Northern District of Texas. Press Release.

DOJ 9 (2009, June 11). Florida man indicted for setting 2003 fire that destroyed Strasburg, Virginia Restaurant. U.S. Attorney's Office. Western District of Virginia. Press Release.

DOJ 10 (2012, January 23). Members and associates of Hell's Lovers motorcycle club indicted for firearms and drug crimes. U.S. Attorney's Office. District of Colorado.

DOJ 11 (2009, April 4). Motorcycle gang national president indicted: 17 others members charged in criminal complaints. U.S. Attorney. Eastern District of Michigan. Press Release.

DOJ 12 (2009, June 3). Two more motorcycle club members plead guilty to meth conspiracy. U.S. Attorney. Western District of Missouri.

DOJ 13 (2009, November 25). Two motorcycle club members plead guilty to meth trafficking. U.S. Attorney. Western District of Missouri.

DOJ 14 (2008, June 26). Two iron Horsemen Bikers sentenced to five years for dealing speed. DEA News Release.

DOJ 15 (2009, December 2). Massachusetts man receives life sentence for cocaine trafficking. U.S. Attorney. District of Maine.

Downsley, A. (2013). Australian-based bikie gangs clash in Asia. *Herald Sun*.

Droban, K. (2007). *Running with the devil: The true story of the ATF's infiltration of the Hells Angels*. Guilford, CT: The Lyons Press.

DW Staff (2008, December 15). Tensions high as German gang trial begins. www.dw-world.de.

Edwards, P. (2008, December 26). Hells Angel found guilty. NiagraThisWeek.com.

Edwards, P. (2009a, August 25). Hells Angels lose bid to have logo items returned. Thestar.com.

Edwards, P. (2009, August 8). "I am invincible," Bandidos murder suspect told police. *The Star*, www.thestar.com.

Edwards, P. (2010). *The Bandido Massacre: A true story of bikers brotherhood and betrayal*. Toronto, Ontario, Canada: HarperCollins.

Edwards, P. (2012a, June 7). Hells Angels clubhouse now federal property. Insidethestar.com.

Edwards, J. (2012, November 7). Rebels targeted by police taskforce. *ABC News*.

Edwards, P. (2013). *Unrepentant: The strange and (sometimes) terrible life of Lorne Campbell, Satan's Choice and Hells Angels biker*. Toronto, Canada: Random House.

Epting, C. (2012, August 6). In the pipeline: A resurrected Hells Angel. *Huntington Beach Independent.*

European Police Office (2012). *Europol review: General report on Europol activities.* Luxembourg: Office of the European Union.

Europol (2005, October 25). 2005 EU organized crime report: Public version. The Hague.

Europol (2010). *2010. EU Organized crime reports.* The Hauge July 30, 2010.

Europol (2010). *2010. EU Organized crime reports.* The Hague October 8, 2010.

Fagan, K. (1995). When Jailbirds Sing. *San Francisco Chronicle,* www.sfgate.com.

Falco, C., & Droban, K. (2013). *Vagos, Mongols, and Outlaws: My infiltration of America's deadliest biker gangs.* New York: Thomas Dunne Books.

Farquhar, P. (2012, April 27). Bikies bringing war to the suburbs—and why the states are powerless to stop it. *Herald Sun.*

FBI (2012, May 18). Enforcer for Sons of Silence motorcycle group sentenced for drug, gun offenses. Indianapolis Division Press Release.

FBI Boston Division. (2012, April 27). Hells Angel sentenced to 15 years in federal prison on firearms charge. Press Release.

FBI Charlotte Division. (2012). Hells Angels members and associates arrested on 91-count federal RICO indictment. Press Release.

FBI San Francisco Division. (2012, April 5). Santa Rosa Angels leader sentenced to prison in mortgage fraud scheme. Press Release.

Fisher, A. (2009, February 27). Gang wars rage in Denmark. *News Europe,* http://english.aljazeera.net/news/europe.

Foote, S. (1974). The civil war. *Red River to Appomattox: Vol. 3.* New York: Random House.

Forkner, W. (1987). Easyriders: Video interview. Cited in Reynolds (2000).

Foster, D. (1999, October 18). Actions speak volumes for Sons of Silence arrests for guns, drugs Thwart biker gang's attempt at new image. *Denver Rocky Mountain News.*

Foy, S. (2009). Local nurse embroiled in bikie warfare. http://moruya.yourguide.com.au.

Fuglsang, R. S. (1997). *Motorcycle menace: Media genres and the construction of a deviant culture,* Unpublished Ph.D. Dissertation, University of Iowa.

Garmine, S. (2008, December 18). Suspected Mongols accept plea agreement. *Times-Standard.*

Gibbs, S. (2006). Sydney's big bikie gangs are armed and dangerous. And now the Hells Angels are rolling into town. www.smh.com.au.au/news/national.

Gilbert, J. (2013). *Patched: The history of gangs in New Zealand.* Auckland, New Zealand: Auckland University Press.

Gills, D. (2009, August 23). Anna Bligh gets tough laws to wipe out bikie gangs. *The Australian.*

Godfrey, T. (2012, March 13). Renewed hunt for Canadian fugitive. *Toronto Sun.*

Grant, J. (2009, August 23). Hells Angels come to Bridgewater for fundraiser. myCentralJersey.com.

Grover, P. (2009, January 14). Goff willing to work on gang ban. Nzherald.co.nz.

Guisto, B. (1997). *My vida loca: An insider ethnography of outlaw bikers in the Houson area.* Unpublished Ph.D. dissertation University of Houston.

Hall, J. (2008). *Riding on the edge: A motorcycle outlaw's tale.* Minneapolis, MN: MBI Publishing and Motorbooks.

Hall, N. (2007). Low-ranking Hells Angel gets six years. *Vancouver Sun.* April 11, 2007. Found at http://www.canada.com.

Hall, N. (2011). *Hell to pay: Hells Angels vs. The Million-Dollar Rat*. Mississauga, Ontario: John Wiley & Sons.

Hamilton, K. (2011, October 27). Hells Angels and Vagos motorcycle gangs fueding… over Starbucks? *Seattle Weekly.*

Hammer, K. (2008, December 13). Hells Angels bosses guilty on drug charges. *The Globe and Mail,* www.theglobeandmail.com/servlet/story/LAC.2008.Hell13/TPStory/National.

Harris, M. (1985). *Bikers: Birth of a modern day outlaw.* London, UK: Faber and Faber.

Haut, F. (1999). Organized crime on two wheels: Motorcycle gangs. *International Criminal Police Review, 28,* 474–475.

Hayes, B. (2005). *The original wild ones: Tales of the Boozefighters motorcycle club.* St. Paul, MN: Motorbooks.

Hayes, B. (2007). The Riverside Riots. In A. Veno (Ed.), *The mammoth book of bikers.* New York: Carroll & Graf.

Hayes, R. (2008). *Outlaw biker: My life at full throttle.* New York: Citadel Press.

Hayes, B. (2010). *American biker: The history, the clubs, the lifestyle, the truth.* Birmingham, MI: Flash Productions.

Hayes, B. (2011). *The One Percenter Encyclopedia.* Minneapolis, MI: Motorbooks.

Hayes, R., & Gardner, M. (2008). *Outlaw biker: My life at full throttle.* New York: Citadel Press.

Heinz. (2006). Angels "share Cody values" in peaceful rally. www.codyenterprise.com.

Hench, D. (2010, September 20). Police kill biker club member from Maine: Harvey Seaway, 51, of South Portland dies in a shootout outside a Cincinnati bar. *Portland Press Herald.*

Hendley, M. (2012, March 30). Hells Angels Kevin Augustiniak gets 23 years up the river for 2001 slaying of Cynthia Garcia. *Phoenix New Times.*

Hensley, J. J. (2012, March 29). Mesa Hells Angel gets 23 years for murder. *Tucson Citizen.*

Herendeen, S. (2006). Murder suspect built life on the coast. www.modbee.com.

Hernandez, R. (2008, December 17). Hells Angel guilty of assault: Brawl took place in Newbury Park. *Ventura County Star.*

Hernandez, R. (2009, August 23). Hells Angels president's case heats up. *Ventura County Star,* www.venturacountystar.com/news.

Hessians, M. C. (2005). Hessians West Coast. www.Guerilladocs.com.

History Channel (2008). Bandido army. Gangland—Season Three: Bandido Army.

Holthouse, D. (1992). Smashing the Shamrock: A massive federal indictment names the senior leadership of America's most frightening prison gang. But will it work? Intelligence Report. Southern Poverty Law Center. Fall (2005).

Hopper, C. B., & Moore, J. (1990). Women in outlaw motorcycle gangs. *Journal of Contemporary Ethnograpy, 10*(4), 363–387.

Humphries, A. (2012, December 6). Hells Angels members deported as refuge board declares bike gang a criminal organization. *National Post.*

Humphreys, A. (2009, June 30). Appeals court quashes Hells Angels' anti-gang law challenge. *National Post,* www.nationalpost.com/story.

Hunt, N. (2013, March 30). South Australian Police action to have the Finks declared a criminal organization. *The Advertiser.*

Interpol (1984). *Motorcycle gangs.* ICPO-Interpol General Secretariat.

Ivens, A. (2010, July 26). Hells Angels linked to man found guilty of smuggling ecstasy into the U.S. *The Province.*

Jacobson, S. (2009, September 15). Warlocks gang member and a security guard have been arrested for death of a man in Apopka. Orlandosentinel.com.

Jaspan, E. (2007). *Buried in the bitter waters: The hidden history of racial cleansing in America.* New York: Basic Books.

Jenkins, P. (1992). The speed capital of the world: Organizing the methamphetamine industry in Philadelphia. *Criminal Justice Policy Review,* 6(1), 18–19.

Joans, B. (2001). *Bike Lust: Harleys, Women, & American Society.* Madison, Wisconsin: University of Wisconsin Press.

Johnson, W. C. (1981). Motorcycle gangs and organized crime. *The Police Chief,* 32–33, 78.

Johnson, G. (2007, June 11). Guilty Verdicts in Hells Angels' trial. FoxNews.com.

Johnson, C. (2011, August 16). 1 dead, 1 injured in Manteca, shooting. *New10/KXTV.*

Jorge, D., & Frohlingsdorf, M. (2010, October 21). Hells Angles vs. Bremen Mongols: Biker war feared in Germany. *ABC News.*

Kari, S. (2009, October 29). Jury quick to convict 6 in murders of Toronto Bandidos bikers. *National Post,* www.vancouversun.com.

Katrandjian, O. (2011, September 25). Hells Angels dead and two injured in shootings in Nevada casino. *ABC News.*

Kendall, R. E. (1998). The international problem of criminal gangs. *JCPR,* 469–471.

Kessler, R. E. (2002). Feds: Pagans to take a plea deal/nearly all of the 73 bikers to face prison for brawl. *Newsday.*

Kilgallion, S. (2012, March 25). Hells Angels refused permit for gang raffle. *Auckland Now.*

Kleinig, X. (2009, November 28). Criminals hijacking bikie clubs—Bikies in Nikes take over. *The Daily Telegraph.*

Kravetz, A. (2006, February 9). Two Hells Angels members plead guilty. *Journal Star.*

Lambert, S. (2006, June 16). Police charge 3 Winnipeg men in slayings of 8 bikers in Ontario. *National Archive,* www.680news.com/news/national.

Langton, J. (2006). *Fallen Angel: The unlikely rise of Walter Stadnick in the Canadian Hells Angels.* Mississauga, Ontario: John Wiley.

LAPD (2011, July 14). Joint task force targets notorious and violent gang. Press Release.

Lasky, R. (2002). Psychoanalytically informed intervention in violence: Four case studies. *Journal for the Psychoanalysis of Culture and Society,* http://www.highbeam.com/library/doc3.asp?ctrlInfo=R.

Lavigne, Y. (1987). *Hell's Angels, taking care of business.* Toronto: Ballantine Books.

Lavigne, Y. (1999). *Hells angels at war.* Toronto: Harper Collins.

Lerten, B., & Burns, B. (2012, September 9). Biker club confrontation prompts Redmond rally shutdown. Ktvz.com.

Levingston, T. G., Zimmerman, K., & Zimmerman, K. (2003). *Soul on bikes: The East Bay Dragons MC and the Black Biker Set.* St. Paul, MN: MBI Publishing Company.

Lewis, J., & Maticka-Tyndale, E. (1998). Final report: Erotic/exotic dancing: HIV-related risk factors 1998. A Report to Health Canada. Grant #6606-5688.

Lyons, D. (2005). *The Bikeriders.* San Francisco, CA: Chronicle Books.

MAGLOCLEN Assessment (2003). *Outlaw motorcycle gangs,* Publisher not listed.

Mandelkau, J. (1971). *Buttons: The making of a president.* London, UK: Sphere Books.

Manning, S. (1999). Major organized crime network reported. *Scoop Auckland.*

Mantle, R. (2012, July 26). Bacchus president pleads guilty to manslaughter in Pitt St. shooting. *News,* 889.

Marchocki, K. (2007, May 11). Outlaws MC member gets 45-90 yrs for killing man wearing a Hells's Angels T-Shirt. *New Hampshire Union Leader.*

Marin, F. (2007). FBI details threat from gangs in military. *Sun Times*, www.knowgangs .com/news/jan07/0120.php.

Martineau, P. (2003). *I was a killer for the Hells Angels*. Toronto, Ontario: McClelland & Stewart.

Maxton, R. (2009). Hells Angels boss stood aside from $100K RTA job. *Live News*, www .livenews.com.au.

McAloon, C. (2004, January 29). Vic: Slain Mum feared ex-hubby and the Hells Angels would kill her. *AAP General News*.

McCabe, F. (2012, August 1). Judge tosses out case against Hells Angels in wedding chapel brawl. *Las Vegas Review Journal*.

McClure, G. (2000). The role of Interpol in fighting organized crime. *International Criminal Police Review*, 55(481).

McDonald, C. (2007, March 12). Hells Angels leaders on trial today: Biker gang charged with racketeering. *Seattle Post-Intelligencer*, http://seattleepi.nwsource.com.

McFeeley, R. A. (2001). Enterprise theory of Investigation. *FBI Law Enforcement Bulletin*, 70, 19–25.

McGrath, M. (1999, February 12). Riders on the storm. *The Guardian*.

McIntyre, M. (2007). Hell's Angels trial: See the evidence: leaked files no surprise to Ewatski; gangs gather counter-intelligence. *Winnipeg Free Press*, www.winnipegfreepress.com.

McIntyre, M. 2010a. High-tech aids major drug bust: Six people arrested in three provinces following year-long investigation. *Winnipeg Free Press*.

McIntyre, M. (2010, April 10). Hells Angels drug deals out in the open: Bikers conduct illegal activity at restaurants, shops. *Winnipeg Free Press*, www.winnipegfreepress. com.

McIntyre, M. (2012, April 10). Cops make life hell for Angels. *Winnipeg Free Press—Print Edition*.

McIntyre, M. (2012, April 4). Gang linked in slaying. *Winnipeg Free Press*.

McKee, M. (2001). On the side of Angels. *Legal Business*, http://web.lexis-nexus.com .library.eku/universe/document?.

McKnight, P. (2009, July 14). Prosecutor, not the jury, should take the rap here. *Vancouver Sun*, www.vancouversun.com.

McPhee, M. (1999, November 20). Sons of Silence meet Accuser in courtroom. *The Denver Post*, B-06.

Melde, C., Taylor, T. J., & Esbensen, F. (2009). "I Got Your Back": An examination of the protective function of gang membership in adolescents. *Criminology*, 47(3), 565–594.

Melvin, J. (2012, March 20). DA: Hells Angel and rival tussle at Belmont coffee shop. *San Mateo County Times*.

Menginie, A., & Droban, F. (2011). *Prodigal Father, Pagan Son: Growing up inside the dangerous world of the Pagans motorcycle club*. New York: St. Martin's Press.

Miner, J. (2009). Two club members never owned bikes, biker expert testifies. *London Free Press*, http://lfpress.ca.

Miranda, C. (2003). Bikie pursuit as police target the "X-Men" inside. *The Daily Telegraph*.

Morton, J. (1999). Rebels of the road: The biker film. In J. Sergeant & S. Watson (Eds.), *Lost highways: An illustrated history of road movies* (pp. 55–66). London: Creation.

Mulick, S. (2012, June 8). Biker 62, charged in shooting. *The News Tribune*.

Naquin, R. (2012, May 2). More like a business than a club, inside the Hells Angels. CarolinaLive.com.

National Commissioner of Police (2002, September 25). Plan of 25 September 2002 for intensified efforts to combat crime and problems of law and order etc. originating in the biker community. National Commissioner of Police.

National Gang Intelligence Center (2011). 2011 National Gang Intelligence Center. The FBI.

National Police Directorate (2010, December). The Norwegian police force's efforts to combat Outlaw motorcycle gangs, 2011 to 2015.

raids. National Post. www.canada.com.

Neely, T. (1996, August 28). Hell's Angels-type bikers create havoc in Denmark, too. *Knight Ridder? Tribune News Service* (HighBeam Research).

Newbold, G. (1997). The emergence of organized crime in New Zealand. *Transnational Organized Crime, 3*(3), 73–94.

Newton, M. (2013, July 24). Vagos lawyer: Hells Angel killing self defense. KTVU.com and AP Wires.

NGIC (2011). *National Gangs Threat Assessment: Emerging Trends 2011.* National Gang Intelligence Center. GPO.

Nguyen, L. (2007, April 4). Thirty arrested as police raid biker gangs. *Toronto Star,* www.thestar.com.

Nicaso, A., & Lamonthe, L. (2006). *Global mafia: The new world order of organized crime.* Toronto, CA: Macmillan.

Nichols, D. (2012). *The one percenter code: How to be an outlaw in a world gone soft.* Minneapolis, MN: Motorbooks.

Nielsen, B., & Wienberg, C. (2009, March 5). Bullets fly in Copenhagen as drug gang war punctures city, image. www.bloomberg.com.

Nixon, G. (2007, April 5). Hells Angels "reeling" after cross-country raids, but war not over: Expert. *Canadian Press,* www.canada.com.

Nolin, C. A. (2006). Tellecommunications as a weapon in the war of modern organized crime. *Common Law Conspectus: Journal of Communications Law and Policy, 15*(1), 231–260.

Oakes, D. (2013, June 5). Bikie enforcer charged with extortion, assault. *The AGE,* www.theage.com.au/Victoria.

Olivier, C. (2010, October 3). Angels at funeral just family "friends." *The Province.*

Operation Roughrider (1985, May 15). After three years on the road, FBI arrests "Angels" in nationwide raid. *Narcotics Control Digest,* 4–5.

Organized Crime Consulting Committee (1986). 1986 Report of the organized crime consulting committee. Ohio Attorney General.

Orr, S. (2012, June 1). Lawyers for alleged Hell's Angels accused in Chino Valley shootout want case thrown out. *Chino Valley Review.*

Osgerby, B. (2003). Sleezy riders. *Journal of Popular Film and Television, 31*(3), 98–110.

Parra, E., & Williams, L. (2007, March 29). Pagan attorneys seek investigation details. www.delawareonline.com.

Pazzano, S. (2008, December 12). Hells Angels control Niagara drug market: Former member. *Toronto Sun,* www.torontosun.com/news/2008/12/12/7732461.html.

Pazzano, S. (2009, January 29). Biker verdict causes uproar. *Toronto Sun,* www.torontosun.com/news/canada.

Pennsylvania Crime Commission (1980). *A decade of organized crime.* Commonwealth of Pennsylvania.

Phuketwan Reporter (2012, May 31). Bikie Bandidos gang on Phuket triggers police concern. *Phuket Wan Toruism News*.

PM with Mark Colvin.

Prain, E. (2013, November 14). Charity riders "feel like criminal" after police probe event. *NewsMail*.

Pritchard, D. (2007). Cop papers found at Hells Angels home, court found. *Sun Media*, http://winnipegsun.com/News/Winnepeg/2007/03/13/pf-3741887.html.

Queen, W. (2000). ABCNEWS.com. "William Queen Interview". http://more.abcnews.go.com/onair/2020/transcript/2020_00918_queen_trans.html.

Queensland Crime and Misconduct Commission (2004). *Annual report*. Queensland Crime and Misconduct Commission.

Queen, W. (2005). *Under and alone: The true story of the undercover agent who infiltrated America's most violent Outlaw motorcycle gang*. New York: Random House.

Quinn, J. (1983). *Outlaw Motorcycle Clubs: A Sociological Analysis*. University of Miami: Unpublished Master's Thesis.

Quinn, J., & Koch, D. S. (2003). The nature of criminality within one-percent motorcycle clubs. *Deviant Behavior, 24*, 281–305.

Ralston, N. (2012, May 11). Charged teenagers investigated over link to drive-by shootings. crime@smh.com.au.

Ramachandran, A. (2009). Bikie killed at Sydney Airport linked to police officer stabbing. www.wmh.com.au.

Raptis, M. (2012, March 24). Drug smugglers linked to B.C.-based Hells Angels sentenced in Seattle. *The Province*.

Ravensbergen, J. (2012, March 13). Hells Angels "L'animal" still in police custody in Panama. *The Gazette*.

RCMP (1999). Anti-gang legislation: Bill C-95. *Gazette, 61*(Nos 7–12).

Reporter fired over Hells Angels contacts (2009, June 4). The local: Sweden's news in English. http://www.thelocal.se/20090604/19874.

Reynolds, T. (2000). *Wild ride: How Outlaw motorcycle clubs conquered America*. New York: TV Books.

Risling, G. (2006, March 19). Vagos motorcycle club targeted in Southern California crime sweep. SignOnSanDiego.com.

Roberts, M. (2012, January 24). Hell's Lovers: Nineteen suspects appear in court on drugs, weapons, explosives. *Denver Westword*.

Robertson, I. (2006, April 13). Bandidos betrayal? Bloodbath tip-off: A source. *Sun Media*.

Robertson, J. (2012, June 5). Balkan Bandidos rally at Milton tattoo parlour after bikie shooting. *The Courier-Mail*.

Robertson, J. (2012, May 14). Violent Balkan members of Bandidos behind surge in bikie violence in Queensland. *The Courier-Mail*.

Robertson, J., & Baskin, B. (2012, June 12). Bandido suspect linked to execution-style shooting of Jei "Jack" Lee at Brisbane shopping centre flees. *The Courier-Mail*.

Robertson, J., Kyriacou, K., & Vonow, B. (2012, June 5). Bikie terror hits Brisbane residents as Bandidos war spreads to suburbs. *The Courier-Mail*.

Rosenberg, M., & Melvin, J. (2013). 49ers suit: Friend of ex-Raiders player kicked out of Candlestick for Hells Angels gear. *San Jose Mercury News*.

Roslin, A. (2002, June 18). Quebec biker war: A Hells Angels chieftain named "Mom" stands accused of running a $1 billion drug empire. *High Times Magazine*.

Ross, R. (2012, August 1). Outlaw motorcycle gang moves to P.E.I. *The Guardian*.

Rossmann, R. (2008, September 8). Altercation leads to arrest of Hells Angels. *The Press Democrat*.

Rowe, G. (2013). *Gods of mischief: My undercover vendetta to take down the Vagos Outlaw motorcycle gang*. New York: A Touchstone Book.

Salonga, R. (2012, May 22). San Jose man was driver in crash-and-clash with bikers on Peninsula freeway. rasalonga@mercurynews.com.

Salkeld, I. (2010, January 13). BBC reporter dismissed over revelations he was moonlighting as a Hell's Angels Press Officer.

Sanger, D. (2005). *Hell's witness*. Toronto: Penguin Group.

Sawchuk, B. (2013, November 7). Niagara kikers taken in early morning raid. *St. Catherine's Standard*.

SCNow, Staff (2012, May 1). Myrtle Beach Hells Angels arrestees appear for bond hearings. SCNow.com.

Scotland on Sunday (2009, May 17). To hell and back. http://scotlandonsunday.scotsman.com/spectrum/Ja-Dobyns-interview-To-hell.527101.jp.

Scott, M. (2013, October 8). Roberge played a key role in bringing biker gang to its knees. *The Gazette*.

Serna, J. (2009). Biker sentenced, other waiting. *Daily Pilot*, http://www.dailypilot.com/articles.

Seymour, A. (2010, April 21). Brookville cocaine dealer gets seven-year prison term: Blaine Doner worked with Hells Angels. *The Ottawa Citizen*.

Seymour, A. (2012, April 10). Hells Angels boss "Sasquatch" Porter pleads guilty to cocaine possession. *The Ottawa Citizen*.

Shand, A. (2012, May 5). Bikies to show their colours on protest ride. *The Australian*.

Shannon, M. (2007, February 5). Federal agent: No protection after dangerous undercover work. *All Headline News*, www.allheadlinesnews.com.

Shannon, K. (2009, July 18). Bandidos walked silently to their deaths, court hears. *National Post*, www.nationalpost.com/news/canada/story.

Sharp, M. (2012, November 5). Meth ring helped by "good screw" in prison. *Auckland Now*.

Shaylor, A. (2004). *Hells Angels motorcycle club*. London: Hugh Merrill.

Sher, J., & Marsden, W. (2006). *Angels of death: Inside the biker gangs' crime empire*. New York: Carroll & Graf.

Sid (2007, April 16). Bandidos to face court over fire. www.ozbiker.com.

Siegelbaum, D. (2012, May 15). Officer fired for ties to biker gang sues Capitol Police for discrimination. *The Hill*.

Silverman, A. (2008, December 7). Ecstasy traffic booming. BurlingtonFreepress.com.

Sims, J. (2009a). Kellestine cried on the phone, girlfriend of slain biker testifies. *London Free Press*, http://lfpress.ca/newsstand/News/Local/2009/06/10.

Sims, J. (2009b). Biker leader asked to be killed first, witness says: Testimony from informant M.H. continues. *London Free Press*, http://lfpress.ca/newsstand/News/Local2009/07/17.

Sims, J. (2009c). Raposo wounds from two guns, jury told. *London Free Press*, http://ifpress.ca/newsstand/News/Local/2009/08/07.

Sims, J., & Dubinski, K. (2009). Order to kill top Canadian Bandido bikers came from the top, accused ex-cop testifies. *London Free Press*.

Sims, J., & Miner, J. (2009, July 14). Bandido trial: Biker cast as a control freak. *Sun Media*, www.edmontonsun.com/news/canada,2009/07/14.

Small, P. (2013, March 18). *Being a Hells Angel coukd mean no bar licence Appeal Court Rules*. Thestar.com.

Smith, B. W. (1998). Interpol's "Project Rocker" helps disrupt Outlaw motorcycle gangs. *The Police Chief*, (September) 54–56.

Smith, R. (2002). Dangerous motorcycle gangs: A facet of organized crime in the mid-Atlantic region. *Journal of Gang Research*, 9(4), 33–44.

Sonner, S. (2013, August 7). *Biker leader convicted of murder in NV*. The Associated Press.

Soto, O. R. (2005, September 23). Local Hells Angels boss gets prison as Racketeer. *Union Tribune*.

Southeastern Connecticut Gang Activities Group (2000). Pagans motorcycle club. www.segag.org/mcgangs/pagans.html.

Spiegel Online (2009, January 5). Growing links between the Hells Angels and Neo-Nazis. www.speigel.de/international/germany/0,1518,druck-599507,00.html.

Spurgeon, D. C. (2011). *Bikin' and brotherhood: My journey*. Bloomington, IN: Westbow Press.

SPVM (Service de la Ville de Montreal) (2009). Operation AXE. www.spvm.qu.ca.

Staff (2013, November 15). Appeals court upholds Hells Angels convictions. www .newsinenglish.no.

Staff Writer (2010, October 9). Third Mainer pleads guilty to racketeering. *Portland Daily Herald*.

State of New Jersey: Commission of Investigations (2004, May). The changing face of organized crime in New Jersey—A status report.

Stein, L. (2010, August 25). 27 charged in biker gang shootout. *Chino Valley Review*.

Stephenson, R. (2004). *Milperra: The road to justice*. Sydney: New Holland Publishers.

Stidworthy, D. (2003). *High on the Hogs: A biker flimography*. Jefferson, NC: McFarland & Company.

Stolz, G. (2012, May 4). Finks claim Gold Coast bikie shooting accused Mark James Graham a maverick. *The Courier-Mail*.

Stolz, G., & Pierce, J. (2013, November 14). Three Mongols bikies first charged under Queensland's new anit-association laws following arrest at Palazzo Versace. News.com.au.

Sullivan, R. (2009). *Australian police defend response to biker brawl*. The Associated Press, www.google.com/hostednews/ap.

Sutton, C. (2013, August 3). Bikie nation—The outlaw gangs in your backyard. News .com.au.

Synder, A. (2002). Ripped from today's headlines: The outlaw biker movie cyhcle. *Scope: An Online Journal of Film Study*.

Synder, R., & Taylor, J. (2013, June 27). Four-year, multistate probe of Las Vegas motorcycle gangs brings 25 arrests. *Las Vegas Sun*.

The Canadian Press (2012, March 30). Canadian who smuggled cocaine and pot between Canada and U.S. gets 13 years. *Winnipeg Free Press*.

Thesis, L. (2012, May 1). Hells Angels crime bust suspects ask for bond. CarolinaLive.com.

Thompson, H. S. (1966). *Hell's Angels: The strange and terrible saga of the Outlaw motorcycle gangs*. New York: Ballantine Books.

Thompson, T. (2011). *Outlaws: One man's rise through the savage world of renegade bikers. Hells Angels and global crime*. Penguin Books.

Trethewy, S., & Katz, T. (1998). Motorcycle gangs or motorcycle mafia? *The Police Chief*, 66(4), 53–60.

Turner, T. (2012, April 18). Hells Angels prospect challenging peace bond. *Winnipeg Sun*.

United States v. Harry Bowman. (2002, August 20). No. 01-14305. http://www/law .emory.edu/11circuit/aug2002/01-14305.opm.html.

Upright, M. H. (1999). *One percent*. Los Angeles: Anon.

Valdemar, R. (2009). Protecting gang witnesses. *Police*, www.policemag.com.

Vallis, M. (2007, April 5). *Ontario police officials praise informant's help in Hells'*.

Veno, A. (2003). *The brotherhoods: Inside the Outlaw motorcycle clubs*.

Veno, A. (2007). *The mammoth book of bikers*. New York: Carroll & Graf.

Veno, A., & Gannon, E. (2009). *The brotherhoods: Inside the Outlaw motorcycle clubs* (3rd ed.). Crows Nest, NSW, Australia: Allen & Urwin.

Viellaris, R. (2007, April 1). Charities told to outlaw bikie gifts. www.news.com.au/ perthnow/story.

von Lampe, K. (2003). Criminally exploitable ties: A network approach to organized crime. In E. C. Viano, J. Magallanes, & L. Bridel (Eds.), *Transnational organized crime: Myth, power, and profit*. Durham, NC: Carolina Academic Press.

von Lampe, K., & Johansen, P. O. (2004). Organized crime and trust: On the conception and empirical relevance of trust in the context of criminal networks. *Global Crime*, 6(2), 159–184.

Wagner, D. (2006). Informer links top Hells Angel to murder plot. *The Arizona Republic*.

Walker, C. (2006). Hells Angels bikers indicted. *Rapid City Journal*.

Walker, I., & Auerbac, T. (2013, July 24). Five shootings in a fortnight as bikie war rages. thetelegraph.com.au.

Wangkiat, P. (2012, May 20). Police "keeping an eye" on Bandido members. *The Phuket News*.

Weaver, R. (2012, May 10). Shamed MP out of Soc Dem dog house. *The Copenhagen Post*, http://cphpost.dk.

Welch, D., Kennedy, L., & Harvey, E. (2009). Bikie killed in airport brawl. www.smh .com.au.

Wethern, G., & Colnett, V. (1978). *A Wayward Angel*. New York: Richard Marek.

Wilkins, C., Reilly, J., Rose, E., Roy, D., Pledger, M., & Lee, A. (2004). *The socio-economic impact of Amphetamine type stimulants in New Zealand: Final report*. Auckland: Massey University.

Willon, P. (2011, November 6). A tale of two Stephen Kinzeys. *Los Angeles Times*.

Wilson, T. (2006). New cop squad to focus on bad bikies. *The Gold Coast Bulletin*.

Wilson, R. (2012, May 18). Bandido members bailed after bashing. *Fraser Coast Chronicle*.

Winterhalder, E. (2005). *Out in bad standings: Inside the Bandidos motorcycle club the making of a worldwide dynasty*. Owasso, Oklahoma: Blockhead City Press.

Winterhalder, E., & De Clercq, W. (2008). *The assimilation: Rock Machine become Bandidos—Bikers against the Hells Angels*. Toronto, Canada: ECW Press.

Wolf, D. R. (1991). *The rebels: A brotherhood of outlaw bikers*. Toronto: University of Toronto Press.

Wolf, D. R. (1999). *The rebels: A brotherhood of bikers*. Toronto: University of Toronto Press.

Wood, J. (2003). Hells Angels and the illusion of the Counterculture. *The Journal of Popular culture*, 37(2), 336–331.

Wordsworth, M. (2012, June 4). Bandidos HQ targeted in drive-by shootings. ABC.

Wuth, R. (2013, November 13). Teenage "baby bikies" are trafficking drugs, extorting Money as older bikies go underground. *Gold Coast Bulletin*.

Yates, B. (1999). *Outlaw machines: Harley-Davidson and the search for the American soul*. New York: Broadway Books.

Zito, C., & Layden, J. (2002). *Street justice*. New York: St. Martins Press.

Index

Note: Page numbers followed by *b* indicate boxes, *f* indicate figures and *t* indicate tables.

A

Abbott, Roger L., 23, 23*b*
Ablett, Christopher Bryan "Stoney," 80
ACC. *See* Australian Crime Commission
Adam, B. A., 43
ADL. *See* Anti-Defamation League
AFP. *See* Australian Federal Police
Aguilar, Phil, 90–91
Aikman, A., 184
AK81 MC, 209
Alain, M., 14–15
Alexander, Sandy, 80–81
Aliens MC, 32–33
Alliance Ireland, 195
Altamont Speedway, 29–33, 220
American Motorcycle Association (AMA), 23, 35–36, 52–53
    conventional motorcycle clubs and, 13
    Gypsy Tours and, 12–13, 17–18
    one-percenters and, 29
    outlaw MCs and, 14
American Outlaws Association (AOA), 74, 111, 200
Amnesty International, 210
Angels of Death (Sher and Marsden), 133, 213–214
Annihilators MC, 161
Anti-Defamation League (ADL), 128, 129
Anti-gang legislation, 150, 150*b*, 151, 156
Anti-patch laws, 191, 192
AOA. *See* American Outlaws Association
Aryan Brotherhood, 5, 6–7, 112, 221
    OMGs and, 129
    one-percenters and, 125–126
    organizational structure and, 100
Aryan Nation, 129
Associates, 99
Attero National Task Force, 184
Auerbac, T., 184
Australia, 2, 45, 135, 170*f*, 215, 224
    bikies in, 11, 169–171
    criminal organization continuum and, 2
    gang colors in, 43
    HAMC in, 106, 174–175, 183–184
    legislation in, 42
    Mongols MC in, 185
    OMGs in, 169–192
    U.S.-based OMGs in, 140–141
Australian Crime Commission (ACC), 169–171
Australian Federal Police (AFP), 169
Autobiographies. *See* Crooks' books
Avengers MC, 37, 83, 87, 118

B

Bacchus MC, 167*b*
Back Patch Clubs, 193, 198
Baers, M. J., 30, 31
Balin, Marty, 30–32
Bandidos MC, 45–46, 75, 96–97, 107–109, 151, 196
    in Australia, 176–177, 178–179, 183
    chapters outside of continental U.S., 140
    criminal behavior of, 87
    as criminal organization, 75*b*
    as economic criminal organization, 5–6
    formation of, 108*b*
    gang colors and, 43
    in Germany, 205, 206
    insignia of, 108*b*
    massacre of, 160–166
    in Norway, 211, 211*t*
    puppet/support gangs of, 116, 117*t*
    as social criminal organization, 6
    SOS MC and, 114
    in Sweden, 213
    veterans and, 27
    worldwide locations of, 109*b*
Barbarian Brotherhood MC, 102
Barbeito, David Keith "Bart," 83
Barger, Ralph "Sonny," 26–27, 35–36, 88, 220
    Altamont Speedway and, 31–32, 33
    autobiography of, 7–8, 86–87
    on HAMC as criminal organization, 46
    on initiation, 84
    intellectual property and, 105
    RICO and, 37–38
    on righteous bikers, 76–77
    as veteran, 14–15
Barker, T., 1–2, 4, 12–13, 37–38, 75, 91, 98
Barrett, R., 181
Baskin, B., 178
BATF. *See* Bureau of Alcohol, Tobacco, Firearms and Explosives
BC Bud (marijuana), 148, 160
Beardsley, C., 51

Beesley, A., 216–217
*Befriend and Betray: Infiltrating the Hells Angels,
    Bandidos and Other Criminal Brotherhoods*
    (Caine), 90–91
Belli, Melvin, 32
Berglund, N., 212
Berserker Brotherhood, 130
Big Five OMGs, 103–114, 219. *See also specific
    OMGs*
Big Four OMGs, 91, 193. *See also specific OMGs*
Biker clubs. *See* One-percenters; Outlaw
    Motorcycle Clubs; *specific clubs*
Biker Enforcement Unit (OPP), 157
Biker movies, 24. *See also specific movies*
Biker wars, 117–118
    in Canada, 93, 106–107, 147, 149, 152, 153,
        155–156, 222
    in Germany, 206
    Great Nordic Biker War, 207–213, 208*b*, 222
Bikers: Birth of a Modern Day Outlaw
    (Harris), 197
Bikies, 11, 169–171
Bikin' and Brotherhood: My Journey (Spurgeon),
    90–91
Bill C-95, 150, 150*b*, 151, 156
Biographies, of OMG members, 86–96. *See also*
    Crooks' books
Black Guerrilla Family, 5
Black OMCs, 125–128
Black OMGs, 127–128
Black Pistons MC, 54, 116, 116*f*, 129, 164
Blasky, M., 124
Blatnois Maurice MC, 150
Block, 3
Blonks MC, 179
Bolan, K., 160
Boone, Daniel "Snake Dog," 101–102
Boozefighters MC, 15–17, 53–54
    Hollister Motorcycle Incident/Riot and, 18, 19
    patch of, 16*f*
    Riverside Motorcycle Riot and, 22–23
    veterans in, 15–16, 27
Born Killers Motorcycle Gang, 32–33
Boucher, Maurice "Mom," 11, 148, 153,
    155, 222
Boulanger, Sylvain, 157
Bowe, 121
Bowman, Harry "Taco," 88–89, 122, 127, 201, 222
Braithwaite, D., 176–177
Brando, Marlon, 23–24
Los Bravos MC, 148, 149, 151
Breed MC, 87–88, 118, 220
Brenner, S. W., 39

Brotherhood, 77*b*, 128, 157, 164, 174–175,
    219–220
    as rhetoric, 101
    righteous bikers and, 77–78
Brown Wings, 196–197
Bulldog Bash, 42, 201–202, 223
Bullshit MC, 209
Bureau of Alcohol, Tobacco, Firearms and
    Explosives (BATF), 80, 123–124, 226
Burgen, S., 215–216
Buttons: the Making of a President (Welsh),
    196–197

C

Caine, A., 10, 90–91, 215
Campbell, Lorne, 36
Canada, 2, 24, 41–42, 106–107, 123–124, 135,
    145–168
    biker war in, 93, 106–107, 147, 149, 152, 153,
        155–156, 222
    CISC, 146–155
    criminal organization continuum in, 2
    drug smuggling to U.S., 159–160
    efforts against OMGs in, 156–159
    gang colors in, 43
    key events in Niagara, 167–168*b*
    map of, 146*f*
    OMG violence in, 160–166
    puppet/support OMGs in, 115*b*
    recent actions against OMGs, 166–168
Canadian Motorcycle Association (CMA), 13
Cannonballs MC, 222–223
Caparella, K., 112–113
Carrico, Jim, 187–188
Carroll, David MacDonald, 158–159
Carter, Dick, 30
Cavazos, Reuben "Doc," 90–91, 119, 120
Chafin, Raymond "Bear," 88–89
Chambers, Donald Eugene, 107–109, 220
Chapman, Duane "Dog," 86–87
"Charlie" (Outlaws MC logo), 110, 110*f*
*Charlie and the Angels: The Outlaws,
    The Hells Angels and the Sixty
    Years War* (Caine), 90–91
Charter of Rights and Freedoms, 158
Chenault, Clair, 25
Cherry, P., 5–6, 10, 145–146, 158–159
Chinese Triads, 4, 133
Chosen Few MC, 127
Christian Identity, 128
Christie, George, 10, 35–36, 40–41
Christie, George, Jr., 96–97

Christie, George III, 96–97
Church meetings, 99–100
CIB. *See* Criminal investigations branch
Ciccone, John, 80
CISC. *See* Criminal Intelligence Service Canada
Civil Remedies Act, 158
Club de Clichy MC, 109, 215, 221
CMA. *See* Canadian Motorcycle Association
Code of Brotherhood. *See* Brotherhood
Code of Silence, 101
Coffey, Dustin, 85
Coffin Cheaters MC, 173–174, 174*b*, 179, 210, 211–212
Cohen, Stanley, 19–20, 21
Collins, Judith, 190–191
Colnett, V., 27, 29
Colors. *See* Gang colors
Comancheros MC, 173–174, 175
Communications Assistance for Law Enforcement Act, 225
Community-focused policing, 190, 190*t*
Compton, Margo, 221
Confederate Cavalry Corps MC, 129, 130
Conventional motorcycle clubs, 2, 13
Core values of outlaw bikers, 80–83
Corman, Roger, 30
La Cosa Nostra, 94, 102, 133
Coventry Slaves MC, 198–199
Crewe, Della, 12
Criminal behavior and activity, 86–97, 87*b*, 97*t*
    leaders' involvement in planning and execution of, 98–100
    by OMG members, 95*t*
    OMG members' biographies and, 86–96
    types of, 94*t*
Criminal exploitable ties, 3, 5
Criminal Intelligence Service Canada (CISC), 146–155
Criminal investigations branch (CIB), 175
Criminal justice, view of OMGs, 36–43
Criminal organization continuum, 6–7, 108–109
    of OMCs, 73–75, 100–102, 101*f*
    of OMGs, 2
Crooks' books, 7–8, 86–87, 90–91
Cross, Meg, 90–91
Cross, Phil, 90–91
Cunningham, A., 167
Cuts, 9–10
Cyber crime, 137
Cycle Tramps MC, 198–199
"Cyclists Raid" (Rooney), 23–24

D

Dammers MC, 153
Davidson, Arthur, 11–12
Davidson, Walter, 11–12
Davis, D. C., 27
Davis, Johnny, 110
Davis, R. H., 37
De Clercq, W., 107–108
De Vries, Paul "The Butcher," 213–214
Death Riders MC, 147–148
Death's Head Hooligans, 129
Death's head logo, 194–195
Demon Knights MC, 102
Denmark, 24, 135, 208–210, 221, 222
    Great Nordic Biker War in, 207–208
    U.S.-based OMGs in, 140–141, 205
Department of Justice (DOJ), 56–57, 71, 111, 113
Desroches, F. J., 4, 7
Detroit, M., 36–37
Devil Dolls MC, 52–53
Devil's Diciples MC, 53–54, 54*b*, 102, 118, 195–196
Devil's Henchmen MC, 189
Diablos MC, 88, 224
Diehl, J., 206
District councils, of New Zealand, 191–192
Dobkins, Lou, 111
Dobyns, Jay, 48, 90–91, 226
DOJ. *See* Department of Justice
Double-O-Alliance, 39, 39*b*
Downsley, A., 173–174
Dragons MC, 195–196
Droban, K., 90–91
Drug smuggling, from Canada to U.S., 159–160
Drug trafficking, 27–28, 56–57, 73–74, 215
    OMGs involved in, 69*b*
    PMC and, 96
Drug-trafficking organizations (DTOs), 2–3, 71
Dubinski, K., 162

E

Easy Rider (film), 24, 30
Easyriders (magazine), 49
Economic criminal organizations, 5–6, 75, 91
Economics Intelligence Unit, 209
Edwards, P., 36, 41, 45–46, 145, 161, 173–174
EIS. *See* Europol Information System
La Eme (Mexican Mafia), 118
Epitaph Riders MC, 52, 189
Esquire (magazine), 30
EU Organized Crime Report, 135–136
Europe, 2, 203–217, 204*f*. *See also specific countries*
Europol, 134, 135–140, 136*b*, 139*b*, 203, 212

Europol Information System (EIS), 140, 140*b*
Evil Ones MC, 155–156
Expression (newspaper), 47–48

F

Falco, C., 90–91
FARC. *See* Revolutionary Armed Forces of
    Colombia
Farquhar, P., 180
*The Fat Mexican: The Bloody Rise of the Bandidos
    Motorcycle Club* (Caine), 90–91
Federal Bureau of Investigation (FBI), 37–38, 39
5150 Crew, 130
Finks MC, 42, 173–174, 176–177, 180, 183
Finland, 135–136, 140–141, 207–208, 213, 222,
    224
First Kavallerie Brigade, 130
Fisher, A., 209
Florida Warlocks MC, 27, 121–122
Fly-in Wheels MC, 52–53
Folk devils, 19–22, 187
*Folk Devils and Moral Panics: The Creation of the
    Mods and Rockers* (Cohen), 19–20
Fonda, Peter, 24, 30
Forbidden Few MC, 173–174
Forgive Me Father for I Have Sinned (Aguilar),
    90–91
Forkner, "Wino Willie," 14, 18–19
Forsaken Few MC, 116
Foster, D., 114
Fourth Reich MC, 181
France, 158–159, 205, 215
    Bandidos MC in, 109
    EIS in, 140
    HAMC in, 106
    Interpol in, 135
    U.S.-based OMGs in, 140–141
Free Spirits MC, 52–53
Freedom of Information Act, 196–197
Freelancers MC, 88
Friends of the club, 78–79, 99
Fuglsang, R. S., 12–13, 17–18

G

Gallant, Gerald, 222, 226
Galloping Ghosts MC, 209
Galloping Goose MC, 16–17, 17*b*, 28–29
Gang colors, 43, 139
    in Australia, 43
    for HAMC, 43, 104–105, 105*b*
    "no colors" signs, 43, 44*f*

Gang label, 44–46, 47–49
Gangs. *See also* Outlaw Motorcycle Gangs;
        specific gangs
    clubs vs. gangs, 9–11
    prison, 27–28, 91, 128
    single-purpose, 4
    street, 4, 5, 27–28, 94
    super, 5
    support/puppet, 114–117
Gannon, E., 219–220
Garcia, Cynthia, 48
Gardner, 90–91
Garmine, S., 40–41
Garrett, Otis "Buck," 221
Germany, 24, 205–206, 215–216, 223
    EIS in, 140
    HAMC in, 106
    Interpol in, 135
    U.S.-based OMGs in, 140–141
    Vagos MC in, 123–124
    white supremacist groups in, 112
Ghostriders MC, 216–217
Gibbs, S., 178–179
Gilbert, J., 52, 187, 188
Gimme Shelter (documentary film), 31, 32
Glendale Stokers MC, 16–17
Godfrey, T., 158–159
*God's of Mischief: My Undercover Vendetta to Take
    Down the Vagos Outlaw Motorcycle Gang*
    (Rowe), 90–91
Gonzalez, Ernesto, 123–124
Government agencies, view of OMGs, 41–43. *See
    also specific agencies*
Grant, J., 49
Great Nordic Biker War, 207–213, 208*b*, 222
Green Machine Nation MC, 43
Grim Reapers MC, 148
Grondalski, Billy, 221
Guardado, Mark "Papa," 80
Gypsy Joker to a Hells Angel (Cross, P. and Cross,
    M.), 90–91
Gypsy Jokers MC, 28–29, 173–174, 175,
    176–177, 179
Gypsy Tours, 12–13, 17–18

H

Hakaim, Tom, 87
Hall, J., 90–91
HAMC. *See* Hells Angels Motorcycle Club
Hammer, K., 156–157
Hancock, Don, 175
Hanebuth, Frank, 215–216

Hangarounds, 78–79, 99

Harley, William, 11–12

Harley-Davidson Company, 11–12, 13–14

Harlow, Jean, 25

Harper's Magazine, 23–24

Harris, Maz, 84, 197

Harvey, E., 182

HAVMC. *See* Hells Angels Vikings MC

Hawi, Mahmoud "Mick," 182–183

Hayes, Bill, 11–13, 23, 52–54, 90–91

Headhunters MC, 189, 192

Hedstrom, Oscar, 11–12

Hell Bent for Glory OMC, 25–26, 52

Hell Razors MC, 52–53

Hell to Pay: Hells Angels vs. The Million-Dollar Rat (Hall), 90–91

Hells Angels (comic), 105

Hell's Angels: Demon of Lust (film), 105

Hells Angels Model, 52, 98, 131, 188–189

Hells Angels Motorcycle Club (HAMC), 7–8, 10, 21, 28–29, 54, 71, 96–97, 220

   at Altamont Speedway, 30–32

   articles on, 93

   in Australia, 106, 174–175, 183–184

   as Big Five biker gang, 104–107

   biker alliance against, 198–200

   blacks in, 126

   in Canada, 145–146, 148, 149, 152, 154–155, 156–157, 158

   chapters/charters outside of U.S., 106*b*, 140

   clubhouse of, 107*f*

   court's view of, 40–41

   criminal behavior of, 88

   as criminal organization, 78*b*

   in Denmark, 208–209

   early years of, 27–28

   as economic criminal organization, 75

   in Europe, 203

   expansion by continent, 137–138, 137*t*

   gang colors and, 43, 104–105, 105*b*

   gang label and, 47

   in Germany, 205

   government agencies and, 41–42

   independent OMGs and, 117–118

   insignia of, 105*f*

   interactions with, 50–51

   local law enforcement and, 36–37

   in mid-1960's, 29–30

   Mongols MC and, 119

   murder of president, 80*b*

   national law enforcement and, 37–38

   in Netherlands, 214

   in New Zealand, 187–188, 192

   in Norway, 210*t*, 212

   one-percenters and, 25–30

   Pagan MC and, 112–113

   SOS MC and, 114

   in Spain, 215–216

   in UK, 196–198, 196*b*

   worldwide expansion of, 138, 138*t*

Hell's Angels: The Strange and Terrible Saga of the Outlaw Motorcycle Gangs (Thompson, H. S.), 36–37

Hells Angels Vikings MC (HAVMC), 194–195

Hells Angels World Runs, 203–205, 205*b*

Hell's Witness (Kane), 90–91

Henchman Back Patch Club, 195–196

Hendree, George, 11–12

Hermanos de Pistoleros Latinos, 5

Hernandez, R., 40–41, 47–48

Hessians MC, 84

Hicks, Wayne "Joe Black," 89

High Plains Drifters MC, 54

Highway 61 MC, 189

Hill, John Peter, 174–175

Hodges, Ronnie, 108–109

Hollister Motorcycle Incident/Riot, 17–19, 21, 22, 25

   eyewitness account of, 19*b*

   staged photograph of, 21*f*

   trophy of, 18*f*

Holthouse, D., 112

Los Homeboys MC, 96–97, 116

Honor Few, Fear None: The Life and Times of a Mongol (Cavazos), 90–91

Hoover, J. Edgar, 196–197

Hopper, 125–126

Hopper, Dennis, 24

Horizontal differentiation, 6–7

Hotchkiss, Effie, 12

Hughes, Howard, 25

Human, K. M., 91

Humphreys, A., 43

Hunt, N., 42

Hunter, Meredith, 31, 32

I

I Was a Killer for the Hells Angels: The True Story of Serge Quesnel (Martineau), 90–91

Immigration and Refugee Board (IRB), 41–42

Imperial Klans of America, 129

Independent OMGs, 117–125. *See also specific OMGs*

Ingalls, Paul A. "German," 28

Initiation rituals, 84–85
Intellectual property, 105, 137
Intelligence-led policing, 190, 190*t*
International Motorcycle Gang Investigators
    Association, 175–176
International organizations, 134–140. *See also*
    Europol; Interpol
International Outlaw Motorcycle Gang
    Investigators Association (IOMGA), 54, 70,
    96, 212
  Devil's Deciples MC and, 53–54
  OMGs by state, 58*b*, 70*t*
  U.S. Outlaw Motorcycle Gangs, 54, 55*t*
Interpol, 134, 134*b*, 135
Interracial OMCs, 125–128
IOMGA. *See* International Outlaw Motorcycle
    Gang Investigators Association
IRB. *See* Immigration and Refugee Board
Iron Chariot MC, 216–217
Iron Circle MC, 130
Iron Horsemen MC, 37, 88

J
Jackal Manifesto, 209
Jacobson, S., 51
Jaspan, E., 20
*Jay Dobyns v. United States of
    America*, 226
Jenkins, P., 111
Joans, B., 76
Johansen, W. C., 3, 27–28
Johnson, W. C., 36–37
Johnson-Shelton, N., 90–91, 226

K
Kane, 90–91
Kari, S., 165
Katz, T., 133
Kellestine, Wayne, 161, 162–163,
    164, 165
Kendall, R. E., 134
Kennedy, L., 182
Kessler, R. E., 112
King's Crew MC, 148–149
Kinzey, Stephen "Skinz," 53–54
Kleinig, X., 11
Know Nothing Tribe MC, 51
Koch, D. S., 74–75, 91, 95–96
Kozlowski, Darrin, 80
Kramer, Stanley, 23–24
Kravetz, A., 88
Ku Klux Klan, 125–126, 128

L
Lamonthe, L., 106–107
Langton, J., 90–91
Lasky, R., 32–33
Last Chance MC, 151
Last Rebels MC, 117
Latent criminal dispositions, 74–75
Lavigne, Yves, 45, 111, 125–126
Law enforcement, 36–40
Law Enforcement Officer's motorcycle clubs (LEO
    MCs), 117–118
Layden, J., 77–78, 84
LEO MCs. *See* Law Enforcement Officer's
    motorcycle clubs
Lewis, J., 7
Lewis, Lou, 175
Life (magazine), 19, 21, 22, 25–26, 30
Local law enforcement, 36–37
Loki (Norse god of mischief), 122
Lone Wolf MC, 181
Loners MC, 88, 151, 160–161
Lynch, Thomas, 30
Lyons, Danny, 110, 111

M
M. H. (police informant), 162, 163, 164, 165
Maddow, Ben, 23–24
Mafia paragraph, 41, 212
MAGLOCLEN. *See* Middle Atlantic Great Lakes
    Organized Crime Law Enforcement
    Network
Magogs MC, 192
Mandelkau, J., 196–197
Mangu Kaha MC, 192
Manifest criminal dispositions, 74–75
Mannebach, Phillip, 85*b*
Manning, S., 189
Mantle, R., 167
Marchocki, K., 51
Marin, F., 45
Market Street Commandoes MC, 16–17, 25–26
Marron, John Vernon "Satan," 111
Marsden, W., 126, 133, 174, 213–214
Martineau, P., 90–91
Martinez, Anthony "Tiny," 39
Marvin, Lee, 24
Maysles, Albert, 31
Maysles, David, 31
McAloon, C., 176–177
McClure, Robert "Bug Eye Bob," 221

McFeeley, R. A., 37–38
McGrath, M., 199–200
McIntyre, M., 157, 166, 225
McKee, M., 105
McKnight, P., 156
McMahon, John, 145
Medellin Cartel, 87, 116
Menginie, A., 90–91
Merla, Richard, 45–46
Middle Atlantic Great Lakes Organized Crime
        Law Enforcement Network
        (MAGLOCLEN), 94
Miles, James "Mother," 25–26
Miles, Pat, 25–26
Milk-bar cowboys, 187
Millspaugh, Jacob, 80
Milperra Massacre, 175, 176, 221
Miner, J., 164
Miranda, C., 183
Mobile organized crime groups (MOCGs), 137
Mocks, 171
Mofos MC, 28–29
Mongols MC, 45, 52, 71, 75, 86–87, 96–97
    in Australia, 185
    chapters outside of continental U.S., 140
    as criminal organization, 79b
    as economic criminal organization, 5–6
    fight song of, 120b
    France and, 215
    gang colors and, 43
    in Germany, 206
    as independent OMG, 118–120
    insignia of, 119f
    murder of Hells Angels president, 80b
    prospects and, 81
    RICO and, 79
Mongrel Mob MC, 192
Moore, 125–126
Moore, Floyd B. "Jesse," 83
Moral panic, 19–22, 187
Morrison, Jim, 15–16, 22
Morton, J., 30
Muscedere, John "Boxer," 160–161, 162
"Myth and Reality in Motorcycle Subculture"
        (Harris), 197

N

National Alliance of Gang Investigators Association
        (NAGIA), 96
National courts, view of OMGs, 40–41
National Drug Intelligence Center (NDIC), 56–57, 96
National Drug Threat Survey (NDTS), 56–57

National Gang Crime Research Center (NGCRC),
        125–126
National Gang Intelligence Center (NGIC), 54,
        56–57, 66b, 69b, 70t
National law enforcement, 37–40
National Rifle Association (NRA), 20–21
Nationalist Coalition, 129
NDIC. See National Drug Intelligence Center
NDTS. See National Drug Threat Survey
Neely, T., 207–208, 209
Neo-Nazis, 125–126, 128, 205, 206
Netherlands, 135, 159–160, 213–215
Network approach to organized crime,
        2–6, 27–28
New Zealand, 24, 135, 169–192
    district councils of, 191–192
    map of, 186f
    OFCANZ, 190–191
    OMGs in, 187–190, 187b
    organized crime in, 191b
    white supremacist groups in, 112
New Zealand Bill of Rights Act, 192
New Zealand Police, 189, 190t, 191
Newbold, G., 189
Newton, M., 123–124
NGCRC. See National Gang Crime Research
        Center
NGIC. See National Gang Intelligence Center
Nguyen, L., 157
Nicaso, A., 106–107
Nichols, Dave, 49
Nielsen, B., 209
Nielsen, Jorn "Jonke," 207–208, 209
Nietzsche, Friedrich, 168
Nike Bikies, 11
9/11 terrorist attacks, 20
No Angel (Dobyns), 226
No Angels: My Harrowing Undercover
        Journey to the Inner Circle of the Hells
        Angels (Dobyns and Johnson-Shelton),
        90–91
"No colors" signs, 43, 44f
No Surrender Crew, 162, 163–164
Nolin, C. A., 225
Nordic countries, 207–213, 207f.
        See also specific countries
Norway, 173–174, 184–185, 205, 207–208, 210–212
    Bandidos MC in, 211, 211t
    Coffin Cheaters MC in, 174b
    HAMC in, 210t
    mafia paragraph of, 41
    Outlaws MC in, 211, 211t
    Vagos MC in, 140–141

The Norwegian Police Force's Efforts to Combat Outlaw Motorcycle Gangs, 2011 to 2015, 210
NRA. *See* National Rifle Association

O

Oakes, D., 51
Oakland Panthers MC, 26
OFCANZ. *See* Organized and Financial Crime Agency of New Zealand
Olivier, C., 47
Olsen, Arvid, 25
OMCGs. *See* Outlaw Motorcycle Club Gangs
OMCs. *See* Outlaw Motorcycle Clubs
OMGs. *See* Outlaw Motorcycle Gangs
The One Percenter Encyclopedia: The World of Outlaw Motorcycle Clubs from Abyss Ghosts to Zombies Elite (Hayes), 52–54
"1%er" symbol, 142*f*, 143*f*
1% (patch), 29, 29*f*
One-percenters (1%ers), 2, 4, 6, 7, 9–33, 35–36, 45, 48
   Altamont Speedway and, 30–33
   brotherhood and, 77
   creed of, 35
   "Cyclists Raid" and, 23–24
   folk devils and, 19–22
   HAMC and, 25–30
   Hollister Motorcycle Incident/Riot and, 17–19
   interactions with, 49–52, 50*b*
   moral panic and, 19–22
   motorcycle clubs, 11–17
   Riverside Motorcycle Riot and, 22–23
   The Wild One and, 24
Ongoing instrumental acts, 92, 92*t*, 94*t*
Ontario Biker Enforcement Unit, 145–146
Ontario Provincial Police (OPP), 157, 162–163
Operation Abyss, 190–191
Operation Black Rain, 120
Operation Casablanca, 215–216
Operation DE-BADS, 136
Operation Easy Rider, 122
Operation Enmesh, 198
Operation Explorer, 190–191
Operation 4-H, 153
Operation HAMMER, 153
Operation Pure Luck, 124
Operation Ranmore, 181
Operation Rocker, 135
Operation Roughrider, 37–38
Operation SHADOW, 153

Operation SharQc (Strategic Hells Angels Region Quebec), 158–159
Operation Sport Track, 225–226
Operation SPRINGTIME, 10, 154, 155
Operation 22 Green, 123–124
Operation WOLF, 153
Operation Zircon, 175–176
Operational data services, 134
Operational police support services, 134
OPP. *See* Ontario Provincial Police
Order of the Blood MC, 75, 112
Organizational structure, 98, 98*b*, 100, 131, 188–189
Organized and Financial Crime Agency of New Zealand (OFCANZ), 190–191
Organized Crime Consulting Committee, 37, 39
Organized Crime Directorate, 184
Organized Crime in Denmark in 2004, 208–209
Organized Crime Program, 37–38
Original Kings MC, 50–51
Osgerby, B., 24, 30
Out in bad standing, 85–86
Out in good standing, 86
Outcasts MC, 193, 199–200
Outlaw Biker: My Life at Full Throttle (Hayes and Gardner), 90–91
Outlaw Motorcycle Club Gangs (OMCGs), 135–136, 171, 172*b*
Outlaw Motorcycle Clubs (OMCs), 12–17, 35–36, 73–102. *See also specific clubs*
   becoming member of, 76–85, 76*t*
   black, 125–128
   criminal behavior of members, 86–97, 87*b*, 97*t*
   criminal organization continuum of, 73–75, 100–102, 101*f*
   extent of member's involvement, 76–97
   Forkner and, 14–15
   gang label of, 44–46, 47–49
   interactions with other motorcyclists and citizens, 49–52
   interracial, 125–128
   leaving, 85–86
Outlaw Motorcycle Gangs (OMGs), 1–2, 9–10, 35–43, 103–131. *See also specific gangs*
   of Australia, 169–192
   Big Five, 103–114, 219
   Big Four, 91, 193
   biographies of members, 86–96
   black, 127–128
   criminal behavior of members, 95*t*, 96–97, 97*t*
   as criminal gangs, 52–71
   criminal justice view of, 36–43

criminal organization continuum of, 2
cross-membership with white supremacists, 129
defined, 38, 38*b*
drug trafficking and, 69*b*
efforts against, in Canada, 156–159
in Europe, 203–217
independent, 117–125
interactions with other motorcyclists
    and citizens, 49–52
introduction to, 103–104
links with white supremacists, 128*b*
in New Zealand, 187–190, 187*b*
organizational structure of, 131
puppet/support gangs, 114–117
recent actions against, in Canada, 166–168
by state, 58*b*, 66*b*, 70*t*
structural complexity of, 6–7
U.S.-based, 133–143
violence in Canada, 160–166
Outlaws MC, 51, 71, 92, 125–126, 196, 199
articles on, 93
in Australia, 178–179, 183
as Big Five biker gang, 110–111
chapters outside of continental U.S., 140
"Charlie" logo, 110, 110*f*
criminal behavior of, 88–89
as criminal organization, 74*b*
insignia of, 110*f*
intimidation by, 51–52
needle law and, 44
in Norway, 211, 211*t*
RICO and, 39
in UK, 195–196, 200–202
Warlocks MC and, 88–89, 122

P

Pagans Mother Group, 99–100, 101–102
Pagans Motorcycle Club (PMC), 45, 74, 91, 93,
    96–97, 198–199
articles on, 92
as Big Five OMG, 111–113
criminal behavior of, 89
as criminal organization, 83*b*
drug trafficking and, 96
insignia of, 112*b*
puppet/support gangs of, 117
RICO and, 39
Titans MC and, 115*b*
Warlocks MC and, 122
Pammett, Robert "Peterborough Bob," 164
Panzer Task Force, 169–185, 171*b*
Para-Dice Riders MC, 149

Passaro, Allen, 32–33
Patches, 9–10, 11
    anti-patch laws, 191, 192
    of Boozefighters MC, 16*f*
    of HAMC, 26–27
    1%, 29, 29*f*
    of SOS MC, 114
Patchholders, 84–85, 99
Patching over (assimilation), 25–26, 42, 84–85,
    109, 198–199
Pazzano, S., 158
Peckerwoods MC, 130
PEN1. *See* Public Enemy Number 1
Pennsylvania Warlocks MC, 5–6, 75, 121
Peterson, Barney, 19
Phantom MC, 102
Pierce, J., 42
Pike, Jeff, 162
Pioneer clubs, 52–53
Pissed Off Bastards of Bloomington (POBOB),
    16–17, 19, 25, 105–106
Pistelero MC, 129
Pitts, Michael, 85
Planned aggressive acts, 92*t*, 94*t*
PMC. *See* Pagans Motorcycle Club
POBOB. *See* Pissed Off Bastards of Bloomington
Police Act (1886), 189
Porter, Walt, 15–16
Prain, E., 42
President, 98
Prison gangs, 27–28, 91, 128
Pritchard, D., 225
Probates, 80–83
*Prodigal Son, Pagan Son: Growing Up Inside the
    Dangerous World of the Pagans Motorcycle
    Club* (Menginie and Droban), 90–91
Project AMIGO, 153, 154
Project Divide, 159
Project Flatlined, 166
Project Monitor, 138
Project Resurgence, 168
Project RETIRE, 154
Project Tandem, 156–157, 168
Prospects, 80–83, 81*b*, 99
Provincial Biker Enforcement Unit, 157
Public Enemy Number 1 (PEN1), 125–126
Puppet/support gangs, 114–117

Q

Queen, William, 79, 84, 90–91, 100, 119
Quinn, J., 7, 74–75, 84, 91, 95–96
Quiroga, Robert, 45–46

R

Racketeer Influenced Criminal Organization
        (RICO), 37–38, 83, 99–100, 101
    Double-O-Alliance and, 39, 39*b*
    HAMC and, 78
    Mongols MC and, 79
    Outlaws MC and, 39
Ralston, N., 183
Ramblers MC, 52–53
Raposo, Luis, 163
Raptis, M., 160
Ravensbergen, J., 158–159
RDMC. *See* Road Disciples Motorcycle Club
Rebels MC, 42, 84–85, 148, 173–174, 176–177,
        184
Recruitment
    friends of the club, 78–79
    hangarounds, 78–79
    patchholder initiation, 84–85
    prospects, 80–83, 81*b*
Red and Gold World, 117*t*
Red Devils MC, 116*b*, 178, 190–191, 192
Redlined MC, 166
Reed, Leonard "JR," 114
Regional information sharing system (RISS), 94
Renegades MC, 89
Restricted Premises Act, 181
Revolutionary Armed Forces of Colombia (FARC),
        115, 158
Reynolds, T., 14, 15, 17–18, 21, 22–23, 25, 33
Richards, Keith, 31–32
Richardson, Bruce "The Dude," 113
RICO. *See* Racketeer Influenced Criminal
        Organization
Riding on the Edge: A Motorcycle Outlaw's Tale
        (Hall), 90–91
Righteous bikers, 4, 76–78, 219–220
RISS. *See* Regional information sharing system
Riverside Motorcycle Riot, 22–23
Road captain, 99
Road Disciples Motorcycle Club (RDMC), 83
Road Rats MC, 28–29, 193, 195*b*, 197–198
Road Runners MC, 16–17
Road Saints MC, 89
Roberge, Benoit, 168
Robertson, J., 178, 181–182
Rock Machine MC
    Bandidos MC and, 151
    biker war and, 93, 106–107, 147, 149, 152
    Operation Sport Track and, 225–226
Rockers MC, 11, 114–115, 155–156
The Rolling Stones (band), 30–32, 33

Ronald McDonald House Charities, 105
Rooney, Frank, 23–24
Rosenberg, M., 43
Rosga, Jack "Milwaukee Jack," 201, 224
Roslin, A., 93, 155
Rossmann, R., 50–51
Rowe, G., 90–91
*Running with the Devils: The True Story of the
        ATF's Infiltration of the Hells Angels*
        (Droban), 90–91

S

Saddle Tramps MC, 102
Sadilek, Frank, 28–29
Salerno, Frank "Bam Bam," 162
San Francisco Chronicle, 19
Sandham, Michael, 161, 162, 163, 164, 165
Sanger, D., 115
Satan's Choice MC, 36, 84, 148, 149, 151
Satan's Sinners MC, 16–17
Satan's Slaves MC, 28–29, 193, 198
Satan's Syndicate MC, 116
Satudarah MC, 214, 215
Schutzstaffet MC, 130
Scorpios MC, 198
Second Amendment, 20–21
Secretary-treasurer, 98
Secure global police communications services, 134
September 11, 2001 terrorist attacks, 20
Sergeant at arms, 99
Serious and Organized Crime (Control) Act, 180
Shand, A., 181
Shannon, M., 226
Shaylor, A., 196
Sher, Julian, 126, 133, 161, 174, 213–214
Shore Dogs MC, 117
Short-term instrumental acts, 92*t*, 93, 94*t*
Side Winders MC, 16–17
Siegelbaum, D., 48
Silent Few MC, 117
Silent Rebels MC, 117
Silent Thunder MC, 117
Silva, Benjamin "Psycho," 221
Sims, J., 162, 164
Sinatra, Nancy, 30
Sisson, Andrew, 189
Sixteen Hell's Lovers MC, 127*b*
Skinheads, 21, 125–126, 128
Skinner, Pete, 188
Smith, B. W., 133, 135
Smith, Michael "L'Animal," 158–159
Smith, R., 39

SOA. *See* Sons of Aesir MC
Social criminal organizations, 6, 27–28, 74–75
Sonner, S., 1–2
Sons of Aesir MC (SOA), 129, 130
Sons of Hell MC, 81, 195–196
Sons of Silence MC (SOS MC), 27, 45, 54, 71,
        96–97, 113–114
    criminal behavior of, 89
    as criminal organization, 85*b*
    insignia of, 114*f*
    patch of, 114
    puppet/support gangs of, 117
Soto, O. R., 88
Southern Brotherhood MC, 130
Spain, 140, 173–174, 205, 215–216
Spatial differentiation, 6–7
Spontaneous expressive acts, 92, 92*t*, 93, 94*t*
Spurgeon, D. C., 44, 51–52, 90–91
Stadnick, Walter, 164, 167, 168
Stafford Eagles MC, 198–199
Stephenson, R., 175
Stidworthy, D., 23–24
Stolz, G., 42, 183
Street gangs, 4, 5, 27–28, 94
Strikers, 80–83
Structural complexity, of OMGs, 6–7
Sturgis Rally, 12–13
Sullivan, R., 182
Summer Bash, 49
Sundowners MC, 89
Super gangs, 5
Support/puppet gangs, 114–117
Sutton, C., 178
Sweden, 205, 207–208, 212–213, 224
    Europol and, 135–136
    HAMC and, 47–48
    U.S.-based OMGs in, 140–141
    Vagos MC in, 123–124
Synder, R., 24, 124

T

Taskforce Hydra, 181–182
Taskforce Kilo Cajun, 181–182
Tate, Anthony, 37–38
Tattoos, 29, 83, 85–86
Taylor, Mick, 33
Te-ARA: The Encyclopedia of New Zealand, 185
Terrorism, 20, 138, 158
13 Rebels Motorcycle Club, 13, 14, 15, 52–53
Thompson, Hunter S., 29–30, 36–37, 126
Thompson, Michael "Iron Mike," 221
Thompson, T., 197–198, 199, 200–202

Three Points MC, 14
Time (magazine), 30
Titans MC, 115*b*
TMC. *See* Tribes Motorcycle Club
Tobin, Gary "Gentleman Gerry," 202, 223
Tomic, Bernard, 47–48
Trademarks, 105, 139
Tramps MC, 178, 198
Trethewy, S., 133
Tribes Motorcycle Club (TMC), 48, 117
Tribesmen MC, 190–191, 192
Troopers MC, 213
Trudeau, Yves "Apache," 145–146, 222, 226
Turkey, 115, 139, 203, 215–216
Turner, Simon, 201
*2011 National Gang Threat Assessment: Emerging
        Trends* (NGIC), 56–57
Typology of Biker Criminal Activity, 91, 92*t*

U

UK. *See* United Kingdom
Umphries, Travis, 85
*Under and Alone: The True Story of the Undercover
        Agent who Infiltrated America's Most
        Violent Outlaw Motorcycle Gang* (Queen),
        90–91
United Kingdom (UK), 2, 42, 50, 193–202, 221
    biker alliance against HAMC in, 198–200
    HAMC expansion in, 196–198, 196*b*
    map of, 194*f*
    Outlaws MC in, 195–196, 200–202
United States (U.S.), 104*f*, 115, 224–225
    drug smuggling from Canada, 159–160
    government agencies' view of OMGs, 43
    HAMC charters/chapters outside of,
        106*b*, 140
    OMGs based in, 133–143
    organized crime networks in, 4*b*
United States v. Harry Bowman, 127
*The Unlikely Rise of Walter Stadnick in the
        Canadian Hells Angels* (Langton), 90–91
Upright, Michael, 125–126
U.S. *See* United States
U.S. Outlaw Motorcycle Gangs, 2010 Edition
        (IOMGIA), 54, 55*t*, 58*t*
USA PATRIOT Act, 20

V

*Vagos, Mongols and Outlaws: My Infiltration of
        America's Deadliest Biker Gangs* (Falco and
        Droban), 90–91

Vagos MC, 1–2, 43, 90–91, 118, 140–141, 224
  chapters outside of continental U.S., 140
  as independent OMG, 122–124
  insignia of, 123*f*
  mission statement of, 123*b*
Valdemar, R., 221
Vallis, M., 157
Values. *See* Core values of outlaw bikers
Veno, Arthur, 24, 98, 182, 219–220
  on bikies, 11
  on initiation, 84
  on violence, 49
Ventura, Jesse, 119
Vertical differentiation, 6–7
Veterans, 19, 75, 105–106, 113
  in Boozefighters MC, 15–16, 27
  in Galloping Goose MC, 17
  letting off steam and, 14–15
Vice president, 98
Viellaris, R., 48
Vietnam Vets Motorcycle Club (VNVMC), 54,
  56*b*, 57*f*
Vietnam War, 27, 113
Vikings Defence League, 208–209
Vikings MC, 194–195, 195*b*
VNVMC. *See* Vietnam Vets Motorcycle Club
Von Lampe, Klaus, 2–3, 5–6, 27–28, 74–75

W

Wagers, George, 87
Walker, I., 184
Walt Disney Corporation, 105
Wanganui District Council (Prohibiting of Gang
  Insignia) Act, 192
War on Terror, 20
Ward, Gerald, 167, 168
Warlocks Counsel, 99–100
Warlocks MC, 27, 51, 112–113, 117–118
  chapters outside of continental U.S., 140
  criminal behavior of, 87–88, 89
  of Florida, 27, 121–122
  as independent OMG, 120–122
    Outlaws MC and, 88–89, 122
    of Pennsylvania, 5–6, 75, 121
Webb, John Cleve, 88
Welch, D., 182
Welsh, Peter "Buttons," 196–197
Wethern, George "Baby Huey," 27, 28–29, 220
Wheels of Soul MC (WOS), 45, 54, 96–97, 118,
  124–125
White Boy Society, 130
White Knights of America, 128, 129
White Pride Internet users group, 129
White Racists Extremists Gang Members
  (WREGs), 125–126
White Revolution, 129
White supremacists, 91, 94, 112, 128
  biker gangs, 130
  cross-membership with OMGs, 129
  links with OMGs, 128*b*
Widow Makers MC, 122
Wienberg, C., 209
The Wild Angels (film), 30
The Wild One (film), 23–24, 110, 187
Willon, P., 53–54
Wilson, T., 181
Winged skull logo, 195–196
Winterhalder, Ed, 107–109, 116, 127, 161, 162–163
Wolf, D. R., 12–13, 78, 80–81, 82, 84, 98
Wolf Outlaws MC, 198–199, 200
Women, 12–13, 52–53
WOS. *See* Wheels of Soul MC
WREGs. *See* White Racists Extremists Gang
  Members

Y

Yates, B., 13–14, 17, 22

Z

Zig Zag Crew MC, 159
Zimmerman, K., 26
Zito, Chuck, 77–78, 84, 86–87, 182
Zwerin, Charlotte, 31

Lightning Source UK Ltd.
Milton Keynes UK
UKOW07f1202270515

252348UK00008B/311/P